Politics and the Media in Poland from the 19th to the 21st Centuries

International Comparative Social Studies

Editor-in-Chief

Mehdi P. Amineh
(*Amsterdam Institute for Social Science Research, University of Amsterdam,
and International Institute for Asian Studies, Leiden University*)

VOLUME 58

The titles published in this series are listed at *brill.com/icss*

Politics and the Media in Poland from the 19th to the 21st Centuries

Selected Issues

Edited by

Evelina Kristanova
Rafał Habielski
Małgorzata Such-Pyrgiel

BRILL

LEIDEN | BOSTON

Originally published in hardback in 2024.

Cover illustration: 'Facebook Worldwide Data'. Pixabay, Public Domain.

The Library of Congress has cataloged the hardcover edition as follows:

Names: Kristanova, Evelina, editor. | Habielski, Rafał, editor. |
    Such-Pyrgiel, Małgorzata, editor.
Title: Politics and the media in Poland from the 19th to the 21st centuries
    selected issues / edited by Evelina Kristanova, Rafał Habielski,
    Małgorzata Such-Pyrgiel.
Description: Leiden ; Boston : Brill, 2024. | Series: International
    comparative social studies, 1568-4474 ; volume 58 | Includes
    bibliographical references and index.
Identifiers: LCCN 2023052179 | ISBN 9789004683365 (hardback ; acid-free
    paper) | ISBN 9789004687998 (ebook)
Subjects: LCSH: Mass media–Political aspects–Poland. | LCGFT: Essays.
Classification: LCC P95.82.P7 P65 2024 | DDC 302.209438–dc23/eng/20231206
LC record available at https://lccn.loc.gov/2023052179

Typeface for the Latin, Greek, and Cyrillic scripts: "Brill". See and download: brill.com/brill-typeface.

ISSN 1568-4474
ISBN 978-90-04-73838-6 (paperback, 2025)
ISBN 978-90-04-68336-5 (hardback)
ISBN 978-90-04-68799-8 (e-book)
DOI 10.1163/9789004687998

Contents

Foreword

Following the unfortunate conjunction of events in the late 18th century, Poland lost its independence for over a century. And the history of the Polish press in the 19th century reflects the situation of a nation deprived of its statehood. Publishers faced adversities arising from cultural, economic and societal issues (primarily illiteracy and poverty); the interminably slow modernisation of social structure, as well as the policies implemented by the partitioning powers. Aware of the importance of the press – both as a source of information and as an institution able to preserve the culture and national identity in these dire circumstances – these powers had neither the interest nor the intention of making life easier for the Polish press. This situation resulted in a limited number of titles, low circulation figures, and content that had to be in line with the legal restrictions and censorial intervention. These factors, however, hindered but did not entirely preclude the development of the press in the former Polish territories. In the late 19th century, a segment of the daily press – consisting of news dailies and titles controlled by political groups – emerged in those territories that were to become part of the new Polish state in 1918. These were modelled on periodicals that were operating in Western Europe, which were soon followed by the very first sensationalist daily. Another noteworthy phenomenon unique to the Polish press were the sociocultural and literary weeklies, paralleling the emergence of a new intelligentsia, whose representatives were the founders and readers of such publications.

The press would often act as a replacement for those institutions that were deprived of the right to be present in public life, providing both a platform for political activity (to the degree permitted by the governments of the partitioning powers), and a place where geopolitical orientations were forged in the period preceding the outbreak of World War I. Despite the differences of opinions espoused, the press played a role that should not be underestimated; namely, it brought together a nation that was living across territories now belonging to foreign states.

In 1918 the country regained its independence, an event that proved to be a springboard for the Polish press, and not only because it could take a certain amount of credit for the liberation. The financial standing of most citizens in the newly formed state may have been less than satisfactory – thereby preventing a rapid increase in circulation figures – but newspapers and magazines were at last able to operate under relatively favourable conditions, and their editorial boards knew exactly how to take advantage of this. The March Constitution of 1921 did not legislate for preventive censorship, guaranteeing both the right to obtain information and freedom of dissemination. By prohibiting state-support practices, it also provided boundless opportunities to establish new periodicals. Besides the protection warranted by the Constitution, the political situation also worked to the advantage of publishers. The multiparty structure and the parliamentary-cabinet model of the political system stimulated civic activism, which then encouraged the launch of new periodicals and an increase in circulation figures.

Close links between the press and political factions were the order of the day in the 1920s, with the former being a major tool for legitimising politics. Discussions conducted in parliament were typically either the prelude to, or the consequence of debates held in newspapers and magazines. The ferocity and uncompromising nature of these disputes enticed readers and increased circulation, thereby confirming the importance of the press in the political system of a democratic state.

However, the enthusiasm surrounding this new freedom of speech was not its only concomitant manifestation. Shortly after the restoration of independence, the darker aspects of the press and the freedoms it enjoyed were highlighted. The press was often perceived as an exponent of particularistic interests and an instigator of the mounting conflicts and divisions. This was reinforced by the assassination of Gabriel Narutowicz, Poland's first President (elected and killed in December 1922). The event was preceded by numerous attacks in the press, conducted on the limits of the law and sometimes even beyond it, and launched by newspapers hostile to the president. Some of this vilification could be regarded as more than an expression of opinion, as these were attempts to wrest power and evidence of aspirations by the unchecked media acting above the constitutional bodies of the state.

The 1926 coup d'état in Poland and the resultant change in the rule of law within the existing Constitution brought considerable consequences, both for the role of publishers and the liberties they enjoyed. The importance of individual rights was gradually replaced by the concept of 'the welfare of the state'. This shift was felt by all participants of political life, including the press, and the persecution of opposition-run periodicals was a clear manifestation of the process. Any criticism of government policy led to seizure of print runs, especially during pre-election periods. A new class of periodicals emerged – the government-controlled press, which owed its existence to handsome budgetary subsidies. Along with daily newspapers, the dynamically expanding class of state-run periodicals began to include weeklies, e.g., socio-cultural papers, and the sensationalist press, an important instrument of propaganda in the late 1920s and the early 1930s. An increasingly important impact was also exerted by the radio, seized by the state in the mid-1930s; a medium that had reached one million listeners by the outbreak of World War II.

A consequence of the transformations in the political sphere was the new Constitution of 1935. Possessed by a desire to lay the foundations of a strong state, its creators abandoned the concept of unrestrained freedom for the press, reducing it to mere freedom of speech. This included a proviso of the 'common good', a concept vague and difficult to define; true not only for publishers and journalists. Shortly afterwards, in 1938, a new press law came into force, perceived by journalists as a list of imperatives and prohibitions, which – while not completely incapacitating the press – still made it even more subservient to the state.

Even if it is assumed that the 1926 political turmoil in Poland culminated in the establishment of an authoritarian rule, it did not end the pluralism of the press. Despite being subordinated to the demands of the state, the press still enjoyed a considerable degree of freedom, even in the face of the constraints imposed.

World War II brutally ended this chapter in the history of the Polish press (the origins of which dated back to the mid-19th century), as in the post-war communist-run state there was no desire to revive periodicals whose existence had been brought to an untimely end by the war. Several titles did however survive in exile, where – along with newly-established ones – they assumed the duty of penetrating the country through the Iron Curtain.

The press in the People's Republic of Poland was closely modelled on the system developed in the Soviet Union. The media were seen as a 'conveyor belt' – a term that augured their objectiveness – for government propaganda, and were completely subservient to the government. Even prior to the official establishment of the new Polish state, the Central Office of Control of the Press, Publications and Performance, an institution strictly subordinated to the communist party, was founded. Through its arbitrary, unlegislated decisions the press became a unified instrument of propaganda. With this purpose in mind, the press was assisted by the radio, and, in the mid-1950s, by television, which, from the 1970s, gradually becoming the major tool of indoctrination.

After the Polish October (1956), triggered by the transformations in the Soviet Union, the press gained marginally greater freedom. One upshot of this was the socio-cultural weeklies, which, despite remaining under state censorship, were able – through the efforts of some authors – to offer a glimpse of the truth by skilfully selecting genres, language and subject matters, oftentimes seemingly far from the issues they were discussing. This did not mean, however, that the press was relieved of its former responsibilities to toe the state line, and the vast majority of journalists followed the imposed guidelines, sacrificing integrity and honesty to enforced loyalty or conformism.

This condemned readers to a 'world of illusion'. By paradox, or perhaps by natural reaction to the quality and predictability of the propaganda, reinforced by the dislike for its instigator, this proved to have the opposite effect than that desired, prompting citizens to protest against the authorities.

In 1976, Poland faced yet another economically-driven political crisis – just like previous upheavals – which led to the emergence of a democratic opposition and a like-minded press that operated outside censorial oversight. Initially, the number of titles was limited and editions scant. However, this changed with time, and the new press gradually became a counterbalance to the governmental 'propaganda of success'. Thanks to this underground press, *Czarna księga cenzury* PRL (*The Black Book of Communist Censorship*) was published in 1977, revealing how scrupulously all manifestations of political, social and cultural life were being controlled.

Another factor that helped to break the regime's information monopoly were radio stations from the West, the most effective of which was Radio Free Europe, founded in 1950. In the 1960s, it already boasted an audience of up to 14–15 million listeners, despite attempts by the authorities in Poland and the Soviet Union to jam the signal. Western stations were also reporting on the situation in Poland and in the world, broadcasting programmes on political, economic, international and cultural issues. Importantly, these reports were a balance to the lies and distortions of the communist propaganda.

The loss of the state's monopoly on political power exacerbated the loss of its control over the mass media. A unique moment in the history of the Polish media was the brief period between August 1980 and December 1981 when Solidarity was allowed to operate legally. Following lengthy negotiations, Solidarity was granted permission to publish a weekly, while in the autumn of 1981 the government also authorised the passing of a new censorship law that granted publishers the right to highlight which extracts had been exposed to censorship and even to take legal actions against censorial verdicts that they considered unlawful.

Solidarity's legal operations were brutally terminated by the imposition of martial law in December 1981. Its journalists were laid off, their trade union liquidated, and the Solidarity magazine was closed. These acts were compounded by the subjection of the media to governmental control and oversight, just as it had been prior to the Gdansk Agreement of August 1980. This marked a return to the crude and muddled propaganda that included accounts on the external enemy biding its time in the West. Unsurprisingly, these efforts proved counterproductive, thereby increasing the popularity of Western radio stations, and spurring the dynamic development of the underground press after 1981.

In 1989, with the collapse of the communist system, came systemic and economic reforms, which also impacted the mass media. Liberated from political oversight and institutional censorship, the media had to operate in a competitive and commercial world and under pressure from mass culture. Forced to adjust to the demands of the political world, albeit not that of 'real socialism', they could not ignore the expectations of the readers, listeners and viewers, who were now the controlling force on the market. The expectation that these challenges would be easy to overcome was shown to be far from the truth.

Rafał Habielski

Figures and Tables

Figures

Tables

Notes on Contributors

Katarzyna Drąg

holds a post-doctoral degree in media and social communication. A graduate of Polish philology and international cultural studies. Since 2011, she has been working at the Pontifical University of John Paul II in Cracow. She is the director of the Institute of Journalism, Media and Social Communication, and an assistant professor of Media and Social Communication Chair. Her research interests: history of media, history of journalism, the problem of forming and evolving of the ethos of a journalist (since mid XIX century), cross-cultural communicating, theory of communication and information competencies. She is a member of the scientific council of the journals: *Com.Press* (Crakow, Poland) and *Пресознавство* (Press Studies) (Lviv, Ukraine). She is a member of The Polish Communication Association (Head of History of Media Section) and member of Commission on Media Studies at Polish Academy of Arts and Sciences. ORCID ID: 0000-0001-9920-3526

Rafał Habielski

is a professor at Warsaw University (Faculty of Journalism, Information and Book Studies), historian, press and media expert, researcher of Polish political emigration (to Great Britain, France, etc.). His scientific interests include politics, history, press and mass media, and literature, with particular focus on the history of media (press, Radio Free Europe, etc.). Between 1984 and 2012, he was employed at the Institute of Literary Research of the Polish Academy of Sciences (Department of History of Polish Press in the 19th and 20th Centuries). In the years 2003–2010, he was a member of the Scientific Council of the Institute of Literary Research of the Polish Academy of Sciences. In 2009, he became a member of the Committee for Studies on the Polish Diaspora at the Polish Academy of Learning in Krakow and the Scientific Council of the quarterly *Studia Medioznawcze/Media Studies* published through Warsaw University. In the years 2010–2014, he was a member of the Programme and Scientific Board of the National Film Library, and between 2011 and 2015, a member of the Scientific Council of the Polish History Museum. Since 2012, he has been an active member of the Polish branch of the PEN Club. His book publications include: *Audycje historyczne i kulturalne Rozgłośni Polskiej Radia Wolna Europa w latach 1952–1975/Historical and Cultural Broadcasts of the Polish Section of Free Europe Radio between 1952 and 1975* (Wroclaw 2019); *Rozgłośnia Polska Radia Wolna Europa w latach 1950–1975/The Polish Section of Free Europe Radio between 1950 and 1975* [co-author:] P. Machcewicz (Wroclaw 2018); *Wolność czy odpowiedzialność? Prasa i polityka w II Rzeczypospolitej/Liberty or Responsibility? Press and Politics in the Second Polish Republic* (Warszawa 2013). ORCID ID: 0000-0003-3686-9931

Dariusz Jarosz
is a professor of history at the Institute of History of the Polish Academy of Science in Warsaw. He specialised in the social history of Poland after 1945 and the relations of Poland with Western countries. Selected works: *Increase Supply, Reduce Demand and Punish Severly. A Contextual History of Meat in Communist Poland*, Peter Lang Edition, Berlin 2020 (with Maria Pasztor); *Polish-French Relations, 1944–1989*, Peter Land Edition, Frankfurt am Main 2015 (with Maria Pasztor); *Władze komunistyczne w Polsce a chłopi 1948–1956* [The Communist Power in Poland and Peasants 1948–1956], Wydawnictwo DiG, Warsaw 1995; „The Collectivization of Agriculture in Poland: Causes of Defeat", in *The Collectivization of Agriculture in Communist Eastern Europe. Comparison and Entanglements*, Constantin Iordachi, Arndt Bauerkämper, eds., Central European University Press, Budapest - New York, 2014. ORCID ID: 0000-0002-7882-8532

Ewa Jurga-Wosik
(Phd) is an assistant professor at Institute of Media Education and Journalism, Cardinal Stefan Wyszynski University in Warsaw, Poland. Her academic interests involve the local media in Poland and issues of access to information in Poland, information policy and access to documents in the institutions of the European Union, journalistic role performance in Poland. Publications: A. Stępińska, E. Jurga-Wosik, K. Adamczewska, D. Narożna, B. Secler, Polish Journalists' Attitudes Towards Political Actors: Empirical Studies, *Przegląd Politologiczny* 2017 No 1 pp. 127–141; E. Jurga-Wosik, I. Oleksiuk (2022). Wybrane zagadnienia etyczne dziennikarstwa interpretacyjnego na tle badań empirycznych. *Roczniki Nauk Społecznych*, 50 (2), pp. 83–96. ORCID ID: 0000-0002-9307-6009

Joanna Hobot-Marcinek
holds a post-doctoral degree in literature sciences and is a professor at the Jagiellonian University in Krakow. She currently heads the Center for Multimodal Educational and Cultural Research at the Faculty of Polish Studies. She is the editor of publishing series *Figurae* of the *Jagiellonian University Publishing House*. She is the author of books: *Game with censorship in New Wave Poetry (1968–1976)*, *Crone and Goethe: the experience and transgression of old age: Tadeusz Różewicz, Czesław Miłosz, Jarosław Iwaszkiewicz*. She is a co-author of books: *Ant-Beatrice:studies on the cultural history of the old drunken crone, The Old Rebel Women. Studies on the semantics of images*. She holds lectures and classes on censorship in the Polish People's Republic, cultural impact of

stereotypes, polish modern literature and methodology of teaching polish language and literature. ORCID ID: 0000-0002-4057-0070

Monika Kaczmarek-Śliwińska

holds a post-doctoral degree in social sciences (specialisation: research on media and communication) and is an assistant professor at the Faculty of Journalism, Information and Book Studies at the University of Warsaw. Media expert and advisor. Author of publications, coordinator and participant of research projects in the areas of: PR, crisis management, communication ethics, media, political communication. Member of the Polish Communication Association and the Polish Society of Media Education; an expert of the Conference of Rectors of Academic Schools in Poland (KRASP). Juror of the prestigious PR competition "Złote Spinacze" (The Polish Public Relations Consultancies Association). Laureate of PRoton and Lew PR awards. ORCID ID: 0000-0002-9096-9338

Evelina Kristanova

holds a post-doctoral degree in social sciences (specialisation: mass media) and is a professor at SWPS University in Warsaw (the Faculty of Humanities; Department of Culture and Media Studies). She holds lectures and classes on Journalism and Social Communication. In 2007, she received a bachelor's degree in theology from Cardinal Stefan Wyszyński University in Warsaw. Since 2021, she has been part of the editorial board of the bi-annual *Nasza Przeszłość*. Between 2009 and 2012, she worked as an editorial assistant of the academic and didactic series *Acta Universitatis Lodziensis. Folia Librorum*. She has been a member of the Polish Communication Association since 2017, and the Society for the History of the Humanities since 2021. Her research interest focuses on the history of the media, in particular on 20th-century Catholic sociocultural periodicals in Poland and contemporary books in Bulgaria. Recently, she has commenced research into digital versions of periodicals and into the religious broadcasts for Radio Free Europe's Broadcasting Service. Her portfolio of publications consists of 7 books and over 80 papers. ORCID ID: 0000-0003-4935-7417

Cecylia Kuta

is a historian, a holder of a post-doctoral degree in humanities, head of the Historical Research Office in Krakow of the Institute of National Remembrance, assistant professor at the The Pontifical University of John Paul II in Kracow, and member of the Historical Commission of the Katowice Branch of the Polish Academy of Sciences and of the SPI (Information Professionals Association). She is also a member of the editorial board of the following scientific periodicals *Pamięć i Sprawiedliwość, Zeszyty Historyczne WiN-u, Nasza Prz-eszłość*. She researches the history of the Catholic lay association after the Second World War and of the creative and opposition communities in the Polish People's Republic (PRL). Author of many academic and popular science publications on contemporary Polish history, including the books: *"Działacze" i "Pis-maki". Aparat bezpieczeństwa wobec organizacji katolików świeckich w Krakowie w latach 1957–1989* ["Activists" and "Writers". The security apparatus towards the organisation of lay Catholics in Krakow in the years 1957–1989], Kracow 2009; *Niecenzurowane. Z dziejów drugiego obiegu wydawniczego w Krakowie w latach 1976–1990* [Un-censored. From the history of the second publishing circuit in Krakow 1976–1990], Krakow 2019.

Rafał Leśniczak

has a post-doctoral degree in social sciences in the discipline of social communication and media science (UMCS 2020), associate professor and head of the Department of Social Communication, Public Relations and New Media at the Institute of Media Education and Journalism at the Cardinal Stefan Wyszyński University in Warsaw. He is the author of over 90 scientific publications in the field of media, religion, and politics. His research interests focus on political communication, mediatization, and public relations. He is currently a member of European Communication Research and Education Association (ECREA), International Association for Media and Communication Research (IAMCR), and the Polish Communication Association (PTKS). ORCID ID: 0000-0003-0099-4327

Inga Oleksiuk

is Doctor of Humanities (University of Warsaw; School of Journalism), Doctor of Law (SWPS University of Humanities and Social Science). Fellow/ Scolarship holder: Frederico II University,(Italy), British Library, (UK) Carleton University (Canada), Barcelona University (Spain, Catalonia). Fields of scientific interests: civil liberties intellectual property, creativity and AI. ORCID ID: 0000-0003-2682-8968

Rafał Opulski

(Phd) is an employee of the Pontifical University of John Paul II in Krakow and the Institute of National Remembrance, graduate of the Faculty of International and Political Studies at Jagiellonian University and the Faculty of Philosophy at Jagiellonian University. Author of publications on the political propaganda of the Polish People's Republic, Polish history in the 20th century and the anthropology of politics, including symbolic forms of governance: Opulski, R. (2019). Stalinization, de-Stalinization, and re Stalinization. 1953 behind the

"Iron Curtain". *The Person and the Challenges. The Journal of Theology, Education, Canon Law and Social Studies Inspired by Pope John Paul II*, 9(2), 25–39; Opulski, R. Ficoń, M. (2020). In Search of Internal Enemies. Show Trials of the Members of the Communist Parties in Stalinist Poland, Czechoslovakia and Hungary, in: *The European Crucible of Diversities*, ed by. C. Kuta, J. Marecki, L. Rotter, Krakow 2020, pp. 147–159. ORCID ID: 0000-0001-9772-0298

Dominika Popielec

(PhD media studies) holds a master's degree in journalism and social communication from the University of Warsaw. She is a graduate of doctoral studies in political science at Maria Curie Skłodowska University in Lublin, when she works now. She is a member of the Polish Communication Association and the editor-in-chief of the magazine *Com.press*. She is a member of Editoral Council *Media over Language*, which is published by Sofia University St. Kliment Ohridski. She is vice-chair of the Interpersonal Communication and Social Interaction section of the European Communication Research and Education Association (ECREA). She is the author of a monograph on investigative journalism. Her research interests include journalism studies, whistleblowing, selected aspects of communication and social interaction, media and politics. ORCID ID: 0000-0002-9583-0861

Małgorzata Strzelecka

is a Doctor of Humanities (with a specialization in 20th century history and the didactics of history), professor at Nicolaus Copernicus University in Torun. Since 2000, employee of the Institute of History and Archival Studies at Nicolaus Copernicus University. Since 1999, employee of the University High School. Member of the Polish Historical Society & secretary of the Toruń branch. Member of the Commission on the Didactics of History at the Polish Historical Society. Associate of the Commission on the Didactics of History of the Committee on Historical Sciences of the Polish Academy of Sciences. In 2004–2018 co-editor of a collection of scientific and didactic studies (XII volumes) in the series: Toruń Didactic Meetings. In her research work, she focuses on the analysis of the journalistic and social activity of the intellectuals gathered around the editorial offices of *Tygodnik Powszechny* and *Znak* monthly, on the activity of the representatives of the broadly understood social movement Znak, which consisted of, among others. the editorial offices of Catholic magazines (*Tygodnik Powszechny, Znak* and *Więź* monthlies), five Clubs of Catholic Intelligentsia, the environment of the bimonthly *Chrześcijanin w Świecie*, the Center for Documentation and Social Studies and the Znak Parliamentary Circle. Author of three monographs: Difficult Compromises. The environment of *Tygodnik Powszechny* vis-à-vis reforms of the educational system and upbringing in 1945–1989, (2009); *Between Minimalism and Maximalism. Ideological dilemmas of Stanisław Stomma and Janusz Zabłocki*, (2015); *Woldview of Jerzy Turowicz's. Faith, Ideas and Reasons in the Light of Journalism from 1932–1939*, (2023). ORCID ID: 0000-0001-9018-4875

Anna Szwed-Walczak

holds a doctoral degree in social sciences (specialisation: political science) and she is an assistant professor at the Maria Curie-Skłodowska University in Lublin, Poland. In 2011, she received a master's degree in sociology from Maria Curie-Skłodowska University. She has been a member of the Polish Political Science Association since 2012, and the Polish Communication Association since 2016. Her research interests include political communication with focus on the Polish national movement, political press, online political communication. She holds lectures and classes on history of political communication, media policy, public relations, social engineering, network society, international and intercultural communication. ORCID ID: 0000-0002-9878-1401

Małgorzata Such-Pyrgiel

is an associated professor (habilitated doctor) of social sciences in the discipline of sociological sciences, methodologist. Vice-Rector for education and evaluation of research, for student matter, education in branch location and cooperation with the environment at the Alcide De Gasperi University of Euroregional Economy in Józefów. The author of publications on digital society and new technologies, participant of seminars and conferences devoted to this subject. In her works, she presents the social dimension of digital transformation as the 4th industrial revolution, affecting the life of modern human being. She is particularly interested in the analysis of changes in communication, education, media, labor market and public administration under the influence of intensive development of new digital technologies. Conducted research and published texts fit into the area of three sociological specialties: sociology of contemporary societies and modern and new technologies of marketing and economics, as well as lifestyle. As a promoter of the policy of quality and improvement of education, she is a member of the Polish Accreditation Committee, appointed by the Minister of Education, a member of the Polish Sociological Society and the European Sociological Society ESA and well as a manager of many research, development, and implementation projects. ORCID ID: 0000-0001-5435-1154

Rafał Śpiewak

(Phd in the humanities in the field of history, habilitation in social sciences in the discipline of communication and media sciences) is an assistant Professor at the Department of Marketing and Market Research of the University of Economics in Katowice. Priest of the Archdiocese of Katowice. From 2006–2016, academic chaplain, founder and chaplain of the St. Raphael Kalinowski Home Hospice in Rybnik, chaplain to scouts, independence organisations and the Piłsudczycy Association, expert of the Katowice Archdiocese Second Synod Church Heritage Commission. Member of the Polish Communication Association and the Polish Society for Media Education. Since 2021 pastor of the parish of St. Joseph in Chorzów. Dean of the Chorzów deanery. Interested in social and political aspects of the Catholic press in Upper Silesia, media deontology, communicative competence, use of new media in religious communication. Author of *Gazeta Katolicka. Pismo Duchowieństwa i ludu polskiego na Śląsku 1896–1910. Historical and doctrinal study*. Chorzów Museum Publishing House, Kraków-Chorzów 2006; *Społeczeństwo – naród – państwo na łamach „Gościa Niedzielnego" 1923–1939*, University of Economics in Katowice Publishing House, Katowice 2022. Co-author: *Rodzina w kryzysie czy kryzys w rodzinie*, Fidelis Publishing House, Pszów 2013; *W świcie aksjologii, polityki i kultury. Students towards media (based on empirical research)*, Wydawnictwo Uniwersytetu Ekonomicznego w Katowicach, Katowice 2018; *Polskość w narracjach medialnych z perspektywy Górnego Śląska*, University of Economics in Katowice Publishing House, Katowice 2019. Writes poems and paints pictures (oil on canvas). ORCID ID: 0000-0003-2559-8232

Weronika Świerczyńska-Głownia
holds a post-doctoral degree in social sciences (specialization: social communication and media) and is a professor at the Jagiellonian University. Graduate of the Jagiellonian University, Faculty of Law and Administration, Institute of Political Sciences. She has completed Postgraduate Management Studies at the Warsaw School of Economics (SGH) and Management and Business Studies at the Department of Applied Economics of the Jagiellonian University. She works at the Institute of Journalism, Media and Social Communication at the Jagiellonian University. Head of the Department of International Communication and Media; Vice-Dean For Educational Affairs Faculty of Management and Social Communication of Jagiellonian University. University lecturer and author of award-winning monographs and numerous of scientific publications on media functioning and information management. ORCID ID: 0000-0001-8840-703X

Tomasz Walkowiak
is an assistant professor at the Department of Artificial Intelligence, Faculty of Information and Communication Technology, Wroclaw University of Science and Technology, Poland. He is the editor of 9 monographs, author, and

co-author of over 210 papers published in international journals, book chapters, and conference proceedings. His research interests include text mining, stylometry, and out-of-distribution analysis. He is currently involved in the CLARIN (Common Language Resources and Technology Infrastructure) project, which aims to create a pan-European research infrastructure for the humanities and social sciences. It facilitates work with very large collections of natural language texts. ORCID ID: 0000-0002-7749-4251

Monika Wawer

has been conducting research and teaching at Jagiellonian University since 2008. She is associated with the Institute of Media Journalism and Social Communication. For over 20 years, she also worked as a journalist and producer on radio and television. Her main areas of research interest are television content, media genres, television formats, journalistic workshop, and AI in television production and programming. She is a member of the Polish Communication Association. ORCID ID: 0000-0003-4073-4693

Jan Wieczorek

is a linguist, an assistant professor at the Department of Artificial Intelligence, Faculty of Information and Communication Technology, Wrocław University of Science and Technology, Poland. He is an user involvement officer at the CLARIN-PL Language Technology Centre. His research interests relate directly to text semantics, discourse analysis and stylometry. He is particularly interested in the application of natural language processing (NLP) in modern research in the fields of digital humanities and social sciences. ORCID ID: 0000-0001-8709-7754

Introduction

Małgorzata Such-Pyrgiel

Politics and the media are two closely-related fields. At different times and in different places, the interweaving of politics and media was very visible, and politicians always tried to use the media for their own political interest. The book entitled *Politics and the Media in Poland from the 19th to the 21st Centuries. Selected Issues* shows, describes and discusses these links between the media and politics in Poland in the period between the nineteenth and the twenty first centuries. The book presents the latest research and reflects on the relationship between the media and politics, using the case study method. It delves into the interests of Polish researchers from various centres in these fields.

The separate parts of the book focus on different types of both old and new media, including the press, books, and the Internet. The authors are historians, media experts and political scientists, sociologists, lawyers, cultural scientists, philologists and representatives of other disciplines, as a result of which the research methods, as well as hypotheses and research results present a range of points of view.

There is scientific value to this book in an interdisciplinary context. The publication consists of fifteen chapters which show – in a very broad way – the mutual interpenetration of politics and various types of media in our country at different times. It is worth adding that the articles contained in the book are arranged chronologically, covering the most important historical and media events in Polish society. The studies undertaken by researchers are presented both through the prism of theoretical findings and original empirical research.

The first chapter, entitled *The Lviv-based Parisian Fashion Daily (1840–1848) – between Fashion and Politics*, concerns the history of the Galician press in the nineteenth century. It discusses the importance of *Dziennik Mód Paryskich* in propagating democratic ideas in Polish society under the Austrian Partition, where the magazine played an important role in spreading political awareness. It contains a multifaceted analysis of the conditions for the development of the Polish press in the mid-19th century. *Dziennik Mód Paryskich* is a unique example of the struggle for a free press in difficult political conditions.

The next chapter is titled *The Political and Societal Position Taken by the Weekly Gość Niedzielny over the Threats to the Catholic Worldview in the Interwar Period* was established and published in Upper Silesia in the years 1923–1939. It constitutes a rich and important source of historical knowledge, providing a picture of the challenges faced by the Catholic Church and society at that time.

© MAŁGORZATA SUCH-PYRGIEL, 2024 | DOI:10.1163/9789004687998_002

Gość Niedzielny fulfilled important pastoral functions, complementing and deepening the religious and social awareness of lay people. Its most important tasks were education and activation in social and political fields.

The third chapter, named *"For Censors, We Were Never Fringe Papers" – On Censorial Interferences and the Games Played with Censors in Tygodnik Powszechny between 1945 and 1953*, presents the situation around the existence of weekly, which was a Catholic socio-cultural periodical, published in Poland after 1945. The key research objective of this study concerns the purpose and sense behind publishing in the face of harsh preventive censorship. The weekly offered, as far as possible, a Catholic point of view on complex religious, cultural and socio-political issues, and demonstrated an alternative vision of culture. The editorial board used all available means to oppose the distortion of reality and to seek new forms of communication with the reader.

The next part of this publication is titled *Mythologizing the Enemy in Polish Communist Propaganda in the Years 1949–1954*. The aim of this study was to analyse the process of mythologizing an enemy in Polish communist propaganda during Stalinism between 1949 and 1954. The images of enemies shaped by communist authorities can be divided into two basic groups – internal and external ones. While the first group consisted of military and political resistance movements, the authorities of the official Polish Underground State, rich landowners, the Catholic Church, proponents of 'right-wing, nationalistic agendas', saboteurs, spies, and speculators, the second one were grouped around such external enemies as Western countries (especially the USA and the Federal Republic of Germany) and Polish emigrants pushing for independence. Spreading the belief that there was a threat from a real or imaginary enemy had several functions, which are explained and described in detail in this chapter.

The part that follows describes the functioning of a Catholic publishing house in communist Poland. The title of the chapter is PAX *Publishing Institute between 1949–1989 – The Largest Catholic Publishing House in Poland Under the Communist Regime*. The Institute was established in 1949 and run by the PAX Association and was one of the largest and most important publishing houses in Poland under Communism. It was also the only place where, along with religious publications, memoirs and books about the Home Army, works by the greatest writers of the Polish and world literature could be published in great detail. The aim of the study is to recount the history of the publishing house, summarising its achievements while drawing attention to its ambiguous role during the political situation of the time.

The sixth chapter is entitled *The Religious Broadcasts of Rev. Tadeusz Kirschke for Radio Free Europe's Broadcasting Service*. The research purpose of this part

is to analyse the previously unresearched issue of cyclical broadcasts of programmes edited by Rev. Tadeusz Kirschke in 1952–1975 available on the portal
of RFE and in the monthly *Na Antenie*. In addition to identifying the subject
matter, the research questions included determining the unofficial group of
journalists who covered religious issues and the radio genres they most often
employed. The results show that the topics discussed in broadcasts were dominated by issues of Church life in Poland, the countries of the Soviet Bloc and
around the world. These mostly involved the relationship between the Church
and state, the strategy behind the Communists' struggle against religion, and
the lies and propaganda against the Church hierarchs.

The next chapter – *Mass Media under Censorial Surveillance. Politics in Press
in the Polish People's Republic of the 1960s and 70s* – shows the role of censors in
communist Poland. Its main purpose is to analyse the operations of communist censorship in the 1960s and 70s in the Polish People's Republic, including
its impact on the national press of the period. The author takes a keen interest in the complex relationships between censors and editors-in-chief, with
particular focus on the compromises the latter had to accept to escape bans of
single issues or even whole newspapers.

The chapter *The Book Policy of the Cultural Department of the Central Committee of the Polish United Workers' Party in the Final Years of the Polish People's
Republic* constitutes a brief analysis of Communist Party opinions on Polish
book publishing and information dissemination between 1985–1989. An analysis of the documents produced by the appointed teams operating under the
patronage of the Cultural Department of the Central Committee of the Polish
United Workers' Party reveals several characteristics of the attitude of the
Party's elites towards literature.

*Słowo Narodowe (1989–1991): The First Legal Post-War Magazine of the Polish
National Radical Camp* is the next part of our publication. It discusses arrange-
ments made during the Round Table Agreement that influenced the development of the media in Poland, overturning repression against samizdat and
replacing the concession system with the registration system. The new legislation made it possible to establish titles with a range of views. The monthly
Słowo Narodowe [English: *National Word*] appeared in May 1989. It was the first
legal magazine of the national radical camp in Poland, and a platform for the
presentation of nationalist ideas and programmes during the period of political transformation.

The next chapter of the book covers the very interesting topic of investigative journalism. The part is entitled *Investigative Journalism and the Public
Image Crises of Politicians – selected examples*. Investigative journalism is a
form of control for those in public life, in particular in politics. In many cases,

investigative journalists revealed the pathological mechanisms in the world of politics, which, in turn, negatively affected the positively created image of politicians holding high positions. The intention of the study is to examine the correlation between the results of journalistic investigations and the image crisis for politicians on selected examples. Polish investigative journalism not only publicises and introduces discourse on important topics of public interest, but first and foremost stigmatises politicians for certain behaviour, which includes corruption, nepotism, law-breaking and indecency.

The next chapter focuses on the relationship between the media and citizens' crucial right to information. The study entitled *The Media and Citizens' Right to Information. The Reliability and Objectivity of Journalists in the Light of Empirical Research of the Polish Press Between 2010 and 2018* attempts to assess the professionalism of news journalists concerning citizens' rights to information. The study includes an interdisciplinary analysis of source material and the literature. The chapter shows that the professionalism of the local press in terms of citizens' rights to information is similar to that offered by the commercial national press. The analysed press articles allow the conclusion that local news sources contain opinions that may have an adverse impact on citizens' access to reliable information.

The next part of the publication describes the relation between religious media (web portals) and politics. The aim of the research entitled *Political Communication in Selected Polish Religious Web Portals (2019–2020)* is to analyse the process of communication in selected Polish religious portals (deon.pl, gosc.pl, aleteia.pl, Stacja7.pl, wiara.pl) related to political events in Poland between 06/08/2019 and 30/04/2020. Since the selected portals can be treated as active participants in political debate, the analysis undertaken increases the cognitive value in the area of the political involvement of Polish religious websites.

New technologies have enabled the development of new types of media – including social media. Among the many different issues related to social media, one seems to be very crucial. The next chapter, entitled *Fake News and Image Crises in Politics in the Social Media Space*, scrutinises the issue of fake news and its impact on politics. Current political activity is inescapably intertwined with the media space, as this is where politicians are given the opportunity to present themselves and their programmes. Their ideas are also most often disseminated and evaluated through media messages, and then analysed and processed. In the study, this social media space is considered in the context of the institutional media environment and social media. In both of the selected spheres, fake news may threaten the reputation of a politician and their organisation. The aim of the study is to analyse potential image crises caused by fake news.

The next two parts of the publication discuss the connection between the media and political elections. Both chapters focus on the figure of Małgorzata Kidawa-Błońska as a presidential candidate. The first one is entitled *The Presidential Campaign of Małgorzata Kidawa-Błońska in Media Discourse. Analysis Based on Statistical Corpus Analysis and Topic Modelling*. The purpose of the study is to identify the possible reasons behind the candidate's failure in opinion polls. The two main topics presented are how the media discourse on Małgorzata Kidawa-Błońska as a presidential candidate changed over time and the way the media presented her electoral programme. The chapter shows that the insufficient visibility of the candidate's programme in the media can lead to a complete election failure.

The second chapter about elections is entitled *Gender Stereotypes in Polish Presidential Campaigns Based on the Case of Małgorzata Kidawa-Błońska*. The paper aims to investigate the presence of stereotypes in the media discourse that accompanied the presidential campaign of Małgorzata Kidawa-Błońska, a key politician of the opposition. It shows many examples of stereotypes regarding women's role in politics applied in the media discourse. In the analysed case, the study indicates that the candidate herself, politicians from her political camp, and the media that supported her provoked and reinforced gender stereotypes. As a result, this narrative was inconsistent with her party's strategy and was unpalatable to its electorate.

The book does not address all research issues in the field, only those that were most important for the authors in the context of their current research interests, but it expands the existing research in the field of social sciences, political science, media and communications.

The publication is mainly aimed at academics. Individual chapters deal with topics that are of key importance for research and debate, including: political science, media studies, history, cultural studies, sociology and law, amongst others. Thanks to its selected thematic, empirical and innovative approach, the study focuses on revealing the history of the media in Poland in the context of key political events. The book may also be an interesting source of international comparison, especially in Europe.

The editors and authors of individual chapters have made every effort to ensure that the arguments they present, the concepts and theories they describe, as well as the most important historical and political events are digestible for the average recipient, therefore the book arouses interest and is comprehensible not only to the scientific community, students or media scientists, but also to the general public.

The monograph is characterised by its great scientific value, while, at the same time, offering an insight for readers interested in the subject. It complements the existing knowledge of social and political changes in mass media and the information society. The publication is to provide the reader with knowledge about the mutual relationship between the sphere of politics and the media, at the same time as being an inspiration for reflection, discussion and further research not exhausted in the issues presented here.

CHAPTER 1

The Lviv-Based *Parisian Fashion Daily* (1840–1848) – between Fashion and Politics

Katarzyna Drąg

1.1 Introduction

A hundred times better than any similar publication as it offers a careful selection of articles, promotes the mother tongue and thoughts, and describes real life, while others are filled with unbearable babble' (*An extract from Kraszewski's letter / Wyjątek z listu Kraszewskiego*, 1841) – the compliment was written by the renowned writer and journalist Józef Ignacy Kraszewski about *Dziennik Mód Paryskich* in 1841 – the second year of its operation (Drąg, 2015).

A unique example of the struggle for a free press in difficult political conditions, namely the *Dziennik Mód Paryskich*, is covered in this chapter. The described example is very important for the history of the Polish and European press and journalism. It shows the mechanism of journalists' struggle to maintain national identity at a time when Poland did not exist on the map of Europe. To obtain this result, the analysis of the literary criticism and the content of press was used.

Dziennik Mód Paryskich is a periodical worthy of the attention of press historians and political scientists, since it aptly illustrates how an editorial board could link fashion content with literature and patriotism, and importantly, do it under the nose of Austrian censorship. The magazine was of paramount importance for the dissemination of democratic ideas among Poles residing both within and outside the Austrian Partition.

The deeper insight gained into the premise and history of the periodical allows us to recapture numerous significant literary, journalistic, and socio-political contexts that had a considerable impact on the Lviv media market in the early 19th century. At the same time, any reflection on *Dziennik Mód Paryskich* is inseparably intertwined with the great socio-political movement which brought a shift in power and social relationships in various regions of Europe – the Spring of Nations.

© KATARZYNA DRĄG, 2024 | DOI:10.1163/9789004687998_003

1.2   Dziennik Mód Paryskich – Characteristic

Dziennik Mód Paryskich ran for eight years under its original title – between January 1, 1840 and June 24, 1848 – and for several months (intermittently from July 1, 1848 to February 17, 1849), with numbering maintained, but under a different title: *Tygodnik Polski. Pismo Poświęcone Literaturze, Obyczajom i Strojom / Polish Weekly. A Magazine on Literature, Customs and Clothing.*

The periodical predominantly operated as a biweekly, but became a weekly in 1848. The vast majority of the budget came from subscriptions, the number of which changed dynamically. Initially, there were one hundred subscribers, a figure that doubled within the first year, and continued to rise steadily together with the growth of the paper itself. The years 1847–1848 marked the height of its popularity, with a staggering 1,000 subscriptions (Poklewska, 2002, p. 207), at which time it also exerted the greatest impact on its readers' political awareness.

The paper was a Polish counterpart to the popular Western European fashion magazines, mostly French publications: *Journal des Tailleurs, La Mode. Revue du Monde Elegant,* and *Petit Courrier des Dames. Journal des Modes.* Founded and printed in Lviv, not only did it find subscribers in Galicia, but also in other partitioned areas of Poland. Interestingly, similar fashion magazines were also published in the Russian Partition, i.e., the Warsaw-based *Magazyn Mód. Dziennik Przyjemnych Wiadomości / Fashion Magazine. Feelgood News Daily* and *Dziennik Domowy. Poświęcony Życiu Domowemu, Familijnemu i Towarzyskiemu / Home Daily. On Domestic, Family and Social Life* in Poznan (Poklewska, 2002, p. 207).

The target readers included intelligentsia, bourgeois, craftsmen, and sapient landowners. Naturally, women were also an important target audience, not just through the fashion-related nature of the periodical, but primarily for their role in the patriotic upbringing of the next Polish generations.

1.3   Conditions for the Development of the Press in Lviv

The idea to establish a literary journal in Lviv emerged in the 1830s – a time when the Austrian Empire imposed harsh censorship based primarily on the Franciscan Penal Code of 1803 (the so-called *Strafgesetz*). This code (which listed the breaches of the censorship code, including the publication of content compromising public order and that of treason) gave censors the virtually unlimited possibility to redact texts to be published. What is more, censorship in the Austrian partition was based on the Act of Press Law of 20 September

1819 (the co-called *Pressegesetz*) passed by the German Confederation during the Congress of the Holy Alliance in Carlsbad, and customarily named after its proponent, Klemens von Metternich (Tyrowicz, 1978, p. 7). As a result, in Galicia censorial restrictions were a major factor inhibiting the development of the press and, thereby, public opinion. First and foremost, censors curtailed the evolution of political thought, especially the dissemination of the notion of independence. 'The Galician press had no possibility whatsoever to provide the public with direct coverage of current political events' (Tyrowicz, 1978, p. 22).

Journalists had no opportunity to establish their own periodical, since all requests for press permits were rejected out of hand, as 'all authors were suspected of misusing literature to propagate completely irrelevant principles that transgressed (...) boundaries of innocent intellectual entertainment' (Zawadzki, 1961, p. 153). Therefore, a different solution was necessary – one that would allow for the propagation of literature in Polish and the dissemination of socio-political ideas. 'Essentially, there was a need for a publisher who could guarantee that the new periodical would not appear to have any hidden tendencies, and that its main objective would be nothing other than intellectual entertainment' (Zawadzki, 1961, p. 153).

1.4   Tomasz Kulczycki – Founder of Dziennik Mód Paryskich

Dziennik Mód Paryskich was founded and published by Tomasz Kulczycki, who was born on March 19, 1803 in the town of Zwierzyniec within the Lubelskie Region. However, he spent most of his life in Lviv, where he graduated from vocational school and started his tailoring career. Recognised for his excellent craftsmanship, he is remembered both as someone who transformed tailoring, and an editor-in-chief of an interesting periodical, which – despite its title, or perhaps because of it – played an important political role in 19th century Galicia.

Kulczycki owed his immense popularity to the new technique of cut that he had adapted from the renown Parisian tailor Compaing, and which he later developed and propagated across the Polish partitioned territories. Kulczycki's version of the technique was based on the assumption that a measuring tape and a compass were enough for anybody to prepare custom-made sewing patterns; an approach which was truly revolutionary in the 19th century. Not only did he apply the new cut and pattern system in his own studio, but he also devoted time and energy to propagating the solution outside Lviv, in places like Vienna or Warsaw, where he instructed master tailor Straupernicki on the innovative technique, thereby promulgating it among Varsovian tailors (Rogoziewicz, 1933, p. 6). In an attempt to promote the French measuring system, Kulczycki compiled and published a dedicated booklet entitled *A Treatise on the Cut of Male Broadcloth by Mathematical Reckoning / Rozprawa o kroju sukien męskich podług wyrachowania matematycznego* (Kulczycki, 1839). He gained fame as a master tailor who, on the one hand, was able to meet the expectations of the most demanding customer, and on the other hand, gave the readers of his periodical the opportunity to use fashionable sewing patterns to make their own garments.

In 1835, Kulczycki purchased a tenement house on St Mary's Square in Lviv, where he opened a thriving and immensely popular tailoring studio that employed fifty journeymen. However, despite being the owner of a successful sewing business and a wealthy man, Kulczycki never felt completely self-fulfilled, being driven by a desire to pursue his social and political ambitions. As a result, several years later he used the same address to house the premises of another business: 'the editorial office of *Dziennik Mód Paryskich*' (Rosnowska, 1967, p. 64).

This all made Kulczycki the ideal candidate that the penmen from *Ziewonja* – a literary group operating in the Austrian Partition between 1832 and 1838 – had been seeking. The group consisted of Galician democratic conspirators and former participants of the November Uprising. In 1934, the group, led by Augustyn Bielowski, managed to publish the first volume of an almanac of literary texts, which became the group's ideological and artistic manifesto (Witkowska & Przybylski, 2002, p. 573). Four years later, attempts were made to form a centre for Slavophilic Romanticism in Galicia, and the group managed with difficulty to publish a second volume. 'In Galicia, several attempts were made to implement major initiatives that would bring a different, more individual, face to the programme of literary criticism, none of which was ever successful for political reasons' (Witkowska & Przybylski, 2002, p. 573). It was also political repressions that impeded the development of the *Ziewonja* movement.

In all probability, it was either August Wysocki or Józef Dunin Borkowski who hit upon the idea of establishing a new periodical with the help of Tomasz Kulczycki, who owed his professional success in the Austrian Partition to his own financial competences. Being a public-spirited entrepreneur, this exceptional artisan decided to use his personal wealth to support literature and his now subsumed country, and all that on top of his regular charity work. 'His social and patriotic deeds secured Kulczycki a well-deserved place in history' (Rogoziewicz, 1933, p. 6).

An application by a master tailor to run a fashion magazine had high chances of approval, and this is exactly what happened. On April 30, 1839 Kulczycki was granted 'a consent by the president of the highest police authority in Vienna (...) to establish a Lviv-based journal entitled *Dziennik Mód Paryskich*' (Tłuczek, 2005). A few months later, the first issue was published, bringing a new quality to the Polish press market. The periodical is considered the forerunner of the quantitative breakthrough in journalism which followed in 1848 (Tyrowicz, 1979), while some researchers argue that it was *Dziennik Mód Paryskich* that initiated the first shoots of modern journalism in enslaved Poland (Szczerbiński, 1985–1986, p. 4).

Kulczycki was behind the high-quality illustrations, sewing patterns, and cuts in the integral part of the periodical, but he knew next to nothing about literature and journalistic work. These, therefore, became the responsibility of consecutive editors-in-chief: Żegota Pauli, August Bielowski, Jan Dobrzański, Karol Szajnocha, and Jan Zachariasiewicz. The authors who had the greatest impact on the ideological and literary shape of the paper were the Lviv-based journalists: August Bielowski, the Dunin-Borkowski brothers, Dominik Magnuszewski, and Józef Dzierzkowski. At first, the founders focused primarily on piquing the reader's interests while they themselves learnt how to edit a modern style of magazine. The following years were devoted to editorial work aimed at educating the society on democratic ideas, and criticising the egoistic, self-interested attitudes of the nobility.

1.5   Dziennik Mód Paryskich – Content

'The fashion aspect was there to lure wider audiences – especially female readers – for whom literature on its own was not attractive enough. At that time, it turned out to be a shrewd promotion of the journal, since those intrigued readers involuntarily absorbed the extra literary content, became familiar with it, and began to look out for more' (Zawadzki, 1961, p. 154) – accounted Władysław Zawadzki, a diarist of the period, discussing the role the founders attributed to the tailoring theme. He implied that, from the very beginning, it was assumed that combining fashion news with socio-literal content would make the latter more digestible.

Historians studying *Dziennik Mód Paryskich* have expressed conflicting opinions on the profile that allowed the editors to combine a fashion magazine with a biweekly on literature. Janina Rosnowska contradicted the view expressed by Krystyna Poklewska, who supported 'the prevailing belief that the paper's profile had been chosen accidentally, as *malum necessarium'* (Rosnowska, 1967, pp. 61–62). Rosnowska (1967) argued that the group of creators was so diverse that not all members found the specialised profile of fashion magazine 'conspiratorial' enough. On the other hand, Jacek Szczerbiński maintained that, initially, *Dziennik Mód Paryskich* had been 'an advertising and crafts-oriented magazine devoted to tailoring, but soon transformed into a literary and journalistic periodical that did not shun political thought' (Szczerbiński, 1985–1986, p. 30), emphasising the evolution of its profile and role.

An analysis of the magazine's content sheds some light on the topic. The first issue was short – consisting of four pages with a supplement filled with drawings – and was devoted exclusively to fashion. There was a description of winter coats for women to be seen in Parisian theatres, a presentation on fashionable hair decorations, an homage to elastic corset laces, and a revival of classical hatbands. Male readers were advised to wear tailcoats with tetragonal tails, and white silk waistcoats, while descriptions of children's garments, as well as detailed tailoring instructions, cut drawings and sewing patterns completed the issue. Two weeks later, a second issue was published, enriched with four retail advertisements in the column *The National Industry and Trade of Fashion Commodities / Przemysł i handel artykułami mody w kraju*, and the first piece of an unsigned serial novel entitled *Victim to Love / Ofiara miłości*. In 1840, the fourth issue brought the first references to the city's local community – the article *The Lviv Carnival / Karnawał Lwowski* describing a celebration held in the Redoubt.

In the months to come, the magazine published first-person narratives presenting scenes covering family life and romance under the guise of fashion, which posed an opportunity to demonstrate certain patterns of behaviour, choices and values (*The Night of December 24 / Noc 24 grudnia*, 1841; *An Inaccessible Friend / Niedostępny przyjaciel*, 1841). Another novelty was the theatrical reviews – a must-have for any magazine with cultural and political aspirations. Over time, the section on culture was expanded with a music column, and a column on new books, which was particularly eager to inform the reader on newly released dissertations on the tradition and history of Poland, as well as premiering historical novels (*New Releases / Nowości*, 1847). At the same time, the literature section was successively developed, from an unimpressive serialised novel to a column that presented poetry, short stories, extract from dramas, and other literary genres.

The founders went to great lengths to familiarise readers with the world beyond their borders and social relationships in other cultures. An example of which was a series of articles entitled *Several Journeys / Kilka podróży* by Dominik Magnuszewski, who characterised women's role in the social life abroad. The author wrote: 'How do you find the position of women in this part of the world, my Ladies? This abundant collection of sketches will provide you with its accurate image' (Magnuszewski, 1844, p. 35). In general, a woman's role was among the most commonly discussed issues, since it enabled promotion of patriotic and democratic attitudes (*On Upbringing / O wychowaniu*, 1846; Dobrzański, 1841). The same was true for poems, which were peppered with metaphors that the reader could easily interpret through the prism of patriotism. 'My breath scorched with memories / A wraith burning my thoughts. Worn by time,/ Trapped in the coffin,/ Enfolded by deathly air,/ It always returns to ignite the hellfire,/ Always dead, always immortal', wrote Leszek Borkowski in the poem *The Past / Przeszłość* (Borkowski, 1846).

Today, it is extremely difficult to determine what rationale and motives led the founders to establish the magazine. Having analysed its content, Ewa Tłuczek pointed to the literary character: 'The most significant section was devoted to literature, which took 68.2 % of the printed content, out of which 12.2 % was on poetry, and the rest on short stories and (serial) novels, novellas, and other literary genres' (Tłuczek, 2003, p. 84). In 1847, the publishers also mentioned the literary nature of the magazine while informing readers of changes to the frequency of the publication: 'When a fashion magazine is released biweekly, there is no space for a comprehensive section on literature. Therefore, the Publisher appealed to the Government for consent to transform it into a weekly' (*Publisher's Note / Od wydawcy*, 1847). Zofia Sokół stresses its 1846 transformation from 'a women's magazine to a socio-literary journal' (Sokół, 2001, p. 511).

However, the most significant conclusion is that the diverse editorial board of *Dziennik Mód Paryskich* managed to create one of the two most prominent periodicals that were paramount for the development of insurrectionary and democratic ideas in romantic-democratic Galicia. The other being *Dziennik Literacki*, which was published between 1852 and 1854, and then from 1856 to 1870. '*Dziennik Mód Paryskich* was among the first modern Polish publications. Initially, it was a magazine on general culture, before being transformed into a political journal aimed at shaping public opinion. The ideological and literary programme was pro-Western European, orientated towards educating readers on the democratic spirit of precise and logical thinking, while revealing a tendency to link belles-lettres with sociology, without repudiating the ethical, historical and philosophical premises of Romanticism', argued Krystyna Poklewska (2002, p. 209).

1.6   Dobrzański as a Chief Editor

The Revolutions of 1848, which triggered changes in social and political relationships throughout Europe, had a distinct impact on the Galician press,
which became much more politicised. The Spring of Nations turned out to be
too formidable a challenge to be ignored by individual editorial boards, since
the global events 'forced' journalists to hold, as far as it was permitted, an ideological and political debate.

It was during the Spring of Nations that Jan Dobrzański became
editor-in-chief of the magazine (taking the post in early 1847). An extremely
skilful organiser and reformer of the editorial office, Dobrzański supported
the democratic movement, a position concordant with the views presented in
the periodical. 'Stronger accentuation of the programme initiated by the new
editorial board transformed the relatively colourless *Dziennik Mód Paryskich*
into an expressive socio-literary magazine and a pioneer of democratic principles, strenuously defended and vehemently propagated in every single line
and word, by all genres – novels, poems, dissertations, literary and art reviews',
wrote Władysław Zawadzki (1961, p. 165), emphasising the democratic nature
of the periodical, openly glorifying Dobrzański, and overly criticising previous
editors.

Under Austrian censorship, political content had to be concealed behind the
literary character of the magazine. 'There were no possibilities for the Galician
press to provide readers with direct coverage of current political affairs of the
time. However, journalists in *Dziennik Mód Paryskich* still managed to popularise issues related to social development and national culture' (Tyrowicz, 1978,
p. 22). The terrible events of 1846 had an immensely detrimental impact on the
democratic movement but did not directly affect the magazine, which was to
survive another two years – going on to play an even more important role.

A breakthrough for the magazine came in 1848. The Spring of Nations was
spreading across Europe, and eventually the revolutionary spirit reached Lviv,
causing great agitation, which accumulated around the editorial board of *Dziennik Mód Paryskich*. Jan Dobrzański played a crucial role in the foundation
of a revolutionary committee (on March 18, 1848) to write an address to the
emperor. As a result of his personally reading out the address and appealing
for the citizens of Lviv to sign it (to which they responded enthusiastically), he
gained the status of a man of the people.

March 18, 1848 and the events of the following days and weeks made
Dobrzański a well-known man, not only (as previously) as an editor, but
above all, as a social and political activist. Undoubtedly, this was partially
because he understood how to utilise his authority and the possibilities that

came with the position of editor-in-chief. 'The address contained all the demands of the oppressed nation, since it called for a national administration in Galicia and for a Sejm, for a liberal municipal legal framework, a national guard and a Polish army, schools for the people, the reintroduction of the Polish language to all lecture halls and science centres, for a grand jury, the abolishment of serfdom, and the abolition of peasant slavery, for equal justice under the law for all social classes and religious groups, for a free press, freedom of peaceful assembly, civil liberties, a general amnesty, and for legitimisation of the revolutionary committee itself' (Giller, 1887, pp. 11–12).

As stated above, Jan Dobrzański played the dual role of an editor and a social leader during the Spring of Nations. His political commitment translated into a rise in the popularity of the periodical he ran, while, at the same time, his editorial job gave him the opportunity to get politically involved in the first place. Not only did his professional activity give him prominence, but also his political involvement increased the social gravitas of his editorial post. The story of the periodical is intertwined with the story of the Galician community, and its journalistic work made it possible to win over Lviv public opinion. The events surrounding the Revolution of 1848 were vividly described by Zawadzki: 'On March 19, 1848 Jan Dobrzański was no longer an anonymous figure when he stepped out onto the balcony of master tailor Tomasz Kulczycki's apartment on the corner of Mariacki and Halicki Sqaures to read out the address to the emperor to the ecstatic Lviv citizens' (Zawadzki, 1961, p. 165). This was also true for the editorial office of *Dziennik Mód Paryskich*, which on the very same day welcomed crowds wishing to sign the document. At that time, Dobrzański – the appointed man of the people, utterly exhausted yet energised by the crowd, controlling the situation from the balcony of the editorial office during the day, and observing the cheering masses from the window of his own home at night – became not only a symbol of liberation and revolutionary tendencies, but also a sign of a new epoch of journalism in Galicia, particularly in Lviv. This is when the name Dobrzański's and the title 'editor' became inseparable (Szczerbiński, 1985–1986, p. 25).

1.7   Conclusion

A historic moment for *Dziennik Mód Paryskich* came after the public reading of the address and the ensuing signature collection. Following these events, the periodical operated for a few more months only. One may, therefore, conclude that this long-lived magazine, which had played such a critical role in the history of the Polish press within the Austrian Partition, was sacrificed and lost on account of the events that occurred in the memorable year of 1848. The last issues of the paper no longer began with news on male and female fashion. Instead the front pages were filled with politically-oriented articles, e.g., *On Unity and Lack of Civil Courage in Poland / O jedności i braku cywilnej odwagi w Polsce* by Michał Wiesiołowski (1848), and *Future Poland / Przyszła Polska*, whose author wrote openly: 'Falling under the burden of servitude, we could only find consolation in the sheer hope of future restoration, but today, when this hope takes real shape – despite all the ongoing mischiefs and calamities – we should be preparing materialistically to make it happen, and morally for when it eventually happens' (Future Poland / Przyszła Polska, 1848, p. 1).

Issue 24 of 1848 brought a leading article with a meaningful title: *Act One / Pierwszy akt*, whose opening sentence was worded as follows: 'Act one of the great 1848 drama is over' (*Act One / Pierwszy akt*, 1848, p. 1). The author described the revolutionary awakening and its signs across Europe, with particular focus on the fortunes and participation of Poles. The article contained a somewhat peculiar summary of the hopes behind the Spring of Nations: 'In all probability, no other play depicting the real world has raised hopes as high as this revolutionary drama, staged in front of the global audience and commenced in Paris, which played the role of a theatre prompt box for the whole of Europe' (*Act One / Pierwszy akt*, 1848, p. 1). Issue 27 of 1848 was the first published under a new name: *Polish Weekly. A Magazine on Literature, Customs and Clothing / Tygodnik Polski. Pismo poświęcone literaturze, obyczajom i strojom*, which the editorial board had preannounced in late June: 'On July 1, following a change that grants us a wider scope and more transparent mode of operation, the somewhat inaccurate name *Dziennik Mód Paryskich* will be replaced with *Polish Weekly. A Magazine on Literature, Customs and Clothing / Tygodnik Polski. Pismo poświęcone literaturze, obyczajom i strojom*, since it aptly reflects the idea behind a magazine that aims to shape the intellectual life of Poland. Importantly, all supplements with images, drawings, sewing patterns, as well as the price and subscription shall remain the same' (*Announcement / Ogłoszenie*, 1848, p. 1).

In 1849 (the year Jan Zachariasiewicz was appointed the editor-in-chief) the failure of the Spring of Nations at the beginning of the year that followed translated into a drastic decline in subscriptions, which resulted in the financial failure of the magazine. When the very last issue was published on February 17, 1849, Tomasz Kulczycki had lost a total of 10,000 zlotys (*Dziennik Mód Paryskich*, 2020).

Even though prematurely wiped off the Lviv press market, *Dziennik Mód Paryskich* did fulfil an important role, allowing for a transfer of Western thought. The word 'fashion' in the title may be interpreted as referring not only to garments, as initially intended, but also to certain trends and opinions. The magazine transposed Parisian fashion to Polish reality, while, at the same time, propagating the idea of a political independent Polish state. Additionally, the paper sustained the Polish language and promoted reading in it. As a specialised journal, it had its particular practical dimension, but it also played a universal role, shaping public opinion, and promoting the literary works of Galician romantic-democrats. Undeniably, *Dziennik Mód Paryskich* was an exceptional enterprise at that time, and, even today, it remains a valuable source of information for historians of sociology, crafts and trades.

In the history of press and journalism, Tomasz Kulczycki remains an extraordinary figure. For years, this tailor-publisher invested in a magazine that was both specialist and ideological. He managed to combine the dimension of trade and commerce with a political and opinion-forming slant, and during the Spring of Nations he succeeded in transforming the editorial office into a political institution.

References

Borkowski, L. (January 8, 1848) *Future / Przeszłość*. Dziennik Mód Paryskich, p. 3.

Dobrzański, J. (November 16, 1841). *Woman / Kobieta*. Dziennik Mód Paryskich, pp. 173–176.

Drąg, K. (2015). Powieściowy kodeks etyczny profesjonalizującego się dziennikarstwa. "W mętnej wodzie" Józefa Ignacego Kraszewskiego. *Studia Socialia Cracoviensia, 12* (1) 131–142. doi: 10.15633/ssc.985

Dziennik Mód Paryskich. (January 2020) Downloaded from: http://polskaprasa.cba.pl /tytuly/dziennik_mod_paryskich.html

Franke, J. (1999). *Polska prasa kobieca w latach 1820–1918. W kręgu ofiary i poświęcenia.* Warsaw: Wydawnictwo Stowarzyszenia Bibliotekarzy Polskich.

Giller, A. (1887). *Jan Dobrzański: wspomnienie pośmiertne.* Lviv: Przewodnik Gimnastyczny Sokół.

Kulczycki, T. (1839). *A Treatise on the Cut of Male Broadcloth by Mathematical Reckoning / Rozprawa o kroju sukien męskich podług wyrachowania matematycznego.* Lviv: editor's edition.

Magnuszewski, D. (1844, 24 February). *Several Journeys / Kilka podróży*. Dziennik Mód Paryskich, p. 35.

An Inaccessible Friend / Niedostępny przyjaciel. (February 1, 1841). Dziennik Mód Paryskich, p. 23.

The Night of December 24/Noc 24 grudnia. (January 1, 1841). Dziennik Mód Paryskich, p. 1.

New Releases / Nowości. (December 16, 1847). Dziennik Mód Paryskich, p. 171.

On Women's Education. The Current State of Women's Education and its Effect on their Duties / O wychowaniu kobiet. Obecny stan wychowania kobiet, skutki tegoż na ich obowiązki, (September 10, 1846). Dziennik Mód Paryskich, pp. 146–150.

Editor's Note / Od wydawcy. (November 18, 1847). Dziennik Mód Paryskich, p. 256.

Announcement / Ogłoszenie. (June 17, 1848). Dziennik Mód Paryskich, p. 1.

Act One / Pierwszy akt. (June 10, 1848). Dziennik Mód Paryskich, pp. 1–3.

Poklewska, K. (2002). Dziennik Mód Paryskich. W J. Bachórz, A. Kowalczykowa (Eds.) *Słownik literatury polskiej XIX wieku* (pp. 207–209). Wroclaw, Warsaw, Krakow: Wydawnictwo Zakładu Narodowego imienia Ossolińskich.

Future Poland / Przyszła Polska. (May 27, 1848). *Dziennik Mód Paryskich,* p. 2.

Rogoziewicz, W. (1933). Tomasz Kulczycki. Sylwetki zasłużonych rzemieślników. *Sezonowy Żurnal Mód Męskich i Damskich,* 2, 6.

Rosnowska, J. (1967). Twórcy "Dziennika Mód Paryskich". *Rocznik Historii Czasopiśmiennictwa Polskiego,* 2, 61–91.

Sokół, Z. (2001). *Tomasz Kulczycki, krawiec-redaktor i wydawca lwowski.* W. J. Jarowiecki *(Red.) Kraków–Lwów. Książki – czasopisma – biblioteki XIX i XX wieku* (pp. 499–518). Krakow: Wydawnictwo Naukowe Akademii Pedagogicznej.

Szczerbiński J., (1985–1986). Środowisko dziennikarzy lwowskich 1831–1863: narodziny zawodu. *Kwartalnik Historii Prasy Polskiej,* 2, 25–45.

Tłuczek, E. (2003). *Dziennik Mód Paryskich – próba analizy zawartości (komunikat).* W J. Jarowiecki (ed.) Kraków – Lwów. Książki – czasopisma – biblioteki XIX i XX wieku (pp. 79–88). Krakow: Wydawnictwo Naukowe Akademii Pedagogicznej.

Tłuczek, E. (2005). *Lwów w korespondencji Januarego Poźniaka.* W H. Kosętka (Red.) Kraków - Lwów: książki, czasopisma, biblioteki (pp. 413–419). Krakow: Wydawnictwo Naukowe Akademii Pedagogicznej.

Tyrowicz, M. (1978). Austriacka polityka cenzuralna a prasa galicyjska 1772–1849. *Kwartalnik Historii Prasy Polskiej,* 1, pp. 5–26.

Tyrowicz, M. (1979). *Prasa Galicji i Rzeczpospolitej Krakowskiej 1772–1850.* Krakow: Wydawnictwo Literackie.

Wiesiołowski, M. (1848, 20 May). On Unity and Lack of Civil Courage in Poland / O jedności i braku cywilnej odwagi w Polsce. *Dziennik Mód Paryskich,* pp. 1–3.

Witkowska, A. & Przybylski, R. (2002). *Romantyzm.* Warsaw: Wydawnictwo Naukowe PWN.

An extract from Kraszewski's letter of February 4, 1841 to the Editors of 'Dziennik Mód Paryskich' / Wyjątek z listu Kraszewskiego do redakcji Dziennika Mód Paryskich z 4 lutego 1841. (March 16, 1841). Dziennik Mód Paryskich, p. 48.

Zawadzki, W. (1961). *Pamiętniki życia literackiego w Galicji.* Krakow: Wydawnictwo Literackie.

CHAPTER 2

The Political and Societal Position Taken by the Weekly *Gość Niedzielny* over the Threats to the Catholic Worldview in the Interwar Period

Rafał Śpiewak

Founded and published in Upper Silesia between 1923 and 1939, the Catholic weekly newspaper *Gość Niedzielny* is an important and rich source of historical knowledge on the challenges faced by the Church and society at the time.

In the inter-war period, for both liberal and socialist currents, the Catholic Church was the most dangerous opponent in the worldview struggle. Both currents, although ideologically different, were united precisely by the fact that they saw in the Church's teaching and its social position a factor preventing the transformation of society's worldview, and they became *de facto* allies in attacking the Catholic Church. Various ways were sought to undermine the authority of the Church. It therefore became an urgent task for the Catholic press to raise awareness and energise the laity to defend the Catholic Church and the principles of social life it proclaimed. The purpose of this article is to present the main motives behind the journalistic world-view of *Gość Niedzielny* in its initial years of publication. This view was shaped by the challenges faced by the Catholic Church in Upper Silesia after its annexation to the Polish state in 1922, when the Diocese of Katowice was established and was consistent with the attempts of the Catholic Church in Poland to counteract the threat of the secularisation of society.

Gość Niedzielny constantly addressed the various socio-political issues and defended the Church, while exposing the intentions of its opponents and refuting their arguments. In the face of the attempts to undermine the Church's authority and devalue the role of religion in society, *Gość Niedzielny* had the vital role of raising awareness and educating its readers. *Gość Niedzielny* also fulfilled an important function in activating readers to take up the defence of Christian principles.

The process of researching the press as a historical source is, according to Jerzy Myslinski, "[...] labour-intensive, but offering the possibility of tracing the studied phenomena in their multifaceted complexity" (Myslinski, 1974, p. 8). This author is of the opinion that the analysis of journalism of past periods facilitates the reading of selected phenomena or processes embedded in the

© RAFAŁ ŚPIEWAK, 2024 | DOI:10.1163/9789004687998_004

realities of everyday life and comprehending the social climate of the times in which it was published. In his opinion, the press is an important historical source to reconstruct, to a large extent, the social issues and the opinions of the editorial board and the readership (Myslinski, 1974, p. 10), since the press not only reflected the mood of public opinion to some extent, but also shaped that opinion.

The research considered the available issues of the weekly magazine from 1923–1939 stored in the archives of the current editorial office of *Gość Niedzielny* in Katowice. The analysis was based on selected articles from *Gość Niedzielny* and its supplement *Front Katolicki*. The content analysis carried out here is idiographic in nature. An attempt was made to decipher the primary motives and methods of *Gość Niedzielny* in relation to social issues from the perspective of the Upper Silesian region.

2.1   Historical Context

The annexation of a part of Upper Silesia to Poland in 1922 necessitated the creation of an apostolic administration in this area: separate from the Diocese of Wrocław, and then, in 1925, the Diocese of Katowice, headed by Father August Hlond (Królikowski, Paprotna, 2017; Myszor, 2013 (a); Myszor, 2013 (b)). One of his most important initiatives was the founding of the church weekly *Gość Niedzielny* in September 1923 (Myszor, 1999, p. 228; Grajewski, 2008, p. 11; Szczepaniak 2015, p. 322). This was a diocesan periodical of a pastoral nature, whose primary task was to awaken religious life in Silesia and integrate the Catholic community. It was distributed throughout the parish network and thus reached its target readership quickly (Grajewski, 2008, p. 15; Brzoza, 1998, p. 9), with the readership growing year on year. From the information in the pages of this weekly, we learn that it had about 45,000 subscribers after less than a decade of publishing (*Acknowledgement, Request and Wish of the Editor*, 1932, p. 6). From its inception, it became an important tool for resisting the anti-Catholic worldview that was taking place in the sociopolitical sphere.

In the interwar period, there was constant tension between state and Church, especially in political life, despite the ratified concordat (Myszor, 1999, p. 43; Roszkowski 2003, p. 184). With this anti-clericalism being primarily fuelled by left-wing, liberal and masonic circles, it was believed that a deeper religiousness was important, which would lead, among other things, to greater responsibility and involvement in society. This religious revival was to serve not only the Church itself, but also the state as a whole. Its essential motive was not only concern for the salvation of souls, but the good of the state and the protection of the national identity in the face of detrimental worldview currents (*Secret Enemy of the Catholic Church*, 1926, p. 3; *Walka z Kościołem katolickim w Polsce*, 1934, p. 15; *W obronie prawdy, Kościół wstrzymuje pochód cywilizacji*, 1927, p. 3; *Only a Good Catholic Can Be a Good Pole, Only a Good Pole Is Able to Be a Good Catholic*, 1929, p. 3; *Social Democracy and Religion*, 1927, pp. 3–4).

After Poland regained its independence, the spiritual leaders of the Church, in a strong sense of responsibility for the faithful entrusted to them, wanted to awaken awareness of the dangers of the opposing worldviews and expose them for all to see. They did so not only out of concern for the Church, but also, in a broader sense, for the good of society as a whole. Among the most dangerous phenomena was the progressive secularisation of society under the influence of atheistic and materialist ideologies. Among those influencing this were the activities of Freemasonry, Liberalism and Bolshevism. These currents, based on atheistic foundations were intrinsically hostile to the Catholic Church, and formed a certain synergy. The Church became the target of attacks by milieus hostile to its worldview. In turn, the Church considered these currents harmful, not only to their faith, but also to the functioning of society and the state.

The religiosity and piety of the Catholic community was considered to be insufficient to repel the attacks on the Church and the deprecation of its social role during this unfavourable ideological climate (mainly carried out in the anti-clerical press) (Dutka, 2006, p. 57; Podoleński, 1922, p. 207). It therefore became necessary to revive the consciousness of Catholics and to awaken their responsibility towards society. A particular tool for this purpose at this time was the Catholic press. This was exemplified by the journalism of *Gość Niedzielny*, in the pages of which one can find numerous confirmations of the tense socio-political situation.

A well-formed religious awareness, as understood by Father August Hlond and his successors (Bishops Arkadiusz Lisiecki and Stanisław Adamski), was to be expressed and confirmed in various forms of lay social activity. Numerous Catholic organisations and associations were to be used to stimulate and direct the involvement of the laity (Myszor, 1999, p. 161). The lay faithful were to be the most important conduit for overcoming worldview threats, and particularly concerned in this was the development of Catholic Action (Rusin, 2003, pp. 30–36). This organisation was seen as the best way to put into practice the social teaching of the Church (Merkle, 2009, p. 90). The involvement of lay people was to permeate various spheres of social life with the spirit of Christ. Their activity was to overcome the secularisation of the public sphere and to preserve the dominant social status of the Catholic religion (Grzybowski, Sobolewska, 1971, pp. 109–110; Kozerska, 2005, pp. 35–40). Thus, it was intended as an expression of constructive counteraction to the pernicious influence of atheistic and secular ideologies.

2.2   Main Anti-Catholic Trends

Although *Gość Niedzielny* was intended to be a completely apolitical magazine, it could not remain indifferent to the social phenomena and worldviews threatening the Church at that time. This engagement, in the opinion of the editors of *Gość Niedzielny*, was dictated not only by concern for the Church, but also for society as a whole (Szewczyk, 2013, pp. 77–79). In essence, the magazine was intended as an antidote to the so-called *bad press*, which demoralised the faithful and deprecated the role of the Church and Catholic religion in society. (Mysłek, 1966, p. 189; Plis, 2001, p. 28; Adamski, 2008, p. 134). In view of the dangers perceived at the time, it became necessary to raise awareness and activate the broad masses of lay Catholics to take responsibility for the fate of the state and the nation in the spirit of the social teachings of the Church.

At the end of the first year of the publication of *Gość Niedzielny*, in his reflections the editor openly defined the most urgent tasks for the future – the religious and moral rebirth of society motivated by the ability to overcome the worldviews threatening the Church. In *Gość Niedzielny* we read:

> Unfortunately, we are too preoccupied with the existence of our state , with our economic well-being, to concern ourselves as vividly as in other nations with the religious renewal of our society, or with the intensification of the religious fores that seem to live dormant within us. We must openly admit that, despite all appearances, religious thought is weak in our country. How else can we explain this extremely painful, world-wearying fact that *Catholic* Poland attempted to pick a fight with the Church? In what other way can we interpret the actions seen in Poland this year, that perhaps still exist, namely the unlawful taking of Church property? For the time being this danger seems to have disappeared, but, nevertheless, the year 1923 will forever retain for Poland the stain that it wanted to harm the Church. Reflecting on what is happening to us, one still has the impression that Poland, only recently resurrected by God's grace to a new life, wants to repeat all the mistakes that other countries have made, but have corrected, being now ashamed of them. Almost all modern states went through a period of anti-clericalism and struggled against the Church. Today they confess that this was a mistake; even the most liberal press admits it and declares that the fight against the Church

and anti-clericalism was a folly and belongs to history. Today there is no talk of it. Should Poland repeat these slogans which other countries have abandoned with shame? We expect our Catholic society to come to its senses and not to follow this path, but to stand at once where other nations stand today, that is, on the path of closest understanding and friendship with the greatest moral power in the world, the Church. This hope is justified. After hearing of the anti-Church intentions of the government, a powerful movement has arisen in Poland to prevent harm to the Church. May this movement become stronger and stronger, may a deep Catholic thought and vital Catholic action arise in our country too, may a religious revival take place in our country too!. (*At the Close of the New Year*, 1923, p. 3)

It is clear from the above text that Poland, reborn after years of partition, was troubled by the ideas that threatened to secularise society and seemed to reject the centuries-old Christian heritage, and readers of *Gość Niedzielny* were made aware of this tendency to diminish the importance of the Catholic Church in both history and the present day.

One of the most important motives for awakening the consciousness of readers was the dangers of liberal currents. These were nothing new in society, nevertheless, they were steadily increasing (Grzybowski, Sobolewska, 1971, p. 62; Sroga, 2001, pp. 239–251). They were almost always characterised by a kind of antagonism towards the Catholic Church because of its traditional and conservative system of values and solutions to social issues. (Kizwalter, 1989, pp. 50–51; Novak, 1993, pp. 145–154). Pope Pius XI was very critical of Liberalism, especially in his encyclical: *Quadragessimo anno*, in which he always used the word *liberal* in a pejorative sense. He pointed out that Catholic teaching owed nothing to either Liberalism or Socialism (Novak, 1993, p. 149; Kristanova, 2006, p. 67). Nevertheless, at that time, liberalist tendencies were gaining strength, finding their embodiment in various kinds of organisations or political forces. In the religious-moral sphere, this threatened a gradual shift from liberal tolerance to religious indifferentism (Mazur, 1994, pp. 106–115). There was no shortage of people who had faith in the Lord God yet were willing to support organisations with an anti-Christian programme, since these organisations or political forces were seen by some Catholics as modern and attractive.

Liberal ideas influenced the minds of a wide spectrum of people and, therefore, the spirit of Liberalism also permeated the community of the Church (Zywczynski, 1971, pp. 18–55). Since Liberalism strongly accentuated individualistic attitudes in society, it was thought to foster the deconstruction of Christian morality (Novak 1993, pp. 152–153). This undoubtedly constituted one

of the most serious problems for the Church itself. If there was a relativisa-
tion of its teaching, there would also be a loss of its distinctiveness and, consequently, a weakening of its power to influence the faithful and society as a
whole. This blurring of worldviews and axiologies was therefore regarded by
Gość Niedzielny as a very serious threat. "The effects of the poisoning by Liberalism appear clearly in the Catholic system. The Catholic heart is weakening;
arms and legs are becoming lame. We no longer see our aims clearly; we have
become deaf to the words of truth and faith. The place of Catholic activity
has been taken by a weakened Catholic passivity. The army of the Catholic
Church – and each of us belongs to this army – prefers to desert rather than
fight. We need a doctor, we need a cure, we need reconstruction. The Church
must again become a fortress to which all peoples make their pilgrimage" (*III.
Silesian Catholic Convention, Gość Niedzielny* No. 30, 1924, pp. 4–5). With such
an awareness comes the necessity to exert all efforts and activate lay Catholics
in the social realm, on a well-founded knowledge of doctrine. The formative
and activating aspect was to be fulfilled above all by pastors, supported by the
weekly newspaper *Gość Niedzielny*. It had already been very clearly realised at
that time that political or social activity was no longer the role of the clergy,
but was a task for lay people. It was now for the laity, faithful to the teaching of the Church, to actively participate in the political life of the country, a
process that was fostered among the readers of *Gość Niedzielny*. Efforts were
made to ensure that the lay faithful took on the responsibility of shaping society through competent political involvement in the spirit of Church teaching. It was up to pastoral ministers, on the other hand, to preach the gospel
and to awaken the awareness and responsibilities that flow from it. "Whoever
measures and evaluates priestly service and pastoral work only by political or
national or economic yardsticks underestimates the Catholic priest. Therefore,
to appreciate the priest, you must measure him by an eternal yardstick; for the
priest creates values that are eternal; you must look at the Catholic priest and
his cause not in a temporal light – but in the light of an eternal lamp" (Kapica,
1925, p. 3). The priest's mission was first and foremost to lead people to eternal
salvation through appropriate Christian ideals; the laity, in turn, should implement the principles flowing from the gospel into the political arena.

In light of the journalistic slant of *Gość Niedzielny*, various circles hostile to
the Church for ideological reasons constantly sought an effective way of weakening its influence on society or even usurping its role through the creation of
social organizations to attack the Church. These organizations were primarily aimed at winning over young people. "At the last congress of the Universal
Masonic League in Vienna, attended by 700 freemasons from 30 lodges, it was
decided to set up a Masonic press agency with the task of supplying the press

from across the world with news about freemasonry. At the same time, it was decided to set up an international union of Masonic writers and journalists. This union will maintain close contact with the above-mentioned agency. It should be noted that the world union of journalistic associations is also in Masonic hands (...) The congress section for youth affairs decided to set up professional departments in a number of countries in order to organize the goal of winning over young people, especially academics, in a planned manner. Particularly important is the resolution of the congress on the establishment of an international placement office, which, among other things, is to combine the offices and institutions of this kind already existing within the Freemasonry of individual countries" (*Freemasonry's Activities in the International Area,* 1929, p. 10). The intention was to effectively discourage young people from the Church and to undermine its authority in their eyes. Various strategies and arguments were used to achieve this goal. Efforts were made to portray the Church as a hypocritical institution, abundant in wealth, using its social position to exert political influence and secure its own benefits (*In Defense of the Truth,* 1929, p. 4). The attacks on the Church were carried out mainly by means of erroneous arguments and manipulation. That is why *Gość Niedzielny* tried to repel unjust accusations with great determination and intensely encouraged its readers to engage in public activity in the spirit of the Church's teaching (*In Defence of the Truth,* 1928, pp. 4–5; *To the Friends of Youth!,* 1928, pp. 6–7).

Efforts to eliminate the Church from public life took various forms. One was to attack the clergy and make every attempt to undermine its authority and credibility in the eyes of the faithful. In the context of class struggle and material inequality, the topic of Church property was not infrequently raised (Olszar, 2004, p. 30). Accusations of immense wealth were levelled by opponents of the Church to discredit the clergy by portraying them as possessing great wealth while society was simultaneously poor. This disproportion was intended to show the hypocrisy and insincerity of priests, ultimately destroying their authority in the eyes of the faithful and undermining the effectiveness of their teaching. They were even accused of being the root cause of the social and material crises of the time, as can be seen in the extract quoted in *Gość Niedzielny*: "If the Church had spent its billions, the treasury would soon have been filled and the nation's poverty would have ended" (*If the Church Had Spent its Billions,* 1925, p. 8). To counteract this attack, *Gość Niedzielny* tried to demonstrate the absurdity of such accusations, and, at the same time, identify the political forces and circles that formulated them. "Only a crafty Jew could have come up with the idea of writing and talking about the Church's alleged billions" (*If the Church Had Spent its Billions,* 1925, p. 8). It was also claimed that the newspapers funded by anti-Catholic organisations fostered this belief in society in order to simultaneously distract people's attention from the "enormous Jewish capital" (*If the Church Had Spent its Billions*, 1925, p. 8). The question of the Church's wealth was raised, "but they were carefully silent about the fact that one Rothschild alone in Paris had 10 million francs. There was an outcry from Jews and socialist farm labourers that there were 40,000 hectares of land for just 190,000 friars, but nothing was said about the fact that one Rothschild alone owned 80,000 hectares for hunting next to Loigny-la -Bataille" (*If the Church Had Spent its Billions*, 1925, p. 8). It was also emphasised that the vast wealth of individuals was primarily for their personal benefit, whereas the Church's property constituted a common good and was used for the implementation of the Church's various charitable or pastoral initiatives. "At the same time, it had to be remembered that these friars did not spend their money on hunting, perfumes and banquets, but supported 25,000 of the sick, elderly and orphans and educated two million poor children free of charge" (*If the Church Had Spent its Billions*, 1925, p. 8). The article defended the Church against the accusations and, at the same time, identified the interest groups and political forces behind them and exposed their intentions and methods. Firstly, it was about demonstrating the inconsistency and hypocrisy of the attackers. The accusations were formulated not by ordinary people, but by political and ideological enemies, who had a purpose and a clear advantage in doing so. "The friars had their property taken away. But do you think even one poor Frenchman got a shekel from this theft? A quarter of the confiscated church property drowned in the pockets of the so-called liquidators, who were mostly Jews and freemasons" (*If the Church Had Spent its Billions*, 1925, p. 8).

The journalism of *Gość Niedzielny* made readers aware of the gradual and often insidious penetration of materialist and atheist ideas into culture to model society. Through the creation of new cultural trends and patterns, both social and political change was consistently sought. *Gość Niedzielny* warned against the so-called *new culture* flowing from Bolshevik ideology in opposition to Christian values. These new ideas were to replace the cultural patterns and hitherto determinants of Western culture. Under their influence, attitudes, perceptions of reality and patterns of behaviour were to gradually evolve. The fundamental problem was that it completely eliminated the spiritual and supernatural element from human life. Such atheistic and anti-Christian culture was presented in the pages of *Gość Niedzielny* as a kind of neo-paganism.

The main objectives of the process of the atheisation of culture were explained in the article: *Culture in the Wilderness* (Culture on the Roadless Path, *Front Katolicki*, 1924, Issue no. 41, p. 165) within *Front Katolicki* which was a free supplement to *Gość Niedzielny*. In it, the author recalled the clash (propounded by St Augustine) between *Civitas Dei et civitas mundi* – that is, a civilisation based on the gospel of Christ, and a civilisation built on purely secular principles. The latter conception, according to the author of the article, "harnessed to its service the allurements of everyday, earthly life, human effort, the lure of technology, the development of the mind, aesthetics, health, physical education, the cult of sport" (Culture on the Roadless Path, *Front Katolicki*, 1924, Issue no. 41, p. 165). In the author's understanding, this meant that various areas of life, now devoid of the spiritual, supernatural element, would be subordinated only to hedonistic and utilitarian values. As a consequence, technology and aesthetics would begin to focus people's attention only on temporal values, among which the cult of health and consumerism would become the most important. According to such a vision, a world would emerge in which spiritual and religious values would gradually be completely eradicated. Such a conception of the evolution of culture, it was explained, would also have broader consequences, affecting many other areas of life. According to the author, such a secular culture was to be very expansive: "It has brought into existence thousands of ways of earning a living; it opens the doors to science, to the arts, to corporate life; it has built huge, uniform, unsympathetic blocks of flats, barrack-like apartments, new monotonous streets; whole cities in which churches, at rare intervals, hide low among the colossi of modern skyscrapers. It creates clusters of strangers, divested of faith, morals and solid traditions" (Culture on the Roadless Path, *Front Katolicki*, 1924, Issue no. 41, p. 165). The vision of reality thus outlined was to exemplify a new culture growing out of a materialist and atheist vision of the world. Its realisation was to constitute a form of social engineering based on the assumptions of an atheistic and materialist ideology. This was to be achieved by severing the link with tradition in the area of culture, by completely deprecating religious values, and by deepening anonymity and mutual alienation among vast swathes of humanity. In the discourse of *Gość Niedzielny*, the ally of such a conception of culture was the fomentation of lust for money, the pursuit of material goods, the awakening of carnal desire, ultimately degenerating into licentiousness and, further, the loss of all sense of evil and sin. As one wrote: "This chaos of contradictory ideas is tossed about by the devil of money, passions, the desire to use, filthy pleasures, like sin by souls in a Dantean hell" (Culture on the Roadless Path, *Front Katolicki*, 1924, Issue no. 41, p. 165).

Another serious challenge to the Catholic worldview for *Gość Niedzielny* was Bolshevisms. A great many articles in the pages of *Gość Niedzielny* were devoted to combating Bolshevism, exposing its causes and preventing its consequences, taking the form of analyses, memoirs and accounts. Such journalism proved necessary, as the growing Bolshevik ideology was reflected in the programmes of certain political parties. At the end of the 1930s, Pope Pius XI published the encyclical *Divini redemptoris* / *O bezbożnym komunizmie* (*Two Important Encyclicals on Hitlerism and Communism*, 1937, p. 305; Cf. Kozerska, 2005, p. 234). It was the Church's response to the emerging threat in Europe of the ideology of Bolshevism, which sought to eliminate the Catholic Church and change the existing shape of society. *Gość Niedzielny* wrote: "Communism and Marxism, which has defined history and the social structure as a function dependent on economics and rejected the independence of any religious ideology, is itself becoming a religion, only a religion without God, atheistic, with a belief *in things invisible*, e.g., the ideal proletariat, the kingdom of freedom" ('Truths' of Communism, *Front Katolicki*, 1924, Issue no. 9, p. 33). In explaining to readers the seriousness of the danger, the effects it had had on Russian society were pointed out. The twenty years of Bolshevism's reign in Russia had caused such an enormous amount of demoralisation that there arose a peculiar parallel between Communism and Christianity. This became a necessity because Bolshevism, in rejecting faith, denied at the same time everything that was natural and compatible with common sense. By rejecting religion, it paradoxically became a religion itself, but without moral principles. For the followers of this ideology, it became a substitute for religion but without God, with the difference, however, that this pseudo-religion was based on completely irrational dogmas and, in its consequences, was disastrous for society. "Bolshevism destroyed all the moral foundations of life, awakened passions and the basest instincts; jealousy, hatred, egoism, sexual desire in its lowest form and, according to Bukharin's view, instilled only moral nihilism and anarchy" (*From the Tares Grows Wheat*, *Front Katolicki*, 1924, Issue no. 33, p. 130). A clear example of how erroneous ideas first seduce people before revealing their true face was the tragic situation prevailing in Soviet Russia (*Moscow without a Mask*, 1929, p. 7). In view of this fact, an article in *Gość Niedzielny* stated that, in the form of a warning, the social consequences of socialist ideology were foreseeable. Evidently, the falsity of the values professed by Socialism became apparent in the effects that the revolutions brought about in those societies in which they were either adopted voluntarily or introduced by means of violence: violence and manipulation (*Sowiecki raj!*, 1924, p. 4).

The content published in the pages of *Gość Niedzielny* stated that religiosity required a constant deepening of awareness of the conditions in which faith had to be professed. Superficial and customary Catholicism, limited only to practices in the *sacred* space, was endangered and, in view of the ever stronger tendencies towards secularisation of society, possibly already doomed to failure. Growing in strength and integrating wide swathes of the population, atheist and anti-church worldview currents promoted the principle that "faith is a private matter." Consequently, they believed that the public arena should be freed from the influence of the Catholic Church and the social principles it preached. The Church needed an effective antidote in the form of an engaged Catholicism, but first there had to be a wide and clear awareness among the faithful. Such a situation required galvanising the laity and making them aware of the importance of the challenges and responsibilities. For *Gość Niedzielny*, this became an essential and crucial task.

2.3   Catholic Defensiveness

The antidote to the spread of the above tendencies was initially awareness. Subsequently, readers' perception and understanding of the worldview threats would mobilise them to take concrete defensive countermeasures. It was emphasised that without proper awareness, it is impossible to counteract the destruction of culture. The idea, therefore, was to show readers that "true culture grows only on the basis of Christian values, and that it is organically connected to them." [Ibid.] It was argued that one of the key missions of Christianity was, and still is, the building of culture, by highlighting all the beneficial influences of religion and the spiritual realm on human life and society as a whole. True Christian faith spurred believers in their duty of apostleship, i.e., involvement in society. The believer was to become a *soldier of Christ* (*Soldiers in Action*, 1924, p. 165). "And who does not know that the soldier should not only exert himself and fight for himself but above all for others" (*Soldiers in Action*, 1924, p. 165). A call was therefore made to boldly manifest one's faith in the public space and to intensify all social initiatives undertaken from its motives and in its spirit in defence of Christian culture. Genuine religious life was shown to be inseparable from the apostolic mission.

The founder of *Gość Niedzielny*, Father August Hlond (the first Bishop of Katowice), addressed a pastoral letter to the faithful, which, in its essence, was an attempt at a diagnosis of the condition of both the Church and society in Silesia. It was published in its entirety in the pages of *Gość Niedzielny* over several consecutive issues in March 1924. It was, in particular, to raise religious awareness and the social involvement of Catholics in the face of serious worldview threats. This unity was to confirm the maturity of faith, which required responsibility in the social dimension for the common good. Above all, Fr Hlond wanted to revive religious enthusiasm and motivate the faithful to become more involved in the process of shaping social reality, instead of passively and uncritically submitting to the emerging anti-church ideologies. He preceded his reflections and analyses with a long period of observation and understanding of Church life in Silesia. "I have been following our religious life for fourteen months. I was not concerned with appearances and vain forms. I was concerned with the content of Silesian religiosity, its depth and the power of its influence on the thought of the people and on their lives. I have encountered both pleasant and unpleasant phenomena, and today, encompassing with my thoughts all my observations, I come to the conclusion that, by reducing faith only to religious practices, often experienced without depth, religious life in Silesia has reached a serious crossroads" (Hlond, 1924, p. 3). He saw this crisis above all in lack of conscious action. He regarded such Catholicism as shallow and insufficient in view of the challenges facing the Church at the time, which was incapable of resisting the increasing wave of secularisation of society. Observing religious life in Silesia, he concluded that grassroots Catholicism, although rich in various pastoral forms, "has ceased to be a profound conviction and has become a view that is changeable and so weak that it has no orienting force and gives no power for religious action" (Hlond, 1924, p. 3). In view of the above, the pastoral programme outlined in Fr Hlond's letter was very concrete and fundamental (Olszowski, 2013, p. 38). *Gość Niedzielny* was also fully behind it. (Olszowski, 2013, p. 41). It was to give impetus to various pastoral activities aimed at revitalising the broad masses of the Catholic community. A very concrete initiative to revive the lay faithful was the creation and promotion of the so-called Catholic League in Silesia, referring to the Catholic Action proposed by Pius XI. This was to be an organisational formula of a pastoral nature, strengthening cooperation between clergy and laity in defence of the Church and society against all threats to faith and morals. (Olszowski, 2013, p. 42).

Fr Hlond's courageous strategy aroused fears and even hostility from various circles associated with atheistic and anti-Catholic worldview currents. Consequently, from the very beginning, opponents of the Church tried to weaken Fr Hlond's influence by discrediting him in the eyes of the local community. From the article entitled: *Who is right?* of May 1925, we learn of the attack on the person of Apostolic Administrator Fr A. Hlond (who was widely regarded as the natural candidate for the first bishop of the Silesian diocese at the time). In the face of the accusations formulated in one of the articles that appeared in the pages of the magazine *Lodge of the Knights of the Spirit* in Königsberg, *Gość Niedzielny* stood up in his defence. From the polemic of *Gość Niedzielny* against the claims made in the unfavourable article, we learn about the motives behind criticism of Fr Hlond. "Fr Hlond PhD, the candidate for bishop, talked so much foolishness that one has to wonder if it is possible in the 20th century to say such things to the people. Fr Hlond literally said that Freemasonry is a school of murder and every Freemason must carry poison, a knife, a dagger..." (*Who is right*, 1925, p. 2). To accusations formulated in this way, *Gość Niedzielny* replied: "I don't want to correct this folly, because no one, not even a child, will believe it." ..." (*Who is right*, 1925, p. 2). In passing, we learn that this referred to Fr Hlond's speech at the Catholic Convention in Katowice, during which he quoted excerpts from the statutes of the Order of Liberation, a secret youth organisation operating on the premises of a secondary school in Swiecany near Vilnius. This organisation was identified as being under the strong influence of Jewish Freemasonry. To dispel readers' doubts, excerpts from these statutes are quoted: "What do the statutes of the Order of Libera-tion, of its members urge them to do? – Tell him (the disciple) to commit some crime, to kill or whatever. Let him stab at least one. Teach everyone to wield a gun, a revolver, a knife, poison, etc. A great uproar arose in the Masonic-Jewish press when the Fr Hlond dared to publicly pillory the foul criminal work of Jewish Freemasonry." ..." (*Who is right*, 1925, p. 2). To confirm the seriousness of the problem, the article reminded readers of the then famous tragedy that took place in one of the Vilnius secondary schools, when students with revolvers in hand attacked their teachers. *Gość Niedzielny* asked: "Who, then, is right, the Most Reverend Apostolic Administrator or the Masonic organ of the Knights of Liberation? For whom will every good Christian and Pole declare himself, for the one who stands for order; order and morality, or for the one who tells the youth to wield guns and revolvers?" ..." (*Who is right*, 1925, p. 2). The polemic concludes with a statement in the form of questions demanding sobriety: "The Knights of Liberation in Królewska Huta, Ruda, Rybnik, Pawłowo, Knurów, do you know under whose command you stand? Do you know that Jews manipu-late you, even though you cannot see them, by selling you 'New Testaments'? Do you want to establish the same order here in your native land by order of the Jewish Freemasons as there is in Vilnius?" [Ibid] Although the Masonic lodges officially dissociated themselves from the above-described actions, sim-ilar incidents nevertheless took place. It was difficult to prove the connection between these facts and their inspirers, between secret youth organisations and Masonic lodges, but for *Gość Niedzielny,* this interdependence was not in doubt.

A very important form of reinvigorating lay involvement and integrating all Catholic organisations were the so-called Catholic Conventions (Olszowski, 2013, p. 41). They played an important role in the process of activating and directing the activities of the laity (Merkle 2009, p. 90; Myszor 1999, p. 137). Their specific tasks, complementing the mission of the Catholic press, were the integration and activation of Catholic circles. By uniting people around Catholic thought, they built a common social front in the struggle for Chris-tian values in public life, for it was realised that when confronted with various ideological currents, either the Church would integrate people or its enemies would do it instead. That is why, in the journalism of *Gość Niedzielny*, Catholic rallies were intended to serve the purpose of deepening the religious and social awareness of the laity and strengthening their activity in the face of current social challenges. The particular value of this was the involvement of both clergy and laity from different backgrounds and professions.

The Catholic Conventions sought to read and define the most urgent social tasks facing the Church in Silesia. They contributed to the formulation and subsequent promotion of a pastoral action plan (Myszor, 1999, p. 137). Their overriding aim was the widespread involvement of the lay faithful. Every Catholic in Upper Silesia, aware of their faith, should consider defending Church and Catholic thought as his or her own (Myszor, 1999, p. 137). For this reason, *Gość Niedzielny* intensively agitated for participation. In its pages, Apostolic Administrator Fr Hlond appealed: "Today, after a year, I again call upon you Catholics to participate in the Catholic Convention. It will take place in Katowice from 6th to 8th September. I have set great tasks for it, because it is to mark a great step forward on the path to our Catholic revival. We will take a clear stand on a number of fundamental religious questions and we will unambiguously define the role of Catholicism in the life of the nations and in Poland in particular. We will oppose the deliberate poisoning of the Silesian spirit by sects, by theosophical and occultist delusions and by Masonic lodges. Starting from the necessity of endeavours to promote Catholicism, we will, among other things, lay the foundation for a systematic fight against drunkenness and immorality in the street, in dress, in dancing" (Hlond, 1924, p. 1). The III Silesian Catholic Convention held in Katowice in 1924 was a manifestation of the potential of the laity in the Church. It created new spaces for cooperation between the clergy and the laity in the implementation of the Church's social mission and in opposing anti-clerical and nativist socio-ideological tendencies (Myszor, 1999, p. 137). It defined the most important tasks of Catholic organisations to oppose the activities of Freemasonry, the propagation of godlessness, Communism and Liberalism. Thus, the whole population was called upon to fight vigorously against their propaganda, to vigilantly and resolutely repulse all such ideologies presented by *Gość Niedzielny* as highly harmful to the Catholic faith and the Polish state (*Interesting Resolutions of the Catholic League Section*, 1924, p. 5).

In order to mobilise Catholic society, *Gość Niedzielny* suggested the example of lay Catholics in the Netherlands be adopted as a model for the activity of the laity. Particular attention was paid to the urgent need to publish and promote a press with an explicitly Catholic profile (*In the Netherlands Every Catholic Family Subscribes to a Catholic Magazine*, 1937, p. 320). With a note of regret it was rhetorically asked: "When will such a spirit come to us!?" (*Catholic Life in the*

Netherlands, 1925, p. 7). It was noted that despite the relatively small number of Catholics in that country, their involvement in public life was disproportionately greater than in Catholic Poland. "The best organised in Europe, if not in the whole world, are the Catholics in the Netherlands. They number two and a half million only, compared to five and a half million Calvinists and Protestants. In spite of such a small number, they have managed to organise Catholic education in a simply astonishing way. They have more than 20 Catholic grammar schools, in addition to the comprehensive schools. No Catholic thinks of an inter-denominational school as some of our Catholics do. They have even managed to establish a Catholic university in Nijmegen, which already has three faculties: theology, philosophy and law, and a fourth faculty, medicine, in the pipeline. Catholics publish 34 dailies, 70 weeklies and 50 other periodicals!!! And how brilliantly edited they are" (*Catholic Life in the Netherlands*, 1925, p. 7). The richness of religious life was emphasised. The consistency of faith and morals manifested in daily life was held up as a model. "A Dutch Catholic woman would be ashamed to show herself in such clothes as we see on the streets in our *Catholic* Polish women" (*Catholic Life in the Netherlands*, 1925, p. 7). A conscious Catholicism was emphasised, which was contrasted with the merely traditional, reflexive and superficial Polish Catholicism (*Only a Good Catholic Can Be a Good Pole, Only a Good Pole Is Capable of Being a Good Catholic*, 1929, p. 3). "The Dutch do not go to church out of habit, but out of conviction. To the Holy Sacraments not once a year, but every month, or even every day" (*Catholic Life in the Netherlands*, 1925, p. 7). Given the political context of the time, such a state of affairs was considered not only appropriate but even necessary. Therefore, with a note of regret it was asked: "When will such a spirit come to us? We need to wake up for once and show that we are true Catholics and not just those who were accidentally baptised in the Catholic Church. May the Holy Spirit inflame our hearts and incline us Poles to such work for our church and for the good of our souls" (*Catholic Life in the Netherlands*, 1925, p. 7). This reflection was a confirmation of the awareness of the various shortcomings of Polish Catholicism, which on the one hand was very traditional and widespread, but often shallow and passive. There was therefore a desire to overcome this condition.

The issue also became a topic of debate in the Church-wide forums – the aforementioned Catholic conventions (Myszor, 1999, p. 137). This is confirmed in the account of the Third Convention, which addressed the problem of the increasing attacks on the Catholic Church in Western Europe. "The French politician Briand described in 1905 the position of the Church at that time in very harsh words: the Church is a sleepy fortress. Its ramparts are without cannons, its arsenals empty. The army of the Church is scattered; the leaders have fallen asleep" (*III. Silesian Catholic Convention*, 1924, pp. 4–6). Such a bold critical diagnosis against the Church was refuted by the claim that it did not reflect the essence of the real state of the Church. Nevertheless, the seriousness of the situation was not underestimated. Yes, *Gość Niedzielny* was aware of the serious crisis in Christian society at the time. The first diagnosis of this kind was expressed in Western Europe, for example in France a number of years back, and they were also considered symptomatic and dangerous for Poland on the threshold of its independence, and particularly for the staunchly Catholic Silesia. After all, it was believed that the whole Catholic world was in a stage of aggravation. "For 100 years a poison has been administered to us Catholics. That poison was Liberalism, the new-fashioned spirit of indifference and superficiality" (*III. Silesian Catholic Convention*, 1924, pp. 4–6). An exceptionally dangerous phenomenon was that the anti-church ideologies were absorbing the intelligentsia circles and elites of society. As *Gość Niedzielny* wrote: "The intelligentsia often regarded the Church as something outlived, outmoded, a bloodless body, aged and respectable admittedly, but a moldy institution. Ordinary folk, on the other hand, were sometimes content to be present at Sunday services and flag consecration ceremonies" (*III. Silesian Catholic Convention*, 1924, pp. 4–6). The "Enlightened Class" (e.g., historians and political leaders) seemed to underestimate and even depreciate the importance of the Catholic Church's role in the formation of the Polish national and state identity (*Inteligencja i Kościół*, 1927, p. 7; *Inteligencja i Kościół*, 1923, p. 4). From the intelligentsia, political leaders were often recruited, who, in the opinion of *Gość Niedzielny*, fooled the people with their harmful and noxious convictions. This was also an important motive for the activation of lay Catholics, who, being aware of the complexity of the socio-political context, should be ready to take responsibility for the fate of the state and society in the spirit of the Church's teaching.

The laity's involvement in social life was to defend the Church against any attempt to deprecate its social role, but ultimately they wanted to protect the whole of society from atheisation and secularisation. In this perspective, special care was given to the family and the educational system. The bishops' position on the need to defend the family, the model of upbringing and the educational system, as well as their appeals to the faithful and the state authorities at all levels, were immediately taken up by many Catholic organisations (*Silesia's Statement on Marriage*, 1929, p. 5). This was confirmed by the fact that the concern for the family was invariably a fundamental topic at conventions and congresses of Catholic associations. As *Gość Niedzielny* reported on the proceedings of the Catholic Congress in Warsaw: "The axis of the congress and its deliberations was the family and youth" (*Proceedings of the Catholic*

Convention. Resolutions and resolutions, 1926, p. 3). The issue of the family was considered in its broadest context, without reducing it to the religious dimension alone. When talking about the family, thought was given to legislation on marriage, organisations that support the family, the upbringing of children, youth issues and health. The challenge of the time was to defend the sacred character of marriage. The tendency to secularise the heart of the family – which is marriage – was seen as a very serious danger with far-reaching social consequences. "It must be strongly emphasised that whenever a word was said about divorce and civil weddings, whether in plenary or during panel discussions, thousands of Catholic fathers and mothers from all over Poland directly showed their indignation and protested. The Law Commission was seized with the same spirit. The eminent jurists came to the only possible Catholic resolution, namely, that the sacramental nature of Catholic marriage precluded any possibility of compromise with the liberal currents of secular legislation [...] The lack of religious education in universities was also raised with concern". (*Proceedings of the Catholic Convention. Resolutions and resolutions,* 1926, p. 3). This showed that the official voice of the Church in the form of the bishops' teaching was also an expression of the feelings and expectations of the Catholic community. At the same time, the reception of these teachings in Church organisations and associations confirmed how important a role the organisations played in the socio-political field. The bishops' voice in defence of the family and marriage was immediately taken up by lay Catholics, who transposed it into the political space. Without the involvement of lay people, without this social background, the episcopal voice could have been treated merely as a voice without much political significance.

Another important impetus for the involvement of the laity in public life was the perceived progressive secularisation of education. This was seen as contrary to the Polish national heritage. In one issue of 1923, an article entitled *The Farmer and the Teacher* (*Rolnik i nauczyciel,* 1923, p. 3). *Gość Niedzielny* praised the long tradition of Polish education. Readers were reminded of the merits of one of the first institutions of this kind in Europe, which was the Commission of National Education. The article extolled Poland's achievements in comparison with other nations. "Poland can boast outstanding educators, especially since the time of the Education Commission, whose centenary jubilee schools celebrated this year. The Germans have the Pestalozzi, the Czechs Komenskis, the Poles have Father Konarski, Father Piramowicz, Trentowski, Sniadeckis, Estkowski and others who have been famous in the field of education of young generations" (*Rolnik i nauczyciel,* 1923, p. 3). *Gość Niedzielny,* drawing on the intellectual achievements of those eminent Poles recalled from history, sought to join actively and competently in the current of propagating education. "I wish, in the beloved *Gość Niedzielny*, to acquaint our readers with the most distinguished educators and their principles of national upbringing, in order to give parents and young people more than one sound thought of this so important field of upbringing, and thus to support the work of the family, the school and the Church around the upbringing of the latest generations" (*Rolnik i nauczyciel*, 1923, p. 3). Given the various emancipatory tendencies emerging at the time that were subordinated to worldviews contrary to Christianity, this was a particular challenge. *Gość Niedzielny* was clearly aware that the state of schooling, in the long term, shaped and conditioned society as a whole – intellectually, but also spiritually and morally. School not only teaches, but shapes views, attitudes, sensitivity to values. It was therefore of paramount importance who would have a say in shaping curricula, in defining priorities, in determining educational methods. The Church was keen that parents should naturally take precedence in this regard. This was part of the Church's mission regarding the state and the nation (Bartnik, 1999, p. 170). The Church, through the stimulation and awareness-raising of parents and then through their influence, wanted to ensure that society had an adequate level of spiritual education and thus also resistance to erroneous ideologies. Various efforts were therefore made to reach the consciousness of parents and to stimulate their involvement in the educational process, especially in its first, and most sensitive, stage. The upbringing of young people was therefore of interest to Catholic associations and organisations (Koperska, 1923, pp. 3–6). The pages of *Gość Niedzielny* often published reprints of proclamations and speeches by Catholic activists devoted to this subject, with one important text published in one of the first issues of *Gość Niedzielny* being the speech of MP Janicki during the Catholic Convention in Katowice (*Speeches and Papers at the II. Silesian Catholic Convention*, 1923, p. 4). It represents, in a sense, the quintessence of *Gość Niedzielny's* position on the shape and role of school in society. The article emphasised first and foremost that the family and the school are two complementary institutions, and it was the task and responsibility of parents to ensure that the school met their expectations and that it never contradicted the values nurtured in Catholic families. Harmony between educational values at school and home life was the main demand of the state (which was responsible for organising the education and schooling system). It was reasoned that the influence of parents on this system was one of the key manifestations of the independence of the state and the real freedom of citizens (*For the Good of Our Children*, 1928, p. 7). The concept of a so-called *world-neutral* school was strongly opposed. It was believed that such aspirations were in fact dictated by a desire to eliminate Christian values from the educational system and replace them with ones in line with a materialist and atheist vision of society.

Attempts were made to protect young people from the influence of atheistic and materialistic ideologies to counteract the secularisation of the educational system. This was done systemically. It was realised that Catholic youth associations played a most important role in the formation of young people. *Gość Niedzielny* reported on their aims, the forms and scope of their activities. They were supposed to integrate, educate and activate. On the one hand, Catholic youth associations were to shape the religious and social consciousness of young people, and on the other, they were to prepare the youth to take on public roles in the future. Catholic youth organisations were to deepen the religious and community life of the youth of the time and thus protect them from the influence of aggressive secular ideologies.

Such educational activities of Catholic youth associations were to help young people achieve religious and civic maturity (Myszor, 1999, p. 161; Kiedos, 1997, p. 23). This is why appeals to young people to willingly join the ranks of Catholic youth associations were constantly repeated in the pages of *Gość Niedzielny*. In his proclamation to the Convention of Catholic Youth, Father Wawrzyniec Pucher, (Wycisło, 1996, pp. 337–339) guardian of youth associations, wrote: "Nothing can better manifest your Catholic worldview than this year's Catholic convention. So turn out in great numbers, make yourselves as numerous as possible for the convention, let no one be missing! Let the enemies of Catholicism become convinced that there is no success for them here, that the soil of the Piast land is not fertile for pernicious sowings" (*Proclamation to All Polish-Catholic Youth Associations in Silesia*, 1924, p. 3). Catholic youth organisations were to be an effective tool for providing a Catholic grounding and education. The aim of such a strategy was that, in the longer term, the youth would be harnessed to their responsibility for the fate of the state and the nation. Involvement in a Catholic association was to be a preparatory stage for conscious participation in political life or other public activities in a Catholic spirit. "With the wings of our Catholic youth it is a striving to realise the ideal of Christ; it is a striving to develop spiritual fortitude; it is work on oneself, on one's character. For the character developed on the model of God-man will bring to the Church and to our society educated people; people who are conscientious and capable of occupying any position in society. All Catholic Youth Associations in Silesia operate according to this principle" (*The Consecration of a New Pitch for the Catholic Youth Association at St. Mary's Church*, 1924, p. 7). Hope for the future was therefore pinned on young people who were properly educated, committed and took social responsibility.

The associations were to be schools of civic awareness and a preparation for political commitment in a patriotic spirit directed towards the good of the

Polish state. "Every one of you can become a mayor or alderman, a councillor, a civil servant, even a member of the Sejm and a minister in Poland" (*Why Every Young Man Should Belong to the Polish-Catholic Youth Association*, 1924, p. 7). Both challenges and adversities were highlighted when belonging to a Catholic organisation. It would develop in young people fortitude and resistance to adversity, however, there was a realisation that boldly affirming one's faith could be associated with resistance from the peer community. "After all, almost every young man who openly admits to the Catholic faith today, who goes to services every Sunday, is exposed to ridicule and even persecution from his peers!" (*Why Every Young Man Should Belong to the Polish-Catholic Youth Association*, 1924, p. 7). The strength to successfully overcome this was to belong to youth organisations that guaranteed a sense of unity and community. The aim was to ensure that those young people with Christian values were not left on their own and thus not exposed to a sense of alienation or helplessness. Catholic organisations were intended not only to give a sense of security, but above all to show that they were not alone in their views – "here we will meet colleagues who will not ridicule us [...]. A common religious life gives our members encouragement and spirit, will make them an impregnable fortress for life, defending itself bravely even against the fiercest communist" (*Why Every Young Man Should Belong to the Polish-Catholic Youth Association*, 1924, p. 7). In the face of any adversity, intolerance, mockery among peers, young people were given encouragement. When confronted with mockery of their religious values and piety, they were expected to maintain their courage and sense of dignity.

The profile of *Gość Niedzielny* in the interwar period was an important tool of the Church in Silesia in revitalising and directing religious life; informing and activating readers were prominent features of its journalism. *Gość Niedzielny* sought to raise awareness of the important challenges and even dangers to faith and morals. Since religious life cannot be lived in isolation from the complex social context, readers were made aware of the need to take responsibility for this religious sphere in the spirit of Church teaching. Various organisations served this purpose, including Catholic Conventions, Catholic Action and the numerous youth organisations associated with it. *Gość Niedzielny* constantly promoted and justified all activities of the laity in its pages. Very evident in *Gość Niedzielny* of this period was a particular focus on young people, as harnessing the potential of young people was a very important task for the Church. It was to develop the young and systemically prepare them for future social roles. The importance and momentum of lay involvement was constantly demonstrated.

2.4   Conclusion

An analysis of the content of *Gość Niedzielny* from the inter-war period on socio-political and ideological issues has revealed what an important tool for defending Christian values and the place and role of the Church in public life the Catholic press was. It served not only to arouse awareness of the importance and consequences of the ideas permeating political and social life, but also to activate readers to defend the Christian values conditioning social life. *Gość Niedzielny* made its readers aware of the most urgent tasks of the lay faithful in the Church and society. It was a great integrative and formative support for numerous Catholic associations and organisations. Much attention in its pages was devoted to the issues of shaping and educating the young generation; a generation which was particularly vulnerable to the influence of atheistic and liberalist ideological currents. There was a conviction that an authentic, conscious and deepened faith intrinsically demands externalisation in the form of involvement in public life. The rights of the Church and the Christian principles of social life were consistently and determinedly defended, in particular the traditional family model and an educational system based on Christian values. In doing so, it unmasked all the intentions of those that wanted to reduce religion to a purely private matter. Aptly reading the challenges of the time, *Gość Niedzielny* became an exceptional example of the Catholic press, whose mission was to defend not only the rights of the Catholic Church, but also Christian values in social life. The journalism of *Gość Niedzielny* was to provide an important impetus for the activities of numerous associations and organisations of lay Catholics to resist the ideological offensive against the Catholic principles of social order. The pastoral care of the Church at the time strongly emphasised the need to combine piety with activity in the public sphere, which was to be a space for manifesting faith and defending Christian values. The active cooperation of the Church's shepherds of that time with a wide range of people in the community was to confirm the dynamism and specificity of the socio-religious life of the time. The Catholic weekly *Gość Niedzielny* became an important tool for stimulating this. It did so in two ways: on the one hand, by drawing the attention of its readers to the fact that a deepened and authentic religiousness requires an awareness of social challenges; and, on the other, by involving its readers in various forms of activity through which they would imbue public life with the spirit of the Gospel. Thus, although *Gość Niedzielny* was a periodical with a religious-pastoral profile directly subordinate to the bishops of Katowice, from the very beginning it fulfilled a social mission in the spirit of faith and Church teaching. Its editors, in line with the Church's teaching of the time, were convinced that the nurtured development of both individuals and entire societies could only be realised if "everything is renewed in Christ" (Kozerska, 2005, p. 35). This slogan of Pope Pius XI also set out a mission for the Catholic press.

Society is constantly subjected to processes which result in the evolution of world views. In the public space, there is a constant political struggle in which different ideologies and their resulting visions of man and society clash. The media (in the interwar period it was mainly the printed press) has a special place in this confrontation of ideologies/worldviews (Habielski, 2009, p. 94; Mysliński 1974, pp. 5–8). Reaching into the past and, on the basis of an analysis of the content of the press in the interwar period, learning about the political image of the world constitutes an interesting and important field of research (Myslinski, 1974, p. 8). This is important not only from the historiographical point of view, but also from the need to understand contemporary social processes and to grasp the evolution of political and worldview ideas. The study of the past and the discovery of the past issues of social life can shed light on the phenomena occurring in socio-political life today. This is undoubtedly a pressing issue for the contemporary Catholic Church and its media. Evangelisation is essentially the imbuing of people's lives and entire societies with the spirit of the Gospel. An exemplification of this task is the social teaching of the Church, which should be reflected both in the Catholic media and in the activity and conscious social engagement of the laity (Goban-Klas, 2009, p. 169).

As Henryk Seweryniak and Katarzyna Sitkowska optimistically note in their article *Contemporary contexts of media culture*, citing Janusz Marianski's view (Marianski, 2012, p. 81): "Modernity is shaping religious pluralism, with the phenomenon of *spillover of the sacred*. The linear secularisation theory of the 1970s must therefore be transformed: no longer *the more modern, the more secular*, but *the more modern, the more religiously productive*." And further: "Despite the religious crisis in Western Europe, there are still many people for whom secular culture is not enough; who are searching anew for the lost Transcendence. The 21st century does not have to be the century of indifferentism and atheism; perhaps it will be the century of many deities and many spiritualities" (Marianski, 2012, p. 39] Nevertheless, it seems that one cannot underestimate the dynamic impact of phenomena unfavourable to the Church, such as the secularisation of social life, ethical relativism, consumerism and the religious indifferentism of broad swathes of society, especially the youth now emerging under their influence. In the face of these highly complex phenomena, it is difficult to imagine the realisation of the Church's mission in the contemporary world without the following two programme directives, which emanate from the journalism of *Gość Niedzielny* between 1923 and 1939, and which are: the awakening of awareness and the involvement of lay people. Today, *Gość Niedzielny* is a well-known weekly with a nationwide circulation. Celebrating the 25th anniversary of the Koszalin branch of *Gość Niedzielny*, its current editor-in-chief, Adam Pawlaszczyk, defined its main programme profile, stating that "the basic assumption of *Gość Niedzielny* is to unite people, i.e., not to take the side of any political grouping or other party, but to bring the word of God to people" (Parfianowicz, 2023). This task, however, does not contradict the need to make readers aware of specific challenges and to inspire and even initiate joint ventures that constitute a space for lay social activity in the spirit of faith. The pre-war *Gość Niedzielny* in the very turbulent political dispute of the time, invariably tried to make its readers aware of the ideological tensions that were affecting the Church and society as a whole. The example of the pre-war *Gość Niedzielny* provides an interesting point of reference in which one can find many valuable inspirations that are worth considering when defining the current mission and objectives of the Church media in the current social and political context. The mission of contemporary Catholic media is still a very interesting field for discussion and reflection (Hanas, 2012, pp. 117–122).

References

Sources of Gość Niedzielny

Acknowledgement, Request and Wish of the Editor (1932). "Gość Niedzielny", No. 1, p. 6.
At the Conclusion of the New Year (1923). "Gość Niedzielny", No. 17, p. 3.
Catholic Life in the Netherlands. (1925). "Gość Niedzielny", No. 21, p. 7.
Culture in the Wilderness. (1924). "Front Katolicki", No. 41, p. 165.
Dedication of a New Pitch for the Catholic Youth Association at St. Mary's Church. (1924). "Gość Niedzielny" No. 40, p. 7.
Farmer and Teacher. (1923). "Gość Niedzielny", p. 3.
Fight Against the Catholic Church in Poland. (1934). "Gość Niedzielny" No. 12, p. 15.
For the Sake of Our Children. (1928). "Gość Niedzielny", No. 18, p. 7.
Freemasonry's Activities in the International Area. (1929). "Gość Niedzielny" No. 16, p. 10.
Hlond A. (1924). *On Catholic Life in Silesia,* "Gość Niedzielny", No. 10, p. 3.
Hlond A. (1924). *Proclamation of the Most Rev. Apostolic Administrator on the III. Silesian Catholic Convention,* "Gość Niedzielny" No. 34, p. 1.
If the Church Had Spent its Billions. (1925). "Gość Niedzielny" No. 23, p. 8.
III. Silesian Catholic Convention. (1924). "Gość Niedzielny", No. 30, pp. 4–6.
In Defence of the Truth. (1928). "Gość Niedzielny", No. 23, pp. 4–5.
In Defence of the Truth. (1929). "Gość Niedzielny", No. 4, p. 4.

In Defence of Truth, the Church Halts the March of Civilisation. (1927). "Gość Niedzielny", No. 33, p. 3.

In the Netherlands Every Catholic Family Subscribes to a Catholic Magazine. (1937). "Gość Niedzielny", No. 21, p. 320.

Intelligence and the Church. (1927). "Gość Niedzielny" No. 7, p. 7.

Interesting Resolutions of the Catholic League Section. (1924). "Gość Niedzielny" No. 38, p. 5.

Kapica J. (1925). *Prelate Kapica's Sermon.* "Gość Niedzielny", No. 46, p. 3.

Koperska A. (1923). *The Social Duty of Catholics in the Present Day.* "Gość Niedzielny", No. 11, pp. 3–6.

Moscow without a Mask. (1929). „Gość Niedzielny", No. 5, p. 7.

Only a Good Catholic Can Be a Good Pole, Only a Good Pole Is Able to Be a Good Catholic. (1929). "Gość Niedzielny", No. 25, p. 3.

Proceedings of the Catholic Convention. (1926). "Gość Niedzielny", No. 36, p. 3.

Proclamation to All Associations of Polish-Catholic Youth in Silesia. (1924). "Gość Niedzielny" No. 33, p. 3.

Silesia's Statement on Marriages. (1929). "Gość Niedzielny", No. 4, p. 5.

Social Democracy and Religion. (1927). "Gość Niedzielny", No. 3, pp. 3–4.

Soldiers in Action. (1924). "Front Katolicki", No 41, p. 165.

Soviet Paradise!. (1924). "Gość Niedzielny", No. 32, p. 4.

Speeches and Papers at the II. Silesian Catholic Convention. (1923). "Gość Niedzielny", No. 3, p. 4.

The 'Truths' of Communism. (1924). "Front Katolicki", No. 9, p. 33.

The Intelligentsia and the Church. (1923). "Gość Niedzielny", No. 8, p. 4.

The Secret Enemy of the Catholic Church. (1926). "Gość Niedzielny", No. 35, p. 3.

To the Friends of Youth!. (1928). "Gość Niedzielny" No. 20, pp. 6–7.

Two Important Encyclicals on Hitlerism and Communism. (1937). „Gość Niedzielny", No. 20, p. 305.

Who's Right. (1925). "Gość Niedzielny" No. 21, p. 2.

Why Should Every Youth Belong to the Polish-Catholic Youth Association. (1924). "Gość Niedzielny" No. 1, p. 7.

Elaborations

Adamski A. (2008). *Priest and Journalist*, Loretto Sisters Publishing House, Warsaw.

Bartnik Cz. S. (1999). *Teologia narodu*, Publishing House of the Metropolitan Curia in Częstochowa, Częstochowa.

Bishop August Hlond and his Diocese (2013). Ed. J. Myszor (b), St. Jack's Bookshop Publishing House, Katowice.

Dutka W. (2006). Rise *and Development of the Parish Press of the Roman Catholic Church in the Second Republic*, "Rocznik Historii Prasy Polskiej", No. 9/2 (18).

Goban-Klas T. (2009). *Media and Mass Communication. Teoria i analizy prasy, radia, telewizji i Internetu,* PWN, Warszawa.

Grajewski A. (2008). *Twój Gość. 85 lat „Gościa Niedzielnego",* Publishing House of the Metropolitan Curia, Katowice.

Grzybowski K., Sobolewska B. (1971). *Doktryna polityczna i społeczna papiestwa (1789–1968),* Wyd. PWN, Warszawa.

Habielski R. (2009). *Polityczna historia mediów w Polsce w XX wieku,* Wyd. Akademickie i Profesjonalne, Warszawa.

Hanas Z. (2012). *Dwa światy: media kościelne a media świeckie,* in: *Media w Kościele i Kościół w mediach,* eds. M. Przybysz, J. Kloch, Katowice.

Kiedos J. (1997). *Zanim powstała Akcja Katolicka. Zarys dziejów polskich młodzieżowych organizacji katolickich na Górnym Śląsku do 1933 roku,* Bielsko-Biała.

Kizwalter T. (1989). *The Church and the French Revolution,* "Catholic Life", No. 10, pp. 50–51.

Kozerska E. (2005). *Państwo i społeczeństwo w pogladach Pius XI,* Wyd. Uniwersytetu Wrocławskiego, Wrocław.

Kristanova E. (2006). *Program społeczny i kulturalny „Tęczy" (1927–1939) na tle prasy katolickiej w II Rzeczypospolitej,* Łódź.

Marianski J. (2012). *Europe: Religions on the Free Market,* "Znak", No. 681, p. 81.

Mazur J. (1994). *Tygodnik „Myśl katolicka" (1908–1914). Problemy religijne, społeczne i polityczne,* Wyd. Naukowe Papieskiej Akademii Teologicznej, Kraków, pp. 106–115.

Merkle SNDdeN J. A. (2009). *From the Heart of the Church. Catholic Social Tradition,* PAX Publishing House, Warsaw, p. 90.

Mysłek W. (1966) *Kościół katolicki w Polsce w latach 1918–1939. Zarys historyczny,* Wyd. Książka i Wiedza, Warszawa.

Myslinski J., *Notes on the Polish Press at the Turn of the 19th and 20th Centuries as a Historical Source,* "Rocznik Historii Czasopiśmiennictwa Polskiego", No. 14, pp. 5–26.

Myszor J. (1999). *History of the Katowice Diocese,* Katowice.

Nieć M. (2010). *Komunikowanie społeczne i media. Perspektywa politologiczna,* Wyd. LEX, Warszawa.

Novak M. (1993). *Liberalism – Ally or Enemy of the Church,* W drodze Publishing House, Krakow, pp. 145–154.

Olszar H. (2004). *The Church in Poland in the Interwar Period (1918–1939),* "Symposium", No. 1 (12), p. 30.

Olszowski G. (2013). *Fr August Hlond – Pastoral Programme for the New Diocese,* in: *Biskup August Hlond i jego diecezja (Bishop August Hlond and his Diocese),* ed. J. Myszor, Księgarnia św. Jacka, Katowice.

Parfianowicz W. (2023). Jubileusz 25-lecia koszalińskiej redakcji „Gościa Niedzielnego" świętowany w Skrzatuszu, https://koszalin.gosc.pl/doc/5858690.Jubileusz-25-lecia -koszalinskiej-redakcji-Goscia-Niedzielnego (20/06/2023).

Plis J. (2001). *Kościół katolicki w Polsce a prasa, radio i film 1918–1939*, Wydawnictwo UMCS, Lublin.

Podoleński S. (1922). *Catholic Press in the Present Day*, "Przegląd Powszechny", No. 153/154, p. 207.

Rev. August Hlond in Upper Silesia 1922–1926. Listy pasterskie – odezwy – przemówienia. (2013). Ed. J. Myszor (a), Emmanuel Publishing House, Katowice.

Roszkowski W. (2003). *Najnowsza historia Polski 1914–1945*, Świat Książki, Warszawa.

Rusin E. (2003). *Akcja Katolicka*, in: *Encyklopedia Nauczania Społecznego Jana Pawła II*, ed. A. Zwoliński, Polskie Wydawnictwo Encyklopedyczne, Radom, pp. 30–36.

[*Siedemdziesiąt pięć lat*] *75 lat Gościa Niedzielnego 1923–1998.* (1998). Ed. J. W. Brzoza, Curia in Katowice, Publishing House of the Metropolitan, Katowice.

Sroga P. (2001). *The Church and Liberalism: the Beginning of a Dispute*, "Studia Warmińskie", No. 38, pp. 239–251.

Szczepaniak A. (2015). *Katowicki "Gość Niedzielny" wobec społeczno-politycznych wyzwań epoki w latach 1925–1939*, in: *Katowice in II Rzeczypospolitej*, ed. A. Barciak, Studio NOA Publishing House, Katowice.

Szewczyk L. (2013). *Diecezja śląska (katowicka) na łamach „Gościa Niedzielnego" w latach 1923–1926*, in: *Biskup August Hlond i jego diecezja*, ed. J. Myszor, Księgarnia św. Jacka, Katowice.

Wycisło J. (1996). *Pucher Wawrzyniec (1875–1941)*, in: *Słownik biograficzny katolickiego duchowieństwa śląskiego XIX i XX wieku*, ed. M. Pater, Wydawnictwo Księgarnia św. Jacka, Katowice, pp. 337–339.

Zywczynski M. (1971). *Studies on Catholic Modernism (2). Its Nature and Genesis*, "Life and Thought", No. 11(209), pp. 18–55.

CHAPTER 3

"For Censors, We Were Never Fringe Papers"

On Censorial Interferences and the Games Played with Censors in Tygodnik Powszechny between 1945 and 1953

Małgorzata Strzelecka

3.1 Cognitive Value

Tygodnik Powszechny was launched by clerical and secular Catholics who, acknowledging the specific geopolitical location of Poland in 1945, prioritised the needs of the nation and the existence of the state over all factions. With this in mind, the establishment of the new Cracow-based periodical was based on the pragmatism of the hierarchs of the Catholic Church, in particular, Adam Sapieha – the Metropolitan Bishop of Cracow, and Rev. Jan Piwowarczyk – the editor-in-chief of the post-war *Głos Narodu*, an activist of Christian trade unions, and a member of Christian Democracy and the Primate Board of Trustees. In February 1945, in the death throes of the war and amidst preparations for the Yalta Conference, the archbishop supported the concept of founding a Catholic weekly, based around the former editorial board of *Głos Narodu*. Not only did he provide a venue and funds, but by also offering spiritual support, he gave a clear signal that it was the dawn of a new era. What he thought imperative was active participation in Polish social life through the affirmation of its cultural identity on the basis of the canon of moral standards rooted in Christian culture (Sapieha 1945, Issue no. 1, p. 1).

The editorial board of *Tygodnik Powszechny* presented a Catholic perspective on complex religious, cultural, and socio-political issues (Turowicz 1945, Issue no. 11, p. 1; 1946, Issue no. 16, p. 3; 1947, Issue no. 46, pp. 1–2; 1947, Issue no. 51–52, p. 11; 1949, Issue no. 3, p. 1–2; 1950, Issue no. 13, pp. 1–2). The sway and the standing of the periodical stemmed from the fact that it offered an alternative vision, and it opposed the communist distortion of the truth and dumbing down of the society, by especially targeting Catholic intelligentsia. Without doubt, the weekly also owed its popularity to its editors, who were fully aware of distortions resulting from preventive censorship, and yet never ceased to seek forms of communication with their readership. The intentions

© MAŁGORZATA STRZELECKA, 2024 | DOI:10.1163/9789004687998_005

and opinions of the editorial board can be fully appreciated when its publication policies are interpreted not only through the prism of its headline articles, and those pieces of news that escaped the censors' rigorous attention and control, but also through an analysis of the texts and regular columns that were either successfully published or removed. A visible sign of intensified censorial interference was the printing of articles on tourism, environmental protection, or people's attitude to the Tatra Mountains which suddenly replaced the expected news on current issues of Church life, or important issues related to history, philosophy, and culture.

Analysis of the weekly's individual issues across its years of publication is an excellent source of knowledge on the history of 20th century Poland, even more so in that it may facilitate the comprehension of numerous contextual meanings of the country's socio-cultural events between 1945 and 1989. What is more, it also allows for multi-faceted research on the interpretation of articles published in *Tygodnik Powszechny* along with the evolution of the opinions and statements expressed by the editorial board and other contributing authors (of various ideological orientations) (Pawlicki, 2001, pp. 26–33; Stefaniak, 1998, pp. 49–196; Strzelecka, 2009, p. 82; Strzelecka, 2015, pp. 136–137; Kristanova, 2012, pp. 11–23; Kristanova, 2016, pp. 91–103; Kamińska-Chełminiak, 2019, pp. 202–214).

3.2   Scientific Objective

The decision to establish the periodical, with its mere existence as the core objective, was quite controversial and was subjected to harsh criticism, even among its co-founders (Kozłowski, 1998; Hennelowa, 1998). Its launch remains controversial, especially when we take into account the fact that the board were fully aware of having to deal with the ongoing situation in the post-war reality in Poland, i.e., a desire for active participation in society through the publication of articles on the transformation alongside a rather passive acceptance of preventive censorship. In this context, it seems justifiable to delve deeper into the matter by asking how the editorial board managed to communicate with its readers; whether the manner of communication was readable to the recipient; what content could be successfully conveyed despite censorship, and whether the efforts taken by the editorial board in such difficult political and social circumstances (quite often perceived as controversial and severely criticised), was both adequately justified, and beneficial to the preservation and development of the Polish culture *per se*.

3.3 Research Methodology

In order to conduct their analysis, the author examined both archival issues of *Tygodnik Powszechny* published between 1945 and 1953, and collections of documents compiled, inter alia, for the needs of the Main Office for the Control of the Press, Publications, and Public Performances (MOCPP&PP), and the Regional Office for the Control of the Press, Publications, and Public Performances in Cracow, which are stored in the Archives of Modern Records in Warsaw (AMR) and the National Archives in Cracow. The two databases contain extremely valuable archival collections of minutes, accounts, and reports documenting censorial interventions and the original proofs of the submitted articles complete with the censor's numerous corrections and strikethroughs. An important point of reference for modern analyses are also the materials stored in the Institute of National Remembrance Archives in Warsaw (INRA) and its Cracow-based branch (INRA Cr), as well as academic monographs on the current state of research (Kuta, 2009; Graczyk, 2011). Another significant supplement to the sources were witnesses' accounts (Hennelowa, 1998; Kozłowski, 1998; Zabłocki, 2012; Wielowieyski, 2012), the Jerzy Turowicz Archives (JTA), and memoirs of the journalists involved, directly and indirectly, which were published years after the actual events (Gołubiew, 1971; Hennelowa, 2001; Jasienica, 2007; Kisielewski, 2001; Stomma, 1991; Wielowieyski, 2015; Woźniakowski, 2008; Żakowski, 1990).

3.4 Introduction

To begin with, it must be emphasised that the weekly's editorial board commenced its operations in March 1945, as an institution that had to declare loyalty, at least superficially, to the new Polish government. The consent granted by the communist authorities for a Catholic periodical that aimed to present independent opinions to be published when the State was governed by a political camp which promoted a secular worldview was intended to prove that freedom of the press and democratic liberties were well respected in Poland and, additionally, legitimise the new political setup. In later years, the government's attitude towards the editorial board would change and, depending on the then current policies and strategies applied to the Polish Church, evolved from one of acceptance to one of rejection of the concept of the co-existence of multiple worldviews within the country. As a result, the periodical that was published by the Cracow Curia between 1945 and 1953 became a political instrument in the hands of communist authorities, who aimed at an open confrontation with the Church and wished to monopolise those institutions that shaped the social awareness of the nation.

Tygodnik Powszechny, together with *Tygodnik Warszawski* and *Dziś i Jutro*, which were founded in November 1945, were 'flagship titles of social Catholicism' (Sikorski, 2013, p. 17). Even though the three periodicals claimed the right to the post-war legacy, each formulated its own, varying, ideological and strategic vision for social Catholicism (Kosicki, 2016, p. 159). In the new geopolitical situation, those intellectuals gathered around *Tygodnik Powszechny* strived to find space for the propagation of Christian humanism, through adjusting post-war ideas of the Catholic worldview – mainly of the *Revival* Catholic Academic Youth Association – to the post-war reality (Friszke, 2015, pp. 203–219; Kosicki, 2016, pp. 159–176, 413–418). Not only did the editorial board dissent from the radical Catholicism of *Tygodnik Warszawski*, which sought direct confrontation with the ruling party (Kristanova, 2012, pp. 196–199; Wiszniewski, 1998, pp. 111–113; Ciechomski, 1983, p. 4), but also from the avantgarde views of *Dziś i Jutro*, which postulated that the Catholic and Marxist worldviews be reconciled (Piasecki, 1953, pp. 1–2; Garlicki, 1993, pp. 16–21).

All along, the editorial board of *Tygodnik Powszechny* showed a favourable attitude towards the concept of co-operation with all social forces, but stood in constitutional opposition to Marxist ideology (*Opposition and Social Resistance in Poland (1945–1980)/Opozycja i opór społeczny w Polsce (1945–1980)*, pp. 9–10). However, from the weekly's foundation (determined by market survival) its editors had taken a vague, unstipulated and an insufficiently specified path (Gołubiew, 1971, p. 339; Murzański, 1998, pp. 21–29). They based their operations on the simple premise of 'presence', which – on the one hand – constituted a bold and risky long-term approach, and on the other hand, it also meant accepting partial responsibility for the reality that was being formed. The board stressed the fact that they felt responsible for the matters which they could influence directly. In this context, culture was to become a battle ground in a war waged by the weekly's authors against the totalitarian system, and a platform where they competed for the readership's spirituality (Jagiełło, 1986, pp. 62–88). Their opinion-formers believed that, in the new reality, one should seek compromise with the ruling party. They declared a readiness to co-operate in the process of constructing a new socio-political order, but only under the condition that they could, at the same time, preserve their own ideological and cultural identity.

Due to its precarious situation, the board never published a detailed list of programme theses, but only outlined the general directions of projected actions (Gołubiew, 1975, p. 16). Its priority lay with a desire to shape the worldview of

Catholics, despite full awareness of the distortions due to preventive censorship. The editorial team were convinced that the periodical does not have to be published at any cost. It is meant to serve the nation and the Church, but it also must determine the bounds of its remit (Stomma, 1999, p. 15).

The only clearly stipulated goal, stressed on more than one occasion, was to remain in opposition to the ideology of the ruling party. Confronted with reality, the board were convinced that it was necessary to abandon any direct reference to current socio-political affairs. The members decided to object to restrictions on liberty or to express their opinions through apolitical means rather than by commenting on the news. According to Turowicz, this silence to avoid disseminating falsehoods became the programme itself' (Żakowski, 1990, p. 69).

From the very beginning, the policy of surviving for as long as possible, or 'floating' – as described by Stomma, caused great controversy among the editorial board (Stomma, 1946. *Znak*, Issue no. 3, pp. 257–275; 1947, TP, Issue no. 16, p. 5; Rabiński, 2006, pp. 111–112), and the Catholic community (Braun, 1947, *Tygodnik Warszawski*, Issue no. 13, pp. 3–4; T. Ketlicz, 1947, *Tygodnik Warszawski*, Issue no. 15, p. 6).

Despite the harsh preventive censorship and imputations of reactivism, *Tygodnik Powszechny* always had the reputation of being the most significant Catholic periodical among Catholic intelligentsia and governmental authorities. The former perceived the weekly as representative and influential, which most reflected their opinions, whereas the latter regarded it a formidable opponent and an adversary in debate and polemics (Jagiełło, 1988, pp. 13–16). Censors' notes reveal that the paper was classified as threatening for the ruling party, because it aims to create an ideological base for Catholic circles, later to be used to influence public opinion (AMR, MOCPP&PP, File no. 1102, Part I, Vol. 122–9, p. 36).

Analysis of the weekly's archival issues with highlighted censorial corrections and comments allows us to understand the mechanism of the operations behind MOCPP&PP (Strzelecka, 2010, pp. 103–119), a governmental body which, for many Poles, was a symbol of an institution that stifled freedom of speech and all manifestations of independent thinking. 'Armed' with red pens, censors were appointed by the government to ensure the guidelines were not breached. On behalf of the ruling party, they decided what could and could not be published (Fik, 1995, pp. 1 and 5; Hera, 2007, pp. 111–118). Following the top-down imposed guidelines, they adjudicated what issues should be eschewed, whose unwelcome views must be crossed out, who ought to get a publication ban, and which debate is inconsistent with the propagated ideology.

MOCPP&PP prepared a book entitled *A Handbook of Notations and Recommendations/Książka zapisów i zaleceń* where censors could find detailed instructions on the types of information that must not or should be disseminated in the mass media (*The Black Book of Censorship in the Polish People's Republic/Czarna księga cenzury* PRL 1977, p. 7). A substantial number of these instructions were devoted to religious, ethnic, and socio-economic content, with the intention of cutting Polish people off from any independent information. The censors were instructed to eradicate:

> any criticism of Marxism in religious publications, all attempts to politically diversify the nation through denominational or broader political criteria, any statements on the privileges that the religious majority was entitled to (...), every implication that Polishness should be related to Catholicism, including all attempts to exclude anything that is non-Catholic from traditions and national life, any releases on the Church's contributions to current affairs and the realm of the Polish People's Republic, any manifestations of an extremely clerical interpretation of the history of the Church in Poland etc. (*The Black Book of Censorship in the Polish People's Republic/Czarna księga cenzury* PRL 1977, pp. 69–71)

A profound analysis reveals the purposefully vague nature of the guidelines, as they were meant to provide a framework for executive dictates that were convoluted, draconian, and prone to change, depending on the current circumstances. Most customers (here: publishers and journalists) were not familiar with the recommendations, which led to confusion, disorientation, and some unpleasant surprises (quite frequently, publications by popular authors were suddenly banned). Other adverse effects included a complete helplessness on the side of editorial boards, and a total lack of any legal oversight of the ever-changing policies of the censorship office, which, in fact, had become a state within a state.

Due to its opposing ideological principia, the authorities placed *Tygodnik Powszechny* and its team under close surveillance. Archival files generated and collected by the Ministry of Public Security reveal that, initially, the Security Service showed little interest in the journalists gathered around Rev. Jan Piwowarczyk and Jerzy Turowicz. In June 1947, a single case (code-named *Struggle/Walka*, INRA Cr 010/10093/1, pp. 5–424) was filed in court against the team, and only for *pro forma* reasons. The situation changed in 1953–1956, however, when, upon taking control over the journal, the authorities were still unable to break the spirit of the group of authors surrounding Turowicz (JTA, *A Letter to Jacek Woźniakowski from Jerzy Turowicz/List Jacka Woźniakowskiego od Jerzego Turowicza;* JTA: *A Letter to Jerzy Zawieyski from Jerzy Turowicz/List Jerzego Zawieyskiego do Jerzego Turowicza;* Żakowski, 1987, p. 10; Graczyk, 2009, pp. 489–501). In 1955, an espionage class-action lawsuit (code-named *Pen/ Pióro*; INRA Cr 010/10093/1, p. 342; Piotrowski, 2004, pp. 67–68; Kuta, 2006, p. 24) was filed against the leaders who had held regular meetings in the home of Zofia Starowieyska-Morstinowa. The list of investigated journalists included Jerzy Turowicz, Jacek Woźniakowski, Antoni Gołubiew, Jan J. Szczepański, Józef Święcicki, Rev. Jan Piwowarczyk, and Stanisław Stomma. A formal decision sanctioning the lawsuit brought forward charges including 'political sabotage activities in socio-political life' and stated that the defendants 'have been committing acts of subversion in the socio-political life of the Polish People's Republic since its foundation' (INRA Cr 010/10093/1, p. 342). In the documentation of the *Pen/Pióro* lawsuit, the installation of a listening device was justified as follows:

> to determine the nature of current activities undertaken by journalists contributing to *Tygodnik Powszechny*, to recognise their aims and the scope of their operation, to establish whether the group intends to use the process of democratisation of political and economic life for hostile purposes; and whose ideological impact could incur irrecoverable losses on the working class and socialism. (INRA Cr 010/10093/1, pp. 34–35)

The ideological 'law-abidingness' of the weekly's team was monitored by an army of governmental officials, who undoubtedly were rewarded and even promoted up the ranks of MOCPP&PP for their commitment. During the period that was called *Mikołajczyk's era* by Cracow-based journalists, i.e., until October 1947, when Stanisław Mikołajczyk – former Prime Minister of the Polish government in exile – was forced to leave Poland, the content of successive issues was most frequently perused by Roman Szydłowski, the head of the Regional Office for the Control of the Press. In the Stalinist period, the weekly was supervised by Ignacy Próchnicki, the Head of the Censorship Office in Cracow, whom the journalists nicknamed 'word slasher'. Próchnicki was later replaced by Bohdan Gutkowski, who was promoted to vice-head and transferred to the central headquarters in Warsaw (JTA, Kisielewski, p. 3). At the height of this period of repression, decisions on seizures of the entire circulation of individual issues, the so-called repressive-educational or penal confiscations, were made by the highest authorities, in the offices of Jakub Berman, an MP, member of Politburo and Secretariat of the Polish United Workers' Party, Deputy Prime Minister of the Republic of Poland (since March 25, 1953), and Franciszek Mazur, member of Politburo and Secretariat of the Polish United Workers' Party, and Deputy Marshal of the Sejm of the Republic of Poland (1952–1957) (Mołdawa, 1991, pp. 79, 107). The editorial board of the weekly usually delegated the same representatives to discuss and negotiate terms with censors, namely Jerzy Turowicz and Antoni Gołubiew (JTA, Kisielewski, p. 3; Frazik, 2009, p. 13).

The co-founders of the weekly were well aware of the moral price to be paid for the mutually agreed and unwritten arrangement with the ruling party (*Turowicz's Team/Krąg Turowicza*, 2012, pp. 34–39; Żakowski, 1990, pp. 68–69), which also involved a conscious acceptance of the numerous difficulties involved in communication with readers. In practice, the journalists developed an ability to self-censor, which could be described as strategic, reasonable and deliberate avoidance of direct references to controversial or forbidden subjects. The desire to survive stemmed from a strong conviction that it was imperative to pursue the possibility to impact reality, against all odds, and regardless of the extraneous and often hostile political circumstances (...), the instinct of self-preservation, which pushed them to save the existence of the whole nation despite adversities and the political fiasco (Kozłowski, 1995, p. 167).

On order of the authorities, the editorial board had to support the official governmental policy by publishing commemorative texts on various anniversaries, or by sending its representatives to numerous assemblies (e.g., meetings of the Committee of the National Unity Front), major state ceremonies, and official trips abroad.

The initially tolerative policy towards the weekly was manifested by the ruling party's consent to increase the paper's volume. In early July 1945, the authorities officially granted an increase in the number of pages from 4 to 6, which lifted the price from 3 to 5 zlotys. What remained unchanged was the format, which stayed at 47 x 32 cm. Three months later, on October 13, 1946, the print run was expanded again, this time to 12 pages. This was shortly before the parliament elections scheduled for January 1947, and for the very first time, the editorial board was officially permitted to express their views and opinions, although within a framework of controlled freedom of speech. As a result, the team could carry on a polemic with Leon Chajn, the junior minister of justice, who, on his stay in Cracow, declared that in the overall hierarchy, the Church must be subordinated to the State. The commentary on the front page retorted that Nobody can think of subordinating the Church to the State, since it is virtually impossible and would be an absolute disaster. (...) Today, only two solutions to the problem are viable: either an agreement between the Church and the State, or a complete separation' (Editors, 1945, Issue no. 20, p. 1).

For strategic reasons, the authorities temporarily tolerated this dialogue with the Marxists, e.g., the dispute over ideas propagating a new model of the State published in *Kuźnica*. At that time, the unquestioned leader among the weekly's polemicists was Rev. Jan Piwowarczyk, the author of numerous analytical articles on Marxism (Piwowarczyk, 1985, pp. 98–138). He did not represent the conservative wing in the editorial board, and had already been referred to as the 'red priest' in the pre-war era. Paradoxically, even though he entered into the debate over Marxist ideas, he still supported the programme of radical social reforms based on papal encyclicals. At that time, Jerzy Turo-wicz competed with Piwowarczyk as the leading overt critic of the propaganda campaign conducted by the ruling party under the banner of 'fighting off reactionism'. In April 1946, Turowicz was still able to boldly conclude that the deliberations above will most probably trigger a fierce response among our opponents (...); they will massively accuse us of reactionism. We are not afraid of their response and such accusations. After all, we have got used to them. (...) On the other hand, an honest debate over our theses is more than welcome. We will eagerly join it. We might be mistaken. Prove us wrong. (Turowicz, 1946, Issue no. 14, p. 1).

This was the time when the pages of the weekly were filled with debates and polemics: Stefan Kisielewski was able to discuss authenticism and realism in literature (Kisielewski, 1946, TP, Issue no. 4, p. 1; Issue no. 6, p. 2), and Paweł Jasienica could initiate a debate on various ways of defining the moral values that determine Polish honour in response to earlier deliberations on the issue published in *Kuźnica* (Jasienica, 1946, Issue no. 13, p. 3). Despite censorship, several debates took place that were crucial for the Polish national awareness, and were inspired by such works as Kieslowski's novel entitled *Confederacy/Sprzysiężenie* and Szczepański's short story *Shoes/Buty* (Gołubiew, 1947, Issue no. 2, p. 7; Szczepański, 1947, Issue no. 6, pp. 6–9). The latter countered the image of the unblemished, honourable and patriotic guerrillas, 'boys from the woods', and well-disciplined troops of the Home Army (HA). The editorial board triggered this discussion regardless of the fact that many HA soldiers were incarcerated at that time, and the critical message conveyed by the story coincided with the propaganda slogans released by the ruling party. Equally controversial was the situation with Kisielewski's novel, which created tensions in the Curia and among the outraged readers and resulted in the author being temporarily suspended by the weekly. The book shocked with its blatant eroticism and bitter moral settlement, with the 1939 September Campaign in its deeper layers.

In order to keep up the appearance of openness in those discussions, the authorities sent their representatives and emissaries to participate in debates (Żakowski 1990, pp. 83–84). Attempts were made to criticise the ruling party's policy; joining its opponents in formulated objections against the national legal system under construction, and the economic solutions proposed, for instance, by minister Hilary Minc, including – in particular – implementation of the national retail and wholesale commerce bill, which resulted in the State becoming the sole monopolist controlling both production and the market (Krasiński, 1947, Issue no. 24, p. 2; Turowski, 1947, Issue no. 26, p. 7).

Deprived of the possibility to directly comment on certain issues, or to reveal any censorial corrections and interferences, the editorial board often tried to signal to the reader, e.g., by applying Aesopian language. We can find numerous examples of such tactics, e.g., an observation formulated by Hanna Malewska about the fact that Joseph Goebbels never stood in the dock of justice during the Nuremberg trials. In her commentary, she wrote:

> I believe that the horrible experience of recent years should teach us to approach *all* propaganda with extreme caution. (Malewska, 1946, Issue no. 9, p. 5)

A huge amount of important news was covered in the commemorative issue published on the weekly's first anniversary. With a provocative wink to its readership, the editors used the fact that the jubilee coincided with April Fools' Day to alert them to new, concealed and indirect forms of communication. In the column *Amidst Journals/Wśród czasopism*, Jan Piess applied a puckish tone, writing that *Tygodnik Powszechny* wants to return to the ignorance and obscurantism of the Middle Ages, (...) to eradicate the postulate of educating the masses, (...) to propagate regression to serfdom, adobe huts, and female slavery (Piess, 1946, Issue no. 13, p. 8).

The editorial board showed more prudence in using the anniversary to reveal the traits that depicted the life of Catholics in 1946. The column *Letters to the Editor/Listy do redakcji* contained extracts from letters and dispatches sent to the editor-in-chief. The selection was quite meaningful, as was the order in which they were arranged. This was designed to help the reader to evaluate their importance and intentions. The extracts were published in the following sequence: Stefan Żółkiewski (*Kuźnica*), Stanisław Mikołajczyk, Jerzy Borejsza (*Czytelnik*), Bolesław Piasecki (*Dziś i Jutro*), and others. Żółkiewski wrote:

> Even though your weekly has been on the market for a year now, it still remains absolutely aimless. In today's Poland, the only dialecticians that keep their raison d'être are those who, on the basis of adequate semantics, achieve methodological, empirical and logical correctness and the sole objective veracity to cognise the mechanism of revolutionary social evolutions, which are possible through dialectic philosophical materialism (...) Whoever does not possess these fundamental, semantic essentials of scientific thinking makes a fool of himself on entering any debate. In fact, your vagueness and free-thinking is there only to cover up obscurantism,

philistinism, ignorance, and the class egoism of your caste, the remnants of which will soon vanish, making room for the modern and scientific people's democracy (...) I repeat: your weekly is absolutely pointless, not to say harmful.

Mikołajczyk argued that On the anniversary of your widely-read paper, I wish to stress once more that P. S. L. is a peasant party, whose programme does not differ in any way from platforms of any other peasant political groups. (...) Nobody can be forbidden to vote for P. S. L. – and nobody can call us a reactive party.

Borejsza argued that Elections are not just a mechanical count of votes: elections are a conscious act of creative work. Their results will not change the positive path of the overall Polish democracy: there might be minor, but no fundamental ones. The sooner you understand that, the better for you and for the State. We shall not let the hydra of reactionism raise its head. On the jubilee of your weekly, I wish to reemphasise these basic truths to be digested by the camp of young Polish Catholics.

Finally, Piasecki – the leader of the liberal Catholics – wrote:

On the jubilee of *Tygodnik Powszechny*, I am sending my hopes that the appropriate attitudes will be adopted towards the directional and energetic tensions of the epoch that show great results from the revolutionary transformations and its actual corresponding consequences, which should not be ignored by any Pole who represents a Catholic worldview or who does not want to miss out on the spirit and direction of the transformational ideas in the history of our nation, and the worldviews that are structural with regard to the course of these transformations within their ideological content and outlook. The sooner we become aware of this, the better. May this clear and simple historical truth motivate the entire Catholic camp in Poland. And may it do so before it is too late. (Letters to the Editor/Listy do redakcji, 1946, p. 8)

In all probability, the censors did not interfere with those wishes, and readers had a clear insight into the state of affairs before the 1947 elections. Five months later, well aware of the futility of debating with journalists contributing to *Kuźnica* and *Odrodzenie*, Kisielewski used his typical sense of humour to advise the editors of *Tygodnik Powszechny*:

if you cannot stand it any longer – stick your tongue out at them. (Kisiel, 1946, TP, Issue no. 36, p. 8)

Censorial oppression was increased steadily, which forced the weekly's editors to use new means of expression. Jan Piwowarczyk – its leader, a lecturer in Catholic social ethics, and the rector of a divinity school in Cracow – remained an implacable opponent of communism, and never avoided openly disputing the theses of the Marxist doctrine, at least to the extent allowed by the censors (Piwowarczyk, 1945, TP, Issue no. 36, p. 2). The titles of his 1945–1946 articles show the vast scope of interests and the essence of the issues he discussed: *The Sin of Being Unfaithful to the Nation/Grzech niewierności wobec narodu, Primacy of Ethics/Prymat etyki, Liberty and Ownership/Wolność i własność, Raising a New Man/Wychowanie nowego człowieka, Prison and the Creative Spirit/ Więzienie i twórczy duch, The Crucial Issue of Ownership/Wielkie zagadnienie własności, Palestine and the Jewish Problem/Palestyna i problem żydowski, The Nuremberg Verdict/Wyrok w Norymberdze,* and *Support for Catholics/O stronnictwo dla katolików* (Piwowarczyk, 1985, pp. 98–138). He showed the keenest interest in discussing issues related to shaping Catholic awareness of hatred perceived from the ethical and sociological perspective, hostility towards Marxism, and property, polity, liberalism, religion, philosophy, as well as problems of the papacy and the Church itself.

In the column *New Books/Nowe książki*, he managed to publish information on two works by Roman Szydłowski, a local censor, the head of the Regional Office for the Control of the Press, Publications, and Public Performances. *The Issue of Leverage in Law and Teaching Comparative Law/Zagadnienie wpływów w prawie a nauka prawa porównawczego,* and *The Issue of Purpose of Law/ Zagadnienie celowości prawa* were published in 1939 in Cracow (J. P. 1946, Issue no. 18, p. 5). Hidden behind his initials, Piwowarczyk drew the reader's attention to the fact that – despite having been released under the German occupation – both works, and the latter in particular, were quite noteworthy. Reporting on the analytical and experimental nature of the issue discussed by Szydłowski, the reviewer found the study a valuable contribution to the general debate on the purpose of positive law. He emphasised the thesis formed by the censor, who argued that the main purpose of law is »perfection of humankind and progress« (...) Namely, he believed that law aimed at »people leading better lives and being better. The purpose of law is to guarantee well-being for all people, and to improve their mores.

Since Piwowarczyk could not refer directly to the analysed publication, he chose to compare its theories with the standpoint of the Catholic philosophy of law, and thus, in the end, he stated that 'we find Saint Thomas' view on the matter closer to our hearts and more reassuring. Concatenation of law and ethics is much more likely to prevent situations when lawlessness is sanctioned as law'. He also provided the reader with a though-provoking conclusion:

Nevertheless, we must admit that Szydłowski's study constitutes a serious contribution to the debate on the purpose of law, characterised by high scientific quality and nobility of approach. Additionally, we must stress that the author made use of a vast spectrum of jurisprudential and philosophical literature, especially Russian works on the matter, which is quite exceptional among Polish scholars.

It is the comparative analysis of the two reviews that allows us to grasp the essence of views expressed by the weekly's team. Piwowarczyk, who opted for negation of the new polity, was in favour of moderate participation of the Church in the political life of the country (Bankowicz 1990, Issue no. 12, p. 8). Outside the weekly, he coined the shortest definition of bolshevism: 'the square of socialism' (*Turowicz's Team. The Weekly, Times and People 1945–1989/ Krąg Turowicza. Tygodnik, czasy, ludzie 1945–1989*, p. 70), and his most fundamental work was *Catholic Social Ethics/Katolicka etyka społeczna*, published in London just after his death (Piwowarczyk, 1960).

Besides our major deliberations, it also seems noteworthy to mention the work by the relatively unknown name of Dr Stefan Zuzelski, (Zuzelski (S. Wyszyński), 1945, p. 132), which appeared in the column *New Books/Nowe książki* in October 1945, as it was common practice in the post-war Catholic press to publish articles under a pseudonym or initials. Another example that illustrates the need to hide behind pseudonyms are publications by Stanisław Stomma, who adopted the pen name of Marjan Jedlicz to presented his views on interdisciplinary subjects in the weekly *Dziś i Jutro* between 1945 and 1947 (Stomma, 1945, DiJ, Issue no. 1, p. 2, Issue no. 3, pp. 2–3; 1946, Issue no. 1, p. 1; 1947, Issue no. 8, p. 1). Other authors who used a nom de plume in *Tygodnik Powszechny* were Jan Piwowarczyk, alias J. P., and Jerzy Turowicz, who had several pen names, including 'jet', J. T., (jt), and Paweł Brudzewski. Jacek Woźniakowski hid behind the name of Kornik, while Stefan Kisielewski employed his surname abbreviated to Kisiel, but also used: Teodor Klon, Julia Hołyńska, and Tomasz Staliński. Additionally, the editorial board created the fictional figure of Mikołaj Strebejko, who – from October 1946 to December 1952 – served as a collective pen name for Antoni Gołubiew, Paweł Jasienica, Stanisław Stomma, and Zofia Starowieyska-Morstin in various articles on international affairs; written individually or in co-operation. In later years, censorship became even stricter, which forced an increasing number of authors to write under a pseudonym, including such weekly's contributors as Karol Wojtyła (alias Andrzej Jawień), Czesław Miłosz (alias Adrian Zieliński); Anna Morawska (alias as Maria Garnysz), Janusz Zabłocki (alias Karol Zajczniewski).

A figure that made a unique and exceptional contribution to the discourse and battles with the censors was Stefan Kisielewski, a confirmed polity contrarian and a master of polemics. Initially, he wrote music reviews and reportages, but in Issue no. 20, he debuted as a columnist, and most readers soon got into the habit of reading his contributions first. In his column, he expressed his dislike for socialism, and revulsion towards what he called mindless collective thinking. He appealed for a style and language that would realistically describe the socialist reality, and he turned his caustic and stinging sense of humour into a tool to fight against the totalitarian political system. Thanks to his unique ability to write between the lines, he ridiculed the communist newspeak, e.g., music must express the brand new, great and supreme ideas and emotions of the masses', and gobbledygook slogans like 'labourer's culture is nation's culture', by asking what they actually meant, and if the whole nation should apply the labourer's culture: 'And what about Mickiewicz, Słowacki, Chopin? They were no workmen, after all. Nope, I just don't get it! What worries me even more is that nobody else seems to be perplexed by that slogan. There must be something seriously wrong with me (Kisiel, 1946, TP, Issue no. 7, p. 7).

Unable to covey his message directly, he tried to make the reader ponder more deeply. For instance, in the column *Against the Grain/Pod włos*, he referred to commonly known sayings and proverbs, arguing that these words of wisdom took on a new meaning in the socialist world, and yet still remained surprisingly accurate (Kisiel 1946, TP, Issue no. 6, p. 4). In the spirit of the 'brand new reality', he interpreted the old rhyme:

> *To a painting once spoke this old guy, and what he got was no reply. That's how the talking went by...*', stating that 'more or less, this paints an accurate picture of the current political debate between the two media camps. Another apt quote is *Tell me more... No one can hear us*. (That's my recommendation for a sad motto, dedicated especially to *Piast, Gazeta Ludowa, Tygodnik Warszawski*, and *Tygodnik Powszechny*)

Analysing another popular saying – to ram something down somebody's throat – Kisielewski concluded that the 'editors of *Kuźnica* shove the Marxist doctrine and culture down the readers' throats, despite the fact that they could not be less interested. The same thing happened in the Polish Army Theatre in Lodz, when Adam Ważyk strived to ram his infantile, propaganda play *In the Old Mansion/W starym dworku* down the managers' throats. Fortunately, they turned it down, instantly realising that the theatre would *choke on* a drama which contorted history in the most provocative manner, as it would most likely infuriate the audiences. The rejection caused comrade Ważyk, who so courageously and yet carelessly fought against the decision, crumble completely (The humorous effect in this sentence in Polish was achieved by strong alliteration: 'Ważyk, który tak odważnie a nierozważnie odważył się przeciwważyć opinię – zważył się po tej porażce zupełnie').

Not only did Kisielewski enter into disputes with Stefan Żółkiewski, the editor-in-chief of *Kuźnica* (Kisielewski, 1946, TP, Issue no. 4, pp. 1–2), Jerzy Borejsza, (Kisiel, 1945, TP, Issue no. 31, p. 6; Kisielewski, 1946, Issue no. 6, p. 2), Wojciech Kętrzyński (Kisiel, 1945, TP, Issue no. 24, p. 2), but he also polemicized with Kazimierz Wyka, Jan Kott and *Odrodzenie*, taking a keen interest in such issues as authenticity and realism in literature and social life (Kisielewski, 1945, TP, Issue no. 9, p. 3; 1945, Issue no. 17, p. 5;1945, Issue no. 22, p. 7; 1949, Issue no. 1, p. 3). With his rational and pragmatic approach to reality, Kisielewski maintained an open and free mind, and yet remained reticent regarding liberalism. In the weekly, all of his texts that may court controversy were published with the following warning:

> The editorial board does not share all opinions expressed by the author.
> (Kisielewski, 1945, TP, Issue no. 9, p. 3)

Kisielewski undoubtedly found it difficult to fit in with the weekly's team, with his liberal views and unique sense of humour. On numerous occasions, his rebelliousness would transform into flippancy, and his struggle against the system and independence of thinking caused great tensions, which the rest of the team considered a threat to the weekly's existence. However, if we delve deeper into his attitude, we can conclude that he was actually quite a representative journalist for the Cracow-based team, bearing the paper's openness in mind, being an adversary of the system and a political pragmatist whose opinions were convergent with the views expressed by Turowicz and Stomma. Deeply concerned about the fate of his homeland, he perceived liberalism as a supplementation to Christianity, and mastered the Aesopian language to an extent that allowed him to escape the shackles of censorship. His column cannot be read and interpreted solely through the prism of his situational jokes, however. In order to propagate his opinions, he founded a discussion group named the *The Insane Liberals' Party/Partia Wariatów Liberałów*. The major idea behind his articles was the thesis that a liberal economy cannot be implemented without liberalism in politics and culture. As far as he was concerned, until liberalism has been achieved in the socio-political life, one has to weave between pragmatism and extreme disobedience.

Some found Kisielewski's proposals regarding the future unacceptable, disagreeing with his belief that there should be no fatalism, but no uprisings

either – let's get on with our business. And let's do it armed with humour'
(Kisielewski, 2013, Vol. 1, p. 11), and that the Polish needed 'a high-quality sense
of humour that is both powerful and gives power (Kisielewski, 2013, Vol. 1, p. 11).

He argued that satire and opposition are prerequisites of national life (…)
since there is no such thing as satire *for*, satire can only be *against*. Without this
spice, our national dish will be bland. Without the right to oppose, we won't
be able to inspire the youth. This justifies the need for a legal opposition (…)
The opposition of a buzzing mosquito is still an opposition (Kisielewski, 2013,
Vol. 2; p. 16).

Years later, he bitterly accounted:

> Censorship broke me and grossed me out. Censorship made it virtually
> impossible for me to perform my duties as a political journalist, which
> had always been my vocation. Censorship falsified, skewed, and spoilt
> ninety percent of what I ever published. Censors made the weekly arti-
> cles that I wrote for *Tygodnik Powszechny* for 32 years look mutilated –
> a distorted version of my intentions. And I could neither rectify it nor
> insinuate what I wished to say in any other way, since the censors oper-
> ated behind the scenes, eradicating even the slightest clues that would
> reveal their interference. (JTA, Kisielewski, *Against Censorship/Przeciw
> cenzurze*, p. 1)

He called the whole phenomenon of censorship 'the factory of fake texts', an
enormous and camouflaged mystification that had two major objectives: 'a) to
imply to the reader that what authors think is exactly what they write; b) to
make authors become accustomed to thinking and formulating their opinions in a strictly stipulated manner, because writing in any different way will
be eradicated or thoroughly re-edited' (JTA, Kisielewski, *Against Censorship/
Przeciw cenzurze*, p. 2). What is more, he also argued that it was an institution
that wished to 'educate' both readers and authors.

This 'rationed freedom of speech' of the Polish press was curtailed after the
parliament elections of January 19, 1947. Awareness of malpractices and rigged
results could not see the light of day, and thus, the weekly was denied permission to publish even the shortest text on the event. In fact, the word 'elections'
appeared only once, in reference to the political triumph of communists in
France (Żak, 1947, Issue no. 3, p. 12). The editorial board used this situation to
send an oblique message to the public. Apparently in response to an inquiry,
allegedly sent in by a reader interested in French matters who wondered how it
was possible that the communists had won there, the weekly quoted statistical
data on elections in France between 1928 and 1946, and concluded that This

result shows one typical feature (...) Non-Marxist groups divide and respawn, while the extreme left wing always maintains an admirable discipline. As a result, the former are regular losers, and the latter win. The analysis of these dry facts and figures can be quite meaningful and thought-provoking (Żak, 1947, Issue no. 3, p. 12).

The fact that censors did not permit the weekly to publish even the shortest article on the long-awaited elections was a clear sign, heralding the new policy being applied by the ruling party.

It was not until July 1947 that the editorial board managed to inform their readers about the evolution of the authorities' approach towards the Catholic press. The editor-in-chief reported on a governmental 'campaign to save paper'. The initiative, which, apparently, did not affect other periodicals, forced the weekly to decrease its volume (J. T. 1947, Issue no. 30, p. 8) by two pages, to a total of 10 pages. In reality, it began to be published alternately as an 8- and then 12-page newspaper, a custom which survived till the 1990s.

In those uncertain times, Kisielewski's New Year's wishes for 1948, written with his typical sense of humour, were worded as follows:

> May this new year be no worse than the old one. We can't really expect more – let's be perfectly realistic about that. (Kisiel, 1948, TP, Issue no. 1, p. 12)

With censorship becoming ever more stringent in 1948, it was quite an achievement for the editorial board to have been granted permission to print Jerzy Zawieyski's text on the newly born State of Israel (Zawieyski, 1948, Issue no. 25, pp. 3–4). The censors granted a delayed publication of the article *To Israel, our Brother – in Brotherhood/Izraelowi, bratu naszemu – braterstwo* a month after the actual declaration of independence, announced on May 14, 1948 (*Citizen KK, aka. Krzysztof Kozłowski's Thoughts on Poland/Obywatel KK czyli Krzysztofa Kozłowskiego zamyślenia nad Polską*, 2011, p. 48).

An event that marked another step in the tightening governmental surveillance over the Catholic press was the repressions against *Tygodnik Warszawski*, whose offices were raided and whose editorial team dismantled in August 1948 by the Department of Security. Since *Tygodnik Powszechny* could only comment on these happenings in an indirect and veiled manner, the following was published:

> In response to the news being spread by various foreign sources (radio, press) on the closure of *Tygodnik Powszechny* and the arrest of its contributors, it is the editorial board's desire to assure readers that – in reference

to *Tygodnik Powszechny* – none of it is actually true. *Tygodnik Powsze-chny* has not been closed down, and all members of its editorial board remain free, including Rev. Jan Piwowarczyk, Paweł Jasienica, and Stefan Kisielewski. (Editors/Redakcja, 1948, TP, Issue no. 39, p. 3)

Delaying permission to publish certain materials on current affairs related to the Church and culture became common practice among the censors, who hoped to discourage readers and turn them away from the weekly. In reality, it was counterproductive, as people began to feel more attached to the paper. Another significant example of the dirty tricks that censors played on Turo-wicz's team was the delay in their consent to publish information on Stefan Wyszyński designation for Primate of Poland. The death of his predecessor, primate August Hlond, on October 22, 1948, was not reported – by Piwowarc-zyk (Piwowarczyk, 1948, TP, Issue no. 44, p. 1) – until as late as on October 31, which was after the tragic death of Hlond's natural successor, Bishop Stanisław Kostka Łukomski, killed on October 28 in a mysterious car accident. In such circumstances, on November 12, Pope Pius XII appointed Bishop Wyszyński, the Archbishop of Gniezno and Warsaw, as the new Primate of Poland. How-ever, it was not until early 1949 that censors lifted the publication embargo imposed on the weekly and allowed news of the new primate to be shared with the public. The very first, unsigned, details on the event was a short and laconic notice at the bottom of the front page of Issue no. 1 in 1949 (*New Primate of Poland/Nowy Prymas Polski,* 1949, TP, Issue no. 1, p. 1). In the next issue, two months after his actual appointment, Piwowarczyk introduced the relatively unknown figure of Wyszyński, (Piwowarczyk, 1949, TP, Issue no. 2, p. 1).

December 1949 brought another turning point when the People's Republic of Poland, together with the whole Eastern Bloc, entered the zenith of Stalin-ism. In January, during the Penmen Congress in Szczecin, socialist realism was declared to be the main literary trend. As a result, Turowicz warned that the content of culture is not part of politics' (Turowicz, 1949, Issue no. 3, pp. 1–2), while Kisielewski mockingly commented on Turowicz's and Zawieyski's par-ticipation in the event: I didn't go to the congress in Szczecin, because I don't like talking to a brick wall (Kisiel, 1949, TP, Issue no. 7, p. 8).

And Piwowarczyk, in a text massacred by censors, pondered over the essence of the separation of the Church and the State announced in December 1948 (Piwowarczyk, 1949, TP, Issue no. 3, p. 2).

In 1949, the affirmation of Stalinist ideals took place during the celebrations of his 70th birthday, an event which dominated the Polish press. Even though his actual date of birth was December 18, the authorities postponed the main event to December 21 in order to distract people from traditional Christmas celebrations (*The Foundation of the National Committee to Commemorate the 70th Anniversary of Joseph Stalin's Birthday under the Auspices of the President of the People's Republic of Poland./Powołanie Ogólnopolskiego Komitetu Uczczenia 70lecia urodzin Józefa Stalina pod przewodnictwem Prezydenta PL*, 1949, Życie Warszawy, Issue no. 306, p. 1). Despite that, the weekly expressed its allegiance to Polish customs and traditions by publishing an issue entirely devoted to Christmas and the celebration of Christ's birth, full of thematic articles and iconography (Swieżawski, 1949, Issues no. 50–51, p. 1).

In his encounters with censors, Turowicz had to show great patience and strategic thinking, while his team was forced to make each issue print-ready well in advance, since it had to be delivered to the censors' office upon the initial page make-up. The fundamental role of the editor-in-chief at that time was accounted by one of his associates:

> And what if censors reject something? They often do, and late in the day so that we wouldn't know what to substitute it with. And yet Turowicz always knew, thanks to this huge black leather bag of his, bulging and bursting with stuff. Neatly drawn alternative plans of future issues of the paper, lists of articles which had already been submitted, or were yet to be commissioned, calendars highlighted in pencil and synchronised with timetables full of activities for a few days ahead, piles of manuscripts to be read and discussed with their authors whenever time permitted, and, finally, piles of newspapers in various languages that had been successfully smuggled into Cracow. As a result, Turowicz leaned asymmetrically under the heavy burden of the bag, but still he managed its content perfectly. (*Turowicz's Team/Krąg Turowicza*, 2012, p. 31)

When recalling the late 1940s, the weekly's editorial assistant Jacek Woźniakowski accounted that – due to the tightening grasp of government censorship – not only was the paper forbidden to publish ideological polemics, but also reportages on parishes, theological deliberations, or any global news on the Church (Woźniakowski, 2008, pp. 141–143). Harsh censorial interferences soon forced the weekly to abandon articles on economy, and later also any issues related to the arts (Graczyk 1990, *Stages of Censorship/Cenzura w kilku odsłonach*, TP, Issue no. 5, p. 5).

In reports submitted by the censors on preventive inspections, they were obligated to formally justify their decisions. Censorial comments and conclusions from 1948–1950 can be sorted into a logical sequence that forms a peculiar dialogue illustrating the battle between the author/editors and the censor:

> the weekly wouldn't change its aggressive manner, trying to maintain a measured tone (AMR, MOCPP&PP, File no. 1102, Part I, Vol. 122–9/19b, *Assessments of the Religious Press in 1948–1950/Oceny prasy wyznaniowej w latach 1948–1950*, p. 67),
>
> a few recent issues may have been less aggressive (…), but the reviewed one takes a very rebellious tone, even though three articles have already been banned (AMR, MOCPP&PP, File no. 1102, Part I, Vol. 122–9/19b, *Assessments of the Religious Press in 1948–1950/Oceny prasy wyznaniowej w latach 1948–1950*, p. 46),
>
> following an aggressive issue, the current one is noticeably less subversive (…), standing up for the oppressed against bureaucracy (…), or attempting to sway the mob's (TP's readers) attitude towards Marxism and the current reality (AMR, MOCPP&PP, File no. 1102, Part I, Vol. 122–9/19c, *Assessments of the Religious Press in 1948–1950/Oceny prasy wyznaniowej w latach 1948–1950*, p. 65),
>
> 'the militancy (…) of the recent issues is visibly lower, and yet, under the pretence of literary analyses, the weekly gets involved in politics and socio-political campaigning' (AMR, MOCPP&PP, File no. 1102, Part I, Vol. 122–9/19b, *Assessments of the Religious Press in 1948–1950/Oceny prasy wyznaniowej w latach 1948–1950*, p. 243),
>
> basically, the issue is quite orderly, which stems from the censor's firm intervention (AMR, MOCPP&PP, File no. 1102, Part I, Vol. 122–9/19b, *Assessments of the Religious Press in 1948–1950/Oceny prasy wyznaniowej w latach 1948–1950*, p. 281),
>
> the issue bears every stamp of the previous militancy, fighting on all battlefronts (AMR, MOCPP&PP, File no. 1102, Part I, Vol. 122–9/19b, *Assessments of the Religious Press in 1948–1950/Oceny prasy wyznaniowej w latach 1948–1950*, p. 318).

In the early 1950s, as a result of strict censorship, the pages of the weekly were filled with literary works by Antoni Gołubiew, travel reportages of Leopold Tyrmand, and Stefan Kisielewski's essays on music. A dispute between Kisielewski and Tyrmand resulted in the reappearance of articles on jazz, a forbidden subject under Stalinism (Tyrmand, 1951, Issue no. 10, p. 8). At that time, the editorial board opted for texts that could be an antidote and counterreaction to the obtrusively propagated socialism (Gołubiew, 1951, Issues no. 12–13, p. 9). In consequence, the weekly promoted jazz and published a serialised version of Gołubiew's historical novel on Boleslaw the Brave.

The fifth anniversary of the newspaper fell during the apogee of Stalinism, and the resultant difficulties ('with phenomena that are spiritually foreign to Christianity') were discussed by Turowicz in an article entitled *Nihilism, Culture, and Catholicism/Nihilizm, kultura i katolicyzm* (Turowicz, 1950, Issue no. 13, pp. 1–2). A dramatic change in the weekly's position came with a rather unexpected covenant concluded on April 14, 1950 between the government and the Episcopate of Poland on terms dictated by the ruling party. The more obvious it became that the deal would not come up to the expectations of the Church, the more difficult it was for the weekly to operate, as it started to suffer the brunt of the unsuccessful experiment conducted by the authorities and the episcopate. Despite this, in June 1950, the editor-in-chief still found the courage to write that the agreement is not an excuse for Catholics to refrain from analytical thinking and being active in all areas of everyday life (Turowicz, 1950, Issue no. 23, p. 1).

In December 1950, he co-published a balanced but expressive text with Stomma, where he wrote:

> Catholics may give up, and in the current Polish reality, they actually do give up on their struggle for political goals (...) Under no circumstances should they, however, abandon their struggle for their Christian culture (...) We are neither Marxists nor socialists (...) the socialist ideal is not our ideal'. (Stomma, Turowicz, 1950, Issue no. 50, pp. 3–4)

Two years later, the authors stated that As for the issue of Catholicism, Marxism gives little to no hope (...) it still seems too early to assess the results of the Polish experiment. The situation may still take a completely surprising twist (Stomma, Turowicz, 1952, Issue no. 5, p. 1).

In the period when most front pages in Poland contained affirmation of Stalinism and communism, the statement that the socialist model may not be an ideal solution combined with a sceptical assessment of reality were particularly weighty and telling.

In the early 1950s, censorial interference intensified, increasing tension around the weekly and its contributors, and imposing a heavier price on the editorial board for the survival of the paper. The crisis entered its next stage in 1951, when the censors no longer restricted themselves to crossing out parts of articles, but began to dictate to the team what they should write about and which texts/announcements to publish. For instance, the weekly was forced to reprint on its front page *A Manifesto to the Polish Nation/Manifestu do narodu polskiego*, agreed during a plenary session on March 31, 1951 by the Polish Committee for the Defence of Peace (The Polish Committee for the Defence of Peace/Polski Komitet Obrońców Pokoju. 1951, Issue no. 20, p. 1). Another effect of censorial pressure was the fact that Piwowarczyk left the team in August 1951. Harassed by the Department of Security for his contacts with Adam Doboszyński – a member of National Democracy, who illegally returned to Poland – Piwowarczyk resigned from his seat on the editorial board and left Cracow.

The authorities' unsatisfied expectations of the editorial board grew, and in early 1952 the relationship with censors entered a new phase, during which the censorial office began to question the legality of whole issues and block their publication at short notice. However, Turowicz was prepared for such circumstances, as he possessed a selection of back-up articles, already verified by the censorial office. In order to obtain permission to publish an issue, he would use a ploy and send censors these articles, which they could not really turn down. Such exchanges with censorship can be illustrated with Issue no. 1 in 1952, where the editor-in-chief replaced the whole rejected issue with another one, already prepared and print-ready. It contained a five-page leading article of an excellent short story by the publicist and prose writer Karol Ludwik Koniński, who died during the war. Its genre differed so significantly from typical editorials in the weekly that it highlighted a clear sign of the conflict between the board and the censorial office (Koniński, 1952, Issue no. 1, pp. 1–5).

The policy of silence became a survival tactic. The noticeably different format used for the following issues, often as a result of the refusal to allow articles to be published, once again turned into a form of protest, reflecting the situation of the Catholic press. In March 1952, for the weekly's birthday, the board expressed its opposition to the drastic measures taken by the censors, and devoted the entire issue to the situation in the Polish highlands – the regions of Podhale and the Tatras (Woźniakowski, 1952, Issue no. 13, pp. 1–2). The front page presented a series of three engravings entitled Morskie Oko Lake – 1842 – 1860 – 1867, which were meant to reflect the current position of the editorial board, and had an ironic unsigned caption:

> we believe that these problems are crucial, burning, diverse, and that their significance exceeds beyond the geographical boundaries of the Tatra and Podhale region. (Unsigned text within a border/Niepodpisany tekst w ramce, 1952, Issue no. 13, p. 1)

In the issue of March 23, 1952, the usual annual recaps and summaries were replaced with an article devoted to two masters: Ludwig van Beethoven and Karol Szymanowski. Kisielewski wrote there that We are facing the anniversary of two deaths in the world of music: the 125th of Ludwig van Beethoven's and the 15th of Karol Szymanowski's death. Even though these anniversaries differ greatly, (...) we put them in one article in order to mechanically fulfil our *com-memorative* duty. What absolves us, however, is the widely accepted struggle to remain relevant. (...) We must reminisce both events with a commemoratory text, and thus, follow custom and perform our duty (Kisielewski, 1952, Issue no. 12, pp. 1–2).

In March 1952, the weekly was forced to propagate the project of a newly developed constitution (*The Project of the New Constitution/Projekt nowej konstytucji* 1952, Issue no. 11, p. 1). The journalists drew the reader's attention to Article 70 that stipulated the position of the Church in the People's Republic, and in particular, to Item 3, which was worded as follows:

> overusing freedom of conscience and religion to prejudice the interests of the Polish People's Republic shall be punishable by law.

Recapping on the entirety of the normative solutions, they expressed hope for 'the possibiity of reaching appropriate *modus vivendi* between the State and Church in People's Republics'. A laconic piece on the adoption of the Constitution of the Polish People's Republic by the Legislative Sejm on July 22 was placed at the very bottom of the front page, juxtaposed with a comprehensive article on the first anniversary of Cardinal Adam Sapieha's death. This layout made it obvious that, in the face of the new constitution, the editorial board wished to communicate their loyalty to Sapieha's ideals (Starowieyska-Morstin, 1952, Issue no. 30, pp. 1–2). Just like all other periodicals in Poland, the weekly participated in posting provisions of the new constitution. The unabridged text of the Constitution of the Polish People's Republic was published in early August 1952 (*The New Constitution/Nowa Konstytucja*. 1952, Issue no. 31, p. 1). The editorial board celebrated July 22 (National Day of the Rebirth of Poland) in a non-committal manner, devoting the whole issue to the Recovered Western Territories (Editors/Redakcja 1952, Issue no. 29, pp. 1–2). In September, before another pseudo-elections to the Sejm, the weekly managed to offer an opinion on current affairs in the form of a brief but caustic front-page heading: 'Nothing Polish is neutral to us' (*Nothing Polish is neutral to us/Nic co polskie, nie jest nam obojętne*. 1952, Issue no. 38, p. 1).

In mid-1952, shutdown became a truly possible outcome for the weekly, discussed locally among Cracow-based censors, and nationally, by representatives of various governmental institutions in Warsaw. The closure seemed inevitable even though some courtesy talks with the editors were still conducted, aimed at breaking the resistance of the editorial team and enforcing compliance with the ruling party's policy. At the height of the crisis, i.e., during negotiations with minister Antoni Bida, head of the Office for Religious Denominations, the editors were scornfully referred to as 'Tatra lovers' (*Turowicz's Team/Krąg Turowicza*, 2012, p. 127). Finally, the situation became so tense that on October 16, 1952 the ideological management of the weekly (Turowicz, Stomma, Gołubiew, Zawieyski, and Woźniakowski) decided to travel to Krynica to consult further strategy with Cardinal Wyszyński (Wyszyński, 2017, pp. 370–376). The primate encouraged them to persevere in their attempts to promote Christian culture, saying:

> you must rehabilitate Christian naturalism and philosophical realism; you must be sensitive to the inherent community of the social life. You must show man as a social being against the background of this inherent community, which is propagated a certain way nowadays, but distorted by the propaganda. (Wyszyński 2017, p. 372)

The weekly managed to survive beyond the end of 1952, and its 400th issue – excellent in terms of content – opened with 'A Letter from the Primate of Poland to the Editorial Board of *Tygodnik Powszechny*' (*A Letter from the Primate of Poland to the Editorial Board of 'Tygodnik Powszechny'/List Prymasa Polski do redakcji 'Tygodnika Powszechnego'*, 1952, Issue no. 46, pp. 1–2). A month after the consultations in Krynica, Wyszyński stated that 'today, joy and achievements should not be measured by time and numbers, but by the effort and commitment to the cause, by love for the deed, by spirit of sacrifice and dedication, and by overcoming difficulties.

In addition, the jubilee issue owed its great value to Antoni Gołubiew's prose, Jan Paczuski's essay on Krzysztof Kamil Baczyński, a sketch on reading *The Holy Bible* by Zygmunt Kubiak, and another column article by Stefan Kisielewski (Gołubiew, p. 2; Paczuski, p. 5; Kubiak, p. 7; Kisiel, p. 12). Later in 1952, Józefa Golmont managed to express her objection against the *madness of socialist realism* that she had noticed, together with Kisielewski, during the Poznan Convention of Young Experts in Polish Studies. Somehow the censors failed to erase her conclusion that one must learn not to assume what one wants to find, one must know how to notice a separate way of making each writer individually (Golmont, 1952, Issue no. 49, p. 5).

In the very last Christmas issue the editors also managed to sneak in the *Episcopal Statement/Oświadczenie Episkopatu* on the exposed malpractices of some employees in the Cracow Curia (*Episcopal Statement/Oświadczenie Episkopatu*. 1952, Issue no. 51–52, p. 1).

The pressure exerted on the weekly regarding the subjects it should write about reached its climax in the early 1953. Finally, the authorities abandoned the previously applied strategy of tolerating the co-existence of Catholic and Marxist worldviews (Dudek, 1992, pp. 282–284; M. Strzelecka, 2001, pp. 120–121). The ruling camp sparked a conflict that became an element of a massive campaign aimed at open confrontation with the Catholic Church, with the intention of taking full control over all institutions that shaped social awareness in Poland. At the beginning of 1953, all texts began to be censored to an extent that completely distorted their initial meaning, which forced the members of the editorial board to conspicuously demonstrate their resistance. The very first issue of January 4, 1953 foreshadowed a new chapter of the conflict, leading directly to a full-scale confrontation. The front page contained an unsigned editorial declaration entitled *The Matter of Accountability/Sprawa odpowiedzialności*, alluding to the statement published by the Episcopate and the announced show trial of the Cracow Curia (*The Matter of Accountability/ Sprawa odpowiedzialności*, 1953, Issue no. 1, p. 1). The authors managed to sneak in the following, though-provoking sentence:

> We must all be fully aware of the great extent to which the diversionary actions of foreign intelligences are against the interest of the Polish nation.

Commenced on January 21, 1953, the show trial of the Cracow Curia was part of a larger propaganda campaign against the Church. The authorities planned to weaken its position by removing church administrators in the Recovered Western Territories, closing lower divinity schools, intensifying censorship, decreasing the circulation of Catholic periodicals, and shutting down certain titles. In January, the weekly's editorial board was subjected to bullying, and the situation turned from bad to worse when other Polish newspapers began to print mendacious articles on the trial. The authorities demanded that *Tygodnik Powszechny* should also release a critical statement on the matter, and the censors blocked new issues until this occurred. The three-week embargo lasted from January 25 to February 15, and led to talks between the weekly's leading journalists and prominent governmental representatives. The subject of the controversy and the effect of the talks was the text of the statement following the show trial of the Cracow Curia, which the newspaper eventually published on February 15 (*After the Cracow Trial/Po procesie krakowskim*, 1953, Issue no. 5, p. 1). At that time, the team behind most statements included Turowicz, Stomma, Gołubiew and Woźniakowski. Facing such tense circumstances, Stomma found the wording of the statement tolerable, realising that the survival of the paper was at stake. Many years later, however, he described it as indecently outrageous. The dominating after-the-fact opinion among the authors of the statement was that they should have conveyed their *non possumus* message earlier, when the first arrests were made in the Curia (Stomma, 1991, p. 98).

The crisis culminated when the authorities used the weekly's refusal to print Stalin's obituary as a pretext to dismantle its team and shut the paper down. Following an order from the ruling party for a photograph and a commemorative article, the editorial board once more tried to negotiate terms with the censors, offering to reprint an official governmental statement that glorified the late Russian leader. The ruling camp accepted the idea, but also demanded the text to be placed within a mournful black frame (Stomma, pp. 98–99). The weekly's *non possumus* reply in the matter meant the liquidation of the periodical, whose last issue was published on March 8, 1953. The editorial board was evicted from their headquarters in Wiślana Street, and the weekly was closed. Contrary to the authorities' expectations, the shutdown period of three and a half years did not break the community gathered around the periodical, but it made it even more consolidated.

When analysing the censors' attitude towards the two Cracow-based periodicals, the weekly *Tygodnik Powszechny* and the monthly *Znak*, Tomasz Fiałkowski, the editorial assistant of the latter, stated that for censors we were never fringe papers (For censors, we were never fringe papers/Dla cenzorów nie byliśmy elitarni, 1990, TP, Issue no. 8, p. 2).

The authorities were well-aware that even though both periodicals were aimed at a narrow audience, they still had a far greater impact on the whole of society, regardless of their limited circulation. Fijałkowski believed that the censorial operations were characterised by the reluctance to leave uncontrolled any channels of communication with society (...) The attitudes of the censors were also shaped by our position among the Polish press at that time. We were perceived as a title linked with the opposition. In all probability, that is why they also tampered with our non-political texts, e.g., religious and theological articles (*For censors, we were never fringe papers/Dla cenzorów nie byliśmy elitarni,* 1990, Issue no. 8, p. 2).

Openness combined with silence to avoid spreading falsehoods had been an intrinsic philosophy applied by the editorial board ever since *Tygodnik Powszechny* was founded. Władysław Bartoszewski reminisced that if it was impossible, for censorial reasons, to tell the truth, it was a moral obligation to remain silent in a way that screamed it from the rooftops, and to use any methods available to help the reader find the path leading to the truth (Bartoszewski 1999, Issue no. 6, p. 7).

3.5   Conclusions

The key topic of this study is understanding the meaning and sense of publishing in the face of harsh preventive censorship. However, there is no unambiguous answer to that. The decision to print a Catholic periodical that presents independent opinions, at such variance from the views of the ruling party's propaganda machine, led to numerous problems and provoked truly extreme reactions. What the editorial board found exceptionally difficult was to determine at what point they should say 'enough' – no more compromises; the time of the debate was over. To keep the weekly alive, the leaders took many controversial decisions, which even they bitterly criticised years later.

The fact remains that the team of Cracow journalists faced a formidable challenge in communicating with their readers due to the obstacles imposed by harsh censorship. They negotiated with the authorities and tried to outwit the censors, making attempts to circumnavigate the imposed rules and bans in defence of freedom of speech, and in a desire to provide their Catholic audience with vital information. The editorial board developed various methods of communication with the audience. The more censorial restrictions and intrusions there were in the weekly's articles, the more varied the signals and messages the journalists sent to the public. The authorities hoped that the paper's enforced detachment from current affairs and issues of everyday life would put readers off, and yet the effect was counterproductive. Even though the release of news on issues fundamental for Poland's development, and the situation of Catholics and the Church was distorted and symbolic, the weekly remained an indispensable source of knowledge and information in the sphere of Polish culture. The authors promoted the development of Catholic culture through propagating intellectual output, the art of thinking, and exchange of opinions. At that time, *Tygodnik Powszechny* published the views of the most prominent figures of scientific, cultural and religious life, including some outstanding and rebellious journalists.

References

State Archives - Archives of New Records (*Archiwum Akt Nowych - AAN*)

AAN, Główny Urząd Kontroli Prasy, Publikacji i Widowisk (GUKPPiW):

AAN, GUKPPiW, sygn. 1102, cz. I, t. 122–9, *Oceny prasy wyznaniowej w latach 1958–1950*.

AAN, GUKPPiW, sygn. 1102, cz. I, t. 122–9/19b, *Oceny prasy wyznaniowej w latach 1948–1950*.

AAN, GUKPPiW, sygn. 1102, cz. I, t. 122–9/19c, *Oceny prasy wyznaniowej w latach 1948–1950.*

Archives of the Institute of National Remembrance (*Archiwum Instytutu Pamięci Narodowej* - AIPN)

AIPN Kr 010/10093/1, *Sprawa obiektowa kryptonim „Biegun", „Pismak", „Pióro". Postanowienie o założeniu sprawy agenturalno-grupowej,* Kraków 28 IV 1955.

AIPN Kr 010/10093/1, *Zamówienie na założenie P.P. do sprawy kryptonim „Pióro",* Kraków 16 II 1957 r.

Jerzy Turowicz's Archives (*Archiwum Jerzego Turowicza w Goszycach* - AJT)

AJT, S. Kisielewski, *Przeciw cenzurze – legalnie (garść wspomnień).*

AJT, *List Jacka Woźniakowskiego od Jerzego Turowicza,* Zakopane 21 VII 1953.

AJT, *List Jerzego Zawieyskiego do Jerzego Turowicza,* Warszawa 27 XI 1953.

Reports

Hennelowa J. (1998).

Kozłowski K. (1998).

Wielowieyski A. (2012).

Zabłocki J. (2012).

Memoires

Bardecki A. (1995). *Zawsze jest inaczej,* Kraków.

Gołubiew A. (1971). *Unoszeni historią,* Kraków.

Gołubiew A. (1975). *Na Franciszkańskiej i na Wiślnej,* w: *70 żywotów.* Red. A. Paluchowski, Kraków.

Hennelowa J. (2001).*...bo jestem z Wilna. Z Józefą Hennelową rozmawia Roman Graczyk.* Kraków.

Jasienica P. (2007). *Pamiętnik.* Warszawa.

Kisielewski S. (2001). *Dzienniki.* Warszawa.

K. Kozłowski K. (1995). *Przemówienie Krzysztofa Kozłowskiego na zebraniu redakcji na 30-lecie „Tygodnika Powszechnego",* w: A. Bardecki, *Zawsze jest inaczej.* Kraków.

Krąg Turowicza. Tygodnik, czasy, ludzie 1945–1989. (2012). Red. W. Bereś, K. Burnetko, J. Podsadecka, Limanowa-Kraków.

Obywatel KK czyli Krzysztofa Kozłowskiego zamyślenia nad Polską. (2011). Red. W. Bereś, K. Burnetko, Kraków-Limanowa.

Stomma S. (1991). *Pościg za nadzieją.* Paryż.

Wielowieyski A. (2015). *Losowi na przekór.* Warszawa.

Woźniakowski J. (2008). *Ze wspomnień szczęściarza.* Kraków.

Żakowski J. (1987). *Anatomia smaku czyli o losach „Tygodnika Powszechnego" w latach 1953–1956.* Warszawa.

Żakowski J. (1990). *Trzy ćwiartki wieku. Rozmowy z Jerzym Turowiczem.* Kraków.

Journalism

Bartoszewski W. (1999). *Żyjący pośród nas,* TP, nr 6.

Braun J. (1947). *W cieniu dekadencji (Psychoza klęski w katolicyzmie francuskim),* Tygodnik Warszawski, nr 13.

Ciechomski W. (1983). *„Tygodnik Warszawski" 1945–1948,* Ład, nr 29.

Dla cenzorów nie byliśmy elitarni. Z Tomaszem Fiałkowskim, sekretarzem redakcji miesięcznika „Znak" rozmawia Krzysztof Burnetko. (1990). TP, nr 8.

Fik M. (1995). *Cenzor jako współautor,* TP, nr 4.

Golmont J. (1952). *Żołędzie i ogrodnicy czyli nico o krytyce.* TP, nr 49.

Gołubiew A. (1951). *Emnilda (Fragment cyklu powieściowego o B. Chrobrym),* TP, nr 12–13.

Gołubiew A. (1952). *Księstwo w worach (fragment z „Bolesława Chrobrego"),* TP, nr 46.

Gołubiew A. (1947). *„Sprzysiężenie" Stefana Kisielewskiego,* TP, nr 2.

Graczyk R. (1990). *Cenzura w kilku odsłonach,* TP, nr 5.

Jasienica P. (1946). *Honor,* TP, nr 13.

Jedlicz J. (Stomma S.). (1945). *Cząstka własnej winy,* Dziś i Jutro, nr 3.

Jedlicz J. (Stomma S.). (1946). *Myśli o zwycięstwie,* Dziś i Jutro, nr 1.

Jedlicz J. (Stomma S.). (1945). *O t. zw. „neokatolicyzmie",* Dziś i Jutro, nr 1.

Jedlicz J. (Stomma S.). (1947). *O właściwych drogach porozumienia,* Dziś i Jutro, nr 8.

Jedlicz J. (Stomma S.). (1946). *Ziemia jest kulista,* Dziś i Jutro, nr 10.

Ketlicz T. (Przeciszewski T.). (1947). *Minimalizm czy maksymalizm społeczny?,* Tygodnik Warszawski, nr 15.

Kisiel. (1952). *Cztery setki,* TP, nr 46.

Kisiel. (1945). *Jeszcze o realizmie i formalizmie (na marginesie ostatnich dyskusji literackich),* TP, nr 17.

Kisiel. (1945). *Kott – wieczny rewolucjonista,* TP, nr 22.

Kisiel. (1945). *Pod włos: Jerzy Borejsza mówi,* TP, nr 31.

Kisiel. (1946). *Pod włos: Pokazujcie język!,* TP, nr 36.

Kisiel. (1945). *Porachunki narodowe (artykuł dyskusyjny),* TP, nr 24.

Kisiel. (1949). *Pod włos: Felieton megalomański,* TP, nr 7.

Kisiel. (1946). *Pod włos: Przysłowia i powiedzonka,* TP, nr 6.

Kisiel. (1946). *Pod włos: Sprawy trudne,* TP, nr 7.

Kisiel. (1848). *Pod włos: Z Nowym Rokiem,* TP, nr 1.

Kisiel. (1949). *Realizm, ale jaki?,* TP, 1949, nr 1.

Kisielewski S. (1952). *Beethoven i Szymanowski,* TP, nr 12.

Kisielewski S. (1946). *Sytuacja polityczna,* TP, nr 6.

Kisielewski S. (1945). *Tematy wojenne*, TP, nr 9.

Kisielewski S. (1946). *Żółkiewski – prawdziwy marksista*, TP, nr 4.

Koniński K. L. (1952). *Straszny czwartek w domu pastora*, TP, nr 1.

Krasiński K. (1947). *Na marginesie pewnego wyroku*, TP, nr 24.

Kubiak Z. (1952). *O drogocennym „pięknoduchostwie"*, TP, nr 46.

Listy do redakcji. (1946). TP, nr 13.

List Prymasa Polski do redakcji „Tygodnika Powszechnego". (1952). TP, nr 46.

Malewska H. (1946). *Dziś: Propaganda*, TP, nr 9.

Nic co polskie, nie jest nam obojętne. (1952). TP, nr 38.

Niepodpisany tekst w ramce. 1952, nr 13.

Nowa Konstytucja. (1952). TP, nr 31.

Nowy Prymas Polski. (1949). TP, nr 1.

Oświadczenie Episkopatu. (1952). TP, nr 51–52.

Paczuski J. (1952). *Krzysztof Baczyński*, TP, nr 46.

Piasecki B. (1953). *Dwie drogi katolicyzmu*, Słowo Powszechne, nr 52.

Piess J. (1946). *Wśród czasopism: Tygodnik Powszechny*, TP, nr 13.

Piwowarczyk J. (1945). *Dyskusja nad marksizmem*, TP, nr 36.

J. P. (Piwowarczyk J.). (1946). *Nowe książki: Studia prawne*, TP, nr 18.

Piwowarczyk J. (1949). *Nowy Prymas Polski*, TP, nr 2.

Piwowarczyk J. (1949). *Rozdział Kościoła od państwa*, TP, nr 3.

Piwowarczyk J. (1948). *Żałoba Kościoła w Polsce*, TP, nr 44.

Polski Komitet Obrońców Pokoju. (1951). *Manifestu do narodu polskiego*, TP, nr 20.

Po procesie krakowskim. (1953). TP, nr 5.

*Powołanie Ogólnopolskiego Komitetu Uczczenia 70lecia urodzin Józefa Stalina pod prze-
wodnictwem Prezydenta PL*. (1949). Życie Warszawy, nr 306.

Projekt nowej konstytucji. (1952). TP, nr 11.

Redakcja. (1945). TP, nr 20.

Redakcja. (1948). *Od redakcji*, TP, nr 39.

Redakcja. (1952). *Odra i Nysa*, TP, nr 29.

Sapieha A. (1945). *Błogosławieństwo dla zespołu redakcyjnego*, TP, nr 1.

Sprawa odpowiedzialności. (1953). TP, nr 1.

Starowieyska-Morstinowa Z. (1952). *Ksiądz Kardynał*, TP, nr 30.

Stomma S. (1946). *Maksymalne i minimalne tendencje społeczne katolików*, Znak, nr 3.

Stomma S. (1947). *O pozornym maksymalizmie i urojonym defetyzmie*, TP, nr 16.

Stomma S. (1999). *Pożegnania: Jerzy Turowicz (1912–1999)*, Polityka, nr 6.

Stomma S. Turowicz J. (1952). *Eksperyment polski*, TP, nr 5.

Stomma S. Turowicz J. (1950). *Katolicy w Polsce Ludowej*, TP, nr 50.

Swieżawski S. (1949). *Z rozważań nad wcieleniem*, TP, nr 50–51.

Szczepański J. J. (1947). *Buty*, TP, nr 6.

Turowicz J. (1947). *Humanizm, realizm, interesy*, TP, nr 51–52.

Turowicz J. (1947). *Kultura i plan*, TP, nr 46.

Turowicz J. (1949). *Kultura i polityka*, TP, nr 3.

Turowicz J. (1950). *Myśli o kulturze*, TP, nr 51–52.

Turowicz J. (1950). *Nihilizm, kultura i katolicyzm*, TP, nr 13.

Turowicz J. (1950). *Porozumienie*, TP, nr 23.

Turowicz J. (1946). *Reakcja i »reakcja«*, TP, nr 14.

Turowicz J. (1945). *Sprawa katolicyzmu*, TP, nr 11.

Turowicz J. (1946). *Światopogląd, tendencja, ortodoksja*, TP, nr 16.

J. T. (J. Turowicz). (1947). *Zmniejszenie objętości*, TP, nr 30.

Turowski K. (1947). *Bitwa o handel*, TP, nr 26.

Tyrmand L. (1951). *Jazzowe swawole*, TP, nr 10.

Woźniakowski J. (1952). *Tatry*, TP, nr 13.

Zawieyski J. (1948). *„Izraelowi, bratu naszemu - braterstwo"*, TP, nr 25.

Żak J. (1947). *Jak to szło?*, TP, nr 3.

Scientific Studies

Bankowicz B. (1990). *Ks. Jan Piwowarczyk – romantyk sprawiedliwości*, TP, nr 12.

Czarna księga cenzury PRL.(1977). Cz. 1, Londyn.

Dudek A. (1992). *Polityka władz komunistycznych wobec Kościoła katolickiego 1945–1955*, Wiadomości Historyczne, nr 5.

Garlicki A. (1993). *Z tajnych archiwów*, Warszawa.

Frazik W. (2009). *Struktura organizacyjna Urzędu Bezpieczeństwa w województwie krakowskim w latach 1945–1956 w świetle aktów normatywnych*, w: *Strażnicy sowieckiego imperium. Urząd Bezpieczeństwa i Służba w Małopolsce 1945–1990*. Red. F. Musioł i M. Wenklar, Kraków.

Friszke A. (2015). *Między wojną a więzieniem 1945–1953, Młoda inteligencja katolicka*, Warszawa.

Graczyk R. (2011). *Cena przetrwania. SB wobec „Tygodnika Powszechnego"*, Warszawa.

Graczyk R. (2009). *Próby wpływania na „Tygodnik Powszechny" przez TW „CK"/"Kace"*, w: *Strażnicy sowieckiego imperium. Urząd Bezpieczeństwa i Służba w Małopolsce 1945–1990*. Red. F. Musioł i M. Wenklar, Kraków.

Hera J. (2007). *Narodziny cenzury*, Biuletyn Instytutu Pamięci Narodowej, nr 5/6.

Jagiełło M. (1986). *Program kulturalny środowiska inteligencji katolickiej (krąg „Tygodnika Powszechnego") jako forma realizacji polityki kulturalnej Kościoła*, red. W. Leszczyński, t. 1, Warszawa.

Jagiełło M. (1988). *„Tygodnik Powszechny" i komunizm (1945–1953)*, Warszawa.

Kamińska-Chełminiak K. (2019). *Cenzura państwowa wobec „Tygodnika Powszechnego" w okresie Października '56*,w: *Nie tylko Po prostu. Prasa w dobie odwilży 1955–1956*. Red. M. Przeperski i P. Sasanka, Warszawa.

Kisielewski S. (2013). *Felietony*, t. 1–2, Warszawa.

Kosicki P. H. (2016). *Personalizm po polsku. Francuskie korzenie polskiej inteligencji katolickiej*, Warszawa.

Kristanova E. (2012). *Książka na łamach katolickich czasopism społeczno-kulturalnych w Polsce w latach 1945–1953*, Łódź.

Kristanova E. (2016). *On Literary Issues in Tygodnik Powszechny (1945–1953)*, Saarbrücken.

Kristanova E. (2016). *W kręgu zagadnień literackich „Tygodnika Powszechnego" (1945–1953)*, Warszawa.

Kuta C. (2009). *„Działacze" i „Pismaki". Aparat bezpieczeństwa wobec katolików świeckich w Krakowie w latach 1957–1989*, Kraków.

Kuta C. (2006). *Jak bezpieka rozbijała „Tygodnik Powszechny"*, Gazeta Polska, nr 24.

Murzański S. (1998). *Wśród łopotu sztandarów rewolucji. Rzecz o „katolewicy" 1945–1989*, Kraków.

Opozycja i opór społeczny w Polsce (1945–1980). (1991). Ed. A. Friszke i A. Paczkowski, Warszawa.

Pawlicki A. (2001). *Kompletna szarość. Cenzura w latach 1965–1972. Instytucja i ludzie*, Warszawa.

Piotrowski M. (2004). *Syndrom PRL. Wybór artykułów*, Warszawa.

Piwowarczyk J. (1960). *Katolicka etyka społeczna*, Londyn.

Piwowarczyk J. (1985). *Wobec nowego czasu (z publicystyki 1945–1950)*. Wybór i układ J. Kołątaj, Kraków.

Rabiński J. (2006). *U początku sporu o „minimalizm" i „maksymalizm" w polskim katolicyzmie społecznym*, „Roczniki Humanistyczne: Historia", t. 54, z. 2.

Sikorski T. (2013). *Przedmowa*, w: *Niezłomni w epoce fałszywych proroków. Środowisko „Tygodnika Warszawskiego" (1945–1948)*, Warszawa.

Stefaniak J. (1998). *Polityka władz państwowych PRL wobec prasy katolickiej w latach 1945–1953*, Lublin.

Strzelecka M. (2010). *Cztery cenzorskie kreski – o ingerencjach Głównego Urzędu Kontroli Prasy Publikacji i Widowisk na łamach „Tygodnika Powszechnego" w latach 1945–1989*, w: *VII Toruńskie Spotkania Dydaktyczne: Obraz, dźwięk i smak w edukacji historycznej*. Red. S. Roszak, M. Strzelecka i A. Wieczorek, Toruń.

Strzelecka M. (2001). *Powstanie „Tygodnika Powszechnego" i jego rola w powojennej prasie katolickiej (1945–1953)*, w: *W kręgu prasy. Przeszłość-teraźniejszość-przyszłość*. Ed. G. Gzella i J. Gzella, t. 2.

Strzelecka M. (2015). *Między minimalizmem a maksymalizmem. Dylematy ideowe Stanisława Stommy i Janusza Zabłockiego*, Toruń.

Strzelecka M. (2009). *Trudne kompromisy. Środowisko „Tygodnika Powszechnego" wobec reform systemu oświaty i wychowania w latach 1945–1989*, Toruń.

Strażnicy sowieckiego imperium. Urząd Bezpieczeństwa w Małopolsce 1945–1990. (2009). Red. F. Musiał i M. Winklar, Kraków.

Wiszniewski J. (1998). *Z historii prasy katolickiej w Polsce: „Tygodnik Warszawski" 1945–1948*, Kraków.

Wyszyński S. (2017). *Pro memoria*, t. 1: 1948–1952, Warszawa.

Zuzelski S. (Wyszyński S.). (1945) *Watykan a świat powojenny*, Włocławek.

CHAPTER 4

Mythologizing the Enemy in Polish Communist Propaganda in the Years 1949–1954

Rafał Opulski

4.1   Introduction

During one of his speeches, Joseph Goebbels, Reich Minister of Propaganda, concluded that while it is good when authority is based on power, it is much better to win over and retain the heart of the nation. When the Communists assumed power in post-war Poland, they faced the necessity of legitimating their authority. From the very beginning of their regime, they employed a number of brutal methods in order to strengthen their rule. After the end of the Second World War, the new government destroyed the structures of the legitimate Polish Underground State and arrests, torture and killing of political opponents were common. The Ministry of Public Security (*Ministerstwo Bezpieczeństwa Publicznego*), which included the Department of Security (*Urząd Bezpieczeństwa*), was the most important institution in Poland during the period of Stalinism. It could even have been considered a state within a state. In May 1945, there were about 11,000 functionaries (Dudek, Paczkowski, 2005, p. 242), whereas the Office of Public Security employed over 37,000 officers in 1953. The number of all uniformed services of the Ministry of Public Security reached over 320,000 officers (Dudek, Zblewski, 2008, p. 16). Additionally, the Ministry had 70–75,000 paid informants in 1954 (Paczkowski, 2000b, p. 257). One of the most important areas of activity of this Ministry was the "files" it compiled on its citizens. It is estimated that on 1 January 1953 there were files on 5.2 million people (out of 26.5 million citizens of Poland) (Dudek, Paczkowski, 2005, p. 250) and there were over one million people kept in prisons run by the Department of Security under Communist rule. While this apparatus of terror was being built and expanded, the Communist authorities were also trying to win the nation's heart, as proposed by Goebbels in his famous speech. After having assumed real political power in Poland, the Polish Communists began their attempts to "conquer society" – in order to validate their position. This second task turned out to be far more difficult.

The main condition for effective governance is legitimacy of power - a set of rules that entitle an authority to take binding decisions which are approved

by its citizens. One of the effective methods for legitimizing power is the creation of an "imaginary reality", which, as Bronisław Baczko noted is "a strategy
of a paramount significance" (Baczko, 1999, p. 16). This reality includes political
myths which are spread in the form of narratives and rituals. The purpose of
this article is to outline the process of the mythologization by which the Communist authorities attempted to legitimize their rule by disseminated images
of enemies through propaganda. This refers specifically to the Polish version
of Stalinism (Dudek, Zblewski, 2008, p. 74). Between 1949 and 1954, the Communist authorities in Poland became increasingly totalitarian and sought to
control and ideologize all aspects of social life.

4.2   Political Myth

Contrary to the statements from some researchers (Tudor, 1972, p. 137; Flood,
1996, p. 44), a political myth is not only a dramatized narration of political
events, but also a form of collective imagination, which - through the use of
propaganda - can effectively influence not only individuals but also whole
societies. As a response to such fundamental human needs as the need for
meaning, the need for life goals, or the need to create and understand the
workings of the world (Wierciński, 2004, p. 88), a political myth is an "emotionally motivated means of observing and evaluating socio-political reality".
Political myths serve a practical purpose by giving meaning to certain political
experiences (Opulski, 2013, pp. 202–203). They especially allow individuals to
identify themselves with a collective narrative, and they provide individuals
with certain norms of behavior. A political myth is understood as a socially
framed, shared and spread form of social consciousness which influences the
way of perceiving political reality as well as the actions of members of a certain
community. These members - who are not always aware of this influence – can
receive and process collective imagination[1].

Stanisław Filipowicz has stressed that political myths can constitute an
extremely effective instrument for psycho-, and socio-engineering influences,
because people do not necessarily consider the accuracy of these myths, which,
therefore, achieve the status of "unshakeable truths" (Filipowicz, 1988, p. 22;

---

1   There are several characteristics of a political myth. Political myths are: universal, genuine,
    compulsory, ambiguous, emotional, firmly connected to rituals, sacral, specific to their time,
    space and human relationships. Researchers who define political myths as a form of social
    consciousness are for example: Tadeusz Biernat, Ewa Nalewajko and Marian Golka (Biernat,
    1989, p. 68).

Topolski, 1991, p. 244). Political myths encourage the building and strengthening of individuals' conviction that the values shared by a certain community are of meta-empirical descent. Political myths are also a means of communication between the authorities and society, as well as among individuals, groups, and institutions. Among the most important functions of political myths there are: explaining reality, strengthening the bonds within a community, mobilization (which is especially important in crisis situations), establishing and upholding a collective identity, and providing legitimation or delegitimation of a political order. Political power has various techniques to mythologize reality for its own interests (Duda, 2010, p. 28). According to Ernst Cassirer, the political myths of our times are not products of an unawareness or unconsciousness, but rather "artificial things fabricated by very skillful and cunning artisans". Additionally, they "can be manufactured in the same sense and according to the same methods as any other modern weapon – as machine guns or airplanes" (Cassirer, 1961, p. 282). These tasks are carried out by the propaganda apparatus, which included all the institutions that produce and transmit the content of propaganda via the available means. Jerzy Topolski shares Cassirer's views and concludes that political myths are narrative entities which are created through the activity of "social, political, or other forces" (Topolski, 1991, p. 244). Political myths emerge especially during crisis situations when the existing order is undermined, or when there are attempts to introduce a new order. This is when the "mythogenic" human tendency to seek new solutions that grant a person certainty and a sense of meaning, is enhanced. "In all critical moments of man's social life, rational forces that resist the rise of the old mythical conceptions are no longer sure of themselves. In these moments the time of myth has come again" (Cassirer, 1961, p. 280). The process of mythologizing is easy to observe during the initial (crisis) years following World War II, when the process of mythologizing enemies who threatened the new order was one of the means used to legitimize the new Communist power.

4.3   Process of Mythologizing

The process of mythologizing reality is an attempt to change the social consciousness. Tadeusz Biernat describes three stages of this creation: creation of the basis of the myth, transformation of initial content into the principle of the myth, and expression of the myth (Biernat, 1989, pp. 89–111). The first stage of mythologizing shapes the basis of the myth, which results from the set of initial information concerning the current and previous socio-political reality. The basis of the myth includes current or historical events, which – according to the process of the "stolen language" suggested by Roland Barthes – receive additional meanings. The set of initial information consists of two elements, which can be defined as a static and a dynamic element. The first one includes the general state of the social consciousness of a certain society, its knowledge concerning reality (real and deformed), its historical consciousness, and its traditions. The second term includes the information that is currently being transmitted in order to change, supplement or shape social consciousness (Biernat, 1989, p. 90).

The emergence of this dynamic element is either the effect of a spontaneous process within a certain group or of an intentional transmission of information by a sender who has control over the information channels used. The content of messages can be literal or covert, and cause certain mental attitudes to be created (Biernat, 1989, p. 91). Not only do these political myths affect current events but also historical events. Historical events in a political myth are, however, presented very selectively (Bal-Nowak, 1996, p. 169). The outcome of the mythologizing process is the transformation of facts into a set of symbols, patterns, and precedents (Szacka, 2006, p. 169). The transformation of the initial information into the basis of a political myth which can be viewed as conventional wisdom about the socio-political reality is the second, and most complicated, stage of the process of mythologization. The most important factors which influence the transformation of the "myth's basis" into "its principle" are: the character of the information that is being transformed and the external circumstances which the process is accompanied by (Biernat, 1989, p. 100). The external circumstances which foster the transformation of the initial information into a norm of a semiologic system are periods of instability. The principle behind a successful political myth is a logical conclusion drawn from the data given. The principle of a myth does not allow for alternatives, therefore also the process of generalization proceeds differently. Information that reaches individuals is filtered through an interpretative system that has been shaped by a certain worldview. Thanks to this process, the data gain a specific meaning. This stage of mythologizing consists in placing a certain phenomenon in a certain mythological system and in discarding any information which is contradictory to this system (Piątkowski, 1994, p. 124). What is more, accepting and upholding of a myth comes through faith in the system of delivery (Tudor, 1972, pp. 123–124). Mythical narration is an important element of interpretative schemes which mediate in the process of perceiving reality. Political myths may defuse informational conflict that is an occurrence of contradictory information. Individuals who believe in the myths analyze all stimuli that reach them and choose only those that confirm the principle of the accepted myth.

The third and final stage of the process is the analysis of the articulation of the emergence of and functioning of myths. Such articulation includes specific statements, political behavior, as well as material objects (such as rituals and art). However, ideologies, doctrines, political programs can also epitomize the articulation of a myth. These latter ones, according to Tadeusz Biernat, are the best illustration of such articulation (Biernat 1989: 106–107). Political propaganda obviously plays a fundamental role in disseminating and articulating certain forms of political myths. Although this influences the process of formulating a myth in a significant way, the people responsible for propaganda are strongly influenced by the collective imagination present in a certain society.

Propaganda constitutes a fundamental element of every political system, as it serves in the gaining of power and the strengthening thereof. The goal of propaganda is accomplished through convincing society to accept a specific worldview. Such operations are especially evident in totalitarian systems where the omnipresent propaganda and ideological struggle are - together with repressions and violations of human and civil rights – basic elements of exercising power. During the period of Stalinism in Poland, the most important means of propaganda were: the press, books, radio and visual arts.

4.4   Internal Enemy

One of the elements that was exploited by the Polish Communist propaganda was the image of the enemy. Peter Berger noted that every social order is endangered by (the threat of) unreality (Kehrer, 1997, p. 30). There is a tendency to exaggerate the threat from this danger because – from the authorities' point of view – the need for an enemy is much more important than its actual existence or its actual strength. In order to increase the effectiveness of the propaganda, it either presents or creates a threat by: demonizing ("the personification of Evil", "Satan", "Antichrist"), dehumanizing (an enemy does not possess human attributes, therefore it is acceptable not to treat them equally), attributing cruelty greater than in reality (Jarecka, 2008, pp. 199–223). This ideology of 'defining an enemy' has constituted the basis of many totalitarian systems, and if there had been no such element, it would have been necessary to create it (Olszewski, 2011, p. 47). One of the features of the Communist propaganda during the period of Stalinism was the dichotomous presentation of reality. This was bound with a need to flatter the receivers by conveying their group's superiority when compared to other communities via the message (Thomson, 2001, p. 448). Kazimierz Braun, using the example of the theatrical arts, drew attention to the fact that political propaganda during the period of Stalinism concentrated on the victorious struggle between "the new" and "the old", "the socialist" and "the reactionary", "the progressive" and "the bourgeois", and finally between "the soviet" and the "imperialistic". According to Braun, "both historical and contemporary times are painted only in black and white" (Braun, 1994, p. 65). The opponent has been demonized and presented as a "tyrant", "the true enemy of freedom", "evil" or "an ominous force". The dissemination of a conviction that the threat posed by a real or imaginary enemy is real serves several functions: it legitimizes the system, channels social dissatisfaction, unites and mobilizes society to act against a common external or internal threat.

The images created of the enemies by the Communist authorities can be divided into two groups - internal and external enemies. The first group included a certain image of the military and political resistance movement, the authorities of the legitimate Polish Underground State, rich landowners, the Catholic Church, proponents of a right-wing, nationalistic agenda (*zwolennicy odchylenia prawicowo-nacjonalistycznego*), saboteurs, spies, and speculators, while the second grouped such external enemies as Western countries (especially the US and the Federal Republic of Germany) or emigres promoting Polish independence.

Political propaganda during the period of Stalinism presented those military resistance forces which refused to give up the armed struggle at the end of World War II, but continued their fight against the Communist regime, as "gangs from the forest" (*leśne bandy*), "fascist assassins" (*faszystowscy skrytobójcy*), "counterrevolutionary elements" (*element kontrrewolucyjne*), "thugs from the underground" (*bandyci z podziemia*), "bandit groups" (*ugrupowania bandyckie*), or "from a vanishing world" (*umierający świat*). The resistance movement was also accused of having collaborated with Germany during World War II. Even before the war was over, Antoni Ruszkiewicz published an article in *Odrodzenie*, where he suggested that there is "an amazing convergence of the reactionary propaganda with that of Goebbels" which "most vocally concerned the Katyń massacre" (Fik, 1989, p. 22). In order to present these "gangs from the forest" as enemies of Poland, the authorities organized multiple political trials which were intended to change social consciousness. The often forced testimonies given both by witnesses and the prosecuted themselves were to convince the receivers of the Communist propaganda that the command of Polish Home Army (*Armia Krajowa*) were continuing with the subversive policies of *Sanacja*[2], who were accused of cooperating with

---

2   *Sanation* was a political movement that came to power after Józef Piłsudski's May 1926 *Coup d'État*.

Hitler's Germany; that the Warsaw Uprising happened with the agreement of the Germans, and that Communists were the only true patriots. As opponents of the Communist authorities in Poland, political independence organizations were also repeatedly attacked by the Communist press. In his 1944 speech, Władysław Gomulka used several terms to describe his political opponents, which later were widely used and disseminated: "Komorowski's nobles" (*hrabiowie Komorowscy*) "reactionary criminals" (*reakcyjni zbrodniarze*), "noble landowners" (*panowie obszarnicy*), "fascist bandits" (*bandyci faszysto*wscy), "mercenaries of the fascist" (*faszystowscy najmici*), "landowners' daddy's-boys and their servants" (*obszarniczy synalkowie i ich pachołkowie*) (Gomułka, 1961, pp. 119–122).

Members of independent parties were accused of: causing the defeat of Poland during the September 1939 Campaign, collaborating with the Nazis, reluctance to fight against the invaders, and hindering Polish Communists during World War II. According to the Communist authorities, the aim of the Polish authorities who ran the country before 1939 was to establish an alliance with Germany prior to World War II in order to fight against the Soviet Union (*Kuźnica*, 1949, p. 2). Similarly to the actions against the representatives of the military resistance movement, members of the political opposition were prosecuted during the show trials. These trials were organized in such a way that the political opposition could be ridiculed. For example, during the famous show trial of 1949, Adam Doboszyński was accused of: anti-Semitic activity, promoting a fascist ideology, collaboration with the Germans during World War II, and cooperation with American intelligence after the war. The trial was widely reported, and commented on, in the Communist press. The press additionally used the situation to accuse the entire opposition of implementing policies that were "criminal and anti-Polish".

Other sections of society which opposed Communist policy were also considered as enemies, and presented as such. This was especially true of the "kulaks" (a category of relatively affluent farmers who opposed the idea of cooperative farms), and landowners who had been deprived of their lands in order to conduct the agricultural reform. Satire was one of the tools of the Communist propaganda used to discredit their opponents. In Communist publications, people who were born into the "wrong social class" were depicted as being fat, with ridiculous hats (made from beaver pelts), and with cigars in their mouth.

As well as the resistance movement, political opposition, "kulaks" and "bourgeoisie", the propaganda attacks of the Communist were also directed against the Catholic Church. The Church, especially between 1949–1954, was presented as a primary supporter of "reactionary forces". According to the

Head of the Ministry of Public Security, Stanisław Radkiewicz, the Church "constitutes the most active, most organized part of reactionary forces today" (*Aparat bezpieczeństwa*, 1996, p. 127). During one of the meetings at the Office of Public Security, the Head of the 5th Department of the Ministry of Public Security, Julia Brystyger, said that "the fight against the Church is undoubtedly one of the most difficult tasks (...). Not only because the clergy has huge material resources (...). The difficulty of this fight against the hostile activity of the clergy is that the Church can provocatively use every step taken against itself and present it as a fight against religion" (Dudek, Gryz, 2003, p. 30). The Office of Public Security received an order to investigate Church institutions, including monasteries and convents. From 1949, the Catholic Church was considered the main institutional enemy (Dudek, Paczkowski, 2005, p. 267), with censorship of its activities being pervasive and strictly enforced.

The "anti-clerical campaign" in the Polish Communist propaganda concentrated mainly on depicting priests as class enemies, who not only opposed "modernization", but also disseminated anti-government propaganda and kept people in "religious fanaticism", provided "spiritual leadership to the bandits", were "agents of the Vatican" as well as "spies in cassocks" (Kornacki, 2002, p. 161; Czocher, Dyrcz, Kwilosz, 2008, p. 49). Accusations of spying, especially for the Vatican and for the USA, were repeated during the many show trials against clergymen. These trials were aimed at frightening and dividing the clergy, discouraging society from attending religious ceremonies, and at coercing the Catholic hierarchy into pursuing policies according to the Communist Party's guidelines. One of the show trials - concerning the Wolbrom case - took place between January 14th-17th, 1951. On December 15th, 1949, a 15-years-old boy, Waldemar Grabiński, had been murdered near Wolbrom. According to the Communist press, the victim was sent to his death by his mother, "beguiled" by two priests who abused their authority (*Przyjaciółka*, 1951, Issue 4, p. 9). Supposedly, the murder of Grabiński was not the only crime committed by the two clergymen. According to the Communist press, the priests had begun to lead the local underground unit in mid-1949, which was responsible for planning and organizing murders, robberies, terrorist attacks and anti-government propaganda (*Przyjaciółka*, 1951, Issue 4, p. 9). Between January 21st and 26th 1953, the show trial of the two priests was conducted. They were accused of murdering members of the People's Army[3]; of cooperating with "bandits", and of spying for the Vatican, the USA, and "anti-Communist emigres".

---

3   The *People's Army* was a Communist partisan force set up by the Polish Workers' Party (PPR) during World War II.

It was repeatedly remarked through the Communist propaganda that the Catholic Church had always been an institution which had opposed any modernization and democratization tendencies. According to this propaganda, the clergy never considered the common people, was against social transformation in the country (*Trybuna Ludu*, 1949), and "orders citizens to wait for paradise in heaven while allowing for the hell of poverty, ignorance, and degradation in this world" (*Trybuna Ludu*, 1949). The Church was also accused of disseminating anti-government propaganda and of slandering the government.

In November 1949, Boleslaw Bierut said that the most important task was to find all enemies who were hiding in the cracks of the social machine because the hostile imperialist centers were trying to use their "masked tentacles" in order to organize their conspiracy and terrorist activities (Dudek, Zblewski, 2008, p. 80). The culmination of the above-described processes was uncovering proponents of a "right-wing-nationalist agenda" within the Communist Party. Allegations against members of the Party, including leaders, in this hunt for new enemies was in line with Stalin's thesis that the class struggle would intensify gradually as the building of Socialism was progressing, therefore, according to Stalin, it was necessary to be alert to threats from all directions. One effect of Stalin's purge was that many Communists who held high position in the Party's apparatus as well as many officers of the Polish Army were arrested at this time (Opulski, Ficoń, 2020, pp. 148–157). Among the accusations levelled against them were terms that occurred most commonly: "an admirer of the West", "ex-policeman", "links to *Sanacja*" (Poksiński, 1992, p. 7). One of the most important trials during this time was the "Trial of the Generals". Over one hundred officers and generals of the Polish Army were investigated, with many of them being arrested, including: former Minister of National Defense, Marshal Michal Rola-Żymierski, former Deputy Chief of the General Staff of the Polish Armed Forces, General Stefan Mossor and former Head of the Intelligence, General Waclaw Komar. According to the press at that time, it was of significant importance that all of the prosecuted were members of *Sanacja*, who, during the period of 1945–50, "worked in the interest of imperialist countries". An article published in *Przyjaciółka* was entitled "Traitors Stand Trial" and informed readers that the activities of those prosecuted were intended to allow imperialists to annex western Polish territories from Poland, and incorporate them to post-war Germany, while creating an Anglo-American colony out of the rest of Poland (*Przyjaciółka*, 1951, Issue no. 29, p. 7).

These accusations and the show trials themselves were communicated by the Communist mass media. The main reason for such show trials, according to Andrzej Paczkowski, was not only to discredit certain activists but also raise Polish society's awareness of the fact that every offence against the authorities or its ideology would be punished. The trials, therefore, can be seen as a form of social education (Paczkowski, 2007, p. 15). The search for and elimination of the "internal enemy" not only helped to maintain an atmosphere of terror within society, but also consolidated the party apparatus for any potential military conflict between the system of Communism and Capitalism (*Przyjaciółka*, 1951, Issue no. 4, p. 3).

4.5   External Enemy

According to Communist propaganda, the most relevant external enemies were the USA, West Germany, and pro-independence Polish emigrees. "Anglo-Saxon imperialists" were one of the groups that was frequently referred to in the Communist press of the Stalinism period. The image of imperialists shaped by the Polish Communist propaganda concentrated around depicting them as warmongers and exploiters of their own societies. In the words of Jan Szelag, American imperialists aimed to return to Japan and Germany the role that they had played before 1945. According to him, in their mad attempts to rule the world, American imperialists wanted to re-arm Germany and Japan in order to be able to send them against the nations of Europe and Asia (*Przyjaciółka*, 1951, Issue no. 4, p. 3). These imperialists were depicted as warmongers and as an anti-democratic force who opposed the "camp of peace" led by the Soviet Union. It was often repeated that for capitalism, which is full of internal contradictions, the only solution is war (*Trybuna Ludu*, 1952, p. 2). According to *Trybuna Ludu*, wars allow "the leading capitalists" to gain huge profits while lowering the living standards of the working class; destroying social advancement and introducing fascism into a country (*Trybuna Ludu*, 1952, p. 3).

The Communist press often recounted the course of "imperialist wars". During the Korean War, it provided constant information on the barbarity and inhumanity of American soldier. In order to intensify the effect of this news, American soldiers were compared to German soldiers and their brutality during World War II. The damage caused by the American forces "was on a par with the ravages caused by Hitler's bandits" (*Przyjaciółka*, 1951, Issue no. 2, p. 7). Americans were also described as "the heirs of Hitler's idea" (*Przyjaciółka*, 1951, Issue no. 5, p. 3) but a thousand times worse than their predecessors (*Przyjaciółka*, 1951, Issue no. 7, p. 5). According to the Communist press, they destroyed all factories and industry, over 100,000 civilian houses, and they murdered tens of thousands of people. "Imperialist crimes" included: murdering helpless Korean and Chinese prisoners-of-war, raping women, burning or burying people alive, starving civilians, crucifixions, the use of torture or even dumping insects infected with cholera, plague, and typhus to infect civilians (*Przyjaciółka*, 1951, Issue no. 29, p. 8; *Przyjaciółka*, 1952, Issue no. 14, p. 11). In order to make this news more believable, the Communist press cited "independent sources". "Anglo-Saxon imperialists" were additionally described as exploiters who worked against their own people (*Przyjaciółka*, 1951, Issue no. 9, p. 2); who attempted to transform the system of government into a fascist one (*Trybuna Ludu*, 1952, p. 2) and who, just like Hitler, created concentration camps where they kept "progressive activists" (*Trybuna Ludu*, 1952, p. 2).

One of the ways of intensifying anti-American sentiments within Polish society was superimposing swastikas on images of American presidents or depicting them together with Nazi criminals. The Communist press often reminded its readers that the USA was a country where slavery was still present. In one issue of *Przyjaciółka* there were pictures of an American slave whose legs had been amputated due to the fact that he had been chained to the prison bars - a punishment for having refused forced labor. There were also pictures of a child suffering from rickets who was left with no care or help, of a child bitten by rats, as well as pictures of five black men who had been killed for refusing to work in a ditch full of snakes. In this very same issue of *Przyjaciółka* it was also stressed that it is easier for the dogs to live in America than people (*Przyjaciółka*, 1952, Issue no. 41, p. 2). The USA was described as a country of several millions illiterates, where six million children had no access to schools (*Przegląd Kulturalny*, 1952, p. 1).

American imperialists used their "poisonous ideological weapons" (*Przegląd Kulturalny*, 1952, p. 1) to spread their model of society in "colonized" countries of the West. Through scholarship programs offered to Western European intellectualists, they attempted to "ideologically and culturally colonize" the subordinated countries (*Przegląd Kulturalny*, 1952, p. 7). The Communist propaganda in Poland repeatedly referred to the examples of protests taking place in the Western countries, e.g., to the protest of workers in Milan who fought against poverty and unemployment; or to the protest of the French dockers who refused to unload American weapons in order to express "the French people's fight for peace" (*Przyjaciółka*, 1951, Issue no. 16, p. 2).

Among the enemies of the Communist system were the spies run by American intelligence. In order to keep Polish society mobilized, the Communist press widely reported on of the trials of "imperialist spies". In one issue of *Trybuna Ludu* we can read that "never before has the People's Republic of Poland witnessed so many trials of bandits, spies, saboteurs, murderers, and villains who had one thing in common – the letters: USA" (*Trybuna Ludu*, 1952, p. 2).

Apart from the USA, West Germany was also described as the enemy of Poland, one that constantly sought revision of the new post-war borders of

Poland. This image of Germany had its roots in the long and difficult Polish-German relations. According to Stalinist-era school textbooks, Catherine the Great decided to partition Poland because she was "a pure-blooded German". The same textbooks called West Germany "German locusts", "German thugs", or "fascist vermin". In order to create this negative image of Germany, Communist propaganda often referred to the long history of wars between Poland and Germany. During national holidays in the People's Republic of Poland, Polish victories over Germans were constantly celebrated, e.g., the victorious battle of 972 near Cedynia or the Polish-Lithuanian victory at Grunwald in 1410. During these national holidays Germans flags were burnt, effigies of Nazi/German leaders were hanged, and portraits of Hitler were destroyed (Osęka, 2010, pp. 119–128). The Stalinist-era press also printed a picture of Konrad Adenauer, the German Chancellor, in which he was wearing a coat characteristic for the Teutonic Order. The creation of the Federal Republic of Germany (FRG) was presented as an attempt to rebuild Prussian militarism and to "revive neo-Hitlerite Wehrmacht" by the Communist propaganda in Poland (*Trybuna Ludu,* 1952, p. 2). This "new Wehrmacht", under the leadership of Adenauer (who supposedly secretly dreamt of revenge) was necessary in the process of the rejection of the new borders. Communist propaganda also claimed that plans to rebuild the German army was actually about rebuilding the Wehrmacht, while the lip-service concerning a "regular army" were only a "smokescreen" (*Trybuna Ludu*, 1952,p. 2).

When describing the FRG, communist propaganda often used terminology that referred to Nazism: its military forces were described as the Wehrmacht, politicians were "Hitlerite rumps", "Hitlerite dogs of imperialism" or "former SS-men" (*Trybuna Ludu*, 1952, p. 1; *Przyjaciółka*, 1952, Issue no. 5, p. 8). Additionally, the Communist press informed the public that Western politicians were planning to free Nazi-criminals and use their help in order to conquer the world, or that West Germany was a country on the brink of poverty, being constantly exploited by "imperialists", with its elites having links to the Nazi regime. *Trybuna Ludu* presented the FRG as a poor country where there was even a shortage of money to fight common diseases; where professors swept the floors, famous scientists were homeless, and where the tragic situation of students forced them to earn money selling newspapers and cigarettes on the streets (*Trybuna Ludu*, 1952, p. 3).

The situation of the FRG was radically different from the situation in the German Democratic Republic (GDR), or so the Communist press reported. The creation of the GDR was presented by Stalin as a turning point in the history of Europe, which prevented the "subjugation of the European countries by the imperialists" (*Kuźnica*, 1949, p. 1). Unlike the FRG, the GDR was presented as a peace-loving country which "has the same dreams as other countries – dreams of peace and freedom" (*Przyjaciółka*, 1951, Issue no. 6, p. 3). According to the Communist propaganda, more and more students from West Germany were coming to the GDR in order to build a progressive Germany together (*Trybuna Ludu*, 1952, p. 3).

According to the Stalinist-era propaganda, it was the members of the "pro-independence emigrees" who were responsible for losing the September Campaign of 1939. They were also responsible for convincing people to desist from military actions against the Germans "while the Soviet Army heroically fought against the Hitlerites" (*Przyjaciółka*, 1951, Issue no. 5, p. 7). Pro-independence emigrees were also accused of promoting an unrealistic and "anti-patriotic" policy which was actually contradictory to Polish interests. One of political decisions cited which was not in the Polish national interest was the decision to carry out the Warsaw Uprising, which led to the "slaughter of the Polish nation and the destruction of Warsaw" (*Przyjaciółka*, 1951, Issue no. 29, p. 7). Pro-independence emigrees were frequently accused of constructing a network of saboteurs and spies in cooperation with Anglo-American intelligence. This network was to prepare actions directed against the Communist authorities. Individuals who worked in the Polish section of Radio Free Europe were listed among the most dangerous and "damaging" enemies of the system. Radio Free Europe was presented by the Communist propaganda as an espionage center and a tool of American and German intelligence. Attacks against this group of people were often based on Nazi terminology. For example, at the end of 1952 there was a text published in *Życie Warszawy*, in which the author asked: "why is Free Europe – Freies Europa – called in such a way? Free Europe? Because on the gates of Nazi concentration camps: Auschwitz, Treblinka, Stutthof, and so on – there was always a sign: *Arbeit macht frei*" (Machcewicz, 2007, p. 89).

4.6   Conclusion

There were several reasons why Communist propaganda attempted to mythologize the image of an enemy during the Stalinist era. First of all, the search for an enemy within the Party was caused by competition within the Party's apparatus. Second of all, the mythologizing of a figure of an enemy in order to mobilize society against a common (fictional or real) danger was caused by the need for legitimation of power: Communist power. The basis of the Communist system during the period of Stalinism was control - control over all aspects of its citizens' lives. As Paczkowski noted, this control was not possible without creating and upholding an atmosphere of fear (Paczkowski, 2000a, p. 428). Since the execution of power was easier within an atmosphere of threat, the Communist authorities attempted to build and intensify this - the third reason for the mythologization of the phenomenon analyzed here. Thanks to this process, the Communist propaganda could present Polish society as one that is threatened by an extremely dangerous enemy, one that keeps changing its mask. It is important to note that one of the characteristics of a myth is its ambiguity, which, according to Barthes, enables an infinite number of meanings to articulate a specific myth. Depending on the situation, an enemy could be explicit (representatives of the rich landholders, the political opposition from the clergy) or concealed (saboteurs, speculators, sluggards, forest bandits), personified (President Eisenhower, Chancellor Adenauer) or abstract (the potato beetle, jazz); external ("Anglo-Saxon imperialists" and their "German or Polish emigrant lapdogs") or internal (the reactionary underground, the kulak landowners, "remnants of the aristocracy and bourgeois", proponents of a right-wing nationalistic agenda) (Paczkowski, 2000b, p. 166). The room for maneuvering with the images of enemies in order to maintain the feeling of being threatened among members of society was one of the most important principles that shaped the political myths of an enemy in Stalinist Poland.

The political myths that have been described above, however, were not internalized by a significant portion of Polish society – especially not to the extent which would be considered satisfactory for the Communist propaganda officials. This was especially evident in the case of followers of the Catholic Church. Worshippers manifested their belief in the Catholic faith despite the constant propaganda aimed at atheizing the country or dividing the clergy by issuing anti-clergy propaganda (Noszczak, 2010, p. 159). The Communist mythologizing process was akin to a "scattergun" approach. Poles who lived under the period of the People's Republic of Poland were to some extent forced into a state of schizophrenia. Despite the fact that they employed the language invented and used by the Communist propagandists ("Newspeak"), most of them did realize that they were repeating empty slogans. The most important reasons for this were: the lack of legitimacy of Communist power for a significant portion of Polish society, the Communist reign of terror in the Stalinist era, and propaganda that was too intrusive, too insistent, and incompatible with the real needs and hopes of Polish citizens.

References

Aparat bezpieczeństwa w latach 1944–1956. Taktyka, strategia, metody. (1996). Ed. A. Paczkowski, part 2, Warszawa.

Baczko, B., *Wyobrażenia społeczne. Szkice o nadziei i pamięci zbiorowej.* (1994). transl. M. Kowalska. Warszawa.

Bal-Nowak, M. (1996). *Mit jako forma symboliczna w ujęciu Ernsta A. Cassirera.* Kraków.

Biernat, T. (1989). *Mit polityczny.* Warszawa.

Braun, K. (1994). *Teatr polski 1939–1989. Obszary wolności – obszary zniewolenia.* Warszawa.

Cassirer, E. (1961). *The Myth of the State.* New Haven.

Czocher, A., Dyrcz R., Kwilosz J. (2008). *Informator o zasobie historycznym archiwum krakowskiego Oddziału Instytutu Pamięci Narodowej i zasadach jego udostępniania,* Kraków.

Duda, A. (2010). *Język mitu w reklamie.* Lublin.

Dudek, A., Gryz R. (2003). *Komuniści i Kościół w Polsce (1945–1989).* Kraków.

Dudek, A., Paczkowski A. (2005). *Poland,* in: *A Handbook of the Communist Security Apparatus in East Central Europe 1944–1989,* ed. K. Persak, Ł. Kamiński. Warsaw.

Dudek, A., Zblewski, Z. (2008). *Utopia nad Wisłą. Historia Peerelu.* Warszawa – Bielsko-Biała.

Fik, M. (1989). *Kultura polska po Jałcie. Kronika lat 1944–1981.* Londyn.

Filipowicz, S. (1988). *Mit i spektakl władzy.* Warszawa.

Flood, Ch. G. (1996). *Political Myth. A Theoretical Introduction.* New York – London.

Gomułka, W. (1962). *Artykuły i przemówienia 1943–1945,* t. 1. Warszawa.

Jarecka, U. (2008). *Propaganda wizualna słusznej wojny.* Warszawa.

Kehrer, G. (1997). *Wprowadzenie do socjologii religii,* transl. J. Piegza. Kraków.

Kornacki, K. (2002). *Polskie kino fabularne lat 1945–1956 wobec katolicyzmu i Kościoła katolickiego,* in: *Blok. Międzynarodowe Pismo Poświęcone Kulturze Stalinowskiej i Poststalinowskiej,* no. 1.

Machcewicz, P., „*Monachijska menażeria". Walka z Radiem Wolna Europa,* Warszawa 2007.

Noszczak, B. (2010). *Polityka państwa wobec Kościoła rzymskokatolickiego w Polsce w latach 1944–1956,* in: *PRL od lipca 44 do grudnia 70,* ed. K. Persak, P. Machcewicz. Warszawa.

Olszewski, H. (2011). *O roli i ideologii wroga w kształtowaniu się systemów totalitarnych,* [in:] *Totalitaryzmy XX wieku. Idee, instytucje, interpretacje,* eds. W. Kozub-Ciembroniewicz, H. Kowalska-Stus, B. Szlachta, M. Kiwior-Filo, Kraków 2011.

Opulski, R. (2013). *Amerykański mit wojny,* in: *Stany Zjednoczone wczoraj i dziś. Wybrane zagadnienia społeczno-polityczne,* eds. A. Małek, P. Napierała. Kraków.

Opulski, R., Ficoń M. (2020). *In search of Internal Enemies. Show Trials of Members of the Communist Parties in Stalinist Poland, Czechoslovakia and Hungary,* in: *The European Crucible of Diversity,* eds. C. Kuta, J. Marecki. Kraków.

Osęka, P. (2010). *Mydlenie oczu. Przypadki propagandy w Polsce.* Kraków.

Paczkowski, A. (2000a). *Funkcje i formy represji politycznych w systemie komunistycznym. Przykład Polski 1944–1989,* in: *XVI Powszechny Zjazd Historyków Polskich.*

Przełomy w historii. Pamiętnik, t. II, cz. II, eds. K. Ruchniewicz, J. Tyszkiewicz, W. Wrzesiński. Toruń.

Paczkowski, A. (2000b). *Pół wieku dziejów Polski 1939–1989*. Warszawa.

Paczkowski, A. (2007). *Departament X – kontekst ogólny i aspekty międzynarodowe*, in: *Departament X MBP. Wzorce – struktury – działanie*, ed. K. Rokicki. Warszawa.

Piątkowski, K. (1994). *Badacz wobec tradycji*, in: *Pożegnanie paradygmatu? Etnologia wobec współczesności*, eds. W. Burszta, J. Damrosz. Warszawa.

Poksiński, J. (1992). *„TUN". Tatar – Utnik – Nowicki*. Warszawa.

Szacka, B. (2006). *Czas przeszły, pamięć, mit*. Warszawa.

Thomson, O. (2001). *Historia propagandy*, transl. S. Głąbiński. Warszawa.

Topolski, J. (1991). *Historiografia jako tworzenie mitów i walka z nimi* [in:] *Ideologie, poglądy, mity w dziejach Polski i Europy XIX i XX wieku*, eds. J. Topolski, W. Molik, K. Makowski. Poznań.

Tudor, H. (1972). *Political Myth*. London.

Wierciński, A. (2004). *Magia i religia. Szkice z antropologii religii*. Kraków.

Press Sources

Kuźnica
Odrodzenie
Przegląd Kulturalny
Przyjaciółka
Trybuna Ludu

PAX Publishing Institute between 1949–1989 – the Largest Catholic Publishing House in Poland under the Communist Regime

Cecylia Kuta

5.1 Introduction

This interdisciplinary study discusses operations of the PAX Publishing Institute between 1949 and 1989 from the perspective of history, bibliography and press content analysis. The author's main aim was to highlight certain activities undertaken by the largest, and, undoubtedly, one of the most important Catholic publishing houses in the Polish People's Republic. Although the institute deserves a dedicated monograph, there is no comprehensive publication that takes into account the latest research results on the matter. Those studies which do exist were published before 1989 and were all written by members of the PAX Association, which must have had an impact on how politicised and biased they were.

The history and operations of the PAX Publishing Institute – the largest Catholic publisher in the Polish People's Republic – were a part of the activities undertaken by the PAX Association. Janina Kolendo[1] – the first manager of the publishing company – stressed 'the earliest direct link between the

---

1 Janina Kolendo, A.K.A. Jasia Zofia Grzybowska (1919–1977) – editor, journalist, publisher. During German occupation, after 1940, a soldier of the Confederation of the Nation/Konfederacja Narodu, a liaison officer for the Home Army, arrested in 1943 by the Gestapo, imprisoned in the death camps of Majdanek and Auschwitz. After the war she was associated with *Dziś i jutro* and the PAX Association, between 1949 and 1952, and from 1963 to 1975 the editor-in-chief of the PAX Publishing Institute, editor-in-chief of the bimonthly *Życie i Myśl* (1954–1956), deputy editor-in-chief of *Słowo Powszechne* (1957–1962), and *Kierunki* (1976–1977). Board member of the PAX Association, and, after 1952, head of the Association's ideological department. Cf. Z. Lichniak, *Pamięć o Janinie Kolendo w dziesiątą rocznicę śmierci*, "Kierunki", Issue No. 3 (18/01/1987), pp. 1, 10–11; E. Bryll, *Tak wierzyła*, "Kierunki", Issue No. 3 (18/01/1987), p. 10; J. Hagmajer, *Bezkompromisowa*, "Kierunki", Issue No. 3 (18/01/1987), p. 11; L. Gluck, *Janina Kolendo. Próba portretu*, "Kierunki", Issue No. 3 (18/01/1987); Z. Łączkowski, *Jasia*, "Kierunki", Issue No. 3 (18/01/1987); M. Kolendo, *Spotkanie po latach*, "Kierunki", Issue No. 3 (18/01/1987); A. Szubowa, *Jej życie było służbą*, "Kierunki", Issue No. 3 (18/01/1987); *Kolendo Janina pseud. Jasia Zofia Grzybowska*, http://tei.nplp.pl/entity/556 (accessed: 11/01/2021).

© CECYLIA KUTA, 2024 | DOI:10.1163/9789004687998_007

[PAX Publishing] Institute [...] and ideological and the worldview-related *Guidelines/Wytyczne* set by the PAX Association, were perceived as fuel for self-development and initiative-taking that noticeably exceeded its current abilities at any given time' (Księga o nagrodzie imienia Włodzimierza Pietrzaka, 1978, pp. 205–206).

A similar opinion was expressed by Zygmunt Lichniak[2], an editor in the PAX Publishing Institute, who stated that:

> The obvious coherent unity of the Association and the Institute to serve the same paramount purposes seems so natural that it is difficult to imagine how it could be questioned. Any attempts to perceive the two inseparable entities separately or independently are impossible, even within the framework of the most relative historical, ideological and cultural objectivization. (Lichniak, 1981, p. 27)

Importantly, these statements came from people who were fully loyal to the communist authorities of the time.

The PAX Association was an organisation of lay Catholics established by Bolesław Piasecki, a pre-war activist of the Falanga National Radical Camp (FNRC), and the circle of people who gathered around him after the Second World War. Initially, the FNRC operated as a group known as *Dziś i Jutro*, publishing – from November 1945 – a weekly under the same name (Kuta, 2009, p. 251). The PAX Association was formally registered on April 9, 1952, and co-operated with the communist authorities, who used it to attack Catholic Church of Poland (more on the PAX Association, cf. Majchrowski, 1984; Micewski, 1978; Reiff, 2007a; Reiff, 2006; Reiff, 2007b; Dudek, 1996, pp. 73–114; Dudek, Gryz,

---

2 Zygmunt Lichniak, A.K.A. Mateusz Żurawiec (1925–2015) – film and literary critic, journalist. Between 1945 and 1950, he studied Polish philology at Warsaw University. During his university years, he started a career as a city reporter in the daily *Wieczór Warszawy* (1946–1947). Next, he co-operated with the weekly *Dziś i Jutro* and *Przegląd Powszechny*. He was closely affiliated with the PAX Association. As a regular contributor to PAX's periodicals, he was the literary head of *Dziś i Jutro*, and editor of the youth supplement to *Słowo Powszechne*. Between 1958 and 1960, the editor-in-chief of *Życie i Myśl*. He also held the post of editor-in-chief of *Kierunki*. From 1960 to 1965, the head of the literary editorial board in the PAX Publishing Institute. He was also appointed head of the Department of Culture in the PAX Association, and its board member and a representative of the Association's Presidium. Member of the Polish Writers' Union. He was granted the W. Pietrzak Award twice (Cf. *Kto jest kim w Polsce*, Warsaw 1989, p. 721). Between 1981 and 1989 he was under surveillance by Section 5, Department 4 of the Ministry of Internal Affairs (cf. AIPN 0248/14, Kwestionariusz ewidencyjny "Recenzent" dot. Zygmunta Lichniaka; AIPN 01228/2385/D, Materiały dotyczące Zygmunta Lichniaka).

2003; Dudek, Pytel, 1990; Komu służył PAX? Materiały z sympozjum "Od PAX-u do Civitas Christiana" zorganizowanego przez Katolickie Stowarzyszenie Civitas Christiana, 30–31 stycznia 2008 roku, 2008; Kuta, 2009), which meant that the Association had no hierarchical approval from the Church and stood in opposition to Primate Stefan Wyszyński.

In November 1944, Bolesław Piasecki[3] had been captured by the NKVD. What saved him from execution was successful negotiations with the NKVD chief representative in Poland – State Security General Ivan Alexandrovich Serov (Dudek, Pytel, 1990, pp. 153–154; Micewski, 1978, p. 25; Przetakiewicz, 1994, pp. 66–68.). In an interview conducted by Stefan Kisielewski soon after Piasecki's release, he accounted: 'Bolsheviks came here and they won't leave earlier than in 50 years, so... you can imagine the rest yourself' (Bankowicz, 1996, p. 53). In this new reality, Piasecki struggled to find a place for himself. The main premise behind his organisation was a belief in reconciliation between Catholicism

---

3 Bolesław Piasecki, A.K.A. Leon Całka, Sablewski (1915–1979) – politician, lawyer. A founder of the National Radical Camp and the leader of the Falanga National Radical Camp. In 1939, he took part in the September Campaign as master corporal of the Warsaw Armoured Motorized Brigade. The founder and leader of the secret resistance organisation: the Confederation of the Nation, commander of the Striking Cadre Battalions, and, after the 1943 merger with the Home Army, the commanding officer of the 3rd Battalion, 77th Infantry Regiment of the Home Army. On November 12, 1944, he was incarcerated by the Soviets and interrogated, on several occasions, by State Security General Ivan Serov. In the summer of 1945, he was released from prison, and after the war he co-founded and ran the so-called Socially Progressive Movement of Secular Catholics, which supported the communist authorities and was associated with the weekly *Dziś i Jutro*. Next, he co-established the PAX Association, which he remained in charge of till the end of his life. Between 1965 and 1979 an MP, and from 1971 to 1979 a member of the Council of the State of the Polish People's Republic. More on B. Piasecki, cf. A. Dudek, G. Pytel, *Bolesław Piasecki. Próba biografii politycznej*, London 1990; J. M. Majchrowski, *Geneza politycznych ugrupowań katolickich. Stronnictwo Pracy, grupa "Dziś i Jutro"*, Paris 1984; A. Micewski, *Współrządzić czy nie kłamać? PAX i ZNAK w Polsce 1945–1976*, Paris 1978; Idem, *Wielki outsider katolicyzmu polskiego*, "Zdanie" 1989, Issue No. 4; Z. Przetakiewicz, *Od ONR-u do PAX-u*, Warsaw 1994; A. K. Kunert, *Słownik biograficzny konspiracji warszawskiej 1939–1944*, Warsaw 1987, pp. 125–129; J. Engelgard, *Bolesław Piasecki 1939–1956*, Warsaw 2015; AIPN, 01305/676, Bolesław Piasecki. Prezes Stowarzyszenia PAX (życie i działalność), ed. K. Piotrowski, Warsaw 1986, Wydział II Biura "C". The study conducted by Piotr Gontarczyk shows that in 1948 Piasecki was registered as an agent of the Fifth Department of the Ministry of Public Security (under the codename 'Tatar'). Cf. P. Gontarczyk, *Zagadka agenta "Tatara"*, "Gazeta Polska" 2006, Issue No. 30. On Bolesław Piasecki's agency and contact with the Security Service, cf. J. Nowak (Zdzisław Jeziorański), *Wojna w eterze wspomnienia*. Vol. I: *1948–1956*, [Wroclaw 1989], pp. 201–210. The thesis of Piasecki's agency is opposed by Ryszard Reiff and Jan Engelgard. Cf. R. Reiff, *Więzień Piasecki rozmawia z gen. NKWD Iwanem Sierowem* [in:] Idem, *Archiwum Stowarzyszenia PAX. Publicystyka polityczna. Tom 1: Refleksje z pogranicza historii, ideologii i polityki Stowarzyszenia PAX*, Warsaw 2006, pp. 49–77; J. Engelgard, *Bolesław Piasecki...*, pp. 161–163.

and Socialism. The group promoted the theory of multi-worldviews and propagated the idea of a collaboration between Catholics and Marxists. Over time, his association accepted the ideological premises of Communism and continued to receive permits to expand and develop the organisation by opening new outposts. From 1947, the Association had its representatives in the Sejm, and this was also when the Włodzimierz Pietrzak Award[4] (More information, cf. *Straty wśród pisarzy polskich (literatów, publicystów, dziennikarzy i redaktorów) w czasie II wojny światowej i okupacji hitlerowskiej 1939–1945*, 1980, p. 64) was established, granted for Christian-related output in various fields (more on the Włodzimierz Pietrzak Award and its laureates, cf. Lichniak, 1978; R. Reiff, 2006, p. 41). In February 1947, the PAX Publishing Company was registered, which later gave its name to the PAX Publishing Institute and Association (Dudek, Pytel, 1990, p. 188; cf. M. Rostworowski, 1968, p. 31). In years to come, Piasecki's group would obtain a series of press permits to publish – besides the aforementioned weekly *Dziś i Jutro* – other periodicals, including the daily *Słowo Powszechne*, the weeklies: *Kierunki*, WTK, and ITK, and the monthly *Życie i Myśl*. In addition, this Association ran an all-boys school – St Augustine Secondary School – in Warsaw, it also owned two thriving trade and industrial hubs – *Inco* – which focused on chemical, metal, timber, and glass-making businesses, as well as *Veritas*, which focused on devotional articles, arts and crafts, as well as sales and distribution of Catholic press and publications operating both on the domestic market and abroad. This was an absolute oddity in the whole Eastern Bloc, and resulted in PAX being called a state within a state; the only private capitalist company between the Elbe and Vladivostok (Dudek, 2013, p. 75)[5].

The story of the PAX Publishing Institute dates back to late 1948 and early 1949. In 1948, Bolesław Piasecki inspired a team of over a dozen associates of *Dziś i Jutro* to begin preparatory work to establish a publishing house. As a result, on May 25 1949, the PAX Publishing Company officially founded the PAX Publishing Institute (Stowarzyszenie PAX 1945–1985, 1985, p. 94.), whose main purpose – according to its originator – was to serve 'intellectual progress and the promotion of Polish Catholicism, ensure the possibility to teach *proper thinking*, supplement philosophical and theological knowledge, and enrich the religious experience through religious thought' (Lichniak, 1981, p. 17).

---

4   Włodzimierz Pietrzak, A.K.A. "Balk" (1913–1944) – poet, author, literary critic; after 1938 a regular contributor to *Prosto z Mostu*; in occupied Poland, a member of the resistance movement and a representative of the Confederation of the Nation; killed during the Warsaw Uprising.

5   A. Dudek, *Program Stowarzyszenia PAX. Realizm, koniunkturalizm czy utopia?*, "Politeja" 2013, 3 (25), p. 75.

5.2   Publishing Offer

The very first book published by the PAX Publishing Institute was *The Holy Bible: New Testament/Pismo Święte Nowego Testamentu* translated by Rev. Eugeniusz Dąbrowski, which – together with a later version translated by Rev. Seweryn Kowalski – totalled over thirty editions with a print run exceeding two million copies[6]. According to Zygmunt Lichniak, the choice of the Bible was not accidental – as this particular book was intended to have a symbolic meaning, heralding the future publishing profile. Lichniak wrote:

> The fact that the Institute chose *The Holy Bible: New Testament/Pisma Świętego Nowego Testamentu* to be its first publication was not only an attempt to meet at least a small fraction of believers' needs, (needs which could not be satisfied even by later reeditions of over one million copies). In fact, the 1949 edition of *New Testament* was so much more: a conscious manifestation and an emphatic accentuation of how vital the religious needs of the Polish nation were. With the birth of the Polish People's Republic, the nation was entering a brand new era of development, which should [...] reasonably and creatively respect principles of historical continuity. Part of this continuity was the co-existence and collaboration between believers and non-believers, where the former's principia of subjectivity should be acknowledged and their right to a self-inspired worldview honoured, as it has potential to enrich the national *bonum commune*. (Lichniak, 1981, pp. 29–30)

These words were written by an editor of the PAX Publishing Institute, which makes them sound slightly exaggerated. The author seems to directly imply that prior to the edition prepared by PAX, Poles had no possibility to encounter *The Holy Bible*, which is clearly untrue.

Besides the *New Testament*, 1949 also brought the first fiction book – a novel by Georges Bernanos entitled *Under the Sun of Satan* and translated by Aleksander Wat. According to Lichniak, this was yet another edition' symbolic for the future operations of the publishing house:

> It primarily demonstrates that the Institute has no intention to limit its operations exclusively to *serving* religious needs, it does not fail to see the vital role of belles-lettres in enriching the development of individuals and the community, it recognises a need for a reasonable and creative

---

6   https://www.iwpax.pl/strona-o-nas-113.html (accessed: 07/03/2019).

symbiosis with the remarkable achievements of Catholic world literature, it comprehends and esteems the imperative of cultural continuity
– and not only in its historical aspect, and it intends to honour and familiarise Polish culture with values that intensify perception of the world
and overworld, values that originate from the profundity of Catholicism.
(Lichniak, 1981, pp. 30–31)

At the same time, in his foreword to Bernanos' novel, Piasecki claimed it to be
the first ideological publication of the house (Piasecki, 1949, p. 2.).

The third book published in 1949 was Bruce Marshall's novel *All Glorious
Within*, which Lichniak also believed to be 'an ideological message from the
Institute that – in an attempt to enrich [...] cultural and literary life with the
output of Catholic writers from other genres – it did not intend to focus exclu-
sively on *classics*, i.e., authors and works already [...] known and recognised.
Thus, the edition of Marshall's book was a sign that the Publisher is to explore
the realms of literature that have not yet been available to the Polish reader'
(Lichniak, 1981, p. 33).

Lichniak argued that this particular book was 'a sign of respect for the
countless shades of Catholicism' (Lichniak, 1981, p. 33), adding that 'the fact
that during its first year, the Institute decided to publish such entirely different
works as Bernanos' *Under the Sun of Satan* and Marshall's *All Glorious Within*
may, or even should, be interpreted [...] as an objective to raise respect for and
a creative comprehension of the multiplicity of forms, manners, styles and
[...] shades that may, and should, manifest Catholicism and reflect its development' (Lichniak, 1981, p. 34).

First and foremost, the Institute's aim was to meet the demand for religious
publications[7]. Apart from the nearly annual re-edition of *The Holy Bible*, it

---

7   More information on books reviewed and recommended in Catholic socio-cultural peri-
    odicals, cf. E. Kristanova, *Książka na łamach katolickich czasopism społeczno-kulturalnych
    w Polsce w latach 1945–1953*, Lodz 2012; eadem, *Książka na łamach krakowskiego "Tygod-
    nika Powszechnego" (1945–1953) w świetle reklamy wydawniczej* [in:]: Краків – Львів: книги,
    часописи, бібліотеки XIX–XX ст., Vol. 10, ред. Г. Врона, О. Колосовська, Г. Косентка, Львів
    2011, pp. 332–345. On books in the Polish People's Republic, cf. Jarosz D., *Dzieje książki w
    Polsce 1944–1989. Wybór źródeł*, Warsaw 2010; Idem, *Władza a książka społeczno-polityczna
    w PRL 1956–1989*, "Z Badań nad Książką i Księgozbiorami Historycznymi" 2013/2014, Vol. 7/8,
    pp. 133–172; Idem, *Jak tworzono "książkę socjalistyczną"? Narady wydawców i księgarzy państw
    bloku wschodniego 1965–1988*, "Z Badań nad Książką i Księgozbiorami Historycznymi" 2016,
    Vol. 10, pp. 317–334; Idem, *Sprawy książki polskiej i jej autorów w sowieckich dokumentach par-
    tyjnych z lat 1954–1971*, "Z Badań nad Książką i Księgozbiorami Historycznymi" 2015, Vol. 9, pp.
    273–285; *Nauka o książce. Antologia tekstów*, eds. D. Kuźmina, M. Tobera, Warsaw 2006.

also issued prayer books, Sunday missals, songbooks, and religious textbooks. In 1951, the first *Catechism of Catholic Religion/Katechizm religii katolickiej* in Poland was published, followed by *Total Apologetics/Apologetyka totalna* by Rev. Wincent Kwiatkowski (Vol. 1–2, 1954–1956), *Ethics/Etyka* by Rev. Józef Keller (1957), and *Catholic Dogmatics/Dogmatyka katolicka* by Rev. Witold Pietkun (1954). As for studies on the Bible, PAX published several books by Rev. Prof. Eugeniusz Dąbrowski: *Biblical Studies/Studia biblijne* (1951), *Prolegomena to the New Testament/Prolegomena do Nowego Testamentu* (1952), *The Acts of Paul the Apostle/Dzieje Pawła z Tarsu* (1953), and *Biblical Glossa and Discoveries/Glossy i odkrycia biblijne* (1954).

Another genre was the classic masterpieces of Christian thought and spirituality by Church Fathers, most prominent theologists, philosophers, historians, biblical experts, anthropologists, sociologists, psychologists and pedagogues, including books by Fathers of the Second Ecumenical Council of the Vatican (1962–1965) and its later propagators: Marie-Dominique Chenu, Yves Congar, Karl Rahner, and Joseph Ratzinger. What is more, PAX also published hagiographic and religious literature based on biblical motifs.

Other publications important for strengthening faith and the dissemination of principles of Christian morality included works on religious education and upbringing, family, marital life, prenatal protection, methods of natural family planning and personal development, as well as a biographical series that presented both saints and larger-than-life figures in the history of the Church (Książki Instytutu Wydawniczego PAX 1949–1989. Przewodnik, 1989, p. VI.).

The institute did not fail to publish masterpieces of Catholic literature either, including such literary giants as Georges Bernanos, Graham Greene, Julien Green, Bruce Marshall, François Mauriac, Gilbert Keith Chesterton, Sigrid Undset, as well as Polish authors: Roman Brandstaetter, Jan Dobraczyński, Antoni Gołubiew, Zofia Kossak-Szczucka, Hanna Malewska, Teodor Parnicki, Maria Kuncewiczowa, and Stanisław Cat-Mackiewicz (Cf. Katalog 1949–1979, eds. A. Małaszewski, M. Piasecka, Warsaw 1980; Książki Instytutu Wydawniczego PAX 1949–1989. Przewodnik, ed. A. Szafrańska, Warsaw 1989). Lichniak emphasised that 'by offering Polish and foreign belles-lettres in this politically peculiar period, the PAX Publishing Institute became not only a proponent and a voice, but also a co-creator of the dialogue on culture and literature, emphasising the fact that they need a multitude of artistic and worldview attitudes' (Z. Lichniak, 1981 pp. 49–50).

The Institute published numerous books on contemporary history, quite often on unwelcome or even taboo topics in the Polish People's Republic, as well as works by Catholic writers and Western European theologians and philosophers which contributed to the preservation of cultural and scientific heritage, and in particular, the vindication of the Home Army and remembrance of the Warsaw Uprising. Lichniak wrote (in 1957): 'From such works as *The Warsaw Uprising of 1944/Powstanie Warszawskie 1944* by Adam Borkiewicz, the album *Days of the Uprising/Dni Powstania* [by Jan Grużewski and Stanisław Kopf – author's note], and Stanisław Podlewski's narrative on the events of August 1944 (*Żoliborz Rapsody/Rapsodia żoliborska*), through accounts from concentration camps (e.g., Jan Domagała's *Those who Survived Dachau/Ci, którzy przeszli przez Dachau*, Czesław Wincenty Jaworski's *Reminiscences from Auschwitz/Wspomnienia z Oświęcimia*, or *Polish Children Accuse/Dzieci polskie oskarżają* by Helena Radomska-Strzemecka and Józef Wnuk), to reports on battles fought by Polish soldiers during the September Campaign and by the underground resistance movement (e.g., Melchior Wańkowicz's *The Battle of Westerplatte/Westerplatte* and *Hubals' Boys/Hubalczycy*, Włodzimierz Wnuk's *I Was with You/Byłem z wami* and *Underground Fight in the Hilltops/Walka podziemna na szczytach*, and Jerzy Łyżwa's *Carpathian Summits/Wierchami Karpat*) – the PAX Publishing Institute co-presented the brutal truth about the Second World War and participated in balancing the political and patriotic experiences of the period' (Z. Lichniak, 1981 pp. 97–98). Interestingly, all publications between 1944 and 1990 were censored in Poland, with authors banned from speaking freely, which makes any attempt to popularise Catholic works and literature on the Warsaw Uprising at that time truly exceptional and noteworthy (cf. Kamińska-Chełminiak, 2019).

The Institute also published the following: *The Military Effort of the Polish Nation during World War 2/Wysiłek zbrojny narodu polskiego w czasie II wojny światowej* (1961) by Wincent Iwanowski, *A March through Hell/Przemarsz przez piekło* by Stanisław Podlewski, *Nazi Nationalistic Strategy in Upper Silesia/Hitlerowska polityka narodowościowa na Górnym Śląsku* (1963), *Life in Warsaw during the Uprising. August – September 1944/Życie w powstańczej Warszawie. Sierpień – wrzesień 1944* (1965), and *Greater Poland in the Shadow of the Swastika/Wielkopolska w cieniu swastyki* (1970) by Edward Serwański, *The Fan – A Monograph on the Separate Diversionary Arm of the Home Army: September 1941 – March 1943/Wachlarz. Monografia wydzielonej organizacji dywersyjnej Armii Krajowej: wrzesień 1941 – marzec 1943* (1983) by Cezary Chlebowski, *The Silent Unseen/Cichociemni* (1984) by Jerzy Tucholski, *Fir/Jodła* (1988) by Wojciech Borzobohaty, and many others.

What is more, the Institute published memoirs and diaries of former soldiers, including *A Gunman-Footman/Artylerzysta – piechurem* (1966) by Tadeusz Sztumbek-Rychter, *The Trail of the Jędrusie Guerrillas/Szlakiem Jędrusiów*

(1966) by Eugeniusz Dąbrowski, *September Roads/Wrześniowe drogi* (1969) by
Bogusław Cierniewicz, *Grenade Shrapnel/Odłamki granatu* (1969) by Cezary
Chlebowski, *The Home Army – in Lodz and Silesia/W Armii Krajowej – w Łodzi i
na Śląsku* (1969) by Zygmunt Walter Janke, *On the Barricades, in the Canals and
the Debris of Czerniakow/Na barykadach, w kanałach i gruzach Czerniakowa*
(1970) by Ryszard Czugajewski, *Poles in the Battle of Britain/Udział Polaków w
bitwie o Anglię* (1968) by Jan Jokiel, *We Were Fated to Survive/Dane nam było
przeżyć* (1972) by Felicjan Majorkiewicz, and *Kedyw/Kedywiacy* (1973) by Henryk and Ludwik Witkowski. These are just examples taken from a long list of
publications (cf. Katalog 1949–1979, 1980; Książki Instytutu Wydawniczego PAX
1949–1989. Przewodnik, 1989). According to Lichniak, they were perceived as 'a
lesson in patriotism, based on factual data and documentation, and aimed at
deepening the nation's identity and unity' (Lichniak, 1981, p. 141).

The fact that they were selected for publication allowed the Institute to
save them from oblivion, since at any other official state-owned publisher
of that time they would have been consigned to the bottom of the drawer
due to censorial rigours. In this case, the Institute's task was to 'throw a lifeline
to authors and works which, God knows where and when, would reach the
Cape of Good publishing Hope, the path to which led – at a certain period –
between Scylla and Charybdis of unilaterally-imposed postulates' (Lichniak,
1981, pp. 80–81).

This can be illustrated with the example of Stanisław Rembek, a writer and
participant in both the Polish-Soviet War of 1919–1921 and the 1939 September Campaign, who was also linked to the conspiratorial organisation Polish
Socialists, which remained active between 1941 and 1943. After the Second
World War, a ban was imposed on all his writings, which condemned him to
a life of poverty. A helping hand was eventually offered by Piasecki, who, in
1956, published a collection of Rembek's stories: *A Ballad on a Contemptuous
Hangman and Two January Tales/Ballada o wzgardliwym wisielcu oraz dwie
gawędy styczniowe*. As a token of gratitude, the author offered the following
acknowledgement:

> To Bolesław Piasecki I dedicate these meagre words of appreciation for
> his gritty determination to help me in the darkest hour. (Rembek, 1956)

It was also PAX that, in 1985, first published a six-volume work *Fighting Poland
1939–1945/Polska walcząca 1939–1945* by Jerzy Ślaski (1924–2002), an ex-soldier
of the Home Army, who continued fighting as a member of the post-war Polish underground anti-communist organisation *Freedom and Independence* in

Lublin Province, and later found shelter with PAX as a long-term board member, and the editor-in-chief of *WTK* (1958–1970), and then *Słowo Powszechne* (1980–1981) (Wernic, 2002, pp. 204–213).

Another publication prepared by the Institute was Lichniak's *Before a Panorama is Created/Zanim powstanie panorama* (1983) on Polish literature in exile, where the author reviewed and assessed critical statements on emigrant literary works. Analysing discrepancies between the various opinions, Lichniak argued there was a demand for agreement and creative debate that could help preserve the values of the Polish literature written abroad, and set its role and place in the national culture (cf. Habielski, 1999).

The Institute's publishing offer also involved larger series, for instance, *The Bookcase of Regained Western Lands/Biblioteczka Ziem Zachodnich*. Initiated in 1960, it included Melchior Wańkowicz's *The Battle of Westerplatte/Westerplatte* and *Hubals' Boys/Hubalczycy*, Romuald Pitera's *Could Hitler Have Taken London?/Czy Hitler mógł zdobyć Londyn?*, Jan Dobraczyński's *Hands on the Wall/Dłonie na murze* and *Judith and the Toy Blocks/Judyta i klocki*, Aleksander Rogalski's *That's What Hitler was Like/Taki był Hitler*, and Władysław Jan Grabski's *The Sawmill Will Commence/Tartak ruszy*. Lichniak accounted that even if the series had 'a cheap form with very poor artwork, way below the ambitious premises of the Institute, and offered a relatively low standard in terms of writing and editing, it still remained an apt and socially useful production, as it was a politically ancillary tool to implement one of the organisation's postulates' (Lichniak, 1981, p. 84).

He also admitted that the series allowed the Institute to meet 'commitments imposed by its ideological programme' (Lichniak, 1981, p. 84).

In 1964, another series – called *Clock/Z zegarem* was initiated in 1964 when Jan Jakub Patz's *A View from the Saxonian Embassy/Z okien ambasady saskiej* was released. Other volumes included Zygmunt Mineyko's *From Taiga to Acropolis/Z tajgi pod Akropol* (1971), Jędrzej Rogoyski's *Memoirs of Mine/Pamiętniki moje* (1972), Ignacy Domeyko's *Letters to Władysław Laskowicz/Listy do Władysława Laskowicza* (1976), Kazimierz Lewandowski's *Memoirs of a Polish Expatriate/Pamiętniki wychodźca polskiego* (1977), Karol Libelt's *Letters/Listy* (1978), and Kajetan Wojciechowski's *My Memoirs from Spain/Pamiętniki moje w Hiszpanii* (1978).

Over time, more series were created, including *Classics of Christian Spirituality/Klasycy duchowości chrześcijańskiej*, *Religious Education/Wychowanie religijne*, the *Labyrinth* series (called after its logo), *Classics of Polish Christian Thought in the 19th and 20th Century/Klasycy polskiej myśli chrześcijańskiej XIX i XX wieku*, *Church Fathers/Ojcowie Kościoła*, and *Diplomats' Diaries/Pamiętniki dyplomatów* (Książki Instytutu Wydawniczego PAX 1949–1989, 1989, p. VII).

Upon Karol Wojtyła's election to the papacy, the Institute initiated a series entitled *John Paul II – the First Pole in the Holy See/Jan Paweł II – pierwszy Polak na Stolicy Piotrowej* to contain the Pope's teachings. In fact, the Institute remained the only organisation to keep full records of all his pastoral journeys (Książki Instytutu Wydawniczego PAX 1949–1989, 1989, p. VII; cf. Kristanova, 2017b, pp. 256–272; Kristanova, 2015, pp. 707–727).

The publications of the PAX Publishing Institute also included periodicals issued under the auspices of the PAX Association, including the weekly *Dziś i Jutro* (1945–1956), and then the daily *Słowo Powszechne* (1947–1993), the weeklies: *Kierunki* (1956–1990), WTK (first published as *Wrocławski Tygodnik Katolików* in Wroclaw between 1953 and 1981, and after 1957 as *Wrocławski Tygodnik Katolicki*; from 1958 printed in Warsaw), ITK – *Ilustrowany Tygodnik Katolików Zorza* (1957–1963 as *Zorza Świąteczna*, 1963–1966 as *Zorza – ilustrowany tygodnik katolików*, and 1982–1991 as *Zorza: rodzinny tygodnik katolików*), and monthlies: *Życie i Myśl* (1950–1999), *Życie Katolickie w Polsce*, and *Biuletyn Wewnętrzny*.

5.3 The Institute's Role and Importance

The story of the publishing house is marked by events that had a substantial impact on its later assessment. A seminal event was the publication of Bolesław Piasecki's *Critical Issues/Zagadnienia istotne* in November 1954, where the author presented his vision of the Catholic share of power, and made an attempt to prove that Socialism was brought about by the Holy Spirit (cf. Piasecki, 1954.). Unsurprisingly, these views triggered a strong reaction, and on June 29, 1955 both this book and the weekly *Dziś i Jutro* were condemned and listed in *The Index of Prohibited Books* by the Sacred Congregation for the Doctrine of the Faith, while Piasecki and his associates faced the danger of excommunication. In response, the managerial board submitted to the verdict and removed the book from the Institute's offer. However, the weekly was not closed down, as the communist authorities did not grant their consent in the matter until May 20, 1956 (Dudek, Pytel, 1990, p. 217), when *Dziś i Jutro* was merged with another periodical – the PAX variant of *Tygodnik Powszechny*[8]

---

8 *Tygodnik Powszechny* – a Krakow-based periodical published from March 24, 1945, and aimed at secular Catholics. Between 1945 and 1953, when its main profile was being formed, the weekly marked its presence in public life by distancing itself from the dominant ideology. Between 1953 and 1956 it was taken over by the PAX Association in retaliation for the editorial board's refusal to publish Stalin's obituary with the deceased's photograph in a black frame. Cf. C. Kuta, *"Działacze" i "Pismaki". Aparat bezpieczeństwa wobec organizacji kato lików*

(unlawfully taken over in March 1953) – to form a new entity entitled *Kierunki* (Dudek, Pytel, 1990, p. 218; Kristanova, 2011, 2012, 2016, 2017b; Micewski, 1978, pp. 71–72; Rostworowski, 1968, pp. 123–124), which was fully controlled by the Association.

The first manager of the PAX Publishing Institute was Janina Kolendo, who held the post between 1949 and 1952, before being succeeded by Teresa Englert (1952–1961)[9]. In 1961, the position of managing director was established and held by Jan Szwykowski until 1968[10], then Zdzisław Borówka in 1969[11], who was later replaced by Witold Jankowski[12] before Zbigniew Czajkowski took over[13],

---

świeckich w Krakowie w latach 1957–1989, Krakow 2009; A. Micewski, *Współrządzić czy nie kłamać? PAX i ZNAK w Polsce 1945–1976*, Paris 1978; M. Jagiełło, *Próba Rozmowy. Szkice o katolicyzmie odrodzeniowym i "Tygodniku Powszechnym" 1945–1953, Vol. 2: "Tygodnik Powszechny" i komunizm 1945–1953*, Warsaw 2001; R. Graczyk, *Cena przetrwania? SB "Tygodnik Powszechny"*, Warsaw 2011; E. Kristanova, *W kręgu zagadnień literackich "Tygodnika Powszechnego" (1945–1953)*, Warsaw 2016.

9 Teresa Englert (1923–1983) – member of the National Party from 1942/1943, A.K.A. "908", "Teresa", in the Home Army (from 1944) in occupied Poland.

10 Jan Szwykowski (1915–1981) – financial manager in the PAX Association, head of the PAX Publishing Institute between 1968 and 1969.

11 Zdzisław Borówka – head of the PAX Publishing Institute between 1969 and 1972.

12 Witold Jankowski (1919–2000) – lawyer, journalist and Catholic activist. During the Second World War he edited the underground press for the Lublin-based division of the Home Army. In 1945 he was employed by the Regional Office of Information and Propaganda in Bydgoszcz. In 1946, he graduated from the Faculty of Law and Economics at the University of Poznan, which he had started before the war. From July 1950 a member of the editorial board of *Słowo Powszechne*, and between 1955 and 1972 the editor-in-chief. In 1969–1985 he was an MP, and between 1972 and 1975 head of the PAX Publishing Institute. He served several terms of office in the supreme authorities of the Polish Association of Journalists. Cf. "Więź" 2000, Issue No. 6; https://bs.sejm.gov.pl/F?func=find-b&request =000004478&find_code=SYS&local_base=ARS10 (accessed: 12/01/2021).

13 Zbigniew Czajkowski, A.K.A. "Dębicz" (1923–1998) – journalists and Catholic activist. During the Second World War, he was a soldier of the Home Army and took part in the Warsaw Uprising. Between 1954 and 1955, the editor-in-chief of *Dziś i Jutro*, and in 1961–1972 the monthly *Życie i Myśl*. He was a regular contributor to *Słowo Powszechne* in Rome and the Vatican (1973–1975). From 1973 editor-in-chief of *Zeszyty Naukowe* run by the PAX Association, of which he was a long-time activist (member of the presidium since 1957, vice chairman from 1986). Between 1976 and 1980 an MP, and between 1975 and 1979 head of the PAX Publishing Institute. In 1958–1983, a member of the National Committee at the Front of National Unity, and from 1971, a representative of the presidium. Between 1988 and 1990 a member of the Council for the Protection of Struggle and Martyrdom Sites. Between 1986–1989 a member of the Advisory Board at the President of the State National Council on behalf of the PAX Association. Between 1985 and 1991 a judge at the State Tribunal. Between 1987 and 1989 a member of the presidium of the National Council of the Patriotic Movement for National Rebirth. Between June 27 and October 12, 1989 a secret

and then the post was held by Józef Wójcik (1979–1981)[14], and finally by Janusz Stefanowicz[15].

The pact that Piasecki struck with communists allowed him to develop a relatively powerful publishing and economic base. In the Communist State, the Institute run by the PAX Association was a unique enterprise that could openly publish Catholic authors, religious works (prayer books, breviaries, The Holy Bible, etc.), memoirs of former Home Army associates, and other publications.

In the self-assessment of the Institute's operations between November 1971 and January 1976, it was stated that 'it plays an important role, among other achievements, in the socially progressive PAX movement. In the reviewed period, the Institute continued its multidirectional work, publishing 415 titles,

---

collaborator with the Security Service (codename: "Wiesław"). Cf. AIPN 00200/1158, Teczka personalna tajnego współpracownika "Wiesław": Zbigniew Czajkowski; *Kto jest kim w Polsce. Informator biograficzny*, Warsaw 1989, p. 189.

14 Józef Wójcik (1929–2015) – journalist and politician. Between 1979 and 1981 the head of the PAX Publishing Institute, in 1982–1989 editor-in-chief of *Słowo Powszechne*, in 1986–1989 the vice chairman of the Executive Board of the PAX Association, after 1989 the head of the *Veritas* Central Sales Office. Between 1986 and 1989 a member of the National Grundwald Committee, and an MP in 1985–1991. Cf. J. Engelgard, *Pożegnanie Józefa Wójcika*, "Myśl Polska" 2015, Issue No. 51–52, http://www.mysl-polska.pl/720 (accessed: 12/01/2021).

15 Janusz Stefanowicz (1932–1998) – journalist, professor in the humanities, PAX activist. After 1955 an editor in the foreign department of *Słowo Powszechne*, after 1956 head of the same department, and after 1960 the associate editor-in-chief. Between 1972 and 1980 editor-in-chief, and between 1981 and 1982 the associate editor-in-chief of *Życie Warszawy*. After 1982 the head and the editor-in-chief of the PAX Publishing Institute. After December 1982 an assistant professor at the National Educational Centre of the Faculty of Political Sciences, Warsaw University. After 1959 a member of the PAX, after 1960 the head of the PAX's foreign department, and after 1962 a board member, between 1968 and 1980 a member of the presidium, in 1971 a member of the secretarial office of the presidium, and after 1976 one of the three vice chairmen of the board. Between 1980 and 1985 an MP, in 1983 a member of the National Council at the Patriotic Movement for National Rebirth, and between 1984 and 1989 the ambassador to Paris. After March 1989 employed in the Institute of Political Studies of the Polish Academy of Sciences. After March 1990 a vice chairman of PAX. Between 1990 and 1998 an employee of the Institute of Political Studies of the Polish Academy of Sciences. Between 1969 and 1980 he was under surveillance by Section 2, Department 4 at the Ministry of Internal Affairs as part of the "Cyklop" Investigation, on July 23, 1979 he became a collaborator, and on July 30, 1980, he was registered as a secret collaborator, named "Seneka", on October 29, 1984, after his arrival in Paris, his collaboration was terminated, and on November 2, 1984 he was removed from the network of secret collaborators. Cf. A. W. Kaczorowski *Janusz Stefanowicz (1932–1998) – kariera dziennikarza PAX-u* [in:] *Nie tylko niezłomni i kolaboranci... Postawy dziennikarzy w kraju i na emigracji 1945–1989*, eds. T. Wolsza, P. Wójtowicz, Warsaw 2014, pp. 172–190 (ibid: Stefanowicz's biography).

which amounts to 6,795 publisher's sheets and a total print run of 4,988,500 copies, including 240,000 copies of *The Holy Bible: New Testament/Pismo Święte Nowego Testamentu*. Many of the books issued by the Institute were winners of various reader's polls organised by different periodicals. Several authors who published their works through PAX have received state awards. [...] We have also expanded our participation in bookfairs abroad, in the Soviet Union and other people's democracies, as well as in Belgium, France, Norway, Yugoslavia, Sweden, West Germany, and Canada' (AIPN, 0639/21, 1976, p. 64.).

The role and the importance of the Institute was also discussed by Lieutenant Janusz Huk in his 1984 master's thesis, written at the Academy of Internal Affairs under the supervision of Colonel Józefa Siemaszkiewicz. Huk stressed that 'the Institute is the largest Catholic publishing house in Poland, with an annual output of 100 publications and up to 1 million copies' (AIPN, 01521/2092/pdf, 1984, pp. 125–126).

He also argued that 'besides religious and philosophical literature, belles-lettres and essays have always been the publisher's flagships. In that respect, the Institute can claim some great achievements in developing and preserving the long-standing values of our culture' (AIPN, 01521/2092/pdf, 1984, pp. 125–126).

The achievements of the Institute between 1949–1989 are unquestionable. The catalogue of PAX's publications compiled by Amelia Szafrańska for the period lists 2,695 titles (with calendars and various guidebooks), including 2,654 books, of which many were reedited (Książki Instytutu Wydawniczego PAX 1949–1989, 1989). The publisher's offer was dominated by belles-lettres (1360 titles) and texts on religion and theology (740 titles). There were noticeably fewer publications on history (309), philosophy (154), socio-political matters (40), psychology (19), and sociology (only 4). The findings of the report are presented in Table 5.1.

A numerical data of the PAX Publishing Institute reveals that the most frequently published author was Jan Dobraczyński (61 titles), undoubtedly the publisher's most popular Polish writer, while Francois Mauriac dominated among foreign authors (28 titles). These two were followed by Roman Brandstaetter, Graham Greene, and Aleksander Rogalski (20 titles each), while other popular writers included: Zofia Kossak, Teodor Parnicki, Maria Kuncewiczowa, Etienne Gilson, Clive Staples Lewis, Ernest Bryll, Francis Clifford, Jean Guitton, Zdzisław Umiński, Sigrid Undset, Józef Maciej Kononowicz, Józef Szczypka, Gilbert Cesbron, Gilbert Keith Chesterton, Julien Green, Zdzisław Łączkowski, Hanna Muszyńska-Hoffmanowa, etc. Table 5.2 contains a list of PAX's authors and the number of their publications.

The possibility to publish freely and extensively came at a price. Not only did the PAX Association have to support the communist authorities, but also

TABLE 5.1   The topics of books issued by the PAX Publishing Institute between 1949 and 1989.

Topic	No. of titles
Belles-lettres	1360
Religion and theology	740
History	309
Philosophy	154
Socio-political literature	40
Psychology	19
Sociology	4

SOURCE: OWN STUDY, BASED ON *KSIĄŻKI INSTYTUTU WYDAWNICZEGO PAX 1949–1989. PRZEWODNIK*, ED. A. SZAFRAŃSKA, WARSAW 1989

TABLE 5.2   Most popular authors (over 5 titles)

Bąk Wojciech	5
Bednorz Zbyszko	5
Bernangos Georges	9
Bocheński Aleksander	7
Bojarska Teresa	8
Boros Ladislaus, Rev.	9
Brandstaetter Roman	20
Brycht Andrzej	9
Bryll Ernest	15
Carretto Carlo, Rev.	5
Cesbron Gilbert	10
Chesterton Gilbert	10
Clifford Francis	15
Cronin Archibald Joseph	8
Czajkowski Zbigniew	9
Czyż Henryk	5
Daniel-Rops Henri	5
Dawson Christopher	6
Dąbrowski Eugeniusz, Rev.	5
Dobraczyński Jan	61
Dolecki Zbigniew	9
Gawecki Bolesław Józef	5
Gilson Etienne	16

TABLE 5.2   Most popular authors (over 5 titles) (*cont.*)

Grabski Władysław	8
Green Julien	10
Greene Graham	20
Guitton Jean	14
Hertz Janina	8
John Paul II	7
Kononowicz Józef Maciej	11
Kossak Zofia	19
Krokiewicz Adam	8
Kucnewiczowa Maria	17
Laurentin Rene, Rev.	6
Lewis Clive Staples	16
Łaszowski Alfred	7
Łączkowski Zdzisław	10
Cat Mackiewicz Stanisław	8
Mascall Eric Lionel, Rev.	8
Mauriac Francois	28
Moore Brian	6
Muszyńska-Hoffmanowa Hanna	10
Parnicki Teodor	18
Piasecki Bolesław	6
Rinser Luise	6
Rogalski Aleksander	20
Rostworowski Mikołaj	5
Saroyan William	5
Stanclik Mieczysław	7
Starzyńska Maria	8
Stefanowicz Janusz	8
Szczawiński Józef	5
Szczypka Józef	11
Szelburg-Zarembina Ewa	5
Śliwicka Anna	5
Teilhard Pierre	9
Umiński Zdzisław	13
Undset Sigrid	12
Wańkowicz Melchior	8
Wnuk Włodzimierz	7
Zientara-Malewska Maria	9

SOURCE: OWN CALCULATIONS, BASED ON *KSIĄŻKI INSTYTUTU WYDAWNICZEGO PAX 1949–1989. PRZEWODNIK*, ED. A. SZAFRAŃSKA, WARSAW 1989

to submit to full surveillance of secret services operating in the Polish People's Republic. Supervision was also exercised over the PAX Publishing Institute to ensure that it remained politically in line and fulfilled the role imposed by the communist party. The main purpose, however, was to use the Institute against the hierarchy of the Catholic Church (Kuta, 2009, p. 275).

Both the Association and the Institute were monitored as part of the investigation codenamed 'Alpha' (AIPN, 0639/21, vol. 1–3). The Security Service officers noted in their reports that 'ideologically, PAX pays great attention to propagating issues related to the German occupation of Poland and publishing books that glorify the actions of the pro-London underground independence movement', and that 'the PAX-related press welcomes former underground activists and reactionists who remain active after the war' (AIPN 0639/223/pdf, 1976, p. 178).

As a result, the officials postulated 'the PAX management should be forbidden from publishing in the press or in books any materials promoting and overstating the armed actions taken by rightist and reactionist political groups that operated both during the war and after the liberation of Poland' (AIPN 0639/223/pdf, 1976, p. 178).

The Security Service took a particularly keen interest in people who were connected in any way with the National Radical Camp, the underground National Armed Forces, the former Home Army conspirators, previous members of the Polish Peasant Party and delegates of the Government of the Republic of Poland in exile, as all those individuals were 'suspicious elements' according to the communist authorities (AIPN Kr 039/1, 1958, p. 144; cf. Reczek, 2008, p. 373). Analysis of available archival documentation allows us to conclude that the Security Service did not show an interest in those individuals due to their work for the PAX Publishing Institute, but more likely because of their former subversive activities.

As noted by Jan Engelgard, PAX 'had always been a haven for political outcasts and members of virtually all underground factions (operating during and after the war)' (Engelgard, 2015, p. 185).

As a result, the PAX Association was not an organisation that can be assessed unambiguously. Even though openly collaborating with the communist authorities, it still gave a helping hand to former Home Army soldiers, underground activists, and all those who could not find employment due to their anti-communist initiatives. Such people were given work for the Institute and the various PAX periodicals and enterprises.

Regardless of the opinion of the PAX Association, the Institute itself was assessed positively. In the 1979 questionnaire for Polish and foreign authors named *My First Book in the PAX Publishing Institute/Moja pierwsza książka w*

Instytucie Wydawniczym PAX, Maria Kuncewiczowa admitted that 'she highly values the whole Institute, which has had the courage to enrich the national market with many works of foreign, mainly Catholic, writers, who had been forgotten or virtually unknown in Poland'. Aleksander Rogalski claimed that 'when it comes to promoting knowledge of German Catholicism, no other publishing house seems to have done more for the matter than the Institute'.

Rev. Prof. Marian Michalski argued that 'the Institute's contribution to the realm of patristics [...] was immense, and not only because of the publications that directly covered the subject, but also owing to the entire department of religious studies, since it helped to understand the background of patristics' (Lichniak, 198, p. 167).

Even the fiercest adversaries of PAX never questioned the achievements and role of the Publishing Institute. In a critical article on the PAX Association in *La Monde*, the French author mentioned its 'grand publishing institute', which could 'certainly be credited with contributions to Catholicism' (Lichniak, 198, pp. 64–66).

Another example can be found in a text on religious literature in Poland written by a German journalist from *Hochland*, who formulated a series of accusations against PAX, and yet admitted that the Institute 'has done a lot of good for the dissemination of religious literature, and not only Polish' (Lichniak, 198, p. 66)·

Finally, there was a columnist of the London-based *Wiadomości* who stated that in PAX not everyone 'was a conscious servant to devilish powers', as 'evidenced by its excellent achievements in the realm of purely religious literature' (Lichniak, 198, p. 66).

This opinion was shared by Jacek Woźniakowski, who translated Graham Greene's *The Quiet American* for the Institute, but rejected the idea of its serialisation in *Kierunki*, as he evidently wished to avoid being suspected of supporting PAX's operations. Nevertheless, he did show his appreciation for its publishing achievements, writing in *Dziennik Polski*:

> For a harmful and foul entity, they have a surprisingly good publishing house (Woźniakowski, 1956).

Amelia Szafrańska rightly argues that 'the position of the Institute in social awareness does not exclusively depend on the number of titles and copies, although they do matter' (Książki Instytutu Wydawniczego PAX 1949–1989. Przewodnik, 1989, p. VI).

More important than the numbers are the role and importance of the published books. It would not be an exaggeration to claim that there is no prestigious library without at least one volume that has PAX's characteristic logo of the Gniezno Doors and the inscription *Gemma viritas Pax*. Similarly, there are probably no Catholics in Poland whose spiritual formation has not been impacted by the PAX books mentioned in this paper (Książki Instytutu Wydawniczego PAX 1949–1989. Przewodnik, 1989, p. VI).

Undoubtedly, PAX's concession for its publishing offer – consisting of religious literature, belles-lettres, and historical studies – was political involvement. The Institute obtained the authorities' consent to have a specific publishing profile, but it was by no means univocal with 'the courage to enrich the national market with many works' as argued by Kuncewiczowa.

Today, it is a formidable task to assess the operations and achievements of the PAX Publishing Institute. Although the organisation was certainly involved in politics, and texts by certain leaders and activists of the PAX Association fitted squarely into the imposed ideology, the Institute continued to publish works by authors that were not politically committed or even represented opposing opinions. The Institute can be said to have unfurled a peculiar 'protective umbrella' over writers, saving them from oblivion by publishing their works, many of which have had a great impact on modern literature.

References

AIPN Kr 039/1, Vol. 9, Sprawozdanie za II-gi kwartał dotyczące aktywu katolickiego, Krakow 12/06/1958.

AIPN, 00200/1158, Teczka personalna tajnego współpracownika "Wiesław": Zbigniew Czajkowski.

AIPN, 01228/2385/D, Materiały dotyczące Zygmunta Lichniaka.

AIPN, 01305/676, Bolesław Piasecki. Prezes Stowarzyszenia PAX (życie i działalność), ed. K. Piotrowski, Warsaw 1986, Wydział II Biura "C".

AIPN, 01521/2092/pdf, Janusz Huk, Stowarzyszenie PAX, praca magisterska, Warsaw 1984.

AIPN, 0248/14, Kwestionariusz ewidencyjny "Recenzent" dot. Zygmunta Lichniaka.

AIPN, 0639/21, Sprawa obiektowa krypt. "Alfa", Vol. 1–3.

AIPN, 0639/21, Vol. 1/pdf, Sprawozdanie Komisji Rewizyjnej na Walne Zgromadzenie Stowarzyszenia PAX 25 stycznia 1976 r.

AIPN, 0639/223/pdf, Organizacja i działalność Stowarzyszenia PAX w latach 1972–1976 –informacje, notatki, korespondencja.

Bankowicz B. (1996). *W labiryncie wieloświatopoglądowości. Stowarzyszenie PAX między marzeniem a rzeczywistością* [in:] B. Bankowicz, A. Dudek, *Ze studiów nad dziejami Kościoła i katolicyzmu w PRL*, Krakow.

Bernanos G. (1994). *Pod słońcem szatana*, Warsaw.

Bryll E. (1987). *Tak wierzyła*, "Kierunki", Issue No. 3 (18/01/1987).

Cenzura w PRL. (2017) *Analiza zjawiska*, eds. Z. Romek, K. Kamińska-Chełminiak, Warsaw.

Chamera-Nowak A. (2019). *Książka a stalinizm. Centralny Urząd Wydawnictw, Przemysłu Graficznego i Księgarstwa i jego rola w kształtowaniu ruchu wydawniczo-księgarskiego w Polsce 1951–1956*, Warsaw.

Dudek A. (1996). *Stowarzyszenie PAX w systemie politycznym Polski Ludowej w świetle dokumentów* [in:] B. Bankowicz, A. Dudek, *Ze studiów nad dziejami Kościoła i katolicyzmu w PRL*, Krakow.

Dudek A. (2013). *Program Stowarzyszenia PAX. Realizm, koniunkturalizm czy utopia?*, "Politeja" 2013, Issue No. 3 (25).

Dudek A., Gryz R. (2003). *Komuniści i Kościół w Polsce (1945–1989)*, Krakow.

Dudek A., Pytel G. (1990). *Bolesław Piasecki. Próba biografii politycznej*, London.

Engelgard J. (2015). *Bolesław Piasecki 1939–1956*, Warsaw.

Engelgard J. (2015). *Pożegnanie Józefa Wójcika*, "Myśl Polska", Issue No. 51–52, http://www.mysl-polska.pl/720 (accessed: 12/01/2021).

Gluck L. (1987). *Janina Kolendo. Próba portretu*, "Kierunki", Issue No. 3 (18/01/1987).

Gontarczyk P. (2006). *Zagadka agenta "Tatara"*, "Gazeta Polska", Issue No. 30.

Habielski R. (1999). *Życie społeczne i kulturalne emigracji*, Warsaw.

Hagmajer J. (1987) *Bezkompromisowa*, "Kierunki", Issue No. 3 (18/01/1987).

Jarosz D. (2010). *Dzieje książki w Polsce 1944–1989. Wybór źródeł*, Warsaw 2010.

Jarosz D. (2013/2014) *Władza a książka społeczno-polityczna w PRL 1956–1989*, "Z Badań nad Książką i Księgozbiorami Historycznymi", Vol. 7/8.

Jarosz D. (2015). *Sprawy książki polskiej i jej autorów w sowieckich dokumentach partyjnych z lat 1954–1971*, "Z Badań nad Książką i Księgozbiorami Historycznymi", Vol. 9.

Jarosz D. (2016). *Jak tworzono "książkę socjalistyczną"? Narady wydawców i księgarzy państw bloku wschodniego 1965–1988*, "Z Badań nad Książką i Księgozbiorami Historycznymi", Vol. 10.

Kaczorowski A.W. (2014). *Janusz Stefanowicz (1932–1998) – kariera dziennikarza PAX-u* [in:] *Nie tylko niezłomni i kolaboranci... Postawy dziennikarzy w kraju i na emigracji 1945–1989*, eds. T. Wolsza, P. Wójtowicz, Warszawa.

Kamińska-Chełminiak K. (2019). *Cenzura w Polsce 1944–1989*, Warsaw.

Katalog 1949–1979, (1980). Eds. A. Małaszewski, M. Piasecka, Warsaw.

Kolendo Janina pseud. Jasia Zofia Grzybowska, http://tei.nplp.pl/entity/556 (accessed: 11/01/2021).

Kolendo M. (1987). *Spotkanie po latach*, "Kierunki", Issue No. 3 (18/01/1987).

Komu służył PAX? Materiały z sympozjum "Od PAX-u do Civitas Christiana" zorganizowanego przez Katolickie Stowarzyszenie Civitas Christiana, 30–31 stycznia 2008 roku. (2008). Ed. S. Bober, preface Z. Zieliński, Warsaw.

Kristanova E. (2011). Książka na łamach krakowskiego "Tygodnika Powszechnego" (*1945–1953*) *w świetle reklamy wydawniczej* [in:]: *Краків – Львів: книги, часописи, бібліотеки XIX–XX ст.*, Vol. 10, ред. Г. Врона, О. Колосовська, Г. Косентка, Львів.

Kristanova E. (2013). *"Tygodnik Powszechny" (1945–1953)*. *W kręgu zagadnień prozy literackiej,* "Rocznik Historii Prasy Polskiej", Issue no. 2 (32).

Kristanova E. (2015) *Wybrane edycje książek św. Jana Pawła II w Polsce w latach 2005– 2014* [in:] *Na co dzień i od święta. Książka w życiu Polaków w XIX–XXI wieku,* eds. A. Chamera-Nowak, D. Jarosz, Warsaw.

Kristanova E. (2016a). On Literary Issues in Tygodnik Powszechny (1945–1953), Saarbrücken.

Kristanova E. (2016b). *W kręgu zagadnień literackich "Tygodnika Powszechnego" (1945–1953),* Warsaw.

Kristanova E. (2017a). *Biographies of Saint Pope John Paul II – Selected Book Editions in Poland between 2005–2014,* "World Scientific News", Vol. 72.

Kristanova E. (2017b) Przepuszczone przez cenzurę. Zagadnienia literackie w "Tygodniku Powszechnym" (1945–1953) jako wyraz starcia światopoglądowego środowiska katolików z obozem marksistowskim [in:] *Cenzura w PRL. Analiza zjawiska,* eds. Z. Romek, K. Kamińska-Chełminiak, Warsaw.

Książki Instytutu Wydawniczego PAX 1949–1989. Przewodnik, (1989). Ed. A. Szafrańska, Warsaw.

Księga o nagrodzie imienia Włodzimierza Pietrzaka z lat 1948–1972. (1978). Warsaw.

Kto jest kim w Polsce. Informator biograficzny. (1989). Warsaw.

Kunert A.K. (1987). *Słownik biograficzny konspiracji warszawskiej 1939–1944,* Warsaw.

Kuta C. (2009). *"Działacze" i "Pismaki". Aparat bezpieczeństwa wobec organizacji katolików świeckich w Krakowie w latach 1957–1989,* Krakow.

Lichniak Z. (1978). *Księga o nagrodzie im. Włodzimierza Pietrzaka,* Warsaw.

Lichniak Z. (1981). *Owocowanie książkami. Trzydzieści lat Instytutu Wydawniczego PAX,* Warsaw.

Lichniak Z. (1987). *Pamięć o Janinie Kolendo w dziesiątą rocznicę śmierci,* "Kierunki", Issue No. 3 (18/01/1987).

Łączkowski Z. (1987). *Jasia,* "Kierunki", Issue No. 3 (18/01/1987).

Majchrowski J. M. (1984). *Geneza politycznych ugrupowań katolickich. Stronnictwo Pracy, grupa "Dziś i Jutro",* Paris.

Micewski A. (1978). *Współrządzić czy nie kłamać? PAX i ZNAK w Polsce 1945–1976,* Paris.

Micewski A. (1989). *Wielki outsider katolicyzmu polskiego,* "Zdanie", Issue No. 4.

Na co dzień i od święta. Książka w życiu Polaków w XIX–XXI wieku. (2015). Eds. A. Chamera-Nowak, D. Jarosz, Warsaw.

Nauka o książce. Antologia tekstów. (2006). Eds. D. Kuźmina, M. Tobera, Warsaw.

Nowak J. (Zdzisław Jeziorański). (1989). *Wojna w eterze wspomnienia.* Vol. I: *1948–1956.* Wroclaw.

Piasecki B. (1954). *Zagadnienia istotne,* Warsaw.

Przetakiewicz Z (1994). *Od ONR-u do PAX-u,* Warsaw.

Reczek R. (2008). *Życie społeczno-polityczne w Wielkopolsce w latach 1956–1970,* Poznan.

Reiff R. (2006). *Archiwum Stowarzyszenia PAX. Publicystyka polityczna,* Vol. 1: *Refleksje z pogranicza historii, ideologii i polityki Stowarzyszenia PAX,* Warsaw.

Reiff R. (2007a). *Archiwum osobiste,* Warsaw.

Reiff R. (2007b). *Archiwum Stowarzyszenia PAX.* Vol. 2: *Polska i PAX na zakręcie dziejowym – Polska obroniła się, Stowarzyszenia PAX - nie,* Warsaw.

Rostworowski M. (1968). *Słowo o PAXie: 1945–1956,* Warsaw.

Stowarzyszenie PAX 1945–1985. (1985). *Informator,* Warsaw.

Straty wśród pisarzy polskich (literatów, publicystów, dziennikarzy i redaktorów) w czasie II wojny światowej i okupacji hitlerowskiej 1939–1945. (1980). Eds. M. Rutkowska, E. Serwański, Warsaw.

Szubowa A. (1987). *Jej życie było służbą,* "Kierunki", Issue No. 3 (18/01/1987).

Wernic A. (2002). *Jerzy Ślaski – żołnierz Polskiego Państwa Podziemnego,* "Przegląd Historyczno-Wojskowy", vol. 3 (54), Issue no. 2 (192).

Woźniakowski J. (1956). *W sprawie tłumaczenia,* "Dziennik Polski" 14/12/1956.

https://www.iwpax.pl/strona-o-nas-113.html (accessed: 07/03/2019).

https://bs.sejm.gov.pl/F?func=find-b&request=000004478&find_code=SYS&local_base=ARS10 (accessed: 12/01/2021).

CHAPTER 6

The Religious Broadcasts of Rev. Tadeusz Kirschke for Radio Free Europe's Broadcasting Service

Evelina Kristanova

6.1 Introduction[1]

From the moment RFE's Polish Broadcasting Service was established, Jan Nowak-Jeziorański "attached great importance" to religious broadcasts. In his memoirs on Rev. Tadeusz Kirschke, he recounted that:

> [...] he proved to be not only an outstanding preacher and editor of religious broadcasts, but also a skilled commentator who knew how to address the public without pathos. (Nowak-Jeziorański, 2006, p. 200)

In another text, Nowak-Jeziorański stated that "he was trusted" (Gawlikowski, 2015, pp. 313–314). He was known as a distinguished chaplain of the Polish Armed Forces in France and a Nazi camp prisoner, sentenced to death for his underground activity. Kirschke also served as editor-in-chief of the religious and cultural weekly *Życie / Life* (1947–1959), published by the Catholic Publishing Centre Veritas in London (Nowak-Jeziorański, 2014). The reverend was only employed by RFE thanks to the efforts of Nowak-Jeziorański – and not without resistance, as the process required official consent granted by Józef Gawlina, the bishop providing pastoral care to the Polish diaspora in exile (Bednarski, 2019). The head of RFE's Polish Broadcasting Service recalled the dispute as follows:

> On day one I chose this academic chaplain from London. [...] All priests in exile were under the jurisdiction of Bishop Józef Gawlina [...]

---

1 This paper was written as part of the research grant entitled *Dokumenty i materiały do dziejów Rozgłośni Polskiej Radia Wolna Europa, cz. II (kontynuacja) t. I–V plus 2/ Documents and Materials for the History of the Polish Broadcasting of Radio Free Europe, Part II (Continuation) Volumes I–V plus 2*, submitted for the competition: *Dziedzictwo narodowe/ National Heritage*, under the programme implemented by the Minister of Education and Science entitled Narodowy Program Rozwoju Humanistyki/National Programme for the Development of the Humanities (project registration number: 11H 20 0148 88; implementation period: 2022–2027; supervisor: Prof. Rafał Habielski, PhD).

I approached him with a request to nominate Rev. Kirschke as chaplain of our broadcasting station. The response was stark and negative. Gawlina had been a military bishop before and during the war, and on that account he was granted the rank of general. Indeed, I felt in his presence like a corporal to a general. He gave orders in a tone that defied all opposition. (Nowak-Jeziorański, 2006, p. 57)

During the meeting, the bishop put forward the candidature of Rev. Juliusz Janusz, whom Nowak-Jeziorański found quite unsuitable. Further correspondence and other candidatures presented by the head of RFE, including the well-known philosopher Rev. Józef Bocheński, did not lead to a consensus either. Eventually, Nowak-Jeziorański made it clear to the bishop that if he kept questioning Bocheński's application, he would entrust the religious broadcasts to a lay person, thus circumventing the obligation to obtain the bishop's approval. "The petty dispute between the secular and ecclesiastical authorities over this candidature did not come to an end until three months after the station was launched"; and later: "To save his credibility, the bishop proposed a compromise. I was to put forward two candidates and he was to make the final choice. Along with Rev. Kirschke, I listed Rev. Rafał Gogoliński, a silver-tongued preacher whom I had once brought into the BBC. I knew that Gogoliński would not accept the appointment because he could not leave London, and so I ended up with Rev. Kirschke, just as I had wished" (Nowak-Jeziorański, 2006, pp. 57–58).

Rev. Kirschke's officially performed his editorial duties at RFE between 1952 and 1975, but he remained a freelance associate until 1981 (Gawlikowski, 2015, p. 315). Kirschke was a commentator on a series of radio broadcasts entitled *Kosciół walczący / Church Militant* (1952–1956), which were later renamed *Wiara i życie / Faith and Life*, but were also known as *Audycje religijne/Religious Broadcasts* (1956–1981). And since Kirschke was also passionate about sport, he would occasionally sit in for absent sports journalists. Undoubtedly, during the period of the Church of Silence, he was the only clerical voice in Polish media.

6.2   Methodology

The selection of religious broadcasts for this paper is based on two criteria, the first being, quite obviously, programmes that focused on strictly spiritual issues and religious (not only Catholic) matters. These include productions reporting on events of the liturgical year, the deepening of faith, matters of the Church, the participation of the laity in religious life, and transmissions of the

Holy Mass and other services. In RFE, the term "religious broadcasts" was also applied to the aforementioned serial programmes *Kościół walczący* / *Church Militant* and *Wiara i życie* / *Faith and Life* presented by Rev. Kirschke. Addressing the issues of Church life in Poland, the countries of the Soviet Bloc and the world, they mainly reported on the relationships between the Church and state, and the strategy behind the Communist struggle against religion, exposing the lies and propaganda against the Church hierarchs (Gawlikowski, 2015, p. 817). Thus, the duality of the term in question stems from the dual nature of these radio broadcasts.

The purpose of this study is to analyse selected broadcasts of RFE's Polish Broadcasting Service prepared by Rev. Kirschke in 1952–1981, some of which are available online in the Radio Liberty service. The audio content is juxtaposed with press materials from the monthly *Na Antenie* / *On Air*, as well as other archival sources, memoirs and studies. The first chronological point of the study is the beginning of Kirschke's work for RFE, while the second is the year when his collaboration with the station ended, just before he left for London. Although he was formally employed until 1975, when he reached retirement age, he continued to edit broadcasts for RFE as a freelance contributor for several more years.

The analysis covers not only broadcasts in which Kirschke participated himself, but also those conducted by an informal team dedicated to religious matters, including Krystyna Miłotworska, Aleksandra Stypułkowska (alias Jadwiga Mieczkowska), Wiktor Trościanko, Włodzimierz Sznarbachowski, Czesław Straszewicz, Tadeusz Zawadzki, Eugeniusz Romiszewski, Tadeusz Nowakowski, and RFE correspondents in Rome: Kazimierz Komła, Karol Wagner and Marek Lehnert. The team employed a variety of radio genres: documentaries, discussions, featured broadcasts, chats, reportages, talks, news bulletins, radio plays, interviews, etc.

The radio broadcasts selected in this study were searched for using various criteria and keywords. The basis is the series of commentaries on events covered in such programmes as *Kościół walczący* / *Church Militant*, *Kościół i świat* / *The Church and the World*, *Refleksje adwentowe* / *Advent Reflections*, *Rekolekcje Wielkopostne* / *Lenten Retreats*, and *Nabożeństwa (Gorzkie żale)* / *Devotions (Bitter Lamentations)*. *Wiadomości kościelne* / *Church News*, prepared on the basis of services provided by the Polish Catholic Information Agency in New York, is also included. Audio materials were searched alphabetically by keyword, series and person's name. Keywords include "Kirschke Tadeusz", "religious broadcasts", "Church", "Millennium", "Wyszyński Stefan", "Piasecki Bolesław", "John Paul II".

Additionally, news on the most important events of the Church are incorporated: the arrests of Primate Stefan Wyszyński in 1953 (e.g., broadcasts by Józef

Światło on the fight against Catholicism) and of Bishop Czesław Kaczmarek, the proceedings of the Second Vatican Council (1962–1965), the radio reading of *Letter of Reconciliation of the Polish Bishops to the German Bishops: "We forgive and ask for forgiveness"* (anniversary broadcasts by Witold Pronobis), the jubilee celebration of the Millennium of the Polish State and Christianisation of Poland, and the election of Cardinal Karol Wojtyła as Pope John Paul II in 1978. Other audio materials include sermons, homilies, speeches by Primate Wyszyński, Popes Paul VI and John Paul II, Bishop Ignacy Tokarczuk, and Rev. Jerzy Popiełuszko's *Mass for the Motherland* (Czaczkowska, 2021), reports on the beatification and canonisation of St Maximilian Kolbe, in 1971 and 1982 respectively, broadcasts on Christian education and mysticism (visits to Padre Pio and Teresa Neumann), and reports on sanctuaries around the world (Lourdes, La Salette).

The issue of the Christian-Jewish dialogue is also presented, as are profiles of popes, priests, Catholic activists and other authority figures. Religious matters were widely discussed and played an important role in the agenda of RFE's Polish Broadcasting Service. This paper addresses only those topics that are related to religious life and the relationship between the Church and state, comprising a general overview of the most important matters and focusing on selected examples, as the subject will be further elaborated on in future publications.

The main methods employed to process the research material were media and press content analysis (Klepka, 2016, Lisowska-Magdziarz, 2004, Pisarek, 1983) and the method of literature analysis and criticism (Cisek, 2010).

6.3 Relationships between the Church and State. Primate Wyszyński in RFE

The religious broadcasts of Rev. Kirschke provided testimony to important events within the Church. On 28 September 1953, a historic programme was prepared on the arrest of Primate Stefan Wyszyński, where his words on "faith certified by martyrdom" were quoted (Kirschke, 1953). In 1954, the radio broadcast the testimonies of Colonel Józef Światło, who had fled to the West, thereby familiarising the audience with the circumstances of the Colonel's imprisonment. Earlier, the Episcopal memorandum of 8 May 1953 and the opposition of the Church hierarchs to the unlawful actions of the Communist government were also publicised. The main mission of RFE was to expose the Communists' efforts to subjugate the Church to the state. As Nowak-Jeziorański observed, the duties of his employees included:

reporting on repression, correcting untruths, advocating for priests accused in political trials, exposing the opponents' methods, communicating speeches from the Holy See, and above all, disseminating authentic documents issued by the Primate and the Episcopate. (Nowak-Jeziorański, 2006, p. 200)

Meanwhile, *The Policy Guidelines for Radio Free Europe Broadcasts to Poland* reads as follows:

It is imperative that RFE's broadcasts in Polish develop, in their listeners, a high degree of approval as an entirely responsible and reliable source of news, commentary and other information. Only when confidence in these broadcasts has become a fact, will it be possible for them, together with other available media, to exert a significant influence on Polish audiences. (Habielski, 2018, p. 270)

From the programme *Za kulisami bezpieki i partii* | *Behind the Scenes of the Security Service and the Party* listeners could learn details of the anti-church operations run by the Communists and the imprisonment of Primate Stefan Wyszyński in the Lidzbark monastery. As argued by Światło, the 10th Department of the Ministry of Public Security employed a variety of methods to suppress religion in Poland. It was this office that plotted the Primate's arrest, for which Bolesław Bierut had unsuccessfully petitioned to Joseph Stalin in Moscow. The dictator refused to grant his permission, and thus, Wyszyński was not interned until September, 1953, i.e., after Stalin's death. RFE reported that at the time of his arrest "his dignified and composed manner made a huge impression on the Security Service agents" (Pronobis, 1993). Two years earlier, Bishop Czesław Kaczmarek had been imprisoned in order to send a message and to intimidate the rebellious Primate. During Kaczmarek's show trial in 1953, the bishop was sentenced to 12 years in prison. As stated by Światło, Wyszyński was moved to various places of isolation so that people could not follow him and gather there to show their support. Only the highest dignitaries knew where he was kept. RFE's broadcasts also familiarised audiences with details of surveillance, wiretapping, interception of correspondence, and denunciations against the incarcerated Cardinal. According to a lieutenant-colonel who later fled to the West, after the Primate's detention, Security Service officers attended masses to listen to what the faithful said and to assess public sentiment (Kasprzak, 2004). When asked why the Primate had been arrested, Światło replied that it was due to his adamant stance as "he had become the spiritual and moral leader of the whole nation in Poland", which posed a real problem to the Communists (Pronobis, 1993). Światło concluded that the authorities had failed to achieve their political goal because the Primate was eventually considered a martyr.

RFE presented events on both sides of the Iron Curtain, and thus, on 4 October 1953, the audience could listen to a propaganda feuilleton by the Warsaw-based activist Wanda Odolska (Myśliński, 1990). The Communist-affiliated reporter argued in a confident tone that party members in Poland "provide religious protection for their citizens". This was allegedly evidenced in "constitution and practice" (Odolska, 1953), which Odolska strived to prove with the example of a young member of the Association of Polish Youth who was reprimanded by party functionaries when an older employee from a factory in Warsaw filed a complaint that he had offended her religious feelings. Odolska then assessed the state's relationships with the Church following the State-Church Agreement of 1950 (Kristanova, 2012, pp. 87–94; Żaryn, 2003). Listeners were informed that "for almost three years the government has demanded compliance with the provisions of the document", and was met with "abuse of his authority by Primate Wyszyński", "an anti-Polish rant delivered from the church pulpit", "fomenting hostility towards the state", "venomous agitation" and exerting "moral pressure" (Odolska, 1953). It was falsely claimed that it was for this reason that the Communist authorities had suspended Wyszyński, replacing him with Bishop Michał Klepacz. The RFE's editors aired the programme without commentary, thus maintaining detachment and objectivity, quite different to the agitational and propagandistic approach taken by the state-controlled media.

6.4 Campaign against "Progressive Catholics" and the PAX Association

During Rev. Kirschke's term of office, the station broadcast a series of 16 programmes about the PAX Association (Gehler, Kaiser, 2004), unmasking the true face of its privileged "leader", Bolesław Piasecki. RFE presented his political genealogy and the Nazi origins of the ONR-Falanga political organisation and its press organ, the weekly *Falanga / Phalange*. The listeners were also informed of Piasecki's totalitarian and anti-Jewish inclinations, the militias he organised, his attempts to dismantle the National Party / Stronnictwo Narodowe from within and his aspirations to take over the leadership of the entire youth front under the Camp of National Unity / Obóz Zjednoczenia Narodowego, as well as to seek co-operation with the Wehrmacht in 1939. Piasecki was portrayed as a "preacher of Polish fascism". For RFE, the disclosure of these ugly facts in Piasecki's political biography was its mission and duty (*Prawda o*

Pax-ie i Piaseckim / The Truth about PAX *and Piasecki,* 1968, pp. 6, 8; Kunicki, 2012).

The role of Bolesław Piasecki, Ivan Serov and Luna Brystygier as so-called "progressive Catholic" activists was discussed by Światło in his series *Za kulisami bezpieki i partii / Behind the Scenes of the Security Service and the Party*, where he presented the disgraceful past of the founder of the PAX Association. Światło explained that Piasecki had been personally supported by Bolesław Bierut when the latter said: "Two NKVD agents put on quite a show, shaking hands over the head of the persecuted Church" (*Za kulisami bezpieki i partii / Behind the Scenes of the Security Service and the Party*, 1955). Światło exposed the methods employed by Piasecki's group to penetrate Catholic circles. The reporter also inquired why the Gestapo and the Soviet counter-intelligence services would always release Piasecki after his arrests, revealing that the Germans freed him upon Benito Mussolini's intervention, while the Russians did so once he had betrayed his friends by divulging their names, and later in exchange for his declaration to establish the PAX Association. The broadcast also included many details indicating that it was General Serov who had recruited Piasecki as an agent and prepared him to execute the plans that involved undermining the Church's position, dividing and dismantling it from within, and eventually subordinating it to Soviet policy. The radio station also reported that Luna Brystygier decided on the funding for the publishing house of the PAX Association. Światło argued that the "leader of progressive Catholics" had proven extremely useful to the Communist authorities. During the liquidation of Caritas, he toned down opinions among the public, while later he took up "dirtier work" (*Za kulisami bezpieki i partii / Behind the Scenes of the Security Service and the Party*, 1955). By presenting the details of Piasecki's shameful past, the station familiarised listeners with the methods applied by the Communist regime to suppress the Church in the Polish People's Republic.

6.5 Proceedings of the Second Vatican Council

Covering the Second Vatican Council in 1962–1965 was one of the major tasks of RFE's Polish Broadcasting Station. The solemn inauguration with a Holy Mass in St Peter's Basilica in Rome was broadcast on 11 October 1962. The liturgy was celebrated by Cardinal Eugene Tisserant with the participation of Pope John XXIII. Commenting on the opening ceremony, Rev. Kirschke mainly confined himself to translating the readings and prayers (*Transmisja uroczystego otwarcia II Soboru Watykańskiego / Broadcast of the Opening Ceremony of the Second Vatican Council,* 1962). A considerable part of the 24-minute recording featured the singing of the choir. The broadcast also included the original papal address in Latin, culminating in a benediction (*Przemówienie papieża Jana XXIII / Address by Pope John XXIII*, 1962). In his brief summary of the event, Kirschke explained that John XXIII reviewed previous Councils in the history of the Church, stating that the Second Vatican Council was being held under more favourable social and political conditions than previous assemblies. The Pope remarked that previous Ecumenical Councils had often been exposed to pressures from authorities, and he outlined the purpose of this Council, which was to transmit and disseminate the deposit of faith through innovative formulas and in the new social situation. John XXIII also recalled the faults that the Church condemned, pointing out that now, deliberations were focused on making the faithful aware of Christian mercy since instruction was considered a more effective method than condemnation or compulsion. "The message of the Council" was to exhibit love, to show the source of divine graces, and to spread reconciliation and the principles of peace. The papal address ended with a traditional appeal to God.

6.6   Coverage of Millennium Celebrations in RFE

RFE's Polish Broadcasting Service extensively reported on the millennium celebrations of Poland's Christianisation of 966 (Wierzyński, 1966 p. 1) which were organised both in Poland and abroad. The broadcast included coverage of the two-day celebrations in Montreal – home to the second largest Polish diaspora (after Toronto) in Canada – namely, speeches given by the Archbishop of Montreal Cardinal Paul-Émile Léger, President of the Canadian Polish Diaspora Jerzy Korey-Krzeczowski, the Mayor of Montreal Jean Drapeau, and a sermon by Bishop Władysław Rubin. Paul-Émile Léger expressed his sympathy for Poland and Cardinal Wyszyński, whom he had met at the Second Vatican Council (*Millenium cz. 3, 1966; Relacja z pobytu w Montrealu, 1966; Tysiąclecie Chrztu Polski, 1966 / Millennium Part 3, 1966; Account of a Visit to Montreal, 1966; The Millennium of the Christianisation of Poland, 1966*). His voice was an expression of solidarity with the Catholic Church and the Polish nation. Léger appreciated the attitude and "adamant stance" of Primate Wyszyński (Nowak, 1966 p. 1), whom Léger perceived as "a symbol of independence and liberty" (*Relacja z pobytu w Montrealu / Account of a Visit to Montreal*, 1966). Jerzy Korey-Krzeczowski emphasised that – regardless of what the Communists claimed – the celebrations harmed nobody, contributing to the strengthening of faith and religious freedom. He stressed the Church's mission, which was to serve the well-being of the faithful and society as a whole. The celebrations united a variety of milieux: representatives of the religious and political scene, and the wartime émigrés from all walks of life, from blue-collar workers to engineers and professors. RFE commented that the event was an attempt to draw the attention of people in Canada to the situation of people in Poland, trapped behind the Iron Curtain.

RFE also broadcast an interview conducted by Edward Kosowicz with Archbishop Władysław Rubin – the delegate of the Primate of Poland during the celebrations in the USA and Canada. The audience learnt how friendly and hospitable the atmosphere of the celebrations was. There was a "keen interest" in the event, not only within the Polish diaspora, but also among Americans and Canadians (*Program specjalny. Rozmowa Edwarda Kosowicza / Special Programme. Interview by Edward Kosowicz*, 1966). Prepared with great panache and boasting an interesting programme, the celebrations were held in such American cities as Chicago, Buffalo, Philadelphia, New York and Boston. The Millennium became an opportunity to foster bonds between the Polish diaspora and the Church in Poland. Americans of Polish descent showed a noticeable understanding of the situation in Poland and expressed solidarity with Primate Wyszyński – "a supreme and spiritual authority figure", whose absence during the celebrations was greatly regretted (*Program specjalny. Rozmowa Edwarda Kosowicza / Special Programme. Interview by Edward Kosowicz*, 1966).

The millennial celebrations were also acknowledged, inter alia, by Archbishops Cousins, Castelli and Cody, and Cardinals Dopfner and King, who sent their official greetings (*Życzenia z okazji Tysiąclecia*, 1969; *Życzenie noworoczne*, 1966 / *Millennial Greetings*, 1969; *New Year's Greeting*, 1966). The coverage of the celebrations in RFE's Polish Broadcasting Station brought international recognition of Polish affairs and drew attention to Poland's difficult political situation behind the Iron Curtain.

6.7   RFE on Popes: The Pontificate of John Paul II

The radio commemorated the elections and lives of popes. An example was the posthumous memoir of John XXIII prepared by Rev. Kirschke in 1963, in which he exaggeratedly called him the "Polish Pope". Kirschke stressed that in his childhood the future pope would often hear of Poland and became acquainted with Polish literature, e.g., through the works of Henryk Sienkiewicz. In his memoirs, John XXIII often referred to his links with Poland. In 1912, he had the opportunity to visit Cardinal Adam Sapieha in Krakow, while in 1929, and he made a trip to Czestochowa, as the Apostolic Delegate to Bulgaria. The Pope was also interested in the history of Poland and the Polish struggle for independence (Kłakus, 2013). His warm regard for the Primate of Poland and Polish bishops was expressed through numerous and often prompt audiences (e.g., in 1957 and 1962), and during a number of meetings at the Second Vatican Council. John XXIII also took a keen interest in the issue of the Polish Western Territories (*Wspomnienie Jana XXIII / Remembrance of John XXIII*, 1963).

Wojciech Trojanowski and Stanisław Zadrożny assisted Rev. Kirschke in reporting on Pope Paul VI's coronation ceremony on 30 June 1963. During the emotional live coverage, listeners were informed about the high attendance of the faithful in St Peter's Square. They could hear the trumpets, the applause, and the singing of the Sistine Chapel choir, and learn about the details of the liturgical settings. Kirschke commented on the Mass while translating the texts of the prayers, litanies and the papal address. Attention was drawn to the Pope's brief statement about "Poland being always faithful" (*Uroczystości koronacyjne papieża Pawła VI 1963 cz. 1 / Coronation Celebrations of Pope Paul VI*, 1963 Part 1). In the second part of the programme, Trojanowski described the atmosphere during the coronation, stating that the moment when the papal tiara was put on provoked great excitement and applause in the crowd, and that the coronation was rich in symbolics. The three-hour ceremony was attended by processions of representatives of various professions (*Uroczystości koronacyjne papieża Pawła VI 1963 cz. 2 / Coronation Celebrations of Pope Paul VI*, 1963 Part 2). In a special edition of the programme, listeners could hear Paul VI's address to the pilgrims at the Marian Shrine in Piekary Śląskie, held in Latin and Polish, and edited and translated by Rev. Kirschke. The papal address was delivered in an elevated tone and closed with an apostolic benediction (*Przemówienie papieża Pawła VI / Address by Pope Paul VI*, 1964). The Pope also made a commemorative speech to the Polish nation on the occasion of the *Sacrum Poloniae Millennium* (*Przemówienie Papieża Pawła VI do narodu polskiego z okazji Millenium Chrztu Pańskiego / Address of Pope Paul VI to the Polish People on the Occasion of the Millennium of the Christianisation of Poland*, 1966).

RFE devoted special attention to Pope John Paul II (Weydenthal, 1979; *Na Antenie* 1978, no 186, p. 1; Stypułkowska, 1978 pp. 1–2). Besides excerpts from the live broadcast announcing the election of the Polish Cardinal to the Holy See (*Habemus Papam*, 1978; Ornatowski, 2009; Stefanowski, 1979), the official inauguration ceremony was also aired. RFE reported on the crowds of the faithful in St Peter's Square, including cardinals, international pilgrims and government representatives. In an emotional tone, Tadeusz Olsztynski listed pilgrims from Poznań, Kraków and Chicago among those gathered. To his surprise, there was a large number of young people in the audience. Listeners also learned about the publication of a special issue of *L'Osservatore Romano* dedicated to John Paul II. The reporter also jokingly remarked that Italians may be concerned that "this Pope will be too Polish". In general, however, Karol Wojty-la's "Slavic origins and individuality" were favourably commented on (*Reportaż z Watykanu / Vatican Report*, 1978; Hall, 2013). Listeners were informed about the course of the traditional homage paid by cardinals to the new pope. The greeting of Primate Wyszyński with Pope John Paul II was also noted as an unprecedented event in the history of the Church, since the former Metropolitan Bishop of Krakow knelt before the Head of the Polish Episcopate. The radio hosts emanated joy and affection while reporting the encounter. A detailed description of the procession during the ceremony was also provided, which was referred to as a "religious manifestation".

6.8   Conclusions

Not only must RFE's Polish Broadcasting Service be praised for the reliability of the news it provided, but also for unwavering perseverance in exposing the methods the Communists employed to suppress the Church in Poland, i.e., propaganda and disinformation in the national media. From broadcasts prepared, inter alia, by Józef Światło, listeners could learn about the covert political persecution of the Church. Considerable airtime was devoted to so-called "progressive Catholics" and the PAX Association, thereby revealing the truth about the attempts to insidiously dismantle the Church from within. However, it was a formidable challenge to convince public opinion in the West due to the completely different socio-political conditions there.

Primate Stefan Wyszyński was portrayed as an unbreakable authority and leader of the nation. At the same time, overt and systematic support for religious matters was also evident.

Objectivity and distance when reporting on current and "hot" political topics related to the relationship between the Church and state were also of considerable importance. RFE's religious programmes of 1952–1981 presented the most significant events with particular focus on Polish affairs, which thus gained wide international coverage.

References

Bednarski, D. (2019). Biskup Józef Gawlina jako opiekun Polaków na emigracji. Katowice.

Cisek, S. (2010). Metoda analizy i krytyki piśmiennictwa w nauce o informacji i bibliotekoznawstwie w XXI wieku. *Przegląd Biblioteczny*, vol. 78, no. 3, pp. 273–284.

Czaczkowska, E. K. (2021). Audycje Rozgłośni Polskiej Radia Wolna Europa o ks. Jerzym Popiełuszce od porwania do pogrzebu (19 x–3 xi 1984 roku) Polish Section of Radio Free Europe broadcasts about Father Jerzy Popiełuszko from his abduction to his funeral (19 October–3 November 1984), *Kultura, Media, Teologia* no. 46, pp. 96–115.

Gawlikowski, L. (2015). Pracownicy Radia Wolna Europa. Biografie zwykłe i niezwykłe. Warszawa.

Gehler, M., Kaiser, W. (2004), In Conflict with the Communist State: The Catholic Church and Catholic Political Organizations in Poland. In: *Christian Democracy in Europe Since 1945*. Routledge, pp. 110–127.

Habemus Papam (1978). Polskie Radio Online [28.03.2023].

Habielski, R. (2019). Audycje historyczne i kulturalne Rozgłośni Polskiej Radia Wolna Europa w latach 1952–1975 (dokumenty i materiały). Wrocław.

Habielski, R., Machcewicz, P. (2018). Rozgłośnia Polska Radia Wolna Europa w latach 1950–1975 (dokumenty i materiały). Wrocław.

Hall, D. (2013). Pope John Paul II, Radio Free Europe, and Faith Diplomacy. In: Seib, P. (eds) Religion and Public Diplomacy. Palgrave Macmillan Series in Global Public Diplomacy. Palgrave Macmillan, New York. https://doi.org/10.1057/9781137291127_3

Kasprzak, M., "Radio Free Europe and the Catholic Church in Poland During the 1950s and 1960s," *Canadian Slavonic Papers* 46.3 (2004): 321.

Kirschke, T. (1953). Aresztowanie prymasa Wyszyńskiego [https://player.polskieradio.pl /kolejka; 10.01.2023]. href="/68/2461/Audio/584413">Aresztowanie prymasa Wyszyńskiego - ks. Tadeusz Kirschke

Kirschke, T. (1954). [https://player.polskieradio.pl/kolejka; 10.01.2023]

Kirschke, T. (1963). Wspomnienie Jana XXIII [Polskie Radio Online; 22.03.2023]

Kirschke, T., Trojanowski W. (1963). Uroczystości koronacyjne papieża Pawła VI, part 1 [Polskie Radio Online 22.03.2023]

Kirschke, T., Trojanowski W., Sowiński K. (1962). Sprawozdanie z zamknięcia pierwszej sesji Soboru Watykańskiego II. [https://player.polskieradio.pl/kolejka ; 10.01.2023].

Klepka, R. (2016). Analiza zawartości mediów: dlaczego i do czego można ją wykorzystać w nauce o bezpieczeństwie i politologii?. *Annales Universitatis Paedagogicae Cracoviensis Studia de Securitate et Educatione Civili VI*, vol. 224, pp. 32–41.

Kłakus, M. (2013). Nuncjusz apostolski Angelo Roncalli wobec problemów polskiej emigracji we Francji po zakończeniu II wojny światowej. *Studia Polonijne*, no. 34, pp. 39–52.

Kristanova, E. (2012). Książka na łamach katolickich czasopism społeczno-kulturalnych w Polsce w latach 1945–1953. Łódź.

Kunicki, M. S. (2012). Between the Brown and the Red: Nationalism, Catholicism, and Communism in Twentieth-Century Poland—The Politics of Bolesław Piasecki. Ohio University Press.

Lisowska-Magdziarz, M. (2004). Analiza zawartości mediów. Przewodnik dla studentów. Kraków.

Machcewicz, P. (2007). „Monachijska menażeria". Walka z Radiem Wolna Europa 1950–1989, Warszawa.

Micewski, A. (1978). Współrządzić czy nie kłamać? Paryż.

Myśliński, J. (1990). Mikrofon i polityka. Z dziejów radiofonii polskiej 1944–1960. Warszawa.

Nowak, J. (1966), Strategia Prymasa, Na Antenie no. 34, p. 1.

Nowak, P. (2014). Katolicki tygodnik religijno-społeczny „Życie". Londyn 1947–1959. Monografia. Toruń.

Nowak-Jeziorański, J. (2000). Wojna w eterze. Kraków.

Nowak-Jeziorański, J., Winowska, M. (2016). Korespondencja 1955–1989. Wrocław.

Nuntio Vobis Gaudium Magnum. (1978) Na Antenie, no. 186, p. 1.

Odolska W. (1953). Felieton na temat wpływu władzy komunistycznej na życie religijne obywateli [Polskie Radio Online; 5.03.2023].

Ornatowski, C. M. , "Rhetoric of Pope John Paul II's Visits to Poland, 1979–1999", in: Joseph R. Blaney and Joseph P. Zompetti (eds.), The Rhetoric of Pope John Paul II (Lanham, MD: Rowman & Littlefield, 2009).

Pisarek W. (1983). Analiza zawartości prasy. Kraków.

Prawda o Pax-ie i Piaseckim. (1968). Londyn.

Pronobis W. (1993). Fragmenty wypowiedzi płk J. Światły. Programy Player Polskie Radio SA [5.03.2023].

Przemówienie papieża Jana XXIII. (1962) [https://player.polskieradio.pl/kolejka 19.03.2023]

Przemówienie Papieża Pawła VI do narodu polskiego z okazji Mellenium Chrztu Pańskiego. (1966). [Polskie Radio Online 25.03.2023].

Przemówienie papieża Pawła VI. (1964) [Polskie Radio Online 25.03.2023]. Puddington A., Rozgłośnie wolności. Tryumf Radia Wolna Europa i Radia Swoboda w zimnej wojnie. (2009). przeł. A. Borzym, Toruń.

Radia Wolności [https://www.polskieradio.pl/68, Radia-Wolnosci 16.11.2021)

Radio Wolna Europa w polityce polskiej i zachodniej. (2009). Ed. A. Borzym, J. Sadowski, Warszawa.

Reportaż z Watykanu. (1978). Polskie Radio Online [30.03.2023].

Stefanowski, R. (1979). "Appendix II: How the East European and Soviet Media Viewed the Papal Visit: Poland", in: The Pope in Poland (Radio Free Europe Research, 1979), p. 117.

Stypułkowska, A. (1978). "Habemus Papam" w Radio Warszawa, Na Antenie, no 185, pp. 1–2.

Transmisja uroczystego otwarcia II Soboru Watykańskiego. (1962). [https://player .polskieradio.pl/kolejka 19.03.2023].

Uroczystości koronacyjne papieża Pawła VI, part 2. (1963). [Polskie Radio Online 25.03.2023].

Uroczystości koronacyjne papieża Pawła VI, part 5. (1963). [Polskie Radio Online25.03.2023].

Uroczystości koronacyjne papieża Pawła VI, part 6. (1963). [Polskie Radio Online 25.03.2023].

Weydenthal, J. B., "The Pope at Auschwitz Hails the Cause and Dignity of Man", in: *The Pope in Poland* (Radio Free Europe Research, 1979), p. 55.

Wierzyński, K. (1966), 966–1966, *Na Antenie*, no. 34, p. 1.

Wspomnienia pracowników Rozgłośni Polskiej Radia Wolna Europa. (2002). Ed. A. Grabowska, Warszawa.

Za kulisami bezpieki i partii. (1955). Part 106 [Polskie Radio Online 13.03.2023].

Zamorski, Z. (1995). Pod anteną Radia Wolna Europa. Poznań.

Żaryn, J. (2003). Dzieje Kościoła katolickiego w Polsce (1989–1944). Warszawa.

CHAPTER 7

Mass Media under Censorial Surveillance: Politics in Press in the Polish People's Republic of the 1960s and 70s

Joanna Hobot-Marcinek

7.1   A Temptation to Censor – Why Plato Disliked Poets

Jacek Bierezin – a representative of the Polish New Wave (aka Generation 68) – in his poem entitled *Plato* wrote:

> I do not hold it against him that he wanted to banish me from the Republic.
> I know that he sacrificed me on the altar of the forces of life and light.
> I know that I was only a shadow, standing between him and the essence of things,
> which he tried to reach so as to gain certain knowledge.
> [...] His one-dimensional state, the brain-child of a ponderous imagination,
> was not the worst of tyrannies. Moreover, it existed only on parchment.
> The Plato of my time is not a philosopher[1].

The extract aptly defines the differences between the Platonian and Communist conception of power and censorship. The Platonian vision of censorship in the Republic remained – as the poet puts it – a philosophical utopia originating from noble motives and the search for the Highest Form of Good and Truth, whereas the implementation of the Marxist utopia led to the birth of a totalitarian authority in its Communist variant.

Bierezin referes to two firm statements *apopempein* ('send away') and *medame paradechesthai* ('to refuse to admit at all') (Platon, 1992, pp. 398a, 595a, 605b; Bartol, 2021, p. 17) uttered by Plato, who considered poets unworthy to stay in his *Kallipolis*. These are as shocking and perplexing today as they would have been to his contemporaneous audience. What makes the stance so striking, or even *pandemic* – as stated by Krystyna Bartol – stems from a number

---

1   The poem *Plato/Platon* was also published in the 1–4 issue of "Nowy Wyraz" in 1972. English translation by Andrzej Busza and Bogdan Czerniawski.

of assumptions the Greek philosopher made, the first of which is strictly connected with an extremely mimetic definition of poetry (Bartol, 2012, pp. 18–19), which he perceived as pseudoscience and pseudo truth (Kőning, 2010, p. 328).

However, Plato's approach to poetry is not his only contribution to the study conducted in this paper. Equally significant are his concepts of the effects and reception of art as a whole, since he entered the realm of political and social thought when he conceived them, expanding his criticism (...) of poets with aspects of their pernicious influence (Bartol, 2012, p. 20).

Plato formulated a thesis that poetic activity nourishes and waters those dispositions that should wither, and offers control over them to the inclinations that need control themselves (Platon, 1992, p. 235), which resulted in poetry and its reception being treated as a *sui generis* tool of social engineering. In that matter, an alternative to banishing poets was to censor literature, for which the philosopher designed specific solutions in his utopian vision of the state. Namely, he recommended poets be allowed to make their works public only after presenting them to judges and law enforcement authorities, and obtaining their approval (Platon,1960, p. 296).

However, it must be noted that in the Platonian approach, censorship is not a negative phenomenon, as it is to serve the purposes of the Highest Form of Truth and Good, and to protect these purposes against poets' delusive visions. Over time, the Platonian perception of censorship has been usurped by an univocally negative definition, one that identified it as a manipulation, aimed at limiting free speech and distorting the truth. What is more, the Platonian concept of the role of the censor as an overseer and guardian of the Highest Form of Good has been replaced with an image of the censor as a servant to authorities, who were often despotic or totalitarian.

The implementation of the Marxist utopia led to the birth of this type of totalitarian authority in its Communist variant. Censors were loyal servants to the Polish government, having been appointed by the Communist Party to control literary output and all information in the mass media. Their duty was to protect the communist raison d'état against 'any attempts to breach it' (Central Archives of Modern Records in Warsaw, MOCPP&PP, *National Conventions, 1966–1973*, File no. 959), and in accordance with the rule that 'the interests of the Polish People's Republic overrides any other motives behind the actions taken by any individual or group (Central Archives of Modern Records in Warsaw, MOCPP&PP, *National Conventions, 1966–1973*, File no. 959).

Therefore, a representative of the Main Office for the Control of the Press, Publications, and Public Performances (MOCPP&PP), working on behalf of a state that encompasses the 'fundamental interests of the whole nation and all workers', was obliged to have appropriate 'political biases'(Central Archives of Modern Records in Warsaw, MOCPP&PP, *Training principles and Schemes,*

1970, 1971, 1972, File no. 1098.) and represent a position that the state's raison d'état is the interests of all individuals separately, and the total interests of all groups, regions, circles, societies, and generations (Central Archives of Modern Records in Warsaw, MOCPP&PP, *National Conventions,* 1966–1973, File no. 959).

7.2   We Burnt Mendacious Newspapers

The background for the reflections on the press in the Polish Peoples' Republic and the complicated censor-editor-author-reader relationship is the socio-political situation in the late 1960s and early 1970s, a period when the first generation raised under the communist regime began to realise that 'disinformation media' (Central Archives of Modern Records in Warsaw, MOCPP&PP, *Evaluative and Analytical Works, VII 1972- II 1973,* File no. 1108)[2] create their own, alternative, version of reality to satisfy those in power. We smoked cigarettes and burned newspapers full of lies, We smoked cigarettes though they poisoned our bodies, We burned newspapers because they poisoned our minds (Krynicki, 1980, p. 81).

– wrote Ryszard Krynicki in the samizdat poem *And we really didn't know/I naprawdę nie wiedzieliśmy,* recalling this symbolic gesture of the 1968 Polish political crisis[3]

– burning those newspapers that distorted events.

The young – having discovered the true face of the untold, falsified world of the Polish People's Republic – channelled their anger, among other things, towards both the press, which was subordinated to the ideological criteria imposed by the communist authorities, and the rulers' loyal tool – the Main Office for the Control of the Press, Publications, and Public Performances. 'Generation 68', the first one raised in the Polish Peoples' Republic, could not imagine any alternative to leftism (Hobot, 2000, p. 333)[4]. Even though Generation 68 became aware of discrepancies between reality and the distorted vision depicted in the press, they knew little about the mechanisms behind censorship. Therefore, they had no conception that the censorial rules imposed on the

---

2   The metaphor comes from Ryszard Krynicki's poem *Flood/Powódź,* removed by censors from the collection *IX Kłodzka Wiosna Poetycka.* Cf. Central Archives of Modern Records in Warsaw, *Prace ocenowe i analityczne/Evaluative and Analytical Works, VII 1972- II 1973,* 1108.

3   The Polish 1968 political crisis was a series of major student, intellectual and other protests against the communist regime in March 1968.

4   Cf. a conversation with Adam Zagajewski, [in:] J. Hobot, *Gra z cenzurą w poezji Nowej Fali (1968–1976),* Krakow 2000, p. 333. In the conversation on the fascination with the myth of leftism among Generation '68, Adam Zagajewski states: 'We could not imagine there was anything else than leftism. We were raised in a cage'.

MOCPP&PP by the ruling party could, at the same time, be both detailed and vague, permanent and yet changeable.

It is only today that modern studies of the so-called censorial guidebooks and other documentation allow us to obtain complete information on the taboo topics or subjects that were to be temporarily removed from social consciousness. The manuals were updated at least annually, in line with the authorities' reaction to the current political situation, a stance which they tried to propagate in the greatest detail. For example, in reference to the August 1968 trials of those arrested during the protests in March, the editorial board of censorial guidebooks published their own reports on court proceedings, making sure the 'events, facts, and lists of witnesses' presented did not differ from the official version given by the Polish Press Agency (PPA). Predictably, also in 1968, special restrictions were imposed on those who wished to inform the public about political transformations, and, later, about the Warsaw Pact invasion of Czechoslovakia. As a result, censors would not permit any, even indirect, polemics from the Czechoslovakian press, or discussions on any topics covered on their radio and television (Hobot, 2000, p. 333).

All commentaries and articles related to the Czechoslovakian issue were to be consulted with the MOCPP&PP, and any reports on self-immolations occurring there could only be taken from the PPA. It was also 1968 when censors exerted great pressure on journalists, demanding 'a cool tone of accounts' (Central Archives of Modern Records in Warsaw, MOCPP&PP, *Schemes, Reports, and Accounts of Organisational Sections within Individual Units*, 1968, File no. 825) so that they would not resemble (linguistically and emotionally) warfront reports (Central Archives of Modern Records in Warsaw, MOCPP&PP, *Schemes, Reports, and Accounts of Organisational Sections within Individual Units*, 1968, File no. 825). The challenges related to monitoring journalists' attitudes were described in *Planach, sprawozdaniach, analizach komórek organizacyjnych własnej jednostki / Schemes, Reports, and Accounts of Organisational Sections within Individual Units*:

For us, the course of the Czechoslovakian crisis posed a serious challenge at work. It wasn't until July, or even August and September that hostile anti-socialist centres and manifestations made some journalists get over their infatuation with these semblances of democracy and to see anti-socialist messages behind 'socialist' slogans.

At times, however, [...] even after the Warsaw Pact military intervention in the Czechoslovak Socialist Republic, we were still forced to interfere in inappropriate political opinions, and above all, in occasional anti-Soviet incidents (Central Archives of Modern Records in Warsaw, MOCPP&PP *Schemes, Reports, and Accounts of Organisational Sections within Individual Units*, 1968, File no. 825).

Another meaningful example was 1971, when censors were instructed to mount close surveillance of press coverages and reactions to the demonstrations that broke out in coastal cities in December 1970, and in particular to redact any information on fatalities. The latter restriction was imposed until further notice, and yet never actually lifted.

When cataloguing censorial notes and guidelines, the researcher must bear in mind that not only did censors meticulously stipulate what and who should not appear in the mass media, but they were also obliged to precisely indicate what language ought to be used in reference to political events and social transformations. As a result, when the brand-new term 'democratisation of life' appeared in the press in 1971, it had to be replaced with such phrases as the 'development of socialist democracy', 'reinstitution of socialist democracy', and 'a complete implementation of principles governing socialist democracy', following the directives in censorial guidebooks. Although a substantial number of censorial records compiled between 1968 and 1971 refer to domestic matters, the censors never failed to concern themselves with an ideologically correct vision of foreign policy. Journalists were not allowed to mention business contacts and commercial relations with countries which were perceived negatively (Greece, Portugal) or very unfavourably (RSA, Rhodesia). Additionally, there was a permanent embargo on publications criticising policies of states with which Poland maintained bilateral ties.

In 1971, on the eve of the 1972 Summer Olympics in Munich, censors began to eradicate any phrases that could be 'discriminatory' towards the German Democratic Republic, e.g., 'German sportsmen', since the issue of relationships between East and West Germany was an extremely sensitive and important topic, especially before the Bundestag ratified the 1970 Treaty of Warsaw on borders on May 17, 1972.

As mentioned above, any significant shift in the internal or external political situation would result in modifications of the accepted language. For instance, the 1973 talks on the Korean Peninsula brought a noticeable change to how Seoul authorities were referred to. The list of previously used expressions – 'the puppet government of South Korea', 'the Seoul regime' – was expanded with more conciliatory terms, e.g., 'South Korean authorities'.

The censorial materials also contain numerous chapters on economic and development issues, including bans on reporting wastage, mismanagement, or misconceived and unaccomplished projects. Following these guidelines, journalists were forbidden to cover the story of the Lenin Mountain Shelter in Markowe Szczawiny near the massif of Babia Gora, whose construction was pompously initiated only to be later abandoned. It was a regular and systemic practice to block news on economic incapacities and resource shortages that made it impossible to complete the development investments which had been announced with much fanfare and initially commenced with great panache.

As a result, censors were obligated to withhold information on the Racławice Panorama and construction works of the exhibition pavilion in Wroclaw, which were delayed 'due to financial difficulties'.

There were also recommendations for certain news items to be confined to a locality. For instance, in 1971 only regional newspapers from the provinces of Szczecin, Koszalin, and Gdansk were allowed to report on the reductions in fish prices for seaside municipalities. The provision on restricted dissemination of information was to prevent news from spreading across the country. Another example was the January 1971 embargo imposed on national and local newspapers, forbidding them to reprint the story initially published in *Dziennik Bałtycki* on the 200 tonnes of rotten canned fish that had been purchased from Portugal.

What is more, in 1974 censors 'cared for' the nation's mental wellbeing by blocking information on exchange rates of national currencies within the COM-ECON when compared to the transferable ruble as the unit of finance. Journalists were expected to write about successes in the realm of civil engineering, and withhold any news on miners' socio-financial privileges (most likely to curb the frustrations of other occupational groups). Out of concern for Polish football fans, sports reporters were expected to refrain from critical comments if the national team were to lose, say to the Argentinians in the World Cup finals.

Besides political and economic matters, censorial guidebooks also focused on social issues. For instance, during the analysed period it was forbidden to publish any texts on the hippie movement in Poland that would show an approving, tolerant, or only slightly dismissive tone. Instead, authors were to print explicitly critical articles. At the same time, however, the guidelines revealed their double standards by recommending censors not ban publications that painted a positive picture of the hippie movement in other countries, especially in the West (Central Archives of Modern Records in Warsaw, MOCPP&PP, *Censorial Guidebook,* 1969–1970, File no. 845. *Censorial Guidebook* 1971, vol. I, File no. 1129. *Censorial Guidebook* , 1972, vol. II, File no. 1130. *Censorial Guidebook* , 1974, vol. I, File no. 1301), as the movement there rejected the accepted Western lifestyle.

Importantly, censors also took a keen interest in the surveillance of the youth press, with particular focus on titles for college and university students. Not only did the MOCPP&PP ensure articles followed censorial guidelines, but it also delved into subjects and topics covered by the periodicals. In the 1972 publication entitled *Prace ocenowe i analityczne/Evaluative and Analytical Works*, the authors emphasised the fact that the Krakow-based magazine *Student* published a series of articles called *Autoportret Pokolenia/Self-Portrait of the Generation*, which – as censors noted – constituted a certain, purposeful, entirety. The censor assigned to assess how dangerous the generational

manifesto was listed the elements common to all articles within the series, indicating the authors' critical attitude towards:
- the path taken by Polish socialism so far,
- the applied human resource policies and models of career progression, and
- those who shaped the face of the generation – educators, pedagogists, ideologists, and creators of the mass media (Central Archives of Modern Records in Warsaw, MOCPP&PP, *Evaluative and Analytical Works*, 1972, File no. 1101).

> The censorial guidelines and notes may appear somewhat chaotic to the reader, since records which the authorities and censors intended to use to shape the internal situation and foreign policies can be found alongside petty bans and regulations that relate exclusively to small, local communities. What is more, the copious documents, records and recommendations and their finicky nature make it nearly impossible to define and determine the rules behind their selection. (Hobot, 2000, p. 30)

The impression of chaos was also felt by censors themselves, who – overwhelmed by the countless guidelines – found them extremely difficult to absorb and remember. Another obstacle was the fact that while some records were preposterously detailed, others remained vague. It was that vagueness and the problems with the practical implementation of the guidelines that low-rank censors would most frequently complain about. At the same time, legislators and senior censors criticised their younger colleagues for their inability to react adequately to sudden problems. This reveals that censorial guidebooks appeared to be manuals that did not actually help censors react and intervene at a sufficient pace.

In view of the above, the communist system attributed editors (and editors-in-chief in particular) with a special role, striving to make them executors of the guidelines and recommendations issued by the MOCPP&PP, and active collaborators with the censors, who had to maintain a balance between allowing publication or needlessly interfering, which – according to their superiors – could pointlessly enrage different circles and societies. Thus, during a national convention held in 1967, the following recommendations were added to the censorial materials:
- the responsibility of editors-in-chief should be increased,
- a suggestion should be made to editorial boards to discuss political interferences during their meetings,
- periodic meetings with editors-in-chief should be held to process and proceed with censorial interventions (Central Archives of Modern Records in Warsaw, MOCPP&PP, *National Conventions* , 1966–1973, File no. 959).

All the recommendations were aimed at eradicating – as censors would euphe-mistically put it – blatant breaches of the principles of community life (Central Archives of Modern Records in Warsaw, 1966–1973, p. 959).

In the era of the Polish People's Republic, it was journalistic obedience to those 'principles of community life' that marked the advent of the grey area of compromise. Obviously, rather than discuss the issue of self-censorship, jour-nalists and other publishing professionals (e.g., writers, literary critics, etc.) are more eager today to speak of their 'game' with the censors, and the impact the censors had on the final shape of their periodicals and individual articles. They deny taking part in self-censorship, even if they reluctantly admit the phenomenon existed.

Similarly, former editors-in-chief are also more prone to mythologise their own stories about their games played against the censors. In the conversa-tion I had with Jan Pieszczachowicz, the former editor-in-chief of *Student*, he described his attempts to come to terms with censors, recalling that:

> There was this unwritten rule that a newly appointed editor-in-chief could have certain requests. I declared that I would take the job only on the condition that censors gave up on the massive interference they had previously exercised. It was when the decision was made (...) that the censorial office in Krakow would review typescripts prior to publication to avoid such drastic situations as after March 1968. (Hobot, 2000, p. 349)[5]

This poses a question to what extent we can trust such recollections today, since editors-in-chief – members of the communist party themselves – were often entangled in complex relationships with censorship, as is illustrated with the example of Tadeusz Leśniak, the head of the censorial office in Krakow, who had – for many years – held the position of the editor-in-chief of *Głos Młodzieży Wiejskiej*. Therefore, one could wonder if Leśniak, as a former editor-in-chief, showed 'some understanding' of the problems his fellow editors (as detailed by Pieszczachowicz) experienced. In the light of the knowledge we possess today, the following part of Pieszczachowicz's account may also raise suspicions:

> Following a tacit agreement, quietly acknowledged by the authorities, I would send Leśniak typescripts of articles to be submitted for publica-tion. These were texts that I believed could be a subject of controversy.

---

5   *A Talk with Jan Pieszczachowicz*, as cited in: J. Hobot, op. cit., p. 349. Talking about 'drastic situations' Jan Pieszczachowicz had in mind censors blocking publication of the whole issue, which under the press law of the time was tantamount to the newspaper's closure.

And then we would haggle over every single sentence he questioned. (Hobot, 2000, p. 333)

The extract shows distinctly that editors-in-chief were expected to select controversial passages, and thus facilitate the work of officials in the MOCPP&PP. Operating as middlemen between censors and authors, they (together with editors in publishing houses) would find themselves in quite schizophrenic circumstances. One day, they acted as proponents of authors, and on another, they would have to coax authors into being more accepting for the good of the newspaper, arguing that sometimes one must 'lose an eye to save the head' (Central Archives of Modern Records in Warsaw, MOCPP&PP, *Evaluations and analyses made on commission*, 1974, Vol. II, vol. II, File no. 1094)[6], i.e., it was advisable to remove an extract or two, use a euphemism, and not refer directly and openly to the shortcomings and drawbacks of the communist system.

All encounters with censors – even those taking place in a seemingly friendly atmosphere – implied a hidden peril that was aptly defined by Adam Zagajewski, and which – quoting the words of Hannah Arendt – can be described as experiencing the banality of evil. Adam Zagajewski discussed this peril in his poem *A Short Song on Censorship/Mała piosenka o cenzurze*. While in a conversation with me he accounted:

I visited a censorial office once only, having had medieval expectations of it being the toughest prison (which I expressed in the poem). And yet, it was just another banal office, where someone was just brewing coffee (Hobot, 2000, p. 331)[7].

This banality (if not friendliness) between the censor and the editor-in-chief made it all so ordinary, thereby de-heroizing any possible resistance, and sadly facilitating entry into the grey area of compromise, making the editor-censor relationship morally ambiguous.

7.3   A Post-Mortem of the Life of Censorship and the Challenges of the Modern Day

Numerous researchers of social issues and media dispute the perception of Plato which I quoted above as an opponent of democracy (Philosophy of

---

6 The choice that Adam Mickiewicz faced while struggling with tsarists censors. In a letter to Jan Czeczot, he accounted how they mutilated his work: 'I let them throw [this extract – M.W] away, just like you let them poke your eye out to save your head'. Parts of Mickiewicz's letter quoted after M. Wańkowicz's sketch *U progu teraźniejszości*, which was reported for censoring by the weekly *Literatura*. Cf. *Evaluations and analyses made on commission/Oceny i analizy dokonane na zlecenie*, 1974, Vol. II, 1094.

7 *A Talk with Adam Zagajewski*, as cited in: J. Hobot, op. cit., p. 331.

Education, 1966, p. 72). The same attitude is adopted by the authors of the encyclopaedia entitled *Philosophy of Education* (1966), who eagerly juxtapose the Platonian way of thinking about censorship with the approach applied by John Stuart Mill, who primarily accentuated its sinister dimension. The English philosopher and the creator of liberal democracy counterposed censorship against the concept of the marketplace of ideas that he used to visually explain and justify the principle of free speech and press, which – in a democratic society – allow for unrestrained discussions, collisions of adverse opinions, the discovery of truth and the best solutions to social problems. However, the Millean metaphor of the marketplace of ideas, with time, also drew criticism. It was argued that a collision of adverse opinions may not, in fact, lead to the discovery of an objective truth, if such exists in the first place, but it may turn into a peculiar consensus that nominates things as true or false (Philosophy of Education, 1966, p. 72).

The Platonian concept of censoring poetry, which raises such great concern today, and the Millean metaphor of the marketplace of ideas, widely questioned by many modern scholars, place the thoughts of these two philosophers in the very heart of the 20th and 21st century disputes related to the ideologization of disputations. These include the areas of mass media, accounts of public discourse and politics, the symbolic organisation of space, shaping attitudes, and education.

The subordination of media discourse in the fight for ideological domination by politicians and bodies, and making this discourse a subject to social consensus remain an irresistible temptation today, when we seem to have prematurely proclaimed the death of all ideology. Alas, ideology – when perceived not as a historical phenomenon, limited in time and related exclusively to totalitarian systems – is still doing quite well and sometimes takes the form of an intellectual orthodoxy that aims to discipline those debaters involved in disputes on particularly controversial social issues (Świrek, 2013).

The effects of this intellectual orthodoxy 'taught a tough lesson' to Hannah Arendt, the author of *The Origins of Totalitarianism*, when she published her account of Adolf Eichmann's trial. Her collision with political correctness was a truly agonising one, triggering public odium upon her and resulting in the loss of quite a few precious friendships. Scientific circles reacted somewhat hysterically to her disquisitions on the banality of evil and the victim's co-responsibility for the crimes (Sosnowska, 2012, p. 158). An army of experts were hired to prove her book erroneous, claiming it was written in a language that did not follow the discourse imposed by the American and Zionist establishment. Referring to her experience of being 'disciplined' by a number of renowned scholars, Arendt wrote to Karl Jaspers: It is quite instructive to see what can be achieved when opinions are manipulated, and how many people, often high-brow intellectuals, succumb to manipulation (Sosnowska, 2012, p. 158)[8].

The experience of the author behind *Eichmann in Jerusalem: A Report on the Banality of Evil* must make us ponder over the temptation – still present in our public life – to use social engineering based on ideologies that, though not necessarily expressed by political doctrines, are still reflected in certain forms of media or scientific discourse and owing to which 'we are expected to become better and happier, not worse and less happy (Platon, 1992, p. 235).

Today, the temptation by a variety of groups to subordinate media discourse does not, however, display the institutionalised nature of the Communist censorship. The latter was convinced that the press should be a loyal and humble servant of the regime, and a monitor sensitive to the needs of the socialist state. That was the attitude adopted by the officials in the Main Office for the Control of the Press, Publications, and Public Performance when they sat to read press articles. On the other hand, those authors who endeavoured to present a truthful account of life and the political situation in the 1960s and 1970s were condemned to walk the tightrope of a morally ambiguous compromise due to both the omnipotence and omnipresence of censorship.

References

Archiwum Akt Nowych w Warszawie (Central Archives of Modern Records in Warsaw)

Książka zapisów cenzorskich/Censorial Guidebook, 1968, File no. 844.
Książka zapisów cenzorskich/Censorial Guidebook, 1969–1970, File no. 845.
Książka zapisów cenzorskich/Censorial Guidebook, 1971, Vol. I, File no. 1129.
Książka zapisów cenzorskich/Censorial Guidebook, 1972, Vol. II, File no. 1130.
Książka zapisów cenzorskich/Censorial Guidebook, 1974, Vol. I, File no. 1301.
Oceny i analizy dokonane na zlecenie/Evaluations and analyses made on commission, 1974, Vol. II, File no. 1094.
Plany, sprawozdania, analizy komórek organizacyjnych własnej jednostki/Schemes, Reports, and Accounts of Organisational Sections within Individual Units, 1968, File no. 825.

---

8 Arendt to Jaspers, 20 June 1963, [in:] *H. Arendt, K. Jaspers*, Briefwechsel 1926–1969, eds. L. Kőhler, H. Saner, München- Zürich 2001, p. 547, as cited in P. Sosnowska, op. cit., p. 158. Interestingly, Hannah Arendt's book on 'the banality of evil' was published as late as in 2000, five years after the Hebrew edition of Adolf Hitler's *Mein Kampf*. Cf. E. Brocke, *"Duża Hannah" – moja ciotka*, trans. E. Rzanna. "Kronos", Issue No. 4, 2013, p. 291. Cf. P. Nowak, Republikanka. Komentarz do republikańskich pism Hannah Arendt, *Kronos* , Issue No. 3, 2017, pp. 193–202.

Prace ocenowe i analityczne/Evaluative and Analytical Works, 1972, File no. 1101.

Prace ocenowe i analityczne/Evaluative and Analytical Works, VII 1972- II 1973, File no. 1108.

Narady krajowe/National Conventions, 1966–1973, File no. 959.

*Zasady i programy szkolenia/Training principles and Schemes,*1970, 1971, 1972, File no. 1098.

Literature

Bartol, K. (2012). *Wypędzić poezję, wygnać poetów. Współczesne interpretacje Platoń-skiego postulatu, Poznańskie Studia Polonistyczne*, Issue No. 19.

Brocke, E. (2013). *"Duża Hannah" – moja ciotka*, trans. E. Rzanna. *Kronos*, Issue No. 4.

Hobot, J. (2000). *Gra z cenzurą w poezji Nowej Fali (1968–1976)*. Krakow.

Kőning, H. H. (2010). *Hesiod: The Other Poet. Ancient Reception of Cultural Icon*. Leiden.

Krynicki, R. (1980). *Nasze życie rośnie*. Krakow.

Nowak, P. (2017). Republikanka. Komentarz do republikańskich pism Hannah Arendt, *Kronos*, Issue No. 3.

Philosophy of Education: An Encyclopedia. (1966). Ed. J.J. Chambliss, New York.

Platon. Państwo. (1992). Trans. W. Witwicki, Vol. 2. Warsaw.

Platon. Prawa. (1960). Trans. M. Maykowska. Warsaw.

Sosnowska, P. (2012). Poprawność polityczna i myślenie o polityce. Przypadek Hannah Arendt, *Kultura i Edukacja*, Issue No. 2 (88).

Świrek, K. *Trzy końce ideologii - najważniejsze dwudziestowieczne ujęcia problemu* [online], https://presto.amu.edu.pl>1654-Tekstartykułu-2969-1-10-20150711.pdf [accessed on: 29/12/2020].

CHAPTER 8

The Book Policy of the Cultural Department of the Central Committee of the Polish United Workers' Party

The Final Years of the Polish People's Republic

Dariusz Jarosz

8.1   Introduction

There is nothing revelatory in the assertion that the exercise of control over the written word was a constitutive feature of the PRL as a so-called socialist realist state. This systemic principle was overseen and enforced by the censor's office, but its practical implementation was also devolved onto lower-rung Party authorities, editors of publications big and small, and not least onto journalists and writers themselves by way of self-censorship. This control was exercised with varying degrees of intensity in the years 1945–1989, depending on the deemed capacity of given political desiderata for sustainable or credible propagation. Certain areas of knowledge, like Soviet war crimes, remained taboo topics to the very end of the PRL.

But, fascinating as an exhaustive study of the PRL's changing scope of censorship and propaganda may be, this article is no more than a toe-in-the-water to ascertain the value of one primary source of information on a topic that represents a fragment of a much greater whole. As such, an attempt is made to reconstruct Party opinions on the situation of the world of books in its various aspects in the period 1985–1989. In the process, the aim is to establish to what extent the Party elites in the PRL's years of decline were enmeshed in their thinking by the ideological-political systemic framework and what was their diagnosis of the situation in regard of book publishing, printing, and dissemination through booksellers and lending libraries.

The basic method employed in this research was a critical analysis of written sources - in this case archival material hitherto almost unknown to historians. It was preceded by a reading of published academic studies of the late 1980s that dealt with the issues addressed in the book. This made it possible not only to reconstruct the communist authorities' discourse on the subject, but also to understand the relevant political, social and economic conditions of the decisions and actions taken.

The source base of this research were mainly the records of the Cultural Department of the Central Committee of the Polish United Workers' Party, particularly the Party Team for Publishing Policy and Book Dissemination (PZP-WUK), set up in 1985 (AAN, LVI-248; AAN, KC PZPR, LVI-1247)[1] and the National Team of Party Librarians and Booksellers (ZPBiK) attached to the Central Committee's Cultural Department which had its inaugural sitting on 24 March 1987 (AAN, KC PZPR, LVI-209, AAN, KC PZPR, LVI-1497). The subject of this inquiry was not just limited to the documents produced by these two teams[2]; materials, for the most part those produced in the Ministry of Culture and Art, which reached the members of these teams, and were the subject of discussion and written opinions, have also come under scrutiny in this analysis.

The article is also based on an analysis of the published secondary sources. They are scarce and concern mainly the broader political context of writing, publishing and distributing books in Poland in the years 1945–1989. So far, they have not dealt with the issue of activities and discussions in the forum of the Cultural Department of the Central Committee of the Polish United Workers' Party (PZPR) in the declining period of the communist system. The subject of censorship of books and breaching its restrictions by the so-called second publishing circuit has been addressed relatively often (Sowiński, 2011; Błażejowska, 2010; Olaszek, 2015). Issues of Moscow's influence on Polish publishing policy have also been of interest to researchers (Jarosz, 2016, pp. 317–334; Jarosz, 2015,

---

1 The surviving documents held in the Modern Record Archives (AAN) reveal that the team met for the first time on 7 May 1985, bringing together over thirty people – representing both the publishing, bookselling, printing and library segments and he literary community which, moreover, had its own party team. Its members included: S. Bębenek (President of the Publishing Cooperative Czytelnik and the Chairman of the Supreme Board of the Polish Society of Book Publishers), Stanisław Czajka (Director of the National Library), Tadeusz Husak (President of the Polish Booksellers' Association), Andrzej Kurz (Director of Wydawnictwo Literackie), Rafał Łąkowski (Director and editor-in-chief of Państwowe Wydawnictwo Naukowe), Eugeniusz Piliszek (Director and editor-in-chief of the publishing house Wydawnictwo Arkady and the Team's chairman), Andrzej Wasilewski (Director and editor-in-chief of the state publishing institute PIW). The chairman, Piliszek, formulated two basic aims of activities at the Team's inaugural meeting: continuous substantive- professional advisory and synchronised synthetic comments, opinions and resolutions flowing from all milieus, concerning programming, producing disseminating books and their readerships.
2 Both bodies were set up in continuation of advisory teams called into being earlier. Information and documents produced by the Team for Book Affairs can already be found in the Cultural Department's files held by the AAN relating to the beginning of the 1980s and the Party Team of Librarians as from 1982.

273–284). Studies on the political management of book affairs during the Stalinist period (1948–1955) have also been published (Chamera - Nowak, 2019; Jarosz, 2011, pp. 43–60; Kondek, 1999).

8.2 Publishing and Publications

The problems with book publishing, distribution and the encouragement of readership growth, were repeatedly raised, as can be seen in numerous documents kept in the records of the various Party bodies duly charged with those concerns over the course of time. In June 1985, the PZPWUK presented its "assessment of the situation in the book publication and dissemination movement" for the early 1980s, to 1985. In the introduction to this document it was asserted that "above all, the Party puts ideological-political, cognitive, educational, cultural and modernisational aims before the publication movement".

It was recalled that in a resolution adopted by the IX Extraordinary Party Congress, the book production rate was to grow to eight books per inhabitant by 1990. The rate of 6.2 books per capita, constituting a cumulative print run of 229.7 million books, was already achieved by 1984. The increase in priority publications, that is, school textbooks, set books, children's and youth literature, dictionaries and encyclopaedias, was also noted (AAN, KC PZPR, LVI-248).

The authors of this assessment pointed to negative phenomena. They included in this, above all, the lack of a central, long-term system of assessment of publication programmes and corresponding principles of paper supply quotas. There was a drop in the volume of published titles from 12 000 in 1980 to 9 000 in 1984, which was particularly painful in the case of academic and technical literature "where one can actually speak of an acute crisis". The book publishing cycle grew longer, coming to about three years (in some branches of literature even up to six year) on average in the period under consideration. Moreover, an increase in the share of brochures (booklets of under 49 pages) from about 20% in 1980 to 32% in 1984, was primarily due to the lack of bookbinding machines and materials. Further deterioration in the durability of publications due to the poor quality of raw materials and printing facilities, was also noted. To remedy this situation, the need was postulated, on the one hand, to call into being a Publications Movement Programme Council, and on the other hand, to increase outlays on the development of printing facilities (AAN, KC PZPR, LVI-248). But, as always, it was easier to diagnose the problem than to implement its recommended cure.

The opinion expressed on the topic in a document produced by this team in December 1986 makes it quite evident how the basic problems in publishing were seen by the PZPWUK. It was asserted in this document that the centre steering the publishing movement had an array of economic and legal-administrative instruments at its disposal, to implement publishing policy "in the new conditions" set out by the so-called phased economic reform plan. In practice, however, the Ministry of Culture and Arts (MKiS) did not fully have these instruments at its disposal. It had no influence on tax policy, it was not the managing authority of the entire stock of paper dedicated to publishing purposes, and it had no direct and effective influence on the promotion of Polish books abroad.

According to this opinion, the Cultural Department had no way of competently assessing the work of publishers, not least because the aims of publishing policy were not elaborated. The resources dedicated to its implementation and the criteria for evaluating publications, printers and libraries, were not specified. Thus, it was concluded, that it was essential to verify from this angle the ministerial assumptions of state publication policy for the years 1986–1990.

The authors of this assessment appealed for at least some rough specification of the resources, notably the limited paper quotas, available for the years 1988–1990. It was not regarded as possible to analyse publishing plans for 1987 due to the degree of their partial early fulfilment (some books envisaged for publication in that year had already appeared or were being printed). Moreover, the document revealed that the growth rate of book prices had already outstripped growth rates in national average wages in 1985. Thus it was essential to bring this negative trend to a halt, fuelled as it was not only by the rising prices of paper, printing services and bookseller mark-ups, but also by income tax which increased from 30 to 60% in 1982–1986. The authors of this opinion thus deemed it essential to reduce taxes` on publications to at least 40 if not 30 percent. Finally, it was asserted that part of the publication production was not in tune with readers' demand, not least Polish contemporary literature, in this particularly popular (factual and fiction) youth literature (AAN, KC PZPR, LVI-249).

Party decision-makers were aware that numerous well-founded postulates as they thought, of earlier years, had not been implemented. No Publishing Movement Programme Council had been set up, no computerised data collection and processing centre on books and analytical-research back-up for the needs of publishing policy and practice, had been organised (AAN, KC PZPR, LVI-249).

8.3   Printing Facilities

The need to modernise printing facilities was postulated in Party documents (AAN, KC PZPR, LVI-249). In a note of information of 4 November 1986 on the current state of implementation of the printing sector's modernisation and development programme for 1986–1990 produced by the MKiS (it was adopted by the Presidium of the Government by resolution of 29 October 1985) (AAN, KC PZPR, LVI-247)[3], more than anything, the non-execution of the postulated volume of supplies of imported printing installations from the GDR in 1986 was highlighted. Plans for further supplies, in this from capitalist countries, were curtailed by the lack of hard currency. Apart from that, import from the GDR and Czechoslovakia, which was easier from the financial point of view, was insufficient, among others due to assortment difficulties. In this situation, attempts were made to develop home production of spares (among others, aluminium printing plates) but that was only possible to a limited degree. The shortage of bookbinding cardboard and fabric remained an unsolved and problematic issue (AAN, KC PZPR, LVI-249).

To supplement the lack of financial resources, the MKiS drafted a Printing Development Fund Act which was to remedy the shortfalls in this area (AAN, KC PZPR, LVI-249).

8.4   Libraries

The quoted PZPWUK opinion on the MKiS study of the book sector's current situation, had already recognised the necessity of accelerating the reconstruction and development of the library network, and the implementation of resolutions of the Party Librarians' Team contained in the document "Status and Directions of Librarianship Development in Poland", published in "Bibliotekarz" (*Librarian*, 1985, Issue no. 2). There was a shortage of basic book selections in libraries of lower rank, and new literature reached them with up to two year time lags (AAN, MKiSLVI-249).

---

3   This document envisaged appropriate activities of various ministries which were to improve and bring about the development of this industry and by the same token increase supplies of paper. Printing was to receive more money to purchase printing machines. It was stressed that this industry's fixed assets were subject to rapid depreciation. In line with the adopted investment programme of the cellulose-paper industry, outlays were to increase considerably.

The ZPBiK looked into this problem area in far greater detail. The most important document that grouping produced, was the position of the Cultural Department's All-Poland Team of Party Librarians and Book-sellers in regard of further dissemination of books and development of libraries with particular regard to rural communities, adopted on 3 May 1988. In it, the ZPBiK discussed the problems raised in the materials produced by the Team's Presidium on the implementation of recommendations regarding book dissemination, and the problems raised in the study "The status of libraries and readership in rural communities".

The ZPBiK asserted that the growing disproportion of library readership figures in the country's diverse regions had been reduced. Analyses revealed that in nineteen voivodships (provinces) readership figures had shrunk, but significant growth in these figures had been registered in nineteen others.

This Team considered it essential to undertake determined steps to integrate library activities to achieve greater work effects and economies of scale in utilising library material and human resources. It was essential to give real effect to the central library hub's organisational and substantive activities in selecting new publications for public, company/works' and school libraries, and in selections of collections. The National Library (BN) was to devolve part of its rights to voivodship-level libraries, in this chiefly to public-academic ones. Support was expressed for the initiative of calling into being library companies in partnership with the BN, which was to take care of computerisation of Polish library stock. The reactivation and expansion of the library and bookshop outlet network and the encouragement of growth of readership in workplaces was postulated.

One of the basic problems of Polish librarianship was recognised to be that of raising the status of books and libraries in rural communities and increasing their readership figures.

The drop in the scope of readership in the countryside in over thirty provinces in the latter years and the drop in sales, is to be treated as a most alarming phenomenon.

Against the background of other cultural outlets in the countryside, libraries were to evince the greatest degree of stabilisation. However, in most provinces, activities were restricted to the quantitative development of networks and, all too often, providing only the most modest of accommodation facilities. On the model of certain regions, it was recommended to concentrate in the immediate coming years on building up a rural library base by dedicating increased resources of the cultural development fund, local governments and cooperatives, to this aim.

Modernised libraries utilising in broader scope professional agrarian literature, periodicals and other library collections equipped with modern technical resources, among others videos, are to constitute basic networks of outlets serving cultural and civilizational rural development. The sale of books in the countryside remained a problem to be solved.

In speaking out in favour of expanding the cultural functions of libraries in rural communities, the ZPBiK argued that this should manifest itself in gathering special collections, in this audio-visual materials as well, which would allow expanding the offer of library services for readers. So-organised libraries were to be the natural places for foreign language tuition and Polish language cultivation.

Restricting the activities of libraries solely to lending books does not pass the test of time. Such a model of the library will not pass muster with the communities of today.

It was argued that booksellers and librarians constitute the most numerous, the most stabilised and relatively well prepared professional groups of workers for spreading culture.

For years, however, low pay causes excessive staff fluctuations with harm to all types of outlets.

A negative phenomenon of departure from the profession of people with good professional and general preparation was observed in connection with this. In numerous places where there was "big pay competitiveness", libraries had to close down due to staff shortages. Thus, the need was postulated to undertake activities to improve the material conditions of that profession.

ZPBiK spoke both in favour of adapting book production to mass readership needs, especially as intended for libraries, and of the utmost urgency to create an electronic information system on books (AAN, KC PZPR, LVI-209; AAN, KC PZPR, LVI-1497). Moreover, governmental decisions on distribution commissions and tax reductions on books were welcomed by Party librarians and booksellers.

8.5   Bookselling

As stems from documents analysed earlier, discussions on book production and dissemination policy in this period did not dodge the problems arising from the economic reforms that were being introduced. The Cultural Department assumed a position in the matter in November 1986 (AAN, KC PZPR,

LVI-208) mindful of the fact that in light of a Xth PZPR Congress resolution, one of the basic tasks in the cultural sphere was to ensure universal access to books. Changes on the bookselling market in 1986 indicated that the further development of readership can "no longer be the simple continuation of the activities to date. All milieus serving to popularise readership in our society (publishers, booksellers, librarians, printers), have the duty to identify new phenomena occurring in the world of books, analyse and evaluate them, and formulate practical ways of giving effect to the resolution of the Xth PZPR Congress in this field".

The new situation found expression in the bookselling market's stabilisation tendency throughout the course of 1986 with the achievement of relative equilibrium in supply and demand:

> The bookselling market is ceasing to be a publishers' market and is clearly becoming a readers' market.

It was pointed out, however, that this could not be regarded unequivocally as positive, because books are not homogeneous products: there are books in great demand and those which do not enjoy the interest of <<Dom Książki>> (House of Books) customers. Booksellers flagged a clear drop in demand in 1986, as could be seen in the growing stockpiles of the <<Dom Książki>> retail chain and in Składnica Księgarska (book warehouse).

This novel situation also obtained on the secondhand book market where supply outstripped demand.

This document reflects the Cultural Department's attempts to explain the growth in stock. The view predominated that high book prices were driven by production costs (the price of paper and publishing services shot up by 40% in 1987). Royalties doubled, general publishing costs and tax burdens increased and rising maintenance costs put book prices beyond the reach of ever more segments of society on a scale that failed to satisfy even minimal educational and readership needs.

The drop in demand was generated by the dwindling financial resources of the intelligentsia, the chief book-buying group, and secondly, supposedly the deteriorating quality of books printed at home. In their mass, books are grey, printed on poor quality paper, in non-sewn bindings, frequently falling apart at the first reading.

The third reason was the failure to adapt a considerable proportion of publications to the needs of the booksellers' and readers' markets. Finally, the concentration of the book trade in towns, particularly big cities, was point to:

Getting through with books to the countryside and to workers' communities, remains a matter of urgency.

The issue of the potential negative consequences of the situation diagnosed so, was raised in this document. Rising book prices put a brake on the process of forming home libraries by social groups for which books were essential to their professional activity. The need for greater coordination between the MKiS with all library networks was highlighted. The need to increase of the influence of librarians on the shape of publishing programmes and for reinforcing the role of the State Library Council was postulated.

The possibility of reducing losses by eliminating deficit titles financed out of publishers' own resources, was mooted. Apart from negative consequences with regard the development of literary and scholarly creativity, it could have caused dissent in authors' milieus. It was anticipated that the economic upkeep of self-sufficiency of publishing enterprises would force publishers to give priority to books satisfying immediate demand on the market. It was feared that a real threat of intensified commercialisation by the rush to satisfy the most primitive readership demand could thereby arise, followed by a restriction in the culture-forming role of publications moulding greater readership discernment. The growing stockpiles of books could force publishers into decisions on reducing mark-ups and even on price reductions on given titles.

What were the ideas for overcoming these difficulties? It was postulated that bookselling chains should proactively organise frequent workplace fairs, street sales, stalls in Houses of Culture at various events, bazaars and markets, to overcome passive forms of sales. A system of book distribution in the countryside with the active cooperation of Dom Książki and Robotnicza Spółdzielnia Wydawnicza (Workers' Publishing Cooperative), Gminne Spółdzielnie Samopomocy Chłopskiej (Municipal Peasant Self-help Cooperatives), pupils' cooperatives in rural schools, was recommended. The sale of books by rural library staff (there were over 6700 such country libraries at the time employing 12000 librarians) was deemed to be a project worthy of consideration. The organisers of such sales were possibly to be Provincial Public Libraries, supplying library sales' outlets with books received directly from book warehouses on the basis of 20% commissions.

The sale of books in big workplaces was to be carried on in broader scope and systematically. Moreover, the greater synchronisation of bookselling and publishing effort was recommended, as based on an efficient system of internal information on books. Finally, it was argued that forthcoming publication announcements containing more exhaustive information on given titles, should be made without delay.

8.6   Political-Ideological Aspects

Thinking on book matters in ideological-political categories found some expression in the formulation of appropriate guiding principles for the unfolding publishing programme. In a manner typical for those times, this was done in an MKiS Book Department document of April 1985, which stated that: "the publishing movement is an essential link on the ideological front. Thus, its ideological line must coincide with the tasks of this front. The most important of them is to safeguard the gains of socialism and the struggle for the consolidation of ideological-moral and socio-political values".

One of the basic criteria in publishing policy was to "observe the principles of Poland's reason of state". This signified the publication of works critically analysing Polish history, but only those "whose intention will not be to strike at Poland's socialist regime, but to verify our history (in a way) that liberates our society from degeneration and deviation from socialist principles." "Publishing programming" was to concentrate on the dissemination of cognitive and educational texts aimed at emphasising "the historical significance for Poland's independent existence, of moulding civic virtues and, in that, the dominant awareness of the indispensable, ceaseless reinforcement of Polish statehood." The requirement of the publishing movement was to be the furtherance of knowledge on "the political and intellectual heritage of the Polish left, and its contribution to the historical successes of the international workers' movement, Polish national culture, and the rebuilding of Polish statehood". It was also "to show the national sources of socialist tradition in Poland". The publishing programme was to accept 'account settlement' literature on PZPR history, but without giving the party's opponents a platform from which to "weaken its political position by preaching historical falsehoods."

The main publishing effort was to concentrate on attracting youth to socialist ideals. An important aim of publishing policy was to educate society regarding the need of economic reform, and hence the need to produce a congruent publishing programmes. The document's authors drew attention to the need of constructing "a role model corresponding to the modern needs of contemporary socialist man, a human-humanist creator of his social environment, a patriot and member of society, the conscious humanistic creator of his work function".

The answer of the state publishing policy "to the ideological threat to the (humanist) worldview, the humanistic values of socialism was to be the intensified production of publications propagating and justifying the scientific, materialistic and secular view of the world, in line with the cognitive rules of Marxism and its hierarchy of ideological-moral values".

The particular addressee of this publishing policy were to be workers. The need to intensify their exposure to books was postulated (AAN, KC PZPR, LVI-249). That ideologically motivated particular interest, in the quoted documents, in disseminating books in the countryside and workers communities, recurred in many other studies in the field of publishing policy, in this also in those quoted earlier (AAN, KC PZPR, LVI-249).

In its principles of publishing policy already postulated in 1985, the PZPWUK proposed "to safeguard the conditions of implementing ideologically, culturally and educationally valuable programmes and titles that grew out of the ideological inspiration of socialism, important for the development of scholarship and technical progress for the rationalisation of social consciousness, historical and economic education and the development of the political culture and reinforcement of the state" (AAN, KC PZPR, LVI-248).

The team proposed to give priority status, in the years 1986–1990, to primary, middle school and first year undergraduate textbooks, children's and youth literature, encyclopaedic-advisory publications, socio-political literature, contemporary Polish literature, academic and academic-technical books associated with the programmes of industrial modernisation and development of new fields of technology and worldview-forming books (AAN, KC PZPR, LVI-248).

If we are to seek symptoms of clear ideological-political deviation in the work of the PZPWUK in the PRL's period of terminal decline, we can also find postulates regarding plans to publish translations of Soviet literature. A particular occasion for such publications was to be the approaching 70th anniversary of the October Revolution in 1987 (Jarosz, 2016, pp. 317–334)[4].

The supreme aim of such cooperation was formulated unequivocally:

> The development of Polish-Soviet cooperation in the area of books is indispensable to the further reinforcement of ideological ties and enhancement of the forms of cooperation in all areas and in deepening Polish-Soviet friendship. (AAN, KC PZPR Wydział Kultury LVI-249)

In the PZPWUK resolution on the evaluation of Polish-Soviet cooperation in the field of books in the years 1982–1985, and its development programme for 1986–1990 (formulated on the basis of the paper delivered and discussed at the sitting of 24 January 1986), it was asserted at the outset that in the past years there had been considerable growth in the volume of translations of Russian

---

4   This literature was published in the decided majority of Eastern bloc states, and representatives of socialist country publishers made up the corresponding discussion forum.

and Soviet literature (from 2.6 million in 1982 to over 6 million in 1985). In spite of that, there were complaints at the small share of Polish publishers in the international publications series: "Real socialism : theory and practice" and "Humanity on the threshold of the XXI Century". The insufficiency of the results achieved in the field of translations of scientific, technical and agricultural literature was also recognised. "Książka i Wiedza's" joint publication with the Soviet publishing house "Progress", of the complete works of Lenin, which was to be completed in 1990 on the 120th anniversary of his birth, was regarded as a success in this field, as was the formation of the publishing concern of the Polish-Soviet Friendship Society's venture "Współpraca" (Cooperation), specialising in translations of Russian and Soviet literature. The publishing house Wydawnictwo Łódzkie initiated the publication of a "Poetry of the Nations of the Soviet Union" anthology (of which the first two volumes were published). The publishers Arkady and Krajowa Agencja Wydawnicza initiated new series of art publications together with Soviet partners.

The availability rate of Polish books achieved in the USSR, chiefly fiction, and not only that translated into Russian, but also into other languages of the nations of the USSR, was hailed as a success. The Polish side enjoyed the printing services of Soviet publishers, but one of the drawbacks of this cooperation was deemed to have been economic determinants, meaning unfavourable settlements in a period of attempted economic reform in Poland of the 1980s.

Popular views spoke in favour of continuing and developing the programme of translating and promoting Marxist-Leninist literature, publishing works documenting and interpreting creatively revolutionary Polish-Soviet working class ties in the struggle for social and national liberation.

Particular stress was to be laid on popularising the ideals and historical role of the October Revolution. This aim was to be augmented by organising, with the help of the joint forces of publishers, booksellers and librarians, of a Soviet Book House, in November 1987. The intensified promotion of Soviet books in Poland, among others by utilising mass media resources, was postulated (Most probably, the first version of this document, see: AAN, KC PZPR Wydział Kultury LVI-208).

Over a hundred titles were arranged thematically in the programme of publications associated with the 70th anniversary of the October Revolution and 55th anniversary of the Soviet state. This programme, devised by the MKiS, comprised the following groups: knowledge on the Revolution, Lenin as a theoretician and leader of the October Revolution: the USSR – the first socialist state; Lenin and Poland: the revolution and the Polish question; the USSR and Poland; problems of international workers' movements and the world socialist system; ideas and visions of the October Revolution in literary fiction;

anniversary publications for children and schoolchildren; the cultural achievements and heritage of the nations of the Soviet Union (AAN, KC PZPR Wydział Kultury LVI-249).

The Cultural Department's advisory team also formulated desiderata on the ideological-educational content of books. This concern extended to children's and youth literature, which occupied an important place in publishing policy. According to a document titled "Ideological – educational content in children's and youth literature, 1982–1985" of 3 September 1986, this segment's output was making up for the production backlog caused by the breakdown of 1981, and achieved the level of 407 titles with a cumulative unit print-run of 52.5 million books in 1985. Such publications were centralised: about 60% of them were published by "Nasza Księgarnia" and Krajowa Agencja Wydawnicza. This document's authors took note of the lack of this type of book on the market and in lending libraries. The situation in this aspect was deteriorating due to the lack of necessary purchasing power at the time.

Moreover, the Party team saw a negative phenomenon "threatening the desired direction of development of the book programme", requiring "decisive counteraction" in the development of religious publications. Catholic publications in particular were deemed to be exploiting the tendency "to create an alternative source of patronage competitive to the state in the sphere of fiction and worldview-forming literature, betraying tendencies to sponsoring oppositionist political activity" (AAN, KC PZPR, LVI-248).

For this reason, the team gave priority to publishing worldview-forming books supporting the introduction of religious studies into school curricula in its plans for 1986–1990 (AAN, KC PZPR, LVI-248). In 1982–1985 it was noticed that apart from the publishing houses mentioned above, other publishers were engaging in publishing children's and youth literature, which, apart from its greater ease of acquisition, brought in train "randomness and shoddiness."

The historical-patriotic contents of these books, propelling to the foreground "a specific <<historiosophy>> cultivating heroic or martyrological characteristics of the nation" that was scarcely rationalised and "stuck uncritically in the messianic-romantic ethos", was deplored. The defect of this literature was also deemed to be that it rarely tackled the realities of the post-World War II period.

Moreover, it was regretted that left-wing/socialist traditions all too rarely served as a basis for crystallising "contemporaneously relevant civic attitudes.

The way of presenting World War II issues, which increasingly approached western conventions, was also criticised. As an example, they pointed to Janusz Przymanowski's books ("Czterej pancerni i pies" Four tankmen and a dog") and Józef Stompor's "Duch baszty" (Spirit of the tower).

Children's and youth literature was also supposed to help rearing society attuned to humanist and rationalist values. Book publishing policy was accused of pushing onto the back-burner worldview-developing and ideological issues, though achievements in this field were generally recognised. The necessity of publishing books propagating correct Polish usage for this segment of readership was also noted, and numerous achievements in this field were actually claimed.

This document also referred to science-fiction, which was popular in the youth segment. Its considerable "educational possibilities" inherent in highlighting the ecological, social and moral threats of the contemporary world were recognised, but a considerable part of it was disdained if not deplored for its naked commercialism based on nothing more than the profit motive (the object of criticism here being the publishing house Alfa). But overall, it was noticed that this direction of writing contributed to animating creative writers' circles (AAN, KC PZPR, LVI-208).

8.7   Conclusions

It seems that the diagnosis of the situation of Polish books made by the Central Committee of the Polish United Workers' Party's "think tank" took into account, at least in part, the basic, real problems in this field. Party decision-makers knew very well what the difficulties of underfunded libraries were, how quickly book prices were rising (in relation to the cost of living). Those in power were aware of the difficulties in producing paper for printing books and magazines. They realised that the book market was no longer a publisher's market and was becoming a reader's market. At the same time, the party leadership persevered in Marxist-Leninist ways of thinking. This meant declaring a drive to increase book readership by peasants and workers, to increase the number of publications promoting a 'materialist and lay view of the world' (including those criticising the Catholic Church), and translations of Russian of works produced in the USSR. The seventieth anniversary of the Bolshevik Revolution of 1917 (in 1987) occasioned intensified efforts in this regard. Was this professed Marxism-Leninism treated more and more as a mere routine ritual? There are many indications that it was. This lack of faith by the state and party elites in a bright communist future stood at the genesis of the bloodless revolution and 'conversion' to the free capitalist market. That was when Poland's second 'paper revolution' (after Stalin's) took place.

References

Archives

AAN, KC PZPR, LVI-249, Opina Partyjnego Zespołu ds. Polityki Wydawniczej i Upowszechniania Książki o opracowaniu Wydziału Kultury KC PZPR pt. „Aktualna sytuacja książki oraz problemy wymagające rozwiązania przez środowisko i instytucje, zajmujące się produkcją wydawniczą, dystrybucją książek i rozwojem czytelnictwa [1987], n.p.

AAN, KC PZPR, LVI-249, Informacja o aktualnym stanie realizacji „Programu rozwoju przemysłu poligraficznego na lata 1986–1990", n.p.

AAN, KC PZPR, LVI-249, MKiS, Departament Książki, Zasady ideowo-polityczne programu wydawniczego na lata 1986–1990, Warszawa, kwiecień 1985, n.p.

AAN, KC PZPR, LVI-249, Wnioski Zespołu d/s polityki Wydawniczej i Upowszechniania Książki w przy Wydziale Kultury KC PZPR w sprawie oceny współpracy polsko-radzieckiej w dziedzinie książki w latach 1982–1985 i programu jej rozwoju w latach 1986–1990 (sformułowane na podstawie referatu i dyskusji na posiedzeniu w dniu 24 stycznia 1986), Warszawa 5 III 1986, n.p.

AAN, KC PZPR, LVI-1497, Lista przewodniczących Wojewódzkich Zespołów Partyjnych Bibliotekarzy, n.p.

AAN, KC PZPR, LVI-208, Aktualna sytuacja książki oraz problemy wymagające rozwiązania przez środowiska i instytucje zajmujące się produkcją wydawniczą, dystrybucją książek i rozwojem czytelnictwa, Warszawa, listopad 1986, n.p.

AAN, KC PZPR, LVI-208, "Ideologiczno-wychowawcze treści w literaturze dla dzieci i młodzieży w latach 1982–1985". Study by the team composed of: Łukasz Szymański, Czesław Wiśniewski, Stanisława Czajka with the cooperation of Jędrzej Bednarowicz, Kazimierz Kochański, Anna Brygoła – Parzyszek and Rena Marciniak, n.p.

AAN, KC PZPR, LVI-208, Założenia programowe i organizacyjne polsko-radzieckiej współpracy wydawniczej w latach 1986–1990, n.p.

AAN, KC PZPR, LVI-209, Deputy Head of the Cultural Department of the Central Committee Zbigniew Domino, Warszawa 5 III 1987, n.p.

AAN, KC PZPR, LVI-209, Stanowisko Ogólnopolskiego Zespołu Partyjnych Bibliotekarzy i Księgarzy przy Wydziale Kultury KC PZPR w sprawie dalszego upowszechniania książki i rozwoju bibliotek ze szczególnym uwzględnieniem środowiska wiejskiego, przyjęte na obradach w dniu 3 maja 1988 roku w Szczecinie, n.p.

AAN, KC PZPR, LVI-247, Postanowienie nr 53/84 Prezydium Rządu z dnia 22 października 1984 r. w sprawie modernizacji i rozwoju przemysłu celulozowo-papierniczego, n.p.

AAN, KC PZPR) LVI-1247, Plan pracy Zespołu ds. polityki wydawniczej i upowszechniania książki przy Wydziale Kultury KC PZPR wrzesień 1985 - marzec 1966 [projekt], n.p.

AAN, KC PZPR, LVI-248, Partyjny Zespół ds. Polityki Wydawniczej i Upowszechniania Książki, Ocena sytuacji w ruchu wydawniczym i upowszechnianiu książek, Warszawa, czerwiec 1985, n.p.

AAN, KC PZPR, LVI-248, Protokół z I posiedzenia Partyjnego Zespołu ds. polityki Wydawniczej i Upowszechniania Książki z dnia 7 maja 1985.

AAN, KC PZPR, LVI-249, Wnioski Zespołu d/s polityki Wydawniczej i upowszechniania książki w przy wydziale kultury KC PZPR w sprawie oceny współpracy polsko-radzieckiej, n.p.

Published Secondary Sources

Błażejowska, J. (2010). *Papierowa rewolucja. Z dziejów drugiego obiegu wydawniczego w Polsce 1976–1989/1990*. Warsaw.

Jarosz, D. (2011). Dni Oświaty, Książki i Prasy w systemie propagandy kulturalnej władz Polski Ludowej 1946–1956, *Polska 1944/45–1989. Studia i materiały*, vol. 10, pp. 43–60.

Jarosz, D. (2016). *Jak tworzono „książkę socjalistyczną"? Narady wydawców i księgarzy państw bloku wschodniego 1965–1988, Z badań nad książką i księgozbiorami historycznymi*, vol. 10, pp. 317–334.

Kondek, S. (1999). *Papierowa rewolucja. Oficjalny obieg książek w Polsce w latach 1948–1955*, Warsaw.

Olaszek, J. (2015). *Rewolucja powielaczy. Niezależny ruch wydawniczy w Polsce 1976–1989*, Warsaw.

Sowiński, P. (2011). *Zakazana książka. Uczestnicy drugiego obiegu 1977–1989*. Warsaw.

Rocznik Statystyczny 1990. (1990). Warsaw, p. 120, table 7 (103).

CHAPTER 9

Słowo Narodowe (1989–1991): The First Legal Post-War Magazine of the Polish National Radical Camp

Anna Szwed-Walczak

9.1 Introduction

The process of the mass media transformation in Poland began in 1989 with the initiation of the change of political system, to which the agreements reached during the Round Table discussions were of great importance. The Sub-team For Mass Media was appointed to deal with this matter. In their report from 22 March 1989, the sub-team recommended the abandonment of the concession system to give way to the system of the registration of press activity. Another result of the sub-team's work was the abolition of the repressive measures taken against the so-called samizdat press. Following this, new press legislation was introduced in May:

> on the attitude of the State towards the Church in the Polish People's Republic (from 17 May 1989) and on the guaranties of freedom of conscience and religion (from 17 May 1989), on amending the Bill on the Control of Publications and Public Performances (from 29 May 1989), on amending the Press Law. (from 30 May 1989) (Słomkowska, 1996, pp. 26–28)

The new legislation made it possible for newspapers representing different worldviews to enter the market, including papers promoting the national democratic thought and the history of the National Democracy movement (prohibited in Poland after 1945), and confessional magazines.[1]

---

1 Roy Atwood (Jun. 1994, pp. 3–5) proves that after the initiation of the political transformation in Poland, the Catholic Church had an influence on shaping the media system, but also on the model of journalistic practice.

Under such circumstances, notwithstanding the system of censorship which still functioned,[2] the first issue of *Słowo Narodowe* [*National Word*][3] appeared in May 1989. The magazine was published until April 1991. Altogether, 24 issues were printed. It was conceived as a monthly newspaper, although in 1989 most editions appeared every two months (in 1990, a double issue appeared only in the summer). The publisher of *National Word* was the company Słowo i Czyn [Word and Action] established on 4 December 1987, headed by the Chair of the Programme Board, Maciej Giertych, the Chair of the Supervisory Board, Marian Szatybełko,[4] and the Board of Directors, Piotr Piesiewicz, Kazimierz Krajewski and Piotr Ołdak (Tomasiewicz, 2003, p. 83). At the same time, the company's management established the Słowo Narodowe[5] publishing house, with Andrzej Kowzan appointed as its director. The permission for the publication of the monthly newspaper was granted on 30 January 1988. While the editorial team was in the middle of preparing the publication of the first issue of the magazine, on 11 November 1988, a commemorative issue of *Gazeta Warszawska* [*The Warsaw Gazette*] was published (for the 70th anniversary of Poland's regaining of independence). It was a sign for the resurgent Polish nationalist movement. It was also supposed to give some validity to the

---

2   The abolition of censorship took place on 6 June 1990, after the entry into force of the Bill from 11 April 1990, repealing the bill on the control of publications and shows, abolishing the control organs and amending the Press Law (*Dz. U.* [*Journal of Laws*] 1990 no. 29 item 173).

3   Due to censorship, some materials were removed, for instance, in the first issue of the magazine from May 1989, a part of the introductory article and the article written by Bogusław Jeznach were cut out, and in the second issue of the magazine from June 1989, some extracts from the article by Piotr Ołdak, "Regionalizm jako podstawa odnowy kultury".

4   Marian Szatybełko (born in 1928) – a soldier of the Home Army, a graduate of Warsaw University of Life Sciences, since 1955 a Ph.D. in the natural sciences, a docent at the National Marine Fisheries Research Institute in Gdynia. A Catholic and social activist. A member of the National Coordinating Commission of Science NSZZ "Solidarity" – the Sector of Departmental Institutes. The chairman of the Gdańsk Branch of the Polish Socio-Catholic Association [further: PZKS], the co-author of the Act of Entrustment of PZKS to the Blessed Virgin Mary – the Queen of Poland. A Sejm deputy of the 9th- and 10th-term Sejm. The co-founder and President of the Supervisory Board of the company Słowo i Czyn ("Marian Szatybełko", 1990, p. 1).

5   It functioned in the period from February 1988 until April 1991. Apart from *National Word* (24 issues), analysed here, the following titles appeared under the imprint of the publisher: five editions of the bi-monthly magazine *Prawica Narodowa* [*National Right Wing*], two issues of the quarterly journal *Zeszyty Historyczne* [*Historical Journals*], commemorative editions of *Gazeta Warszawska* [*Warsaw Gazette*] and *Gazeta Kongresu Prawicy Narodowej* [*The Congress of National Right Wing Gazette*], as well as the following publications: Roman Dmowski, *Kościół, Naród i Państwo* [*Church, Nation and State*], Jędrzej Giertych, *Polski Obóz Narodowy* [*The Polish National Camp*], Władysław "Żbik" [Wildcat] Kołaciński, *Między młotem a swastyką* [*Between the Hammer and the Swastika*] (Kawęcki, 2012, p. 303).

demand for a newspaper representing this ideological trend (Kawęcki, 2012, p. 300; W. L., 1989, p. 8). The newspaper soon issued 20,000 copies.

In the inaugural issue, the editorial board described *National Word* as "the first legal magazine in post-war Poland which openly represented the political trend drawing upon the one-hundred-year tradition of the National Democracy" ("Od redakcji", 1989a, p. 3). They emphasised their affiliation with the nationalist political movement and its national-democratic ideological foundations. The content of the magazine provided the rationale for its categorisation as the representative of the Catholic nationalist ideological strand within Polish national thought (Szwed-Walczak, 2019c, p. 112; Smolik, 2012, pp. 25–26).

Due to the political thought it represented, the legal character of the publisher, the time when its publication was initiated, and also the briefness of the period during which it was issued, the magazine reflected the transformation of the media that took place during the era of political change in Poland. Ryszard Filas noticed that from May 1989 until the first half of 1991, the Polish media market witnessed a huge increase in the number of press titles. He described that period as a phase of unrestrained enthusiasm expressed by new publishers and broadcasters, as well as forced transformation of some old titles (2010, p. 30).[6]

In the case of the periodical that is the subject of analysis in this article, this enthusiasm also resulted from opening up the possibility of legal activity for associations and discussion groups which drew upon the ideological foundation of the National Democracy. The history of *National Word* became an inherent part of perturbations experienced by newspapers and magazines established by the resurgent political movements representing various ideological trends. They struggled with the lack of printing paper, financial difficulties, sudden increases in prices and/or the relocation to more suitable premises and problems with distribution.[7]

---

6 See also: Pokorna-Ignatowicz, K (2012). "From the Communist Doctrine of Media to Free Media: The Concept of a New Information Order in the Round Table Agreements". In K. Pokorna-Ignatowicz (ed.), *The Polish Media System (1989–2011)* (pp. 14–20). Kraków: Oficyna Wydawnicza Akademii im. Andrzeja Frycza Modrzewskiego; Mikosz, J. (2018). "Press Journalist's Profession in Poland After Political Transformation in 1989 and Nowadays". *Studies in Linguistics, Culture and FLT*, vol. 4, pp. 36–37.

7 The editorial team complained about the unequal treatment of publishers, pointing out that the editorial team of *Gazeta Wyborcza* [*Electoral Gazette*] (whose first issue appeared at the same time) was allocated 3,500 tons of print paper for the year, and Słowo i Czyn Sp. z o.o., after several appeals, received only 15 tons and "the information from the President of Warsaw that the applications will not be given any positive consideration 'neither presently nor in the future'" ("Spółka spółce nierówna", 1989, p. 80). On the problems facing the Polish press during the period of the media system's transformation, see: Atwood, R. (Jul. 1994).

The press may be analysed as: 1) transmission channel, 2) broadcasting body, and 3) reception apparatus (Maj, 2015, p. 575). While analysing a political magazine which focused on a particular political milieu, it is necessary to gain insight into its structure, substantive value, and the journalistic competences of the editorial team. The functions performed by the magazine are also of great importance. The aim of this study is to determine the principles of the magazine, its ideological reception and functions, but also the competences of the editorial team. During the research work carried out for the purpose of this analysis, the following hypotheses were tested: 1) the political milieu which initiated the publication of the magazine took advantage of the experiences gained by émigré activists who had published magazines at their own expense, 2) the editorial team of *National Word* was ideologically close to the views held by Jędrzej Giertych, 3) due to the impossibility of legally publishing a national democratic magazine during the period which started after the war and lasted until the era of political transformation, the educational function was a dominant part of the narrative, which resulted from the need to build a political milieu gathered around the magazine.

There seems to be a gap in the existing scholarship when it comes to the national-democratic press during the period of political transformation in Poland. While this kind of political press has been extensively studied with respect to the periods of the partitions, the Second Republic of Poland, and the present moment (to give some examples, see the studies by Aneta Dawidowicz, Jolanta Dzieniakowska, Urszula Jakubowska, Zenon Kmiecik, Ewa Maj, Jerzy Myśliński, Anna Szwed-Walczak, and Wiesław Władyka), there are few comprehensive analyses of the national-democratic press during the period of transformation (especially, the first stage of transformation in the years 1989–1992). The results of preliminary research in this respect have been presented in the book *Obraz wroga Polski we współczesnej politycznej prasie narodowej* [Image of Poland's Enemy in Contemporary National Political Press], but the author focuses mostly on the press outlets after 1989 in her analysis of the images of the enemy of Poland present therein. However, there are no detailed studies of individual periodicals. There is a single article on *National Word* by Krzysztof Kawęcki, a member of the periodical's editorial board.[8] The article

---

"Reconstructing Polish Press Freedom: The Quest for New Models of Free Expression Among Polish Journalists". *Conference: ICA Conference-Sydney, Australia*, pp. 10–13; Jakubowicz, K. & Sükösd, M. (2008). "Twelve Concepts Regarding Media System Evolution and Democratization in Post-Communist Societies". In K. Jakubowicz & M. Sükösd (eds.), *Finding the Right Place on the Map: Central and Eastern European Media Change in a Global Perspective* (pp. 12–17). Bristol, Chicago: Intellect Ltd.

8 K. Kawęcki, *Tradycja narodowa i katolicyzm w publicystyce środowiska „Słowa Narodowego",* [in:] *Nacjonalizmy różnych narodów. Perspektywa politologiczno-religioznawcza,* eds. B. Grott, O. Grott, Kraków 2012.

fails to determine which émigré activists of National Democracy joined the editorial team and whose political experiences were put to use (the members of the pre-war National Party in exile in Great Britain were divided into supporters of the party's leader, Tadeusz Bielecki, or his major opponent, Jędrzej Giertych). What is more, Kawęcki does not pinpoint the sources of the periodical's ideological slant. On account of the time when *National Word* came into being, it seems worthwhile to analyse its functions, which was not attempted in Kawęcki's article.

The current research deployed content analysis, both qualitative and quantitative.[9] The qualitative analysis of the content has made it possible to interpret and categorise the content present in the periodical, to assess the competences of the editorial team, and to decode the periodical's ideological inspirations. Various categories of subjects raised in *National Word* have been enumerated with the help of the created categorisation key. In line with the methodology proposed by Harold D. Lasswell, my research has focused not only on the message itself, but also on the communicator, channel of communication, and the desired effect (Lasswell, 1948). In turn, the quantitative analysis of the content (understood as a strictly press studies method) has made it possible to indicate the ratio of the various content categories as well as the functions played by the periodical (analysis of the structure of generic and thematic content). This enabled an assessment of the monthly's topicality and diversity.[10] Here, Bernard Berelson's methodology (1952) was deployed, in which content analysis is understood as an objective, systematic, and quantitative description of overt content. Due to the monthly's short span, the small number of issues released and limited availability, this article takes into consideration all the issues released.

9.2   The Editorial Team and the Political Milieu of *National Word*

The editorial office was located in a flat owned by a lawyer and pre-war activist for the National Democratic Party, Leon Mrzygłodzki, at 2a/35 Lwowska Street in Warsaw. The function of the editor-in-chief of *National Word* was taken

---

9   Denis McQuail wrote about combining these two methods (2007), pointing to the possibility of drawing multipronged conclusions from the results of research conducted in such a way.

10   For more on quantitative content analysis, see Krippendorff, 2004, pp. 27–30; Kafel, 1969, pp. 112–113, 118–119; Kajtoch, pp. 19–20; J.K., 2006, p. 7; Pisarek, 1983, pp. 43–45; Berelson, 1952.

up by Maciej Giertych,[11] a son of a well-known, pre-war and émigré national writer, Jędrzej Giertych. There is evidence, from many sources, that Maciej Giertych was the main initiator of the magazine. However, Piotr Ołdak, who joined the editorial team in January 1990, emphasised that the originator of the idea of establishing a national democratic periodical was Piotr Piesiewicz, who was appointed deputy editor-in-chief (Rozmowy z laureatami, 1991b, p. 6; M. Giertych, 2005, p. 6). Piesiewicz was also the editor-in-chief of the two final issues of the monthly magazine (23 and 24), which appeared in March and April 1991.[12] Dariusz Sobków became the editorial secretary, in charge of the editorial office, while Henryk Goryszewski headed the political section. In 1990, the editorial staff was expanded when Krzysztof Kawęcki (who had been writing articles for the magazine since 1989), Piotr Ołdak and Leszek Żebrowski officially joined it.[13] Kawęcki selected Piesiewicz, Giertych, Krajewski, Ołdak and Żebrowski for the core team of the editorial board (Kawęcki, 2012, p. 303). Each of them had already taken the first steps towards promoting the political thought and achievements of the National Democracy. Apart from political experience, they had university education, connections with the doyens of the national-democratic movement, or family connections with those who rendered service for the development of the national-democratic ideology, as, for instance, the editor-in-chief of the magazine. Among the editorial staff of *National Word*, one could distinguish three generations of nationalists: senior

---

11   For more on that, see: Szwed, A. (2013). "Opoka w Kraju". *Annales Universitatis Mariae Curie-Skłodowska*, section K, vol. XX, 2, pp. 252–256.

12   Maciej Giertych was not part of the team at that time. The Meeting of the Partners of the company Słowo i czyn held in 1991 appointed Piotr Piesiewicz as the editor-in-chief (Piesiewicz, 1991, p. 1).

13   Krzysztof Kawęcki (born in 1960), a Ph.D. in humanities, in the years 1979–1982 an activist of the Polish Committee for the Protection of Life, Family and Nation, and then of the Polish Self-Defense Committee (KSP). He received a degree in history at Maria Curie-Skłodowska University in Lublin. In 1989, he received his Ph.D. degree in humanities at the Catholic University of Lublin. His research dealt with the Polish national camp. From the 1970s, he became involved in the self-learning groups at the Jesuit church, but he also organised patriotic celebrations. He established Związek Młodzieży Narodowej [the National Youth Association] (bringing together secondary school and university students), which published the magazine *Szaniec* [*Earthwork*]. The co-founder of the Polish Academic Society, and then a member of the board and editorial team of the magazine *Myśl Akademicka* [*Academic Thought*]. After he stepped away from the KSP, he became involved in publishing activity. He was an editor and publisher of the underground newspapers *Wielka Polska* [*Great Poland*] and *Polska Narodowa* [*National Poland*], in 1990 he established *Prawica Narodowa* [*National Right Wing*]. A member and founder of the Roman Dmowski Historical Institute in Warsaw (Kawęcki, 2012, p 303; "Krzysztof Kawęcki", 1990, p. 2).

activists – members of pre-war National Democracy structures, a group of conspirators belonging to the émigré branch of the National Democracy, and the young generation of activists.[14]

It is worth taking a closer look at the profiles of people who influenced the magazine. One of them was Maciej Giertych (born in 1936), brought up in an expatriate community in London, where his family settled after the war. He received a degree in forestry from the Department of Forestry at Oxford University, and after that, he took up postgraduate studies at the University of Toronto, where he started his scholarly career. He was an active member of Polish communities abroad, among others the Polish Scouting Association, and a co-founder and president of the Oxford University Polish Club. He was also the initiator and one of the teachers at Saturday Polish School for Polish children in Oxford, an activist for the Oxford University Eastern Europe Society and the "Balance Club". He was under the ideological influence of his father. While still a postgraduate student, he wrote articles, together with his father, for the magazine *Horyzonty* [*Horizons*] published by Witold Olszewski in Paris. In Poland, he distributed the magazine *Opoka* [*The Bedrock*],[15] which was published by his father in London, and rewrote and promoted the works of Feliks Koneczny, a historian and philosopher admired and valued by the nationalists ("Maciej Marian Giertych", 1990, p. 1; M. Giertych, 2005, pp. 5–6; Wojciechowski, 2005, pp. 7–14).[16] He returned to Poland as a Ph.D. in 1962, and was employed at the Institute of Dendrology of the Polish Academy of Sciences in Kórnik. In 1969, he received his Habilitation degree, in 1981 he became an Associate Professor of forestry, and in 1989, a full Professor. His research area included mostly population genetics, and within this scientific field, he made attempts to, among others, disprove the theory of evolution, advocating the theory of creationism (M. Giertych, 1990d, pp. 29–35; Maciej Marian Giertych, 1990, p. 1). In the years

---

14   M. J. Chodakiewicz, J. Mysiakowska-Muszyńska and W. J. Muszyński pointed out that the movements bringing together young national democrats, which had emerged and developed since December 1981, could be divided into two categories: proponents of Jędrzej Giertych's ideas, who were called "conservatists", and "liberals", who acknowledged the authority of Wojciech Wasiutyński and Wiesław Chrzanowski (2015, p. 435). The milieu of *National Word* belonged to the first category.

15   Its last issue from 1988 included a presentation of the profile of Jędrzej Giertych's son, and also some political articles written by Maciej Giertych, who, after his father's death, continued the publication of the magazine in Poland, with the annotation "in the country" (Szwed-Walczak, 2019b, p. 184).

16   See a more extensive study on the attempts made by the Security Service to obtain Maciej Giertych's cooperation: Sikorski, T. (2013). "Drogi i bezdroża. Trudne życie Macieja Giertycha w Polskiej Rzeczpospolitej Ludowej". *Archiwum Emigracji. Studia – Szkice – Dokumenty*, no. 1 (18), pp. 127–142.

1986–1989, he was a member of the advisory council set up by the Chairman of the Council of State, General Wojciech Jaruzelski.[17] He gained recognition in Catholic circles in 1987, when, in response to Pope John Paul II's invitation, he took part in the Synod of Bishops "On the role of the laity within their church and in the world". He was also appointed Vice Chairman of the Primate's Council in the years 1986–1990. Moreover, he was a founder and member of the Scientific Council of the Roman Dmowski Historical Institute in Warsaw and the Chairman of the Founders' Council of the Jan Ludwik Popławski Association Protector Poloniae (Maciej Marian Giertych, 1990, p. 1). In *National Word*, he took up ideological disputes, made comments and expressed opinions on the current political and social events in Poland and abroad. Moreover, the magazine published some extracts from his speeches (on the Advisory Council and the Congress of the Polish Right Wing), open letters and interviews.

The deputy editor-in-chief and the editor-in-chief of the last two issues of the magazine, Piotr Jakub Piesiewicz (born in 1953), received a degree in law from the Faculty of Law and Administration at the University of Warsaw. He belonged to the Independent Political Group in Gdańsk, was a member of the Polish Academic Society, and a founder of the Youth Commission of The Polish Socio-Catholic Association, in which nationalists had a dominant position (Tomasiewicz, 2003, p. 55). He was one of the columnists of the magazine *Nowe Horyzonty* [*New Horizons*] (Sikorski, 2011, p. 86). From 1978, he was an activist for informal Catholic and nationalist organisations, and until April 1981 ("the Bydgoszcz crisis"), an active member of NSZZ "Solidarity" (he was, among other things, appointed the Chairman of NSZZ "Solidarity" in the District Court in Otwock, and a member of the Board of NSZZ "Solidarity" of the Judiciary within the Provincial Court in Warsaw). In 1981, he founded the St. Andrew Bobola Catholic Publishing House (in cooperation with Kazimierz Krajewski) and the National Publishing House "Chrobry" (in cooperation with Sławbor Cergowski). He was in charge of the publishing companies until 1987. In 1986,

---

17   Maciej Giertych addressed the allegations made against him regarding his cooperation with General Jaruzelski within the Advisory Council, emphasising that it was not a two-man council, but included 56 people, who received no payment for their work (only the travelling expenses were reimbursed). He pointed out that during the activity of the Council, which lasted from December 1986 until July 1989, twelve meetings took place, and the Council did not undertake cooperation with General Jaruzelski or the government, since that was not its objective. It worked overtly and the minutes of each Council meeting were published. Giertych juxtaposed the Council meetings with the Magdalenka agreements, emphasising that the latter were classified. He also admitted that his participation in the Council was a mistake, since it did not bring any results (M. Giertych, 2005, pp. 101–104).

he published *Myśl ideowo-polityczna Jędrzeja Giertycha"* [*The Ideological and Political Thought of Jędrzej Giertych*] in the Publishing House "Bóg I Ojczyzna" [God and Homeland]. He was a founder and board member of the Roman Dmowski Historical Institute in Warsaw and the founder and sponsor of the Jan Ludwik Popławski Association Protector Poloniae ("Piotr Jakub Piesiewicz", 1990, pp. 2–3). In *National Word*, he published articles containing his programme and ideological materials, and expressed his views on the nationalist political movement and the multiplicity of strands inherent in it. As for Maciej Giertych, the publishing house printed some extracts of his speeches.

Piotr Ołdak (born in 1964), a law graduate, had some organisational experience. In 1982, he became active in Catholic and nationalist circles, among others, in the Polish Socio-Catholic Association ("Rozmowy z laureatami", 1991a, p. 6). In 1984, he became involved in the construction of a self-learning centre at the parish of Our Lady of Częstochowa Church at 5 Zagórna Street in Warsaw (referred to as the "Zagórna community").[18] In the years 1985–1988, he was an activist of Narodowe Odrodzenie Polski [National Rebirth of Poland] [(Kawęcki 2012, p. 303). He was awarded the Jan Ludwik Popławski Prize "National Word" by the Foundation Protector Poloniae for his organisational and editorial work ("Nagroda Fundacji", 1991, p. 2). In *National Word*, he published reviews and feature articles.

The historian Kazimierz Krajewski (born in 1955) conducted research on the Polish nationalist underground during World War II. Leszek Żebrowski (born

---

18   In the years 1984–1986, the centre was headed by Rafał Mossakowski, and from 1986 until 1988 by Piotr Ołdak. Within the framework of this institution, they organised lectures on political and social subjects which took place every two weeks, celebrations of national anniversaries, provided people with historical literature as well as political publications of the pre-war National Democracy. Initially, the enterprise was a joint project of the "Zagórna community" and the Warsaw branch of Ruch Młodej Polski [the Young Poland Movement]. The meetings were initiated by Wiesław Chrzanowski. However, Ruch Młodej Polski broke off cooperation in December 1984 when it was proposed that Maciej Giertych should give a lecture. Mossakowski noted that the selection of speakers was "chaotic", and the key factor was the connection with the national idea and self-identification within the nationalist milieu. Apart from the above-mentioned names, the group of speakers included, among others, Major Tadeusz Bednarczyk, Władysław Bruliński, Rev. Henryk Czepułkowski, Rev. Wojciech Giertych OP (Maciej Giertych's brother), Dr. Henryk Goryszewski, Witold Olszewski, Władysław Piasecki, Assistant Professor Mirosław Roszkowski, Bogusław Rybicki, Prof. Witold Staniszkis and Dr. Józef Więcławek. The meetings were open to the public and were attended by from 20 to 185 people, including the representatives of patriotic, conservative and Catholic organisations as well as SB agents, whose participation was unavoidable. After the location of the meetings was moved to the parish of All Saints at Grzybowski Square, the milieu became disintegrated (Mossakowski, n.d.; Chodakiewicz, Mysiakowska-Muszyńska, Muszyński, 2015, pp. 446–459).

in 1955), who was an economist by education, also occupied himself with writing feature historical articles. Since the beginning of the 1980s, he pieced together, by contacting representatives of the nationalist movement, a record of national conspiracy after 1939, which was reflected in his publications in *National Word* (he mainly wrote popular scientific articles and historical book reviews) (Kawęcki, 2012, p. 303).

The magazine was supervised by the Editorial Council comprised of experienced nationalist activists, who represented the group of the oldest writers for *National Word*. Witold Olszewski (1912–1991) was appointed the Chair of the Editorial Council; he was a lawyer by education, a pre-war activist of the National Gymnasium Association, then the manager of the outpost of the Group of Great Poland in Włocławek and a member of the board of the Kujawy and Dobrzyń Land district. During World War II, he served as a soldier of the Home Army, and after the war he became the president of the Polish War Refugee Association. During the inter-war period, he gained his practical experience in journalism while writing articles for *Gazeta Kujawska* [*Kujawy Gazette*], *Gazeta Warszawska* [*Warsaw Gazette*] and the magazine *ABC*. In Oflag, he organised a conspiratorial weekly "spoken magazine" titled *Komentarze* [*Comments*] (after the liberation, the magazine was published in mimeograph under the title *Polak* [*A Pole*]). Within the press section of the Polish 1st Armoured Division of General Maczek, he established a news agency, which published information bulletins for Polish refugee camps in Germany located within the British occupation zone until demobilisation ("Witold Olszewski", 1990, p. 1; Kowzan, 1991, pp. 14–17). As an expatriate in France, he was the publisher and editor-in-chief of the monthly magazine titled *Horyzonty* [*Horizons*], published in Paris in the years 1956–1971. After his return to Poland in 1972, he wrote articles for *Słowo Powszechne* [*The Universal Word*], *Kierunki* [*Directions*], and in the years 1981–1986, he worked as an editor of the weekly magazine *Ład* [*Order*].[19] In *National Word*, he published feature articles dedicated to the nationalist movement and its principles as well as his comments on the political transformation in Poland and its geopolitical situation.

Andrzej Meissner (1923–2008) and Maciej Winiarski (1922–2004) were also members of the council. The former was a graduate of the Main School of Planning and Statistics, and before the war, a member of the National Gymnasium Association and then a soldier of the Home Army and an activist of the émigré branch of Stronnictwo Narodowe [The National Party] (son of

---

19   According to the findings of Sławomir Cenckiewicz, starting in 1958, Olszewski collaborated with the Polish People Republic's secret intelligence. Within the framework of the cooperation, he was given the pseudonym "Wysoki" (2007, p. 382).

Czesław Meissner, an activist and Member of Parliament representing Związek Ludowo-Narodowy [Popular National Union] and senator of The National Party) (Sikorski, 2013, p. 140; "Andrzej Meissner"). He published deliberations on various historical topics in the monthly magazine. The latter, Maciej Winiarski, a doctor of physics by education, was a feature writer for the magazine *Ład* (son of Bohdan Winiarski. a professor of law, a member of Komitet Narodowy Polski [Polish National Committee], a Member of Parliament for the Popular National Union, and then The National Party, and a member of the International Court of Justice) (Krasnowska, 1999; Szymański, 2019). *National Word* published Maciej Winiarski's comments and reflections on the then current politics, as well as notes on his work dedicated to the national idea conceived of by his father, Bohdan Winiarski.

It should be noted that the core team of the editorial staff was comprised of writers who had university education (some were granted science degrees) and experience in editorial and organisational work. Some of them (among others, A. Meissner, M. Winiarski, and M. Giertych), due to their family background, were raised in the spirit of Polish nationalist thought.

Taking into consideration all the authors of articles published in the monthly magazine, they can be divided into the following categories: 1) regular columnists (over 10 publications: Jan Engelgard – pseudonym "Bogdan Zaremba", Maciej Giertych, Leszek Żebrowski, Kazimierz Murasiewicz, Piotr Piesiewicz, Bogusław Jeznach), 2) permanent collaborators (from 4 to 9 publications: Henryk J. Goryszewski, Krzysztof Kawęcki, Andrzej Kowzan, Stanisław Kozanecki, Witold Olszewski, Dariusz Sobków, Marian Szatybełko, Maciej Winiarski, Janusz Zieliński), 3) occasional columnists (from 2 to 3 publications), 4) one-time writers (Figure 9.1).[20]

The vast majority of materials published in the magazine were a result of occasional collaboration, unsigned articles and articles published by some institutions. A small group of permanent columnists, namely J. Engelgard, M. Giertych, L. Żebrowski, Kazimierz Murasiewicz, Piotr Piesiewicz, and Bogusław Jeznach, set the tone for the editorial team.

The political circle gathered around *National Word* derived from many organisations and informal nationalist groups. They included: 1) Unia Nowoczesnego Humanizmu [The Union of Modern Humanism], established in the 1970s by Władysław Bruliński (Chodakiewicz, Mysiakowska-Muszyńska, Muszyński, 2015, pp. 419–425); 2) the previously mentioned self-learning centre at 5 Zagórna Street in Warsaw in the years 1984–1988 (Mossakowski, n.d.);

---

20   The introductory and feature articles, comments, opinions, feuilletons and interviews
      were taken into account, not the readers' letters.

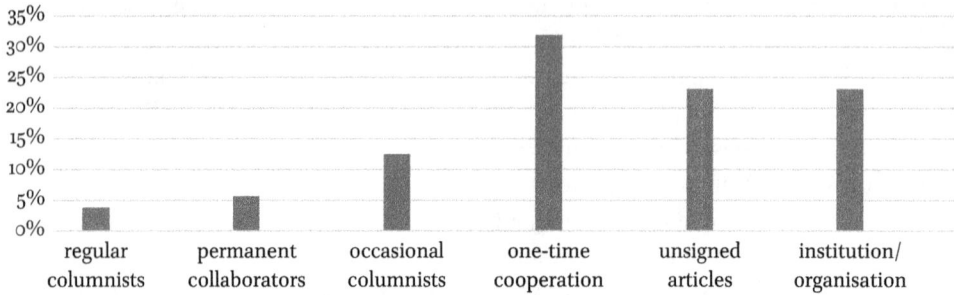

FIGURE 9.1   Categories of columnists of *National Word* (1989–1991)
SOURCE: MY OWN RESEARCH

3) the so-called Napoleon Siemaszko Esq. Political Salon at 4 Piękna Street in Warsaw; 4) discussion-group meetings organised in the 1970s and 1980s in Jan Ostoja Matłachowski's apartment in Warsaw; 5) the editorial office of the unlicensed magazine *Nowe Horyzonty* (1986–1989); 6) St. Andrew Bobola Publishing House and the National Publishing House "Chrobry"; 7) The Polish Academic Society; 8) The Polish Socio-Catholic Association and the editorial office of *Ład*, its press organ; and 9) The Forum of Catholic-Social Thought (Cenckiewicz, 2007, pp. 35, 368; Sikorski, 2011, p. 86; Tomasiewicz, 2003, pp. 55–57; Sikorski, 2016, p. 58).

Along with the development of the magazine, attempts were made to develop its political milieu. Maciej Giertych pointed out that the initiation of *National Word* aimed at creating circumstances in which the voice of the nation could exist in the so-called "first circulation". At the same time, he argued that a party had no *raison d'etre* unless it had its own newspaper. Thus, the periodical was supposed to be a prelude to the subsequent development of an important political power and become "a platform for exchanging ideas and views, open to everyone who identifies with the ideas of the national democracy" ("Wywiad z prof. Maciejem Giertychem", 1990, pp. 53–58). To achieve this goal, the readers were encouraged to initiate Circles of Friends gathered around *National Word*. The first circles were established almost at the same time that the first issue of the magazine was published, as early as in June 1989, in Łódź, Wrocław and Piotrków Trybunalski. The members of those clubs were supposed to be independent, promote the magazine in their regions, and encourage people to buy its subscription. Educational aspects were partially included in the objectives set by the clubs, to mention such aims as promoting the principles of Catholic morality, traditional national values, and money-making. The work of the clubs was supervised by Elżbieta Wilczyńska ("Akt powołania Klubu", 1990a, pp. 72–73 & 1990b, p. 37; "Koło Przyjaciół", 1990, p. 38).

People belonging to the political milieu connected with *National Word* shared the nationalist right-wing self-categorisation, loyalty towards the political programme of the National Democracy, and a critical attitude towards the policy of the left wing, understood as the way of regulating social life, political solutions and the axiological sphere (Piesiewicz, 1990b, p. 5; Kawęcki, 1990b, p. 6). The statements made by those people revealed their common foundation of Polish conservatism and nationalism, namely faith, freedom, law, property and love of the homeland (Ołdak, 1990a, p. 10).

Initially, in their responses to the readers' letters, the editorial team claimed that time was not yet opportune for uniting the national-democratic movement ("Od redakcji", 1990c, p. 1; Majewski, 1989, pp. 60–61). The magazine was considered an essential factor in developing the political movement. There were recommendations made in the magazine to follow the standards of conduct represented by the National Democracy and establish an expanded network of associations, institutes and publishing houses (Murasiewicz, 1989b, pp. 25–30). The editors realised that the nationalist movement comprised a multiplicity of strands.[21] Maciej Giertych pointed out that there was no unanimity of opinion regarding the political and electoral system, as well as the agricultural and military policies of the country (1989a, p. 5). The activists did not hesitate to criticise their own political background (Piesiewicz, 1989a, pp. 77–83). Nonetheless, they decided to present some initiatives worth being involved in, namely the "senior" National Democracy, the Polish Academic Society intended for students, and Młodzież Wszechpolska [All-Polish Youth], addressed to secondary school and vocational school students ("Od redakcji", 1990c, p. 1; P.P., 1989, p. 82). The majority of the editorial team joined the "senior" National Democracy, but it should be noted that the previously mentioned multiplicity of strands within the nationalist movement resulted in organisational divisions. For instance, J. Engelgard joined Stronnictwo Narodowo-Demokratyczne [the National-Democratic Party], H. J. Goryszewski and Dariusz Sobków – Zjednoczenie Chrześcijańsko-Narodowe [the Christian National Union], and P. Piesiewicz and P. Ołdak – Stronnictwo Demokratyczno-Narodowe [the Democratic-National Party] (Tomasiewicz, 2003, p. 83; Sikorski, 2016, p. 68).

---

21   Ewa Maj (2010, pp. 81–82) pointed out that within the contemporary nationalist thought, the following types of nationalisms can be distinguished: liberal, national Catholic, national folk, which she described as "moderate nationalist trends", as well national radical, Slavic and traditional nationalism, which represent political extremism.

The strong representation of *National Word* in the "senior" National Democracy[22] was a consequence of a natural process. It resulted from the closeness of the political milieu involved in the initiation of the project. Tomasz Sikorski's findings indicate that *National Word* "was conceived as the supreme body of the domestic branch of the ND" (2013, p. 40). The members of the "senior" National Democracy considered themselves to be continuators and inheritors of national democratic thought (Tokarz, 2002, p. 13), and Jędrzej Giertych's concepts were popular within their ranks. The beginning of the organisation was marked by the formation of the Senior Caucus on 18 July 1989, which included: J. O. Matłachowski, Tadeusz Krzyszowski, and Adam Krajewski (Sikorski, 2016, pp. 64–65). J. O. Matłachowski was considered the main initiator of the caucus. Its activity began at the Convention held on 18 November 1989. Despite the fact that some prominent pre-war nationalist activists attended the event (namely Leon Mirecki, Rev. Władysław Matusa, Tadeusz Radwan, Andrzej Meissner, Bronisław Ekert and Witold Staniszkis),[23] it did not receive official approval from the émigré branch of the National Democracy in London, although the participants invoked the principle of co-optation, included in the statute of the ND from 1935, regarding the legitimacy of authorities as well as the support of "the oldest living nationalist" – Rev. Władysław Matus (Tomasiewicz, 2003, p. 97; Maj & Maj, 2007, p. 71). The members of the organisation in London were afraid that the nationalist-communist activists of the Grunwald Patriotic Union, which was reactivated all over the country, would join the structures of the party.[24] Due to the doubts regarding the future of the National Democracy in Poland, the president of the émigré

---

22   Stronnictwo Narodowe [The National Party] was registered on 21 August 1990, and Maciej Giertych became the Chairman of the General Council in 1991 (Tokarz, 2002, p. 13).

23   Jan Ostoja Matłachowski died a month before the convention.

24   As A. Tybulowicz noted, the "senior" National Democracy included people who were "suspected of sympathising with the communist party (for example Stefan Jarzębski, Edward Mastej, Bogusław Rybicki)" (Sikorski, 2016, p. 65). As Marian Barański put it, "the Secret Police – Mastej and Rybicki (acted in cooperation with Jan Matłachowski, who, as it turned out, was also a secret police agent) made attempts to form the ND that would be subordinated to the Secret Police. The old national democrats were not adapted to the conditions, they were taken in by the actions of the Secret Police, they were too straightforward, too Latin". He also noticed that "the Giertych family stayed in the background" ("Wywiad z Marianem Barańskim", 2013; cf. Tomasiewicz, 2003, p. 98). Sławomir Cenckiewicz (2007, pp. 354, 356–364) found out that the SB had connections with a group of national democrats: Jan Matłachowski (the pseudonym TW "Maksym" from the 1950s until March 1988), Witold Olszewski (the pseudonym TW "Wysoki"), Napoleon Siemaszko (the pseudonym TW "Teodor" from September 1974), Rev. Henryk Czepułkowski (the pseudonym TW "Henryk" from June 1960), Józef Kossecki, Mariusz Urban, Bogusław Rybicki (the pseudonym TW "Rogulski" from December 1981). The information about

branch of the ND, Antoni Dargas,[25] appointed a team (Albin Tybulewicz and Wacław Całus) whose goal was to evaluate the organisations set up in the country, which directly drew on the ideological legacy of the National Democracy. Albin Tybulewicz initiated talks with Wiesław Chrzanowski, who, according to his view, was capable of taking the lead in developing the centrist wing of the ND, whereas Wacław Całus met the members of the circle gathered around Maciej Giertych, who intended to create a national-catholic organisation. As a result, the émigré branch of the ND supported the idea of forming a completely new faction in the country – Stronnictwo Narodowo-Demokratyczne [the National-Democratic Party] – whose Organizing Committee was set up as early as on 14 April 1989 (Sikorski, 2016, p. 68).

According to the division within the nationalist movement of the 1980s proposed by Jarosław Tomasiewicz, the representatives of *National Word* could be referred to as the paleo-ND (they started their political activity before 1970), defined as "old National Democracy" and a faction which had the dominant role during the Polish People's Republic period. Even though Tomasiewicz made the division according to the criterion of generation, he noticed that the faction also included younger activists. The researcher pointed out that the paleo-ND was characterised by loyalty to nationalist ideology and its conservatism, particular caution in building party structures, which resulted from their fear of being infiltrated by the security service and experiencing repressions, and pedagogical and educational activity including the commemoration of national anniversaries. He also noted that it functioned with the support of "seniors", namely L. Mirecki, N. Siemaszko, L. Mrzygłodzki, and J. Matłachowski, and was ideologically close to Jędrzej Giertych's faction (2016, pp. 277–288).[26]

---

  their activity appeared, for instance, in the "Mrowisko" [Anthill] and "Elite" case files (see
  also Chodakiewicz, Mysiakowska-Muszyńska, Muszyński, 2015, pp. 371–379).

25 Wojciech Wasiutyński (1999, p. 481) points out that despite the appeals made by the members of the émigré branch of the National Democracy (Wasiutyński, Olgierd Dębski) A. Dargas did not cut himself off from Maciej Giertych and J. Matłachowski, connected with "Grunwald", and the magazine *Myśl Polska* [*Polish Thought*] censored articles by W. Chrzanowski, which opposed the opinions of Giertych. As Wasiutyński recalls, the former president Tadeusz Bielecki, before his death, authorised Mirecki, Siemaszko and Chrzanowski to undertake actions for the National Democracy and for the purpose of the distribution of aid in the country. Finally, when Chrzanowski's activity was torpedoed, he backed out of cooperating.

26 It had its antithesis in the faction that J. Tomasiewicz called neo-national democracy which emerged in the second half of the 1970s and in the 1980s. It drew on the traditions of the ND, but also reinvented its ideological heritage, and showed the willingness to build structures and undertake activities in the public sphere in the country. It also cooperated with the émigré branch of the National Democracy (2016, pp. 277–288).

It can be seen that the editorial team of *National Word* comprised people with political experience and with experience in political writing in the immigrant press or in unlicensed publications released in Poland. They included representatives of the young generation (raised in the communist system and deprived of the possibility to become acquainted with the national-democratic thought). They had experience with distributing publications in difficult conditions in Poland, hence they efficiently delivered the periodical to potential addressees. What is more, the activists of the pre-war National Party as well as the politicians of the National Party in exile joined the editorial team. They contributed models of the functioning of the editorial team, such as a low number of constant collaborators, openness to publishing materials sent to the editorial board, the multidimensional character of editorial team (related to the multidimensionality of the Polish national democratic thought) self-identified as the national right, the creation of the political milieu around the periodical to be transformed later into a political party (and the periodical itself – into the party's press outlet), a belief in the necessity to popularise the Polish national-democratic thought in an unaltered form and to interpret the geopolitical reality through the prism of ideas of pre-war ideologues (without taking into consideration political and social transformations).

9.3   The Ideological Premises and Political Notions of *National Word*

The ideological premises present in *National Word* were in line with the premises of the pre-war National Democracy movement. The objectives of the magazine were determined in its first issue: "It is our aim to render our services that will increase the power and strength of our Nation. Only a strong country commands respect among its allies and is held in high estimation among its enemies" ("Od redakcji", 1989a, p. 3). K. Kawęcki pointed out that the continued aim of nationalists was to "maintain the creative continuity of the nationalist movement and remain faithful to its principles" (1990a, p. 5). H. J. Goryszewski included among the set of nationalist political principles such elements as giving precedence to the interests of the nation, independent and autonomous political decisions, a realistic approach to political action and the omnipresence of ethical guidelines (in both public and private life) (1989a, p. 9). *National Word* promoted an array of values such as nation, Catholicism, nation-state, national culture, the Latin civilisation and national economy.

It was emphasised that "the basis upon which national thought is founded is the recognition of the importance of the nation as the lifeblood of national life" (Zieliński, 1990a, p. 8). The nation was perceived as a natural community of free people, the sole political sovereign and the source of the whole political power. It was pointed out that only within a nation can a person "achieve full personal development" ("Od redakcji", 1989a, p. 3). Kazimierz Rokicki stressed that according to the nationalist ideology, the nation is not merely a certain population inhabiting a given territory, characterised by a specific civilisation, culture, set of customs and historical tradition, political system, economy and political interest, but it is a term which refers to "a spiritual community of peo-ple". The community possesses a national self-awareness, filled with collec-tive soul, which is "a source of feelings and moral concepts held by the whole nation". In this idealised community, there is a sense of connection between past, present, and future. All members of the nation fulfil their responsibili-ties to care for and develop the national existence. They feel a deep sense of national solidarity and base their moral conduct upon the Catholic ethical sys-tem. They reject liberalism and communism (Rokicki, 1989, pp. 9–12; Parada, 1991, pp. 4–5).

National Word described the Polish nation as a Catholic nation, pointing out that the Catholic church played a significant role in shaping the nation's consciousness, morality and customs, and influenced its system of values and lifestyle. The magazine drew on the concept of the Catholic State of the Pol-ish People ("Od redakcji", 1989a, p. 4; J. Giertych, 1990, pp. 1–3; Drechna, 1990, pp. 3–5; Kowzan, 1990a, pp. 5–6). The national idea was compared to a reli-gious concept, as it was pointed out that "the national – in Poland undeni-ably means: Catholic" (Zieliński, 1990a, p. 8; Krzepkowski, 1990a, p. 11). Specific references were made to the Primate Stefan Wyszyński's concept of the Polish nation, according to which the nation was defined as a family of families, and thus it was stated that care for the family, its values and property was the essen-tial condition for the nation's rebirth (that is, securing a livelihood) (Kawęcki, 1989a, pp. 30–32).

The state, juxtaposed to the nation, was of secondary value, however, it still had some importance. As the editorial team of *National Word* expressed it, it was "a political form, necessary to organise the Nation". It was assumed that it "ought to serve all citizens, regardless of their background, beliefs and faith. In return, it has the right to demand loyal service to the Polish state and its interests" ("Od redakcji", 1989a, p. 3). The very functioning of the nation-state proved the ability of the nation to build such a state, but it was also an indica-tion of its strength (Rokicki, 1989, p. 12).

The condition of Polish culture on the threshold of the major political change of 1989 met with criticism. Piotr Ołdak pointed out that the causes behind its downfall included the "lack of a religious stronghold" and "the total-itarian concept of exercising power". He saw the opportunity to spark cultural development in going back to the roots of the Latin civilisation and basing the national culture on "vernacular, traditional and regional content, on the close, familiar world, in which the feelings shared by the spiritual community are still stronger" (Ołdak, 1989, pp. 52–56). In this regard, Poland's historical mission was recognised as being a stronghold of the Latin civilisation. Readers were persuaded to choose traditional Polish values such as love, the cult of the Virgin Mary, and freedom (within the limits defined in the Decalogue) (Zarzecki, 1989, pp. 20–24). It was thought that "a situation in which thinking in terms of profit would replace thinking in terms of moral values" was unacceptable. Cultural liberalism was rejected for the sake of a "wise management" of the cultural sector by the nation-state, understood as the protection of national culture from foreign influence, supervision of folk art, financial support of artists, maintenance of museums and artworks, but also concern for values and moral standards (Krajska, 1990, pp. 22–24).

It is worth noting that Catholicism was regarded as superior. Therefore, references were made to the concept of Christian nationalism, which combined the idea of a nation with Catholicism and Latin civilisation. According to this concept, individuals voluntarily accept their duties towards their homeland (Zieliński, 1990a, pp. 9–10). As Maciej Giertych saw it, Catholicism, apart from national interest, was and should be the indicator of Polish national politics. This meant that: 1) politics should be subordinated to the teachings of the Catholic Church, 2) the Church cannot be instrumentalised and used in political power struggles, and 3) Polish politics must manifest tolerance towards ethnic and religious minorities (1989a, pp. 6–8). Krzysztof Kawęcki noticed that despite the lack of institutional forms of nationalist movement during the Polish People's Republic, their task was accomplished by the Catholic Church, which was expressed by "the Jasna Góra vows of the nation taken in 1956 and the millennial celebrations of the existence of the Polish state" (1990a, p. 5). Poland was also referred to as "the eastern bulwark of Christendom" (Sobków, 1989b, pp. 17–25). Starting from issue ¾ from 1989, the magazine introduced its slogan: "Regina Poloniae ora pro nobis" ["Queen of Poland, pray for us"].

Emphasising the importance of Catholicism for the development of the Polish nation was a result of the affiliation of Poland with the Latin civilisation. In this regard, the editorial team of *National Word* referred to Feliks Koneczny's theory of civilisation, pointing out that the Latin civilisation gave birth to certain concepts such as monogamy, respect for women, derogation of slavery and ennobling of manual labour (Sobków, 1989a, pp. 24–25). In the Latin civilisation, the state was based on the society and there was no room for state totalitarianism, which was characteristic of the Byzantine civilisation

(Kawęcki, 1989a, p. 30). Sobków discovered an analogy between restricting the influence of the Catholic Church on nations and the destruction of the principles of social life (1989a, p. 23).

The concept of patriotic and moral upbringing was advocated, likely to be realised only in a religious family, which was capable of "raising national awareness and willingness". The family was given the task of promoting the national traditions, and raising a true Pole and citizen responsible for the fate of the nation and state (Rokicki, 1989, pp. 12–14; "Od redakcji", 1990d, p. 1). Roman Giertych stressed the importance of promoting national pride among young people, who should find the source of this pride in "the great achievements of our ancestors", as well as of shaping the attitude manifested by "sacrifice for the homeland" (1990, p. 11).

Attention was paid to the issue of Poland's future economic system, and the socialisation of state property was recommended as the preferred option. Objections were expressed to Polish national property being sold to foreign companies (M. Giertych, 1989d, pp. 6–9; Szczepaniak, 1990, pp. 26–29). Stanisław Kozanecki expressed his anxiety that the excitement caused by regaining political freedom resulted in a lack of discussions on economic freedom in Poland (1989a, p. 15). References were made to the examples of states which had overcome economic crises (Zaremba, 1989a, pp. 17–20). Economic liberalism was the object of criticism. It was thought that the economic system must be adjusted to suit the needs of the society (Ligęza, 1990, pp. 12–13; Robatyński, 1991, pp. 12–13).

The issue of the geopolitical location of Poland was also addressed in the magazine. It was a significant element of the deliberations regarding the political transformations taking place in close proximity to Poland. Feliks Koneczny's theory of civilisation was also applied to conduct an analysis of international relations. The theme of cooperation between Germany and Russia, which bothered the representatives of the nationalist movement, was explained by reference to one of the assumptions of Koneczny's theory – the permanent inter-civilisational struggle. It was emphasised that hostility towards the Latin civilisation was the cause of the agreement between the Russian and German Byzantinism. Its consequence was the attack launched against Poland. The partitions of Poland and the Molotov-Ribbentrop pact were given as examples (Sobków, 1989a, p. 29).

Germany was regarded as Poland's main enemy. It was pointed out that they used tactics such as "the dulling of vigilance" and "the smokescreen" when offering their economic assistance (Olszewski, 1989b, pp. 13–17; Wertyński, 1990, pp. 19–25; Krzepkowski, 1990b, p. 6; Winiarski, 1990, pp. 44–45; Pukacki, 1990, p. 38; Ruta, 1991, pp. 13–14). There were fears that the fall of the Berlin

Wall might prompt the united Germany to change the existing border with Poland, which the Federal Republic of Germany refused to acknowledge (Kozanecki, 1989b, pp. 11–13; "Od redakcji", 1990a, pp. 3–4; Kurasiewicz, 1990, p. 6; Winiarski, 1989a, pp. 71–73). Maciej Giertych postulated that before the unification of the Federal Republic of Germany and the German Democratic Republic, some treaties should be signed which would resolve the issues of the Polish-German border, individual and collective compensations for the war damage and war crimes committed by the German Third Reich, as well as military guarantees (1990c, p. 3). The threat was seen mainly in Silesia, where the German minority under the leadership of Henryk Król, financed by the Federal Republic of Germany, became active (Zaremba, 1990d, pp. 1–2; "Qui bono?", 1989, p. 81; "Tworzenie", 1989, p. 74). On the threshold of the political transformation, restoring the cooperation with the UK and France, and continuing the cooperation within the Warsaw Pact, were considered appropriate options (Olszewski, 1989b, pp. 13–17; Zaremba, 1990b, pp. 8–9). Maciej Giertych was afraid that the withdrawal of the superpowers from Europe was likely to result in Germany holding the dominant position or in the Russian-German condominium (1989b, pp. 3–6). The postulate made by other political milieus regarding the withdrawal of Soviet troops from Poland did not meet with the approval of the editorial team ("Od redakcji", 1990a, pp. 3–4). They were concerned that Germany posed a potential economic, military, territorial, demographic, ideological, and moral threat (Cofta, 1990, pp. 37–39; (lang.), 1990, p. 43; Urban, 1991, p. 22).

The proposal regarding Poland's accession into the European Economic Community was subjected to criticism, motivated by the fear of losing sovereignty and based on the argument that a "united Europe without the USA and the Soviet Union is German" (M. Giertych, 1990c, p. 3). It was thought that with the aid of the EEC, Germany strove to atomise the Central-Eastern European countries. Instead, a postulate was put forward to approve the concept of the cooperation of small- and medium-sized Central-Eastern European countries, which would take the form of a customs and monetary union, with access to a common market (Rokicki, 1990, pp. 16–17).

National Word addressed some stereotypical opinions regarding the National Democracy, which implied that it was an anti-Semitic, anti-German and pro-Russian organisation (Zaremba, 1990c, p. 3). The allegations regarding the anti-Semitic attitudes, which were formulated against the nationalists by their political opponents (and particularly against Jędrzej Giertych[27]), were

---

27   J. Giertych was repeatedly accused of anti-Semitism and radical views (Dawidowicz, 2012, p. 106).

refuted. Maciej Giertych believed that the Jewish propaganda which implied the alleged anti-Semitism of the National Democracy resulted from the fact that the party refused to acknowledge the Jews' conception of themselves as the chosen and exceptional nation (1989a, p. 5). Witold Olszewski wrote that Jews had a tendency to use the term "anti-Semitic" to describe anything that did not go as they intended. He believed that they did not respect the Pope and the cross, manipulated the results of the genocide committed by the Nazi Germany, refused to acknowledge the suffering of other nations and "had a tendency to exaggerate" (1989a, pp. 3–5).

In *National Word*, the critical stance towards Jews adopted by the national-democratic movement was justified by the attitudes towards Poles and Poland adopted by Jews. Arguments were put forward implying that Jews fought against Poland's interests at the Paris Peace Conference and that they supported the Bolsheviks in 1920 (M. Giertych, 1989a, pp. 5–6; "Obsesje", 1989, p. 81). It was also pointed out that they had a large presence in the Security Office, the military courts and the public prosecution office during the Stalin era, which was the reason behind the fact that, according to Leon Mirecki, "particularly harsh methods" were used for the purpose of investigating and prosecuting the nationalists.[28] Mirecki believed that it was a consequence of the pre-war attitude towards Jews adopted by the National Democracy. However, he refused to call it "anti-Semitism", emphasising that it was "a difficult and dedicated self-defence against taking control of many highly important spheres of national life by people holding different ethical views and representing a different civilisation, which resulted in a terrible disorganisation of national life. During the investigation, we were clearly informed that we would be liquidated not only physically but also in the moral sense, which meant that our honour and good names would be besmirched by using false testimony forced by torture" (1990, pp. 50–53, 55).

On the threshold of the political transformation, there were fears that Jewish capitalists would buy up state property and would take over the media, through which they would gain ideological influence over the society: fighting against Catholicism, formulating false accusations against Poles regarding

---

28   As an example, he recalled the death sentences of Adam Doboszyński (on charges of spying for Germany), Adam Mirecki, Władysław Marszewski and the Chairman of Board of the underground National Party, Prof. Leon Dziubecki. In the latter case, the sentence was changed to life imprisonment. Another example was the accusation of Konstanty Skrzyński of spying for the Gestapo. Prof. Władysław Tarnowski, Leszek Hajdukiewicz, Tadeusz Łabędzki, Leszek Roszkowski, Tadeusz Zawodziński, Jan Morawiec, Janek Kaim and Stanisław Mierzewiński were also imprisoned. They were all murdered. Mirecki also described his own four trials and ten years of imprisonment (Mirecki, 1990, pp. 50–53).

their collaboration with the Nazi Germany and describing the Jewish emigration of 1968 as an expulsion. Maciej Giertych believed that all those activities were a result of a Jewish-German agreement, based on the assumption that the responsibility for Shoah should be thrown on Poland to discredit it in the eyes of the world, provoke it, and destroy it morally (1990c, p. 3). At the same time, it was pointed out that any conflicts with Germany, Russia or Jews were not among the objectives of the nationalist movement but resulted from the necessity of protecting Poland (Piesiewicz, 1990a, p. 67).

The magazine's articles reflected the ideological inspirations of the editorial team. They carefully kept track of the development of nationalist movements in France (Sobków, 1990, pp. 24–28; Le Pen, 1990, pp. 52–53; M. Giertych, 1990a, pp. 18–21), although they did not frequently deal with this matter. First of all, the discourse was dominated by references to the doyens of the National Democracy, which was reflected by ideological postulates, deliberations, the printing of the extracts of works by Roman Dmowski and Jan Ludwik Popławski, as well as making references to the concepts of the ideologues (M. Giertych, 1989a, p. 6; Dmowski, 1991, pp. 9–10). The ideological proximity of the editorial team to the ideas of one of the leaders of the pre-war National Democracy, Jędrzej Giertych,[29] the father of National Word's editor-in-chief, Maciej Giertych, and the grandfather of the president of the All-Polish Youth, Roman Giertych, can also be observed. The impact of Jędrzej Giertych's political thought was expressed, for instance, by promoting Christian nationalism[30] and distancing themselves from non-Christian nationalism. An opportunity for national development was seen in the restoration of moral standards based on the Catholic ethical system, in both private and public life. Zygmunt Balicki's theory of national egoism, as well as apotheosis of the nation, met with criticism (cf. Dawidowicz, 2012, pp. 110–112). Moreover, National Word made references to Feliks Koneczny's theory of civilisation, popularised by Giertych.[31] Some criticism, based on Jędrzej Giertych's publications, was also launched against

---

29   Starting in 1945, he stayed with his family in London, where, apart from doing manual work and then holding the position of a French teacher, he also took up publishing activity. He published both historical and political books, promoted Feliks Koneczny's work, and established two magazines: *Ruch Narodowy* [*National Movement*] (1955–1957) and *Opoka* [*The Bedrock*] (1969–1988). As a result of a conflict with the president Tadeusz Bielecki in 1961, his membership in the émigré branch of the National Democracy was revoked. For a more extensive discussion, see Dawidowicz, 2012, pp. 102–106.

30   Jędrzej Giertych published the brochure "Nacjonalizm chrześcijański" ["Christian Nationalism"] in 1948 in Stuttgart (Cugowski, 2012, p. 37).

31   In November 1945, Jędrzej Giertych promised Koneczny that he would take care of the promotion of his work (1982, p. 248).

Józef Piłsudski (M. Giertych, 1989c, pp. 13–16). The activity of Jewish Masons and Germany was perceived as a source of threat to Poland (Dawidowicz, 2012, p. 113; cf. Cugowski, 2012, p. 156). Much like Jędrzej Giertych, the editorial team distrusted the Workers' Defence Committee. Giertych thought that it was a centre of influence of Trotskyist ideology. He also propagated the view that the milieu surrounding the Workers' Defence Committee took a dominant role in the structures of NSZZ "Solidarity"[32] in order to carry out a Trotskyist revolution using its structures (Szwed-Walczak, 2019a, pp. 578–579; Cugowski, 2012, pp. 204–206, 210).

It can be noticed that the editorial staff of *National Word* still regarded as valid the scenario of the future agenda intended for the nation, as presented by Jędrzej Giertych in the magazine *Opoka* [*The Bedrock*] published in London in the 1980s, which included:

> 1) the development of the productive forces: handicraft, industrial, mercantile, agricultural, 2) raising peoples' awareness of the threats posed by Germans and Jews, 3) explaining some historical mistakes. (Szwed-Walczak, 2019b, p. 193)

The magazine also published some quotes and made references to the magazine *Opoka*, edited by Jędrzej Giertych (Kawęcki, 1990a, p. 5).

The researchers point out that certain specific features of the milieu can be distinguished that had a direct reference to the thought of Jędrzej Giertych. Moreover, terms such as so-called "giertychowszczyzna" [Giertych-ness] or "Giertych's doctrine" are used in scholarly literature. The premises that underlie this doctrine include continuation of the activity and ideological thought of the nationalist movement and loyalty to its agenda (Tomasiewicz, 2003, pp. 214–220; Kawęcki, 2012, p. 299). Czesław and Ewa Maj used the term "giertychow-izmy" [Giertychisms] to refer to the set of views held and presented by Jędrzej Giertych, which included "anti-American, pro-Russian and anti-Solidarity concepts" (2007, p. 69). Even so, the editorial team objected to describing its own milieu as "giertychowszczyzna" or "giertychowcy" [Giertych's people] ("Od redakcji", 1989b, p. 84). Piesiewicz thought that the term "giertychowcy" implied a harmful suggestion that the movement was a sect gathered around "a

---

32   Wojciech Wasiutyński had a different opinion on this matter and thought that the leadership of "Solidarity" should be criticised for a lack of political thinking and not for a conspiracy. Wasiutyński referred to the circle gathered around J. Giertych as "stupid right wing" and described it as "a movement based on superstitions motivated by phobias and manias" (Wasiutyński, 1999, pp. 479–480).

political guru", which was contrary to the national-democratic doctrine (1989a, pp. 81–82).

The qualitative content analysis shows that the ideas propagated in the periodical were primarily in accord with Jędrzej Giertych's political thought. Granted, there were references to the main ideologues and creators of the Polish national-democratic camp – Roman Dmowski and Jan Ludwik Popławski. Still, one can easily note allusions to the notion of "Christian nationalism" propagated by Giertych and to his reflections published in London's *Opoka* [The Bedrock] (mostly on threats to Polish identity, statehood, territory, culture and economy).

9.4 Structure and Functions of the Magazine

In the years 1989–1990, the length of the *National Word* magazine varied from 50 to 88 pages; in 1991, it was reduced to 34 pages. Initially, the monthly was printed in an A4 format, and from April 1990, in an A5 format. A vast majority of the articles published in *National Word* were divided into permanent or occasional columns, whose subject areas reflected the character of the magazine. They included: "Publishers – Documents – Positions", "History", "Comments", "From the Editors", "They Have Written to Us", "Chalk Marks on the Chimney" and "Without Chiaroscuro". In the first column, the editorial team presented appeals, open letters and programme premises of patriotic and nationalist movements that initiated or formalised their activity. In addition, they published Sejm addresses and occasional speeches confirming to their political views.

Within the "History" column, feature writers referred to some important events in Polish history: the regaining of independence, the fights over the borders of the Second Polish Republic, and the military conspiratorial activities during the Second World War. They printed recollections of nationalists' propaganda and publishing activity during the German occupation, as well as accounts of their own arrests and investigations performed by the UB [Security Service]. Moreover, biographical entries about well-deserving patriots were included. Articles written by, among others, Jan Engelgard, Jędrzej Giertych, Lucjan Grabowski, Bogdan Kędziora, Andrzej Meissner, Leon Mirecki, Zbigniew Młot-Kulesza, Rev. Jan Stępień, Stanisław Suszka, Andrzej Tomczyk, and Leszek Żebrowski appeared in this column.

The column under the heading "Comments" mainly addressed political changes that were taking place in Poland, including the reactivation of traditional parties and their struggle to overcome difficulties (for instance, the conflicts regarding the names of the parties or their anachronistic way of thinking).

In addition, comments were made on the current domestic and international political situation of Poland and Poles, including ideological disputes, the dominant position of left-wing parties in the public sphere, parliamentary and presidential elections, problems experienced by compatriots in Lithuania, geopolitical threats, etc. The group of commentators usually included W. J. Engelgard (1989c, pp. 57–60), who also published under the pseudonym of B. Zaremba (1990a, pp. 37–39; 1990e, pp. 72–75) and the initials J.E (1990, p. 58), Roman Giertych (1989, pp. 60–62), B. Jeznach (1990, pp. 71–72), K. Murasiewicz (1989a, pp. 54–57; 1990, p. 31), W. Olszewski, P. Piesiewicz, and M. Winiarski.

The part of the magazine under the title "From the Editors" (1989a, pp. 3–4; 1990a, pp. 3–4; 1990b, p. 1; 1990c, p. 1; B.Z., 1990b, pp. 3–4; Zieliński, 1990b, pp. 5–10) was filled with motivational, demystifying and ideological texts, and articles containing political programmes or assessing opinions. The former aimed at encouraging people to join nationalist movements, whereas the latter contained attempts to present the consequences of political actions undertaken by both the government and the opposition parties from the perspective of the nationalist ideology, as well as the proposed the implemented concrete political solutions. Other articles mainly addressed the fears resulting from the reunification of Germany.

Letters from readers were published in the column titled "They Have Written to Us". They usually contained positive comments on the publishing initiatives of *Warsaw Gazette* and *National Word*. The printed extracts of those letters contained words of praise addressed to the editors, with regard to their effort put into developing the nationalist idea. The readers also encouraged the milieu of *National Word* to make an attempt to consolidate the Polish nationalist movement.

The column under the heading "Chalk Marks on the Chimney" contained feuilletons in which the authors exposed the absurdities of criticism against nationalists as well as Poland and Poles. Negative comments were presented with regard to introducing foreign customs and cultural trends in Poland (Zygier, 1909, pp. 56–59; Majewski, 1989, pp. 60–61; Engelgard, 1989, pp. 43–45; W.W., 1990, pp. 66–67; Urban, 1991, p. 2).

The column titled "Without Chiaroscuro" served the purpose of exposing the inconvenient truths, but also demystifying politicians and their activities that, according to the editorial team, did not serve Poland's interests well. The columnists willingly published some quotes taken from publications in the Polish media (regarding the nationalist movement) as well as publications in foreign media addressing matters related to Poland. The column mostly contained assessing comments written by Maciej Giertych, who used the initials M.G. (1989, pp. 75–76; 1990a, p. 47; 1990c, pp. 75–76; 1990d, p. 76; 1990e, p. 43; 1990f, p. 44; 1991, p. 21) and J. Engelgard (B.Z.: 1990a, p. 44; 1990c, p. 47).

The magazine printed other columns, though less frequently, such as "Camera Obscura" (presenting facts in a sarcastic manner), "Culture" (outlining the profiles of artists, filmmakers, theatre creators) (Skwara: 1990a, pp. 46–40; 1990b, pp. 20–23; 1991, pp. 15–16), "Reviews" (usually of historical books) (Olszewski, 1990, pp. 8–13; Żebrowski: 1989c, pp. 36–42; 1990a, pp. 24–26; 1990b, pp. 59–66; Engelgard, 1990, pp. 34–35; Ołdak, 1990b, pp. 35–37), "The Classic" (presenting the works of the doyens of the nationalist movement, for instance, Jan Ludwik Popławski), and the column titled "Poem", dedicated to poetry.

The above-mentioned columns were started as early as in the first issues of the magazine (in 1989). The following year witnessed the appearance of other columns, such as, "Profiles", "Insult of the Month", "Economy", "Political Milieu of *National Word*", "Novel", "Nation and Politics", "Funereal Page"/"Obituaries". The occasional columns included, among others, "No Comments", "Roads to Independence", "Catholic Ethics"/"Catholicism", "Science", "The Right-Wing Parties in Europe", "From Near and Far", and "Correspondence". Depending on the current political events, there were columns that appeared only once, for instance, articles on the Congress of the Polish Right Wing and on the stance towards the reunification of Germany. Starting with issue no. 6 from 1990, advertisements (usually promoting nationalist publishers) were also printed. In addition, the magazine published interviews and scholarly articles.

The texts printed in the magazine can be divided into eight categories, namely "Ideological deliberations", "Education and upbringing", "Culture", "Economy", "Promotion of political milieu", "Evaluation of politics", "Demystification of reality", and "Statements and appeals" (see Figure 9.2).

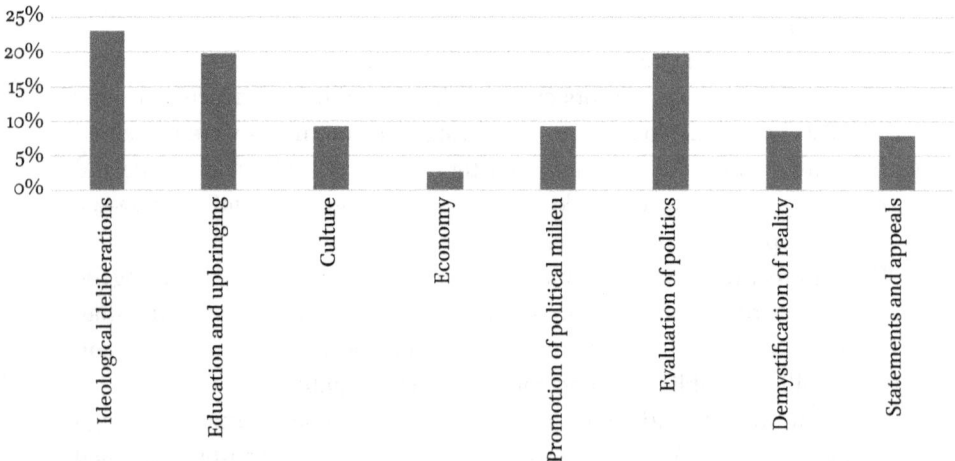

FIGURE 9.2   Frequency of texts in *National Word* (1989–1991) according to subject areas
SOURCE: MY OWN RESEARCH

The dominant position was held by "Ideological deliberations", "Education and upbringing" and "Evaluation of politics". This mainly resulted from the desire to win over new supporters of the nationalist idea, which involved the necessity of introducing the readers to the foundations of the Polish nationalist thought, shaping opinions and building a political milieu around the magazine.

The content of the periodical determined its functions, namely informative, educational, entertaining, opinion-forming, attitude-forming, and milieu-forming functions. The first function was performed by publishing reports on domestic and foreign events. The periodical published statements issued by the nationalist movement, appeals made by patriotic associations, press reviews, and reprinted selected materials. It also published information about the activities of national-democratic and Catholic movements.[33]

The educational function, understood as a combination of historical education and shaping the patriotic attitudes of the readers, played a significant role. The readers were provided with a knowledge of history that was not contained in history textbooks, for instance, as regards the National Democracy, its main ideologues and achievements, and the National Military Organization (Żebrowski, 1989a, pp. 40–55, 1989b, pp. 43–47; Kędziora, 1989, pp. 34–42; Tomczyk, 1989, pp. 42–51; Wituch, 1989, pp. 3–12; Kawęcki, 1989b, pp. 31–33). Patriotic upbringing was combined with religious education (Suszka, 1989, pp. 36–38; Misiuda, 1989, pp. 8–11).

The readers were provided with cultural content in the form of book reviews and novels in instalments (for example, Roman Dmowski's novel *Dziedzictwo* [*Heritage*] written under the pseudonym K. Wybranowski) (Wybranowski, 1990a, 1990b, 1991a, 1991b). The magazine also published patriotic poems (see, e.g., Rostworowski, 1989, p. 86; Norwid, 1989, p. 80).

---

33   See, e.g. "Stowarzyszenie ofiar wojny szansą narodu polskiego (fragmenty memoriału)," *sn* May 1989, no. 1, pp. 62–64; "Apel Poznańskiego Klubu Historycznego im. Dra Franciszka Witaszka (fragment)", *sn* June 1989, no. 2, pp. 67–68; "List emigracyjny Stronnictwa Narodowego do Prezesów i członków wydziałów Wykonawczych S.N., Mężów zaufania S.N. [Stronnictwa Narodowego], członków komitetu politycznego, oraz działaczy narodowych podpisany przez A. Dargasa", *sn* September–October 1989, nos. 5–6, pp. 60–63; P. Szymański, "Polski Związek Akademicki", *sn* May 1989, no. 1, p. 66; Zarząd PZA Poznań, "Chcemy umieć walczyć o Polskę! Polski Związek Akademicki Poznań", *sn* January 1990, no. 1, p. 70; Katolickie Stowarzyszenie Młodzieży Pracującej, *sn* May 1989, no. 1, pp. 64–65; Stowarzyszenie Narodowe im. Romana Dmowskiego, "Apel do studentów polskich o włączenie się do obrony zagrożonych wartości moralnych narodu", *sn* June 1989, no. 2, pp. 68–70.

The attitude-forming function was performed by convincing readers of the validity of the nationalist idea and also the concepts of domestic and foreign politics acknowledged by the editorial office. The readers were encouraged to vote for candidates presented in the magazine through references to the axiological sphere (Goryszewski, 1989, pp. 63–65; Kowzan, 1990b, pp. 20–21). They were requested to take a stand with regard to, for example, the removal of the Carmelite convent from Auschwitz (M. Giertych, 1989e, p. 39; M.G., 1990f, p. 39). The editorial team also became involved in the abortion dispute, since they demanded abolishing the law which permitted abortion and introducing legislation penalising it (Kawęcki, 1989a, pp. 30–32; Chałupka, 1991, pp. 5–7; Szatybełko, 1989, pp. 62–63, 1990, pp. 10–11; M.G., 1989, pp. 75–76, 1990c, p. 44).

The opinion-forming function was of no less importance for the editorial team, since they made a continuous effort to shape the readers' views on current political events, the political transformation, and threats facing the nation and the country. They took a critical stance towards the Round Table discussions, which was expressed in the statement made by K. Kawęcki: "Magdalenka AD 89, was the culmination of an over-thirty-year-long quiet alliance between left-wing communists, social democrats and Catholics, an alliance motivated by the fear of a potential, or rather imaginary, 'populist-nationalist' threat" (1990a, p. 5).[34] S. Kozanecki argued that the "Solidarity" of 1989 did not resemble the movement it used to be in August 1980, but was only one strand of it – "the laic left wing". He objected to politicising the social movement and postulated the so-called renaissance of political trends. He used the term "pink" to refer to the opposition, and the term "red" to refer to the government (1989a, pp. 14–16).

It should be pointed out that the criticism of the political transformation was consistent with many various ideological strands of the nationalist movement. There were fears concerning the direction of the political change. They resulted from the conviction that the "new elites" were not of Polish background, that there was a conspiracy initiated by the government and the opposition during the Round Table discussions, and that the new political power had a cosmopolitan character (Maj, 2008, p. 128). Another issue addressed by the editorial team of *National Word* was the general elections, during which they criticised the appropriation of "the oppositional stance" by the Citizens' Association. It was pointed out that they were not granted the mandate to represent the whole opposition, to mention, for instance, the Christian Democratic milieu. According to the columnists, they solely represented the laic

---

34   They also pointed out the lack of ideological pluralism during the Round Table discussions, as both sides had the same ideological background (Wiśniewski, 1989, pp. 73–79).

left wing. "The Christian democratic, national democratic, conservative and folk camps" were regarded as the "third power" (Zaremba, 1989b, pp. 74–75; Murasiewicz, 1989c, pp. 14–15; Winiarski, 1989b, pp. 70–71). The magazine also published opinions concerning Poland's geopolitical situation and the parliamentary and presidential elections (Jasieńczyk-Krajewski, 1990, pp. 20–21; Zaremba, 1990d, pp. 1–2; Odyniec, 1990, p. 4; "Polska", 1990, pp. 11–17; Jeznach, 1990, p. 32).

The milieu-forming function was equally important to the magazine's editorial staff. K. Kawęcki pointed out directly that the aim of the ideological milieu of the magazine is "to restore a traditional nationalist movement". In his opinion, it should be "an intellectual trend, a stream of social awareness, however, one having a clear ideological outline" (1990a, p. 6). At the same time, it was considered important to initiate the movement's restoration based on national Catholic and social right-wing factions, which recognised not only political but also moral, economic and social threats (Kawęcki, 1990a; Piesiewicz, 1989b, pp. 3–7). On the one hand, all forms of "reinvention" of the thought and concepts of the fathers of the National Democracy – Roman Dmowski and Jan Ludwik Popławski – encountered objections. Bronisław Ekert thought that such a reinvention could lead to "diluting cultural and political imponderabilia, and, what is more, an acceptance of influences foreign to the Polish spirit, of neo-modern and liberal content, will not uplift Polish thought and culture, also in a political sense" (1990, p. 8). On the other hand, some voices were raised saying that being rooted in history was indeed important, however "history cannot be a programme, but merely a spiritual and ideological bond that connects people" (Zaremba, 1990a, p. 39).

The magazine promoted newspapers and books published by the Publishing House *National Word* within the framework of, among others, the National Word Library. The readers were encouraged to purchase a multi-year subscription, under the slogan "Spare some zlotys for the national press!". The Jan Ludwik Popławski Prize was established with the aim of promoting "ideological activity".

As part of the milieu-forming function, the magazine presented profiles of the most deserving activists of the National Democracy (Bondaryk, 1990, pp. 27–28; M. Giertych, 1990e, pp. 28–29; Kaczmarek, 1990, pp. 24–38; Krzemiński, 1991, pp. 17–18) as well as the contemporary political milieu of *National Word*. Some scenarios were designed to win over young people's support (Zacharyasz, 1990, pp. 32–33). In September 1990, Maciej Giertych published an article in which he put forward an initiative aimed at presenting a joint list of national-democratic candidates. For this purpose, he called for a coalition of nationalist parties to run for election to the parliament. He received support from the

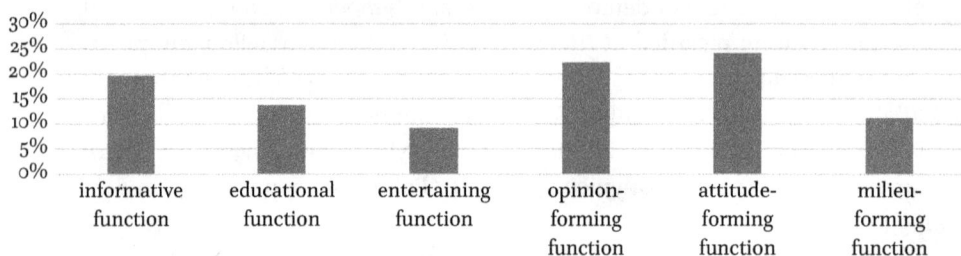

FIGURE 9.3   Functions performed by *National Word*
              SOURCE: MY OWN RESEARCH

All-Polish Youth, the National Liberal Party, and the Odpowiedzialność i Czyn [Responsibility and Action] association (1990b, pp. 1–2). From September, in the column titled "Political Milieu", the editors presented profiles of people who were ideologically close to the editorial staff and might run for election to the parliament, namely M. Giertych, K. Kawęcki, W. Olszewski, P.J. Pisiewicz, Marian Szatybełko, Januariusz Kowalewicz, Leon Mirecki and K. Murasiewicz.

The analysis of the content published in *National Word* made it possible to determine the percentage rate of the share allocated to each function in all their press materials (see Figure 9.3).

It is worth noting that the opinion-forming and attitude-forming functions, which fostered the so-called "political sophistication" of the readers, had a dominant position. Of course, it was political sophistication in line with nationalist ideology. It was, then, the first stage of building the political milieu surrounding *National Word*. This was understandable, though, considering the dispersion of activists and supporters of the national idea during the Polish People's Republic period,[35] and also the intense political competition on the threshold of the political transformation. Only in 1989, claims were made to the political heritage of the National Democracy and the function of its continuator in Poland by groups gathered around Marian Barański, Maciej Giertych and Wiesław Chrzanowski. The activists of the pre-war, and then the émigré branch of the ND as well as some reactivated youth organisations also became active (Szwed-Walczak, 2019c, pp. 85–86).

Even though my research shows that "Ideological deliberations", "Education and upbringing", and "Evaluation of politics" dominated the periodical's content, the third hypothesis has been refuted. The educational function was not of primary importance (it followed the opinion-forming, attitude-forming,

---

35   It should be noted that, as Ewa Maj argued (2010, p. 79), the National Democracy was the only party among the four factions within the Polish Underground State that could not legally restore its structures in Poland.

and informative functions). Content assessment and categorisation enable the conclusion that the periodical was meant, first and foremost, to get the readers interested in the national thought and to shape public opinion in accord with the system of values espoused by the Polish national camp. The periodical was also to shape attitudes in keeping with the national ideology. This stemmed from the primary goal of the editorial team, namely, to build a political party with broad social support. Educational value was thus of a secondary character.

9.5   Conclusion

The monthly magazine *National Word* was a platform for promoting nationalist ideas and a programme based on this during the period of political transformation. It was the second publishing initiative undertaken by the company Słowo I Czyn. Although the first initiative – *Warsaw Gazette* – integrated the nationalist milieu, the second one had a clearly milieu-forming character. The editorial teams connected with both publishing initiatives were comprised of three generations: pre-war nationalists, whose presence legitimised the topicality and validity of the nationalist agenda and an ideological continuity among the editorial team, their followers (who initiated conspiratorial activities all over the country[36]) and the youngest columnists who became active after 1981. It is worth noting that the members of the editorial team and feature writers who worked for *National Word* came from various informal and conspiratorial discussion groups and organisations of nationalist provenance, therefore the first legal periodical was supposed to be a prelude to their unification and then to building political power that would stand a chance of obtaining political legitimacy through the electoral process.

The members of the editorial team had publishing, journalistic and organisational experience. Some of them acquired nationalist views through the process of socialisation and upbringing, like in the case of the sons of prominent ideologues and activists of the National Democracy. They had university education to their credit, however, the issues they addressed in the magazine were often inconsistent with the knowledge they acquired through the process of education.

The ideological premises of *National Word* included the pre-war array of values acknowledged by the National Democracy: nation, Catholicism, nation-state, national culture, and national economy, complemented by Jędrzej Giertych's concept of Christian nationalism and Feliks Koneczny's theory of

---

36   Scholars point out that illegal publications flourished in Poland in the 1970s (Sparks, 2008, p. 52).

civilisation. References were made to the thought of Roman Dmowski and Jan Ludwik Popławski. There was a noticeable influence of Jędrzej Giertych's ideas on the content presented in the magazine, as well as its interpretation of domestic and foreign politics.

The magazine performed numerous ambitious functions for the sake of its readers: informative, educational, entertaining, opinion-forming, attitude-forming and milieu-forming ones.

In the course of the analysis conducted for this article, the first hypothesis was partially verified. My research demonstrated that the team that established the magazine took into account the experience gained by the émigré activists. The representatives of the émigré community became members of the Editorial Council, although the conditions under which the émigré publishers operated differed significantly from those existing in Poland. As much as the domestic magazine regarded as important the technical tips of political feature writers, the experiences gained by the nationalists who performed their first (illegal) publishing activities in the country proved more useful. The second hypothesis was fully verified and was based on the assumption that the editorial team was ideologically close to Jędrzej Giertych's ideas. This ideological proximity was reflected both in numerous references to his publications and in their promotion. The last hypothesis, which was supposed to prove the educational function of the monthly magazine, was not confirmed. This was because the dominant position in *National Word* was occupied by the opinion-forming and attitude-forming functions. The editorial team of the periodical failed to build a permanent political milieu, which was reflected in the fates of the members of the editorial staff, who eventually joined different political parties.

References

Books

Berelson, B. (1952). *Content Analysis in Communication Research*. Gelncoe: The Free Press.

Chodakiewicz M. J., Mysiakowska-Muszyńska, J., & Muszyński, W. J. (2015). *Polska dla Polaków! Kim byli i są polscy narodowcy*. Poznań: Zysk i S-ka.

Cugowski, P. (2012). *Myśl polityczna Jędrzeja Giertycha*. Szczecin: My book.

Kafel, M. (1969). *Prasoznawstwo. Wstęp do problematyki*. Warszawa: PWN.

Krippendorff, K. (2004). *Content Analysis. An Introduction to its Methodology*. Thousand Oaks: Sage Publications.

Maj, C., & Maj, E. (2007). *Narodowe ugrupowania polityczne w Polsce 1989–2001*. Lublin: UMCS.

McQuail, D. (2007). *Mass Communication Theory.* Los Angeles: Sage Publications

Pisarek, W. (1983). *Analiza zawartości prasy.* Kraków: Ośrodek Badań Prasoznawczych.

Smolik, B. (2012). *Naród we współczesnej polskiej myśli politycznej. Problematyka narodu w ujęciu głównych nurtów polskiego nacjonalizmu w latach 1989–2004.* Kraków: Księgarnia Akademicka.

Szwed-Walczak, A. (2019c). *Obraz wroga Polski we współczesnej prasie narodowej.* Lublin: UMCS.

Tokarz, G. (2002). *Ruch narodowy w Polsce w latach 1989–1997.* Wrocław: uWr.

Tomasiewicz, J. (2003). *Ugrupowania neoendeckie w III Rzeczypospolitej.* Toruń: Adam Marszałek.

Wojciechowski, K. (2005). *Maciej Giertych – zarys biograficzny,* Warszawa: Ars Politica.

Articles in Books

Dawidowicz, A. (2012). Jędrzej Giertych jako nacjonalista chrześcijański. In E. Maj, J. Sanecka-Tyczyńska, M. Wichmanowski, & A. Wójcik (Eds.), *Kościół, religia, myśl katolicka. Studia i szkice ofiarowane Profesorowi Antoniemu Mieczkowskiemu z okazji 70 rocznicy urodzin* (pp. 101–121). Lublin: UMCS.

Jakubowicz, K., & Sükösd, M. (2008). Twelve Concepts Regarding Media System Evolution and Democratization inPost-Communist Societies. In K. Jakubowicz, & M. Sükösd (Eds.), *Finding the Right Placeon the Map. Central and Eastern European Media Change in a Global Perspective* (pp. 9–40). Bristol, Chicago: Intellect.

JK [J. Kołodziej] (2006). Analiza treści. In W. Pisarek (Ed.), *Słownik terminologii medialnej* (pp. 6–8). Kraków: Universitas.

Kajtoch, W. (2018). Badanie aksjologicznego wymiaru języka prasy. In A. Szymańska, M. Lisowska-Magdziarz, & A. Hess (Eds.), *Metody badań medioznawczych i ich zastosowanie* (pp. 17–44). Kraków: IDMIKS UJ.

Kawęcki, K. (2012). Tradycja narodowa i katolicyzm w publicystyce środowiska „Słowa Narodowego". In B. Grott, & O. Grott (Eds.), *Nacjonalizmy różnych narodów. Perspektywa politologiczno-religioznawcza* (pp. 299–318). Kraków: Księgarnia Akademicka.

Lasswell, H. D. (1948). The Structure and Function of Communication in Society. In L. Bryson (Ed.), *The Communication of Ideas* (pp. 37–51), New York: Harper & Brothers.

Maj, E. (2008). Myśl narodowa i nacjonalistyczna. In E. Maj, & A. Wójcik (Eds.), *Myśl polityczna w Polsce po 1989 roku. Wybrane nurty ideowe* (pp. 113–148). Lublin: UMCS.

Maj, E. (2015). Prasa: źródło w badaniach historii myśli politycznej. In E. Maj, E. Kirwiel, & E. Podgajna (Eds.), *Myśl polityczna w społeczeństwie informacyjnym* (pp. 575–590). Lublin: UMCS.

Maj, E. (2010). Wielonurtowość myśli nacjonalistycznej w Polsce współczesnej. In E. Maj, M. Mikołajczyk, & M. Śliwa (Eds.), *Idee w procesie kształtowania współczesnej rzeczywistości polskiej. Nacjonalizm* (pp. 74–100). Kraków: Uniwersytet Pedagogiczny.

Pokorna-Ignatowicz, K. (2012). From the communist doctrine of media to free media. The concept of a new information order in the Round Table Agreements. In K. Pokorna-Ignatowicz (Ed.), *The Polish Media System (1989–2011)* (pp. 11–21). Kraków: Krakow Society fo r Education: AFM Publishing House.

Sikorski, T. (2011). "Nowe Horyzonty" (1986–1989) – pismo młodej endecji schyłku PRL-u. Próba zarysu monograficznego. In A. Dawidowicz, & E. Maj (Red.), *Prasa Narodowej Demokracji. Od roku 1939 do początku XXI wieku*, (t. 2, pp. 85–108). Lublin: UMCS.

Sikorski, T. (2016). „Wyznajemy zasady narodowe polskie i uniwersalne katolickie". Stronnictwo Narodowe na emigracji (1939–1992): zarys działalności i myśli politycznej. In *Angielski łącznik. Albin Tybulewicz (1929–2014)* (pp. 11–82). Warszawa: Muzeum Historii Polski.

Słomkowska, A. (1996). Zmiany w mediach w roku poprzedzającym zniesienie cenzury. In A. Słomkowska (Red.), *Transformacja mediów (1989–1995)*. *Materiały Pomocnicze do Najnowszej Historii Dziennikarstwa* (t. XXVI, pp. 25–31). Warszawa: Elipsa.

Sparks, C. (2008). After Transition: The Media in Poland, Russia and China. In K. Jakubowicz, & M. Sükösd (Eds.), *Finding the Right Placeon the Map. Central and Eastern European Media Change in a Global Perspective* (pp. 43–71). Bristol, Chicago: Intellect.

Szwed-Walczak, A. (2019a). Obraz opozycji politycznej w kraju na łamach emigracyjnej „Opoki". W E. Kirwiel, E. Maj, E. Podgajna, & M. Wichmanowski (Eds.), *Myśl polityczna – demokracja – wolność. Księga Jubileuszowa dedykowana Profesorowi Janowi Jachymkowi z okazji 80, rocznicy urodzin* (pp. 567–582). Lublin: UMCS.

Szwed-Walczak, A. (2019b). Obraz Polski niepodległej w emigracyjnym piśmie „Opoka" (1969–1988). In A. Dawidowicz, & E. Maj (Eds.), *Państwo niepodległe. Twórcy – strategie – komunikacja społeczna* (pp. 183–198). Lublin: UMCS.

Tomasiewicz, J. (2016). „Młodzi" przeciwko „starym". Koncepcje ideowo-polityczne i działalność środowisk młodonacjonalistycznych w PRL lat osiemdziesiątych. In B. Noszczak (Red.), *Życie na przekór. Młodzieżowa kontestacja systemu w ostatniej dekadzie PRL (1980–1989) – nowe tropy i badania badawcze* (pp. 277–302). Warszawa: IPN.

Articles in Periodicals

Cenckiewicz, S. (2007). „Endekoesbecja". Dezintegracja Polskiego Związku Katolicko-Społecznego w latach 1982–1986. *Aparat represji w Polsce Ludowej 1944–1989*, 1/5/2007, 343–456.

Filas, R. (2010). Dwadzieścia lat przemian polskich mediów (1989–2009) w ujęciu periodycznym. *Zeszyty Prasoznawcze*, nr 3–4, 27–54.

Mikosz J. (2018). Press journalist's proffesion in Poland after political transformation in 1989 and nowadays. *Studies in Linguistics, Culture and FLT*, vol. 4, 125–140.

Sikorski T. (2013). Drogi i bezdroża. Trudne życie Macieja Giertycha w Polskiej Rzeczpospolitej Ludowej. *Archiwum Emigracji. Studia – Szkice – Dokumenty*, z. 1 (18), 125–142.

Szwed A. (2013). „Opoka w Kraju". (The Bedrock in a Country). The magazine's monograph, *Annales Universitatis Mariae Curie-Skłodowska*,ectiono K, vol. xx, 2, s. 251–270.

Conference Materials

Atwood R. (1994). Reconstructing Polish Press Freedom: The Quest for New Models of Free Expression Among Polish Journalists. Conference: ICA conference-Sydney, Australia. Retrieved from https://www.researchgate.net/publication/278730791 _Reconstructing_Polish_Press_Freedom_The_Quest_for_New_Models_of_Free _Expression_Among_Polish_Journalists [15.02.2021].

Atwood R. (1994). The Transfiguration of the Polish Media. The Catholic Churc"s Intervention into Post-CommunistMedia Practice & Policy Development, Journalism & Media Ethics. Media Issues in Post-Communist Europe. Retrieved from https:// www.researchgate.net/publication/278730786_The_Transfiguration_of_the_Polish _Media_The_Catholic_Churc"s_Intervention_into_Post-Communist_Media _Practice_Policy_Development [15.02.2021].

Legal Acts

Ustawa z dnia 11 kwietnia 1990 r. o uchyleniu ustawy o kontroli publikacji i widowisk, zniesieniu organów tej kontroli oraz o zmianie ustawy– Prawo prasowe (Dz. U. 1990 *[Journal of Laws]* no. 29 poz. 173)

Press

a)   *Słowo Narodowe* (1989–1991)

Akt powołania Klubu Przyjaciół „Słowa Narodowego" (1990, Feb.). *Słowo Narodowe*, no. 2.

Akt powołania Klubu Przyjaciół „Słowa Narodowego". (1990, May). *Słowo Narodowe*, no. 5.

Apel Poznańskiego Klubu Historycznego im. Dra Franciszka Witaszka (frag). (1989, Jun.). *Słowo Narodowe*, no. 2.

B.Z. (1990a, May). Megaloman. *Słowo Narodowe*, no. 5.

B.Z. (1990b, Mar.). Przed wyborami do samorządów. *Słowo Narodowe*, no. 3.

B.Z. (1990c, Apr.). Test Jacka Kuronia. *Słowo Narodowe*, no. 4.

Bondaryk, K. (1990, Apr.). Prezes białostockiego SN ks. Jan Ostrowski (1892–1948). *Słowo Narodowe*, no. 4.

Chałupka, W. (1991, Feb.). Wokół ochrony życia dziecka poczętego. *Słowo Narodowe*, no. 2.

Cofta, W. (1990, Jun.). Rozważania o zagrożeniu niemieckim. *Słowo Narodowe*, no. 6.

Dmowski, R. (1991, Jan.). Walki wewnętrzne a ustrój społeczny. *Słowo Narodowe*, no. 1.

Drechna, L. (1990, Jun.). Nad podmiotowością Narodu... *Słowo Narodowe*, no. 6.

Ekert, B. (1990, Jan.). W płytkim nurcie. *Słowo Narodowe*, no. 1.

Engelgard, J. (1989a, Sep.-Oct.). Bitwa warszawska 1920r. – opinie – relacje – dokumenty. *Słowo Narodowe*, no. 5–6.

Engelgard, J. (1989b, Nov.-Dec.). Casus Kosińskiego. *Słowo Narodowe*, no. 7/8.

Engelgard, J. (1989c, Nov.-Dec.). Nóż w plecy? Na marginesie listu „Solidarności RI" do Polaków na Litwie. *Słowo Narodowe*, no. 7/8.

Engelgard, J. (1990, Apr.). Peter Raina, „Sprawa zabójstwa Bohdana Piaseckiego. *Słowo Narodowe*, no. 4.

Giertych, J. (1990, Jun.). Prymat polityki. *Słowo Narodowe*, no. 6.

Giertych, M. (1989a, May). Dwugłos o naszej tożsamości: co nas wyróżnia?. *Słowo Narodowe*, no. 1.

Giertych, M. (1990a, May). Francuska Prawica. *Słowo Narodowe*, no. 5.

Giertych, M. (1989b, Sep.-Oct.). Geopolityka Brzezińskiego. *Słowo Narodowe*, no. 5/6.

Giertych, M. (1990b, Jul.-Aug.). Inicjatywa prof. dr hab. Macieja Giertycha. *Słowo Narodowe*, no. 7–8.

Giertych, M. (1989c, Jul.). Jak wrócić do normalności. *Słowo Narodowe*, no. 2.

Giertych, M. (1989d, Nov.-Dec.). Komu sprzedać Polskę. *Słowo Narodowe*, no. 7–8.

Giertych, M. (1990c, May). Kongres Prawicy Polskiej. *Słowo Narodowe*, no. 5.

Giertych, M. (1989e, May). List otwarty do sióstr Karmelitanek w Oświęcimiu. *Słowo Narodowe*, no. 1.

Giertych, M. (1990 d, Jan.). W odpowiedzi obrońcy teorii ewolucji. *Słowo Narodowe*, no. 1.

Giertych, M. (1990e, Apr.). Wywiad z ks. prałatem Władysławem Matusem: Najstarszy Narodowiec. *Słowo Narodowe*, no. 4.

Giertych, R. (1990, Jul.-Aug.). Jakie polskiej młodzieży chowanie. *Słowo Narodowe*, no. 7–8.

Giertych, R. (1989, Nov.-Dec.). Najpierw „Polityka", a teraz „Tygodnik Powszechny". *Słowo Narodowe*, no. 7/8.

Goryszewski, H. J. (1989, May). Tezy do doktryny politycznej. *Słowo Narodowe*, no. 1.

Goryszewski, H. J. (1989, Jun.). Deklaracja wyborcza. *Słowo Narodowe*, no. 2.

Jasieńczyk-Krajewski, L. R. (1990, Jan.). Impas. *Słowo Narodowe*, no. 1.

J.E. (1990, Mar.). Nieścisłość zamierzona?. *Słowo Narodowe*, no. 3.

(JEZ). (1990, Jan.). Był Kohl... *Słowo Narodowe*, no. 1.

(jez.). (1990, Jun.). Kiedyś był tylko plan. *Słowo Narodowe*, no. 6.

Jeznach, B. (1990, May). Wałęsa prezydentem?. *Słowo Narodowe*, no. 5.

Kaczmarek, Z. (1990, Jul.). Joachim Stefan Bartoszewicz – pierwszy prezes Stronnictwa Narodowego. *Słowo Narodowe*, no. 6.

Katolickie Stowarzyszenie Młodzieży Pracującej (1989, May). *Słowo Narodowe*, no. 1.

Kawęcki, K. (1990a, Jan.). O polską prawicę narodową. *Słowo Narodowe*, no. 1.

Kawęcki, K. (1990b, May). Przyjaciele Prawicy Narodowej. *Słowo Narodowe*, no. 5.

Kawęcki, K. (1989a, Jun.). Rodzina -własność -szkoła. *Słowo Narodowe*, no. 2.

Kawęcki, K. (1989b, Jul.-Aug.). Ruch Narodowy na emigracji. *Słowo Narodowe*, no. 3–4.

Kędziora, B. (1989, Jul.-Aug.). Kształtowanie się orientacji politycznej Ligi Narodowej w świetle publicystyki „Przeglądu Wszechpolskiego" (1895–1905). *Słowo Narodowe*, no. 3–4.

Koło Przyjaciół „Słowa Narodowego" w Łodzi. (1990, May). *Słowo Narodowe*, no. 5.

Komunikat (1989, Sep.-Aug.). *Słowo Narodowe*, no. 5–6.

Kowzan, A. (1991, Jan.). Rozmawia z red. Witoldem Olszewskim: Narodowe horyzonty. *Słowo Narodowe*, no. 1.

Kowzan, A. (1990a, Jul.). Teologia Narodu. *Słowo Narodowe*, no. 6.

Kowzan, A. (1990b, Dec.). Wybory narodowców. *Słowo Narodowe*, no. 12.

Kozanecki, S. (1989a, Nov.-Dec.). Blaski i cienie polskiej wiosny 1989 (3 VI 1989, Belgia). *Słowo Narodowe*, no. 7–8.

Kozanecki, S. (1989b, Sep.-Oct.). Zawsze naszym kosztem. *Słowo Narodowe*, no. 5–6.

Krajska, E. (1990, May). Jakiej kultury potrzebują Polacy. *Słowo Narodowe*, no. 5.

Krzemiński, Z. (1991, Feb.). Zbigniew Stypułkowski. *Słowo Narodowe*, no. 2.

Krzepkowski, A. (1990, Jun.). Lewica laicka, prawica katolicka. *Słowo Narodowe*, no. 6.

Krzepkowski, A. (1990, Apr.). Zasłona dymna. *Słowo Narodowe*, no. 4.

Krzysztof Kawęcki (1990, Sep.). *Słowo Narodowe*, no. 9.

Kurasiewicz, K. (1990, Feb.). Niemcy, Rosja i sprawa polska – po latach. *Słowo Narodowe*, no. 2.

Le Pen, J.-M. (1990, Mar.). Wolność i cnota. *Słowo Narodowe*, no. 3.

Ligęza, A. (1990, Apr.). Kilka pytań do zwolenników kapitalizmu. *Słowo Narodowe*, no. 4.

List emigracyjny Stronnictwa Narodowego do Prezesów i członków wydziałów Wykonawczych S.N., Mężów zaufania S.N., członków komitetu politycznego, oraz działaczy narodowych podpisany przez A. Dargasa. (1989, Sep.-Oct.). *Słowo Narodowe*, no. 5–6.

M.G. (1991, Jan.). Echa prasowe inwazji masowej na Polskę. *Słowo Narodowe*, no. 1.

M.G. (1990a, Apr.). Ich Prezydent broni lepiej interesów Polski niż nasz Premier. *Słowo Narodowe*, no. 4.

M.G. (1990b, Feb.). Kto zapłaci za urynkowienie. *Słowo Narodowe*, no. 2.

M.G. (1990c, May). Marszałek walczy z Kościołem. *Słowo Narodowe*, no 5.

M.G. (1989, Sep.-Oct.). O obronie prawa do zabijania dzieci. *Słowo Narodowe*, no. 5–6.

M.G. (1990d, Jan.). Pytania. *Słowo Narodowe*, no. 1.

M.G. (1990e, Jun.). Tylko dlaczego tak mało?. *Słowo Narodowe*, no. 6.

M.G. (1990f, May). Wokół Karmelitanek. *Słowo Narodowe*, no. 5.

Maciej Marian Giertych: Bóg – Rodzina – Ojczyzna! (1990, Sep.). *Słowo Narodowe*, no. 9.

Majewski, J. (1989, Jun.). Chcę być Jarońskim!. *Słowo Narodowe*, no. 2.

Marian Szatybełko: Bóg, Rodzina, Ojczyzna!. (1990, Nov.). *Słowo Narodowe*, no. 11.

Meissner, A. (1989, Nov.-Dec.). Traktat wersalski z perspektywy 70 lat. *Słowo Narodowe*, no. 7–8.

Mirecki, L. (1990, Jan.). Białe karty obozu narodowego. *Słowo Narodowe*, no. 1.

Misiuda, W. (1989, Jul.-Aug.). Re quidem vera – odpowiadający prawdzie. *Słowo Narodowe*, no. 3–4.

Murasiewicz, K. (1989a, Nov.-Dec.). Gorące polskie lato A.D. 1989. *Słowo Narodowe*, no. 7–8.

Murasiewicz, K. (1989b, Jul.). My, nieobecni. *Słowo Narodowe*, no. 3–4.

Murasiewicz, K. (1990, Apr.). Okolice jednoznaczności. *Słowo Narodowe*, no. 4.

Murasiewicz, K. (1989cm Sep.-Oct.). Polskie tęsknoty. *Słowo Narodowe*, no. 5–6.

Nagroda Fundacji „Protector Poloniae" i „Słowa Narodowego". Komunikat Jury. (1991, Jan.). *Słowo Narodowe*, no. 1.

Norwid, K. C. (1989, Nov-Dec.). *Słowo Narodowe*, no. 7–8.

„Obsesje" Romana Dmowskiego. (1989, Jul.-Aug.). *Słowo Narodowe*, no. 3–4.

Od redakcji. (1989a, May). *Słowo Narodowe*, no. 1.

Od redakcji. (1989b, Sep.-Oct.). *Słowo Narodowe*, no. 5–6.

Od redakcji. (1990a, Feb.). *Słowo Narodowe*, no. 2.

Od redakcji. (1990b, Apr.). *Słowo Narodowe*, no. 4.

Od redakcji. (1990c, May). *Słowo Narodowe*, no. 5.

Od redakcji. (1990d, Oct.). *Słowo Narodowe*, no. 10.

Odyniec, M. (1990, Apr.). „Schlonzaken, Kaschuben, Goralem i inni. *Słowo Narodowe*, no. 4.

Olszewski, W. (1989a, Nov.-Dec.). Antysemityzm?. *Słowo Narodowe*, no. 7–8.

Olszewski, W. (1990, Jan.). O Dmowskim inaczej. *Słowo Narodowe*, no. 1.

Olszewski, W. (1989b, May). Odpowiedź Mitteleuropejczykom. *Słowo Narodowe*, no. 1.

Ołdak, P. (1990a, May). Co dalej polska prawico?. *Słowo Narodowe*, no. 5.

Ołdak, P. (1989, Jun.). Regionalizm jako podstawa odnowy kultury. *Słowo Narodowe*, no. 2.

Ołdak, P. (1990b, Apr.). Władysław Gauza, Faszyzm w Europie wschodniej i droga wyjścia. *Słowo Narodowe*, no. 4.

P.P. (1989, Jun.). *Słowo Narodowe*, no. 2.

P.P. (1990, Jan.). Wyraźny profil?. *Słowo Narodowe*, no. 1.

Parada, J. (1991, Feb.). Być na prawicy. *Słowo Narodowe*, no. 2.

Piesiewicz, P. (1990a, Jan.). Fragment wypowiedzi Piotra Piesiewicza na seminarium „Idee i wartości współczesnej prawicy polskiej" dnia 4 listopada 1989 r. na Politechnice Warszawskiej. *Słowo Narodowe*, no. 1.

Piesiewicz, P. (1989a, Sep.-Oct.). O nurtach w ruchu narodowym, politycznych dewiacjach, propagandowych manipulacjach i antyendeckich obsesjach. *Słowo Narodowe*, no. 5–6.

Piesiewicz, P. (1989b, Jul.-Aug.). Potrzeba współczesnego „Chjenopiasta". *Słowo Narodowe*, no. 3–4.

Piesiewicz, P. (1990b. May). „Słowo Narodowe". *Słowo Narodowe*, no. 5.

Piesiewicz, P. (1991, Mar.). Zgromadzenie Wspólników Spółki „Słowo i Czyn". *Słowo Narodowe*, no. 3.

Piotr Jakub Piesiewicz: Wszystko dla Polski!. (1990, Oct.). *Słowo Narodowe*, no. 10.

Piotr Piesiewicz. (1991, Jan.). *Słowo Narodowe*, no. 1.

Piotr Ołdak. (1991, Jan.). *Słowo Narodowe*, no. 1. Polska w zmieniającej się Europie. (1990, May). *Słowo Narodowe*, no. 5.

Pukacki, D. (1990, May). Nie sprzedawać Polski Niemcom. *Słowo Narodowe*, no. 5.

Qui bono?. (1989, Jul.-Aug.). *Słowo Narodowe*, no. 3–4.

Robatyński, K. (1991, Feb.). O narodową myśl ekonomiczną. *Słowo Narodowe*, no. 2.

Rokicki, K. (1990, Jun.). Co w zamian za RWPG. *Słowo Narodowe*, no. 6.

Rokicki, K. (1989, Nov.-Dec.). Naród – patriotyzm – solidaryzm. *Słowo Narodowe*, no. 7–8.

Rostworowski, K. H. (1989, Jun.). Naprzód !. *Słowo Narodowe*, no. 2.

Ruta, Z. (1991, Feb.). Prywatyzacja po starcie. *Słowo Narodowe*, no. 2.

Skwara, J. (1990a, Jan.). Dramat Jerzego Gabryjelskiego. *Słowo Narodowe*, no. 1.

Skwara, J. (1990b, Jun.). Dzieje filmu polskiego po wojnie. *Słowo Narodowe*, no. 6.

Skwara, J. (1991, Feb.). Podzwonne dla „szkoły polskiej". *Słowo Narodowe*, no. 2, p. 15–16.

Sobków, D. (1989a, May). Kościół w cywilizacji europejskiej. *Słowo Narodowe*, no. 1.

Sobków, D. (1990, Jan.). Wywiad z Bruno Megret: „Jesteśmy jedynie obrońcami Narodu Francuskiego". *Słowo Narodowe*, no. 1.

Sobków, D. (1989, Jun.). Wywiad z J.E. biskupem Józefem Michalikiem: „Młodzież nasza nie ma motywu aby trwać na klęczkach przed Zachodem". *Słowo Narodowe*, no. 2.

Spółka spółce nierówna. (1989, Jul.-Aug.). *Słowo Narodowe*, no. 3–4.

Stowarzyszenie Narodowe im. Romana Dmowskiego. (1989, Jun.). Apel do studentów polskich o włączenie się do obrony zagrożonych wartości moralnych narodu. *Słowo Narodowe*, no. 2.

Stowarzyszenie ofiar wojny szansą narodu polskiego (fragmenty memoriału). (1989, May). *Słowo Narodowe*, no. 1.

Suszka, S. (1989, Jul.). Historyczna rola Arcybiskupów Gnieźnieńskich i Prymasów Polski. *Słowo Narodowe*, no. 2.

Szatybełko, M. (1990, Jul.-Aug.). Nienarodzony szansą demokracji. *Słowo Narodowe*, no. 7–8.

Szatybełko, M. (1989, Jul.). Troska o poczęte życie nie jest monopolem katolików, przemówienie wygłoszone w Sejmie 26 kwietnia 1989 r. podczas debaty nad projektami ustawy o podstawach prawa wyznaniowego. *Słowo Narodowe*, no. 2.

Szczepaniak, I. (1990, Feb.). Iluzje i mity w rządowym programie gospodarczym. *Słowo Narodowe*, no. 2.

Szymański, P. (1989, May). Polski Związek Akademicki. *Słowo Narodowe*, no. 1.

Tomczyk, A. (1989, Jul.-Aug.). Roman Dmowski w Tokio w 1904 roku. *Słowo Narodowe*, no. 3–4.

Tworzenie i urządzanie mniejszości niemieckiej w Polsce. (1989, Sep.-Oct.). *Słowo Narodowe*, no. 5–6.

Urban, W. (1991, Jan.). Kalendarzyk niemiecki 1990–2000 (studium futurologiczne). *Słowo Narodowe*, no. 1.

Wertyński, A (1990, Feb.). Zjednoczenie Niemiec. *Słowo Narodowe*, no. 2.

Winiarski, M. (1989a, Sep.-Oct.). Iluzje, iluzje... *Słowo Narodowe*, no. 5–6.

Winiarski, M. (1989b, Sep.-Oct.). Refleksje powyborcze. *Słowo Narodowe*, no. 5–6.

Winiarski, M. (1990, Apr.). Utrata instynktu samozachowawczego, czy ... *Słowo Narodowe*, no. 4.

Wiśniewski, P. (1989, Jun.). Pluralizm w jednej „rodzinie". *Słowo Narodowe*, no. 2.

Witold Olszewski: dziennikarz, publicysta, działacz narodowy. (1990, Oct.). *Słowo Narodowe*, no. 10.

Wituch, T. (1989, Jun.). Roman Dmowski – Rola dziejowa z perspektywy 50-lecia. *Słowo Narodowe*, no. 2.

Wybranowski, K. (1990a, May). Dziedzictwo. *Słowo Narodowe*, no. 5.

Wybranowski, K. (1990b, Jun.). Dziedzictwo. *Słowo Narodowe*, no. 6.

Wybranowski, K. (1991a, Jan.). Dziedzictwo. *Słowo Narodowe*, no. 1.

Wybranowski, K. (1991b, Feb.). Dziedzictwo. *Słowo Narodowe*, no. 2.

W.W. (1990, Mar.). Skąd się wzięło święto kobiet. *Słowo Narodowe*, no. 3.

Wywiad z prof. Maciejem Giertychem przedrukowany w całości za „Gazetą Krakowską" z 22 XII 1989 r.: Krajobrazy polityczne. (1990, Feb.). *Słowo Narodowe*, no. 2.

Zacharyasz, M. (1990, Apr.). Stronnictwo Narodowe dzisiaj. *Słowo Narodowe*, no. 4.

Zaremba, B. (1990a, Feb.). Czy jest miejsce dla partii tradycyjnych?. *Słowo Narodowe*, no. 2.

Zaremba, B. (1989a, Nov.-Dec.). Hiszpania – przykład czy ostrzeżenia?. *Słowo Narodowe*, no. 7–8.

Zaremba, B. (1990b, Feb.). Kierunek – Rosja!. *Słowo Narodowe*, no. 2.

Zaremba, B. (1990c, Sep.). My i Rosja. *Słowo Narodowe*, no. 9.

Zaremba, B. (1990d, Apr.). Opolszczyzna – pierwsze starcie. *Słowo Narodowe*, no. 4.

Zaremba, B. (1990e, Jan.). Przeciw monopolowi lewicy. *Słowo Narodowe*, no. 1.

Zaremba, B. (1989b, Jul.-Aug.). Pułapka dualizmu (Chadecja w wyborach). *Słowo Narodowe*, no. 3–4.

Zarząd PZA Poznań. (1990, Jan.). Chcemy umieć walczyć o Polskę! Polski Związek Akademicki Poznań. *Słowo Narodowe*, no. 1.

Zarzecki, W. (1989, Jul.-Aug.). Jak każdy naród, jesteśmy przez Boga wybranym narodem. *Słowo Narodowe*, no. 3–4.

Zieliński, J. (1990a, Jul.). Nacjonalizmy. *Słowo Narodowe*, no. 6.

Zieliński, J. (1990b, Mar.). Spór o jutro. Polemika z Adamem Michnikiem. *Słowo Narodowe*, no. 3.

Zygier. (1989, May). Cywilizacja zaklęć, czyli moje spotkanie z „Res Publicą". *Słowo Narodowe*, no. 1.

Żebrowski, L. (1989a, May). „Cyryl" – Białostocki Okręg Narodowej Organizacji Wojskowej (NOW) 1941–1945. *Słowo Narodowe*, no. 1.

Żebrowski, L. (1989b, Jun.). Dmowski w Chludowie 1922–1934. *Słowo Narodowe*, no. 2.

Żebrowski, L. (1990a, Apr.). Lwowskie AK. *Słowo Narodowe*, no. 4.

Żebrowski, L. (1989c, Nov.-Dec.). Podziemna legalizacja 1939–1945. *Słowo Narodowe*, no. 7–8, p. 36–42.

Żebrowski, L. (1990b, Mar.). „Tajemnica Twierdzy Brześć", książka którą każdy powinien przeczytać. *Słowo Narodowe*, no. 3.

b) *Gazeta Warszawska*

W. L. (1989, 1–15 Jan.). Co inni piszą…*Gazeta Warszawska*, no 1–2.

c) *Myśl Polska*

Szymański, T. (2019, 21–28 Apr.). Bohdan Winiarski – od zaborów do PRL. *Myśl Polska*, no 17–18.

d) *Opoka*

Giertych J. (1982, Dec.). Nowe wydawnictwa Towarzystwa im. R. Dmowskiego. *Opoka*, no 17.

e) *Wprost*

Krasnowska V. (1999, 12 Sep.). Lekcja polskiego. *Wprost*, no 37.

Ideological Writings

Giertych, M. (2005). *Z nadzieją w przyszłość!*. Warszawa: Ars Politica.

Wasiutyński, W. (1999). *Rozstanie z Almą*, [w:] *Dzieła wybrane*, t. 1, oprac. i red. W. Turek, Gdański: Exter.

Internet Sources

Andrzej Meissner. (31 Jan. 2020). Retrieved from https://prepedia.fandom.com/wiki/Andrzej_Meissner.

Mossakowski, R. (31 Jan. 2020). Historia środowiska Zagórnej. Retrieved from https://cep-sklep.pl/news/n/173/Historia.

Original Source

Wywiad z Marianem Barańskim (15. Sep. 2013).

CHAPTER 10

Investigative Journalism and the Public Image Crises of Politicians – Selected Examples

Dominika Popielec

10.1 Introduction

If we look at the history of investigative journalism in its broader context, it is worth noting that the activities of journalists and media publishers have contributed to the underpinning of democratic principles – such as freedom of speech, media responsibility and transparency in the mechanisms of the functioning of the state in the interest of the general public. Freedom of speech, in particular, has a leading place in the constitutions of many democratic countries and is considered a standard of a modern state. The principle of freedom of speech, which appeared in the First Amendment of the US Constitution, was the result of the publisher of *The New York Weekly Journal*, John Peter Zenger, winning a lawsuit brought by Governor William Cosby, who accused Zenger of libel. The governor was portrayed as a corrupt politician in the newspaper (which negatively affected his image). After hearing Zenger's arguments, the court ruled that the publisher had the right to write the truth (Wiggins, 1997, pp. 1–12). In addition to the legal implications, civil rights and media obligations, it is also worth noting another extremely important implication, i.e., image – understood as "a set of information about a person, institution, company or other entity, that is what others think about us, what others know about us, and what they think they know" (Białopiotrowicz, 2009, p. 17). The researcher states that image consists of such elements as:

- appearance, behaviour, manners and interpersonal skills (element 1);
- professional qualifications, skills as well as experience (element 2);
- successes, personal achievements and professional achievements (element 3);
- lifestyle – understood as the quality of relationships with people and ways leisure time is spent (element 4) (Białopiotrowicz, 2009, p. 18).

If any of the above elements are substandard, then it results in the erosion of a positive image, as was the case with the Polish politicians Andrzej Lepper and Kazimierz Marcinkiewicz (Białopiotrowicz, 2009, p. 36).

When observing the contemporary political scene, it must be said that the mentioned examples are not just a historical curiosity. One may also say that the correlation between investigative journalism and the public image of a person or institution is just as strong today as when the scandals mentioned here occurred, with the role of investigative journalism becoming a permanent aspect of a democracy. In the literature on the subject, a number of cases show the clear relationship between the media and various scandals involving politicians. Hans Mathias Kepplinger noted the following relationship which:

> requires information on three key points: the triggering event, the intensity of media coverage, and the perception of the event by the public. (2018, p. 2)

Among the many types of scandals mentioned there are: sex scandals, financial scandals and power scandals (Mancini, 2019, p. 157). One of the most recognizable investigations was the Watergate scandal exposed in *The Washington Post*, which not only destroyed the public image of President Richard Nixon but also his political career. There were many more scandals affecting the public image of presidents and crowned heads in the following years, including the sex scandal involving President Bill Clinton and Monika Lewinsky (McNair, 2006, p. 26). The standards set by the journalistic work of *The Washington Post* found adherents in other editorial offices around the world, including the countries of Central and Eastern Europe, which were aspiring to democracy after 1989 (e.g., Poland). According to Kepplinger, there are various factors that are influenced by the reporting of scandals, e.g., the whole journalistic culture and general political sentiment (Kepplinger, 2018, p. 5). Paolo Mancini also draws attention to this because he believes:

> The surrounding context defined what a scandal is, why and how an illegal or unfair behaviour is transformed into a theme of public debate, how and why it is brought to light, and how it develops. (2019, p. 156)

The intention of this article is to examine the relationship between a journalistic investigation and the public image crisis using selected examples from the Polish political scene in the years 2002–2020.

The crises discussed here are the Rywin affair, the tape scandal and the behaviour of the Minister of Health, Łukasz Szumowski, during the COVID-19 pandemic. We will look at the fallout for the public image of those involved, as well as the impact on the shape of the Polish political scene.

To this end, the following research questions were formulated:

– What information was disclosed by investigative journalists in the analysed examples?

– What impact did this information have on the political scene?
– Did the content of the journalists' exposé affect the image of the public figures under analysis?

The work employs content analysis, case study, and comparative methods to investigate the chosen research material, which consists of investigative journalism published in the *Gazeta Wyborcza* newspaper (digital edition) and the weekly *Wprost*. The results of research carried out by the Public Opinion Research Centres were also used to show the public reception of the scandals analysed.

10.2   Selected Scandals Involving Polish Politicians and the Associated Public Image Crisis between 2002–2014

There have been no shortage of scandals in Polish political life that were revealed by investigative journalists. This is thanks to the control function played by the media and the sense of civic responsibility of the journalists. The multitude of scandals presented in the media may be a signal that something disturbing is happening to democracy, but this is not due to the lack of any journalistic intervention or weakness of the media, which do carry out their primary tasks, i.e., informing and acting as a control mechanism. The work of investigative journalists should include asking difficult questions on behalf of the citizens, especially concerning the standards expected of public figures (Popielec, 2019, p. 11). The content of many media investigative exposés dominated public discourse for weeks, with regular comments and reactions by: politicians, publicists, journalists and invited experts. This was not without impact on society in terms of future election decisions. Those at the centre of these scandals often had their positive image damaged irreparably, and, consequently, lost public positions and political influence.

The Rywin affair was one of the biggest scandals of the Polish political scene at the turn of the 21st century (it was a bribe made by the film producer Lew Rywin to Adam Michnik, the editor of *Gazeta Wyborcza*). At that time, political power was exercised by the Democratic Left Alliance, headed by Leszek Miller, who was then working on an amendment to the Broadcasting Act (on a more strictly anti-concentration provision contained therein) prohibiting a company that had a nationwide daily newspaper from owning a television station (Dudek 2018). The disclosed information in the investigative article in *Gazeta Wyborcza* entitled "The Bribe to Change the Act, or Rywin Propositions Michnik" claimed that the producer had offered to arrange favourable changes for Michnik's company in the government's draft amendment to the Act on

Radio and Television. These changes were to enable Agora to buy Polsat television. The money from the bribe was to be transferred to the Democratic Left Alliance. Other conditions set by Rywin included the cessation of criticism of Prime Minister Leszek Miller by *Gazeta Wyborcza* and a role for Rywin in Polsat television after the takeover of the station by Agora (Smoleński, 2002).

It should be added that the article was the result of weeks of investigation, which is the norm when collecting and verifying information, and testifies to the understanding of its potential impact on the character of those involved. Helena Łuczywo from the editorial office confirmed that: "Investigative exposés are not written quickly. We delayed the publication, hoping that we could complete the transcript of the conversation with specific names, that we would discover at least part of the truth" (Smoleński, 2002). The article is a peculiar kind of calendar of the events, because it was written chronologically, including the content of the bill itself; the opposition to it by the private media community; the criticism expressed by opposition MPs and the President, and the initial conditions of the deal that Lew Rywin proposed, which Wanda Rapaczyńska (Agora CEO) reported to the journalists:

> We talked for maybe ten minutes. Rywin made an offer, which – as he assured – he had heard while fishing. It was as if I had been hit with a club on my head. (Smoleński, 2002)

The Rywin scandal was on the lips of the media and political people and soon became of interest to the relevant public institutions, including the prosecutor's office, which investigated the case. The Sejm established the first parliamentary inquiry commission in Poland since 1989, consisting of selected deputies from various groups: the Democratic Left Alliance, Labour Union, League of Polish Families, Self Defence, Polish People's Party, Civic Platform, Law and Justice (Anon, 2019). The Rywin affair initiated the political collapse of the Democratic Left Alliance, weakened the position of *Gazeta Wyborcza* and broke many political careers (Pawlicka, 2012). It should be noted that many left-wing politicians suffered in terms of image, among others, former Deputy Minister of Culture and Head of the Political Cabinet of the Prime Minister in the government of Leszek Miller, Aleksandra Jakubowska (Mikołajewska 2009), who oversaw the amendment to the Act on Radio and Television. In her interview, Jakubowska stated that "obviously, it (the Rywin affair) led to the government's resignation and my departure from the prime minister's office" (Mikołajewska, 2009). The former deputy minister was sentenced by a final court judgement to eight months imprisonment suspended for two years on irregularities during the preparation of the Law on Radio and Television of

2002 (Anon, 2012). Currently, the former deputy minister is not involved in political activities.

The public perception of the Rywin affair and its impact on the political scene at the time was of interest to the Public Opinion Research Centre (CBOS) to assess the public image of people connected directly (decision-making) or indirectly (party affiliation) with the case. Published research showed that 73% of respondents and no trust in Aleksandra Jakubowska, which was influenced by the findings of the parliamentary inquiry commission into the role of Jakubowska herself. The research also showed that this level of distrust was comparable to the unambiguously negative perception of Rywin by the public (Pankowski, 2003, p. 5). President Kwasniewski's high public support at the time was only slightly weakened as a result of his speech (Pankowski, 2003, p. 5) after his failure to appear before an investigative commission:

> I will not remember anything else. If you want a show, I can dance and sing in front of the Commission, but what for?. (Money.pl, 2003)

It should be added that the decrease in public confidence was noted by Włodzimierz Czarzasty from the Democratic Left Alliance, who was then Secretary of the National Broadcasting Council (Pankowski, 2003, p. 6). The Democratic Left Alliance saw confidence in it drop to 14 percent. 66 percent of those surveyed believed there was a group of politicians behind the Rywin's corruption proposal (Pankowski, 2003, p. 7). This assessment may result from the adopted working report of the aforementioned commission by Zbigniew Ziobro, in which it was stated that "Aleksandra Jakubowska, Lech Nikolski, Włodzimierz Czarzasty and Robert Kwiatkowski formed a *group in power*" (Pawlicka, 2007).

The behind-the-scenes of the Rywin affair – along with other examples of such phenomena, e.g., the Starachowice scandal, the Orlen scandal (Bejma, 2013, p. 115) – adversely affected the standing of the Democratic Left Alliance. This stemmed, for instance, from the emerging public image crisis arising as a result of public discontent, which included: loss of credibility and public confidence in politicians holding key state functions. The unfavourable climate contributed to the poor election result in the parliamentary elections of 2005 – 11.31 percent of votes (PKW, 2005).

Another scandal that caused a serious public image crisis for the ruling camp of the Civic Platform and the Polish People's Party is the tape scandal of 2014, revealed by journalists of the *Wprost* weekly. The figures of the conversations recorded in the *Sowa i Przyjaciele* restaurant were leading politicians of the Civic Platform holding important state positions (ministers), the president of the National Bank of Poland (NBP), and the head of the Central Anti-Corruption Bureau. In addition to the content of the conversations, the attention of the public and the media was also caught by the language of the interlocutors and the dishes served in the restaurants, among others, the infamous "octopus", which became synonymous with the luxury of the then power.

The journalists of *Wprost* decided to disclose the tape transcripts to show the backstage functioning of power in Poland and to stop any attempt to blackmail politicians (Burzyńska, Majewski, Bielakowski, Nisztor, Latkowski, 2014, pp. 15–16). During the recorded conversations (meeting 1: Bartłomiej Sienkiewicz, Marek Belka and Sławomir Cytrycki; meeting 2: Sławomir Nowak, Andrzej Parafianowicz) several threads appeared. The content of the discussion revealed that the NBP president would support the Civic Platform in financing the budget deficit in exchange for the Minister of Finance being replaced. Those involved discussed the Ambergold scandal, the social perception of the government's achievements in the field of infrastructure (road, sports), polls regarding political support, and evaluated the actions of Paweł Graś (Secretary of State for the prime minister) and Jacek Rostowski (Minister of Finance).

As it turned out, no less important than the content of conversations were the behaviour and manners shown; the interpersonal skills, professional qualifications and abilities; the quality of relationships and the ways those involved spent their free time. The language used was publicly criticized, as it contained vulgarities in relation to the persons and events discussed in the conversations (Burzyńska, Majewski, Bielakowski, Nisztor, Latkowski 2014, pp. 17–21). The media cited the statement of Minister Sienkiewicz, who said that "the Polish state exists only theoretically. It practically does not exist because it operates with its individual fragments – and the state is a whole" (Burzyńska, Majewski, Bielakowski, Nisztor, Latkowski, 2014, pp. 20–21). It should be noted that this diagnosis could be interpreted as implying that decision-makers do not have the competence and skills to manage the state.

As great attention was also paid to the lifestyles of those involved – which in this case included: spending time in restaurants, eating fancy dishes and drinking alcohol, telling jokes and commenting on relationships with other people – the following examples were selected:

– "the company orders appetizers: carpaccio made of Dutch herring, anchovies and caviar, pickled radishes, salmon caviar (...) The main dishes will be pork cheeks, oxtails and octopus"
– "I will honestly say that if we invited only those who were permanent, we could order a single person room (comment about Paweł Graś – author's note) ... along with a bottle of something of course"

- "then maybe you have to tell him how he can be robbed more. Maybe he will understand" (about the entrepreneur and investor Zbigniew Jakubas – author's note)
- "do you know what the most popular toast is this winter? To us, to you, to gas, all at once (Burzyńska, Majewski, Bielakowski, Nisztor, Latkowski, 2014, pp. 17–25).

Two days after the publication of the transcripts of those meetings, police and officers of the Internal Security Agency (ABW) entered the editorial office of *Wprost* with the intention of forcibly taking the laptop of editor Latkowski, including data enabling identification of the informer. Latkowski refused, arguing that "protecting the source of information is a journalist's sacred duty" (Latkowski, Majewski, 2014a, pp. 10–13). This raid was strongly condemned by other media, politicians and public opinion. According to Mariusz Janicki, the actions of the ABW were not received positively: "It looks bad, both for the country and for public opinion. The value of the investigation is very questionable, and the loss of image and to the system – very large" (Janicki, 2014).

The tape scandal continued. The journalists involved decided to provide details related to the collection and verification of the information from the tapes and knowledge of other media about tapes, including TVP Info television station and *wSieci* weekly magazine (Latkowski, Majewski 2014b, pp. 12–13). Latkowski explained the purpose of revealing the content of the conversations as follows:

> Our role is not to protect power. No power. Our role is to show where the state works badly. Or does not work at all. Writing the truth, even if it is painful. The image emerging from these recordings is like a bucket of ice water for many people. (Latkowski, Majewski, 2014b, pp. 227–228)

At the beginning of 2015, details of recordings of other public people at restaurants were published in *Wprost*, including former Prime Minister Leszek Miller, former President Aleksander Kwasniewski, businessman Jan Kulczyk and presidents of banks (e.g., at that time the president of the then BZ WBK bank Mateusz Morawiecki), and Radosław Sikorski. Among the topics discussed were the issue of the secret CIA prisons in Poland and even the Rywin affair (Kwasniewski-Miller conversation). The political future of Leszek Miller and Radosław Sikorski was also discussed (Latkowski, Burzyńska, Gielewska, Smolińska, Wasilewska, Dzierżanowski, Łazarewicz, Sadowski, 2015a, pp. 8–11). *Wprost* devoted some attention to the waiters involved, who – at the request of the businessman Marek Falenta – recorded public figures in restaurants in order to obtain information that could be of significance, e.g., for the security services (Latkowski, Burzyńska, Gielewska, Smolińska, Wasilewska, Dzierżanowski, Łazarewicz, Sadowski, 2015a, pp. 14–15).

The Public Opinion Research Centre also displayed an interest in the social perception of the tape scandal shortly after its revelation. Their research showed that the level of interest was related to the political views on the left-centre-right scale and to the attitude towards the Civic Platform-Polish People's Party government. In addition, strong views are most often expressed by respondents who identify with the right wing (61% of them are interested in the tape scandal), secondly with the left wing (53%), and thirdly the respondents with centrist political views (42%). The answers to whether the recorded conversations ought to have been disclosed are particularly important. 65% of respondents believe that it was in the public interest that the contents of the recordings were published, while 19% were of the opposite opinion. It is also important that the majority of opponents of the government of the then Prime Minister Donald Tusk (84%) say that it was good that the contents of the recordings were disclosed (Badora, Omyła-Rudzka, 2014, pp. 2–3). It should be emphasized that this thread was one of the narratives in the upcoming parliamentary (October 2015) and presidential (May 2015) elections, and appeared across various media forms. 80% of respondents believed that the tape scandal discredits the recorded politicians only, while 62% thought it was a government crisis. The attitude towards the media was highly positive (64%), because it was perceived as a journalistic mission (Badora, Omyła-Rudzka, 2014, pp. 6–8). According to the respondents, the most outrageous part of the scandal were: the expensive dishes and alcohol consumed (paid for from the public purse) (32%); the destabilization of the situation in the country and the impact on the image of Poland (25%); the behind-the-scenes policy making (25%); the language and crude vocabulary (23%); inefficiency of security services (22%); the content of the conversations (21%); the Prime Minister's position (18%); the violation of the right to privacy of public figures (15%) (Badora, Omyła-Rudzka, 2014, p. 13).

The Rywin affair and the tape scandal affected the image of the politicians involved, which was reflected in the later election results.

10.3   Political Scandals Affecting the Ruling Party and their Public Image Crisis after 2015

The content of the conversations revealed by investigative journalists from *Wprost* negatively affected the image of individual politicians, with the publication of their conversations dominating the media discourse for many weeks and catching the public's attention. The scandal caused the erosion of the public image not only of the ruling camp as a whole, but also of specific politicians. It would seem that this regularity is a permanent feature of the impact that the media, and investigative journalism in particular, have had on governments and politicians. This is due to the role of watchdog of democracy being fulfilled by investigative reporters. As a result of the efforts of journalists, the information is brought to the attention of not only politicians, journalists, society but also (and equally importantly) the relevant public institutions investigating the described phenomena (corruption, nepotism, illegal activity, etc.).

When looking at the way the publicized corrupt behaviour affected the political scene in terms of the impact of the information on the political class, it is worth recalling the example of the scandal regarding the purchase of farmland during the rule of Law and Justice, the League of Polish Families, and Self-Defence in 2006–2007, when Jarosław Kaczyński was the Prime Minister and the Deputy Prime Ministers were Roman Giertych (the League of Polish Families) and Andrzej Lepper (Self-Defence). The public learnt about this scandal (which concerned a bribe in exchange for changing the legal status of farmland offered by two associates of Lepper suggesting influence in the Ministry of Agriculture) once Deputy Prime Minister Lepper had been dismissed by Prime Minister Kaczyński. The coalition's image at the time was already tarnished by Marcin Kącki's disclosure of a sex scandal involving Andrzej Lepper in December 2006 in the article "Work for Sex" in *Gazeta Wyborcza* telling the stories of abused women (Kącki, 2006). The cited scandals led to the political collapse of the deputy prime minister and his party, as well as the coalition government, which resulted in early elections in which the opposition party (Civic Platform) won. It is worth noting that Self-Defence and the League of Polish Families won no seats in this Sejm (Margraf, 2012).

A number of factors contributed to the election result which saw the Law and Justice win the parliamentary elections in 2015 and 2019. In addition to its social programmes publicised in the media, fragments from the 2014 tapes of the tape scandal were repeatedly returned to, which effectively discouraged voters from trusting Civic Platform politicians.

It should be noted that the scandals whose villains were politicians from the Democratic Left Alliance, Civic Platform, and Self-Defence were important for public opinion in terms of electoral preferences, because they significantly changed the landscape of the political scene. Law and Justice was particularly fierce in condemning Civic Platform politicians involved and their voters strongly identified with this stance.

Law and Justice has seen various scandals and double standards, as revealed by the media during its rule (after 2015). According to journalist Witold

Gadomski, the publicized scandals were irrelevant to Law and Justice voters, since he believes that:

> we have a broken political scene and a broken media scene. For a Law and Justice supporter, the information provided by a newspaper or television sympathizing with the opposition does not matter much. What counts is only what is contained in *our* newspapers and websites. (Gadomski 2020)

Gazeta Wyborcza is the most active editorial office when one considers who investigates the authorities. The Wyborcza.pl website has 27 articles in which journalists revealed scandals after 2015. In 2019 (which was the election year for elections to the Polish and European parliament) nine investigative articles were published, including focusing on ambiguities in the property ownership statement of Prime Minister Morawiecki in the context of the purchase of a plot of Church-owned land at a price five times lower than the parish authorities could have requested. Journalists described the details of the purchase and pointed to the lack of transparency and unclear explanations of both the prime minister and the priest involved in brokering the deal (Harłukowicz, 2019a). Other media, e.g., *Polityka* weekly, *Newsweek*, and *Rzeczpospolita* newspaper also showed an interest in the case. In the opinion of Grzegorz Rzeczkowski from *Polityka*, ambiguities in the prime minister's property portfolio may affect the election result in the autumn (Rzeczkowski, 2019).

Despite the COVID-19 pandemic, the media did not pause its activity in the field of investigative journalism. Although other topics also appeared in the media discourse, the attention of the political class and public opinion was focused on the pandemic (an important reference point in the 2020 presidential campaign). From the beginning of the pandemic, the Minister of Health Łukasz Szumowski was very active, regularly participating in press conferences and informing the public and the media about the details of the serious restrictions on economic and social life that were being introduced.

Minister Szumowski, who is a professor of medical sciences, was positively perceived by the political environment and society as a whole in the initial period of the coronavirus epidemic in Poland. In this way, he became the face of the government in the fight against coronavirus and was top in the ranking of most trusted public figures – ahead of the then ruling president (Lasota-Krawczyk 2020). According to Adam Mitura, an image expert from the InPlus Media agency, the health minister was perceived as:

> Calm, factual, professional, always available to the media, in addition a man practising the profession of social trust; a doctor, not a politician.

Szumowski seemed to be an ideal candidate not only for crisis management, but also – provided that he used the political capital he accumulated very quickly – higher political office. (Goczał, 2020)

So what led to the decline in confidence in Minister Szumowski? Answers to
this question were sought by the team of experts from *Sentimenti*, an organisation that researches emotions on the web based on a specially constructed catalogue, which is key in research into public image (Anon, Senimenti.pl 2020).
Based on research material that contained the name of the Minister of Health
which appeared in social media, news portals, and forums in the period from
February 1, 2020 to June 15, 2020 (Anon, Sentimenti.pl, 2020), it was established
that the public image crisis was caused by: inconsistent communication with
the public; no clear improvements regarding the epidemic when compared to
other countries; the scandal regarding the purchase of masks and respirators
disclosed by journalists (Anon, Sentimenti.pl, 2020).

Personal protective equipment, in particular masks, were becoming a scarce
commodity. In April, the government announced that masks, suits, and disin-
fectants were being purchased from China. The arrival of personal protective
equipment was presented as an unprecedented event due to the number of
items (seven million) and the size of the airplane (Harłukowicz, 2020b). However, journalists alleged that the quality control certificates were forged, and
it appeared that the Chinese producers had falsified the certificates that are
required by the European Union (Harłukowicz, 2020b), which, in turn, raised
questions about the effectiveness of masks and whether they were of a high
enough quality to ensure the safety of medical staff.

In May, journalists from *Gazeta Wyborcza* revealed that the Ministry of Health
had spent 5 million zloty on protective masks that did not meet the required
standards. The villains of this scandal are: the Minister of Health, Łukasz Szumowski; his brother, Marcin Szumowski – operating in the pharmaceutical
industry; the Deputy Minister of Health, Janusz Cieszyński; the Deputy Director
of the Supervision and Control Department at the Ministry of Health, Małgorzata
Dębska; and the ski instructor and personal friend of minister Szumowski who
offered the masks (Czuchnowski, 2020). Journalists recreated the chronology
of the events and revealed the relationships between those involved – from
the submission of the offer to buy the masks for the minister's brother by a
ski instructor friend who had no prior experience of this type of transaction.
Reporters established that Marcin Szumowski assured his ski instructor friend
that he would "talk to his brother" on this matter (Czuchnowski, 2020). Reporters also claimed that this scandal would undoubtedly have a negative effect on
the image of Minister Szumowski (Godusławski, Parafianowicz, 2020).

The public revelations caused greater focus not only on the minister himself, but also his brother. When analysing Marcin Szumowski's activities in detail, the journalist came across information which indicated, among others, the lack of transparency when the minister's brother's company was granted a contract by the National Centre for Science and Development which reports to the Ministry of Higher Education, where Łukasz Szumowski served as deputy minister (Watoła, Jedlecki, 2020).

Based on analysis of the results of the journalistic investigation and publicly-available information, a change in the perception of Minister Szumowski's activities was found. This was detrimental not only for the minister himself, but also for his political associates. According to Monika Kaczmarek-Śliwińska, in Minister Szumowski at the beginning of the coronavirus pandemic:

> we saw a tired doctor, worried about the fate of his patients, which, moreover, brought a significant increase in the trust and popularity of Minister Szumowski. Currently, communication conducted directly by the minister has slowed down a bit – it is less present in the media, which I link with negative information about the finances of the minister's family rather than with a decrease in the government's information needs. (Kalinowska, 2020)

The public image of the minister was based on his professional experience and qualifications but was seriously affected by the revelations from the scandal regarding the purchase of masks. The opaque purchase procedures and the lack of transparency worked to the detriment of Minister Szumowski, which was evident in the decline in public confidence.

10.4   Conclusions

One of the functions of the media, and in particular investigative journalism, is to act as guarantors of a democratic system. There is no doubt that:

> investigative journalism, which relies on freedom of information laws, exposes scandals in government, business, and other institutions, making for a better world. (Cuillier, 2019: 219)

On the basis of the selected examples concerning the Polish political scene, it is impossible to ignore the fact that investigative journalism not only publicizes and sparks discourse on important topics of public interest, but also stigmatizes specific behaviour of politicians, which includes corruption, nepotism, law-breaking and indecency. This requires journalists to be honest and diligent when gathering and verifying information, because this is how public confidence in the media, which is supposed to act in the public interest, is built.

It should be emphasized that investigative journalism in Poland came into existence after 1989, when the political system changed. It was modelled on investigative journalism practiced by the media in more mature democracies. From then on, the media has held politicians to account, which was not without significance for their political careers and, consequently, for the electoral decisions of society. The scandals selected for analysis here are proof of the impact of investigative journalism on the image of politicians. In the analysed investigative articles, journalists have highlighted the corruption, nepotism, law-breaking and unacceptable behaviour of politicians. It is worth noting the fact that the exposed scandals remained present in public discourse for an extended period, greatly affecting the social mood.

The nature and seriousness of the information highlighted in the media had an impact on the erosion of the image of public figures and their political environment. In the case of the Rywin affair, this resulted in a serious decline in voters' confidence in the Democratic Left Alliance, which was reflected in the result of the following parliamentary elections. The next affair, the tape scandal of 2014, negatively affected the image of individual politicians of the ruling camp, which was also visible in the preference of voters. The last of the presented multi-threaded scandals regarding Minister Szumowski also negatively affected his image, which had been very positive at the beginning of the pandemic.

The analysis carried out reveals that investigative journalism has an impact on the political scene. The disclosure of information often generates a public image crisis, which, in turn, results in a number of changes, e.g., accelerated elections, loss of power and resignation from political activity. It is also proof of the need for the media to act as a watchdog of democracy.

References

Anon. (2003). „Członkowie komisji śledczej zdziwieni wypowiedzią prezydenta". At https://www.money.pl/gospodarka/wiadomosci/artykul/czlonkowie;komisji;sledc zej;zdziwieni;wypowiedzia;prezydenta,253,0,61693.html. Accessed 16/06/2020.

Anon. (2012). „Aleksandra Jakubowska skazana - wyrok za „lub czasopisma" prawomocny". At https://wiadomosci.wp.pl/aleksandra-jakubowska-skazana-wyrok-za-lub -czasopisma-prawomocny-6032751877276801a. Accessed 16/06/2020.

Anon. (2019). „Wojna o media, czyli afera Rywina". At https://www.polskieradio.pl/39/156 /Artykul/2243282,Wojna-o-media-czyli-afera-Rywina. Accessed 16/06/2020.

Anon. (2020). „Łukasz Szumowski. Od bohatera do lidera spadku zaufania". At https:// sentimenti.pl/blog/lukasz-szumowski-minister-zdrowia-koronawirus-afera/. Accessed 20/06/2020.

Aucoin, J. (2007). The Evolution of American Investigative Journalism. University of Missouri Press.

Badora, B., Omyła-Rudzka, M (2014). Społeczny odbiór afery podsłuchowej. Komunikat badań CBOS. Nr 104. Warszawa.

Bejma, A. (2013). „Od afery Rywina do katastrofy smoleńskiej – nowe (utrwalone) podziały społeczno-polityczne w Polsce". Studia Politologiczne. Vol. 29.

Białopiotrowicz, G. (2009). Kreowanie wizerunku w biznesie i polityce. Warszawa: Wydawnictwo Poltext.

Burzyńska, A., Majewski, M., Bielakowski, C., Nisztor, P., Latkowski, L. (2014). „Afera podsłuchowa". Wprost no. 25.

Cuillier, D. (2019). Scandals and freedom of information. in H. Tumber, S. Waisboard (eds.), The Routledge Companion to Media and Scandal. London-New York: Routledge.

Czuchnowski, W. (2020). „Wyborcza ujawnia: 5 mln za bezużyteczne maseczki dla znajomego ministra Szumowskiego z nart". At https://wyborcza.pl/7,75398,25936849 ,wyborcza-demaskuje-afere-w-resorcie-zdrowia-5-mln-zl-za-bezwartosciowe .html. Accessed 20/06/2020/.

de Burgh, H. (2013). Investigative Journalism. London-New York: Routledge.

Dudek, A. (2018). „Co po piętnastu latach naprawdę wiemy o aferze Rywina?" At https://opinie.wp.pl/co-po-pietnastu-latach-naprawde-wiemy-o-aferze-rywina -6213459633841793a Accessed 16/06/2020.

Gadomski, W. (2020). „Dla zwolenników PiS afery i skandale w obozie władzy nie mają znaczenia". At https://wyborcza.pl/7,75968,24991915,dla-zwolennikow-pis-afery-i -skandale-w-obozie-wladzy-nie-maja.html. Accessed 17/06/2020.

Goczał, B. (2020). „Łukasz Szumowski z wizerunkowej gwiazdy rządu staje się „czarną owcą" (opinie)". At https://www.wirtualnemedia.pl/artykul/lukasz-szumowski-z -wizerunkowej-gwiazdy-staje-sie-czarna-owca-opinie. Accessed 17/06/2020.

Godusławski, B., Parafianowicz, Z. (2020). „Zakup maseczek nadszarpnął wizerunek ministra Szumowskiego [Opinia]". At https://wiadomosci.dziennik.pl/opinie /artykuly/7701919,zakupy-maseczki-minister-szumowski-koronawirus -covid-19-wybory-korespondencyjne-opinia.html. Accessed 20/06/2020.

Harłukowicz, J. (2019a). „Jak Morawicki uwłaszczył się na gruntach kościelnych". At https://wroclaw.wyborcza.pl/wroclaw/7,35771,24804013,jak-morawiecki-uwlaszczyl -sie-na-gruntach-koscielnych-sledztwo.html. Accessed 17/06/2020.

Harłukowicz, J. (2020b). „Maseczki, które przyleciały z Chin, mają lewy certfikat. Nie wiadomo czy chronią [Śledztwo Wyborczej]". At https://wroclaw.wyborcza .pl/wroclaw/7,35771,25890303,kghm-kupil-maseczki-z-lewym-certyfikatem -nie-wiadomo-czy-chronia.html. Accessed 18/06/2020.

Janicki, M. (2014). *Akcja ABW złym pomysłem*. At https://www.polityka.pl/tygodnikpol ityka/kraj/1583731,1,akcja-abw-zlym-pomyslem.read?backTo=https://www.polityka .pl/tygodnikpolityka/kraj/1583729,1,abw-wkroczyla-do-redakcji-wprost-premier -zabiera-glos.read. Accessed 17/06/2020.

Kalinowska, A. (2020). *Jak w czasie epidemii zmieniała się komunikacja Łukasza Szumowskiego*. At http://www.proto.pl/aktualnosci/lukasz-szumowski-komunikacja -epidemia. Accessed 20/06.2020.

Kącki, M. (2006). *Praca za seks*. At https://wyborcza.pl/duzyformat/1,127290,3767928 .html. Accessed 16/06/2020.

Kepplinger, H. M. (2018). Hidden Traps: An Essay on Scandals. Commentary. *International Journal of Communication*. No. 12.

Lasota-Krawczyk, J. (2020). „Sondaż zaufania IBRiS: Szumowski liderem, na drugim miejscu Duda. Gowin traci najbardziej". At https://www.rmf24.pl/fakty/polska/news -sondaz-zaufania-ibris-szumowski-liderem-na-drugim-miejscu-du,nId,4479972. Accessed 17/06/2020.

Latkowski, S., Burzyńska, A., Gielewska, A., Smolińska, I., Wasilewska, I., Dzierżanowski, M., Łazarewicz, C., Sadowski, G. (2015). Nieznane nagrania kelnerów. *Wprost* No. 12.

Latkowski, S., Majewski, M. (2014a). Taśmociąg Platformy. *Wprost* No. 36.

Latkowski, S., Majewski, M. b (2014b). Afera podsłuchowa. Taśmy „Wprost". Warszawa: Wydawnictwo Zysk i S-ka.

Margraf, M. (2012). „Przed nami wybory - pięć lat temu prezes PiS popełnił największy polityczny błąd?" At https://www.tokfm.pl/Tokfm/1,103087,12298170,_Przed_nami _wybory___piec_lat_temu_prezes_PiS_popelnil.html. Accessed 17/06/2020.

Mancini, P. (2019). Corruption scandals and the media systems in H. Tumber, S. Waisboard (eds.), The Routledge Companion to Media and Scandal. London-New York: Routledge.

McNair, B. (2006). What is Journalism? in H. De Burgh (ed.) Making Journalists: Diverse Models, Global Issues. London-New York: Routledge.

Mikołajewska, B. (2009). *Rozmowa z Aleksandra Jakubowską*. At https://www.polityka .pl/tygodnikpolityka/kraj/299043,1,rozmowa-z-aleksandra-jakubowska.read. Accessed 16/06/2020.

Pankowski, K. (2003). Polacy o tzw. sprawie Rywina w przededniu rozpoczęcia jego procesu. Komunikat z badań. At https://www.cbos.pl/SPISKOM.POL/2003/K_185_03 .PDF. Accessed 16/06/2020.

Pawlicka, A. (2007). „Temat 8. Rywin i inni, czyli korupcja". At https://wyborcza
.pl/1,76842,3981285.html. Accessed 16/06/2020.

Pawlicka, A. (2012). „Milczenie Lwa, czyli bohaterowie afery Rywina 10 lat później". At
https://www.newsweek.pl/polska/milczenie-lwa-czyli-bohaterowie-afery-rywina
-10-lat-pozniej/3k9cb58 Accessed 16/06/2020.

PKW (2005). Wybory do Sejmu Rzeczpospolitej Polskiej. At https://wybory2005.pkw
.gov.pl/SJM/PL/WYN/W/index.htm. Accessed 16/06/2020.

Popielec, D. (2019). Dziennikarstwo śledcze. Istota, funkcjonowanie, perspektywy.
Bydgoszcz: Wydawnictwo Uniwersytetu Kazimierza Wielkiego.

Rzeczkowski, G. (2019). „Mnożą się wątpliwości wokół majątku Morawieckiego". At
https://www.polityka.pl/tygodnikpolityka/kraj/1793482,1,mnoza-sie-watpliwosci
-wokol-majatku-morawieckiego.read. Accessed 17/06/2020.

Smoleński, P. (2002). „Ustawa za łapówkę czyli przychodzi Rywin do Michnika". At
https://wyborcza.pl/1,75398,1237212.html. Accessed 16/06/2020.

Watoła, J., Jedlecki, P. (2020). „Bizensowa ośmiornica braci Szumowskich. Rodzinno-
polityczny układ z setkami milionów złotych". At https://katowice.wyborcza.pl
/katowice/7,35063,25972882,biznesowa-osmiornica-braci-szumowskich.html.
Accessed 20/06/2020.

Wiggins, G. (1997). The Case of John Peter Zenger (1735). A Monkey ... about 4 foot high.
in L. Chiasson (ed.). The Press on Trial. Crimes and Trials as Media Events. Westport
CT: Greenwood Press.

CHAPTER 11

The Media and the Citizens' Right to Information

The Reliability and Objectivity of Journalists in the Light of Empirical Research of the Polish Press between 2010 and 2018

Ewa Jurga-Wosik and Inga Oleksiuk

11.1 Introduction

Freedom of the press is a constitutional law guaranteed by Article 54 of the Constitution of the Republic of Poland (Journal of Laws, 1997, No. 78, item 483, as amended), which ensures to everyone the freedom to express opinions, and to acquire and disseminate information. The bill that regulates the matter is the Act on the Polish Press Law, whose Article 1 states that the press 'realises the right of citizens to reliable information, transparency of public life as well as social control and criticism' (Journal of Laws, 1984, No. 5, item 24). A prerequisite for the successful execution of the right is the professionalism of news journalism (regulated by the Code of Ethics in Media[1], the Code of Ethical Practice of the Polish Journalists Association[2], and the Code of Journalistic Ethics of the Catholic Association of Journalists[3], as of 07/05/2021). According to the literature, journalists are expected to perceive information as the right and interest of all citizens, i.e., they are obliged to collect and disseminate it in a reliable manner (Sarnecki, 2001, Commentary to Article 54, Karatysz, 2014, p. 87, Bauer, 2000, pp. 146–147). However, the literature contains no profound empirical studies of press news content with regard to the right of all citizens to information (Article 1 of the Press Law), and this paper is the authors' attempt to fill that gap.

In view of the mediatisation of political communications, these issues are vital for political discourse in a democratic state (Habielski, 2009, *passim*, Van der Wurff, Schönbach, 2014, pp. 433–451).The purpose of this study is to assess journalistic professionalism with regard to the right of citizens to reliable and unbiased information. into account the normative assumptions stipulated in

---

1 Polish: Karta Etyczna Mediów.
2 Polish: Kodeks Etyki Stowarzyszenia Dziennikarzy Polskich.
3 Polish: Kodeks Etyki Dziennikarskiej KSD.

Article 54 of the Polish Constitution and Article 1 of the Press Law, the authors conducted multistage research of news content published in the local press between 2010 and 2018. The findings were juxtaposed with the results of studies on news items in national daily newspapers (Jurga-Wosik et. al., 2017, pp. 139–142).

11.2 Current State of Knowledge and Research

A journalist is a person engaged in editing, creating or preparing press material. Under the Polish Press law, this notion includes: individuals employed by editorial boards, and media workers hired under a contract of mandate or specific work (the so-called 'junk contracts'). In this study, the terms 'journalist(s)' and 'media worker(s)' are applied in reference to both groups (Bauer, 2000, pp. 146–147; Nowińska et al., 2008) since they perform the same duties, and under the Press Law, their professional conduct is governed by the same regulations, including an obligation to maintain objectivity and reliability in collecting information (Karatysz, 2014, Van der Wurff, Schönbach, 2014, pp. 433–451).

The criterion of objectivity is related to the obligation to present reality regardless of the journalist's beliefs and opinions (under the Code of Ethics in Media, the Code of Ethical Practice of the Polish Journalists Association, and the Code of Journalistic Ethics of the Catholic Association of Journalists, as of 07/05/2021). As argued by Michel Foucault, it must also involve the pursuit of linguistic 'transparency' (Foucault 2006, p. 66; Wacławczyk, 2019, pp. 429–439). Therefore, a crucial aspect of assessing objectivity in the context of journalistic professionalism is the ability to separate verifiable facts from subjective values, as stipulated in Article 12 of the Press Law, which states that 'a journalist is obliged to exercise due diligence and reliability while collecting information' (Journal of Laws, 1984, No. 5, item 24). In the literature, reliability is defined as care, responsibility, trustworthiness, etc. (Sobczak, 2000, p. 267; Kosmus, Kuczyński, 2013, pp. 134–136; Kamiński, 2010, pp. 15–25; Tsfati et al., 2006, pp. 152–173, Sypniewska, 2020, pp. 321–328.). Thus, the objectivity and reliability of news content are core premises of journalistic professionalism.

What seems particularly important in this context is the typology by Wolfgang Donsbach, who distinguished five types of journalist objectivity: functional, real, consensus, relative, and ideological (Donsbach, Klett, 1990, pp. 53–83 ; Kaliszewski, Wolny-Zmorzyński, Furman, 2009, p. 144). The analysis presented herein takes into account two of the criteria: functional objectivity, which adds weight to professional skills and standards; and real objectivity, where news content is prepared in a fashion that makes it easily verifiable empirically (Karatysz, 2014, p. 88).

Importantly, empirical studies conducted in Poland after the political transformation of 1989 show that Polish journalists find the act of informing the public the most significant duty of the press, which was a major conclusion of the project accomplished by Jerzy Olędzki in the 1990s based on the research schedule applied by David H. Weaver for *The Global Journalists* (Olędzki, 1998, pp. 257–276). Weaver's concept of journalistic roles and attitudes was also a starting point for studies conducted in the following decade by media experts from the Faculty of Political Science and Journalism at Adam Mickiewicz University in Poznan (Stępińska, Ossowski, 2010a, 2010b; Stępińska, Ossowski, 2011a, 2011b,; Stępińska, Ossowski et al, 2012; Stępińska, Głowacki, 2014), who confirmed the role of being a provider of current news and views to be most vital for Polish journalists.

Conditions of journalistic work, including legal aspects, were scrutinised by scholars applying qualitative methods and dogmatic analyses of applicable laws (Kononiuk, 1996; Mocek, 2006; Nowińska et al., 2008; Sobczak, 2008; Oleksiuk 2009; Szot, 2010; Barańska, 2011; Skrzypczak, 2013; Zaremba, 2021). There were also studies of local mass media, delving into professional challenges and issues (Chorązki, 1994; Pepliński, 2001; Gierula, 2005, 2006; Jakimowski, 2006; Pokrzycka, 2008; Jaska, Werenowska, 2018). The next decade brought weighty research projects devoted to comparative analyses of Polish and foreign journalism, including 'Media Accountability and Transparency in Europe – MediaAcT' and 'Journalism in Change. Journalistic Culture in Russia, Poland and Sweden' (Dobek-Ostrowska, Barszczyn, 2016). MediaAcT, whose primary objective was to determine the external factors impacting the development of journalistic professionalism (Barczyszyn, Głowacki, Michel, 2011; Głowacki, 2013), proved the growing importance of economic factors for Polish media workers and their professional activity. Other studies included empirical research of various aspects of interpretative journalism (Jurga-Wosik, 2017 et al., pp. 131–144), and analyses of miscellaneous journalistic genres of mixed news and opinion journalism (Wojtak, 2004; Pisarek, 1993), stressing the difference between autonomous and non-autonomous commentary in the news content (Wojtak, 2004). There were also studies of the media's transformation under modern technology (Kristanova, 2009, pp. 113–129), and its role in presenting both the progress and the threats to civilization (Oleksiuk, 2007). Finally, a gradual shift from news journalism towards opinion journalism was also proved (Wolny-Zmorzyńsk Kaliszewski, 2014, Wacławczyk, 2019, pp. 429–439).

11.3 Description of Empirical Research

The aforementioned research objectives could not have been accomplished without a quantitative analysis of press content. The authors focused on the local press in recognition of its social and political role (Michalczyk, 2008, p. 132; Kowalczyk, 2008; Szot, 2013; Kristanova, 2020, pp. 75–87). When selecting specific analytical criteria, the authors referred to the research schedule (and the codebook) developed for the cross-nation Journalistic Role Performance project (JRP). Importantly, studies on journalism – and on relationships between journalists and political actors in particular – were for years based on Four Theories of the Press (Siebert, Peterson, Schramm, 1956) and the concept of the four-dimensional interaction between the media and politics (Blumer, Gurevitch, 1995). Today, researchers mainly rely on three models of the media and politics, a comparative approach proposed by Daniel Hallin and Paol Mancini (2007).

Works by pioneers of media studies were also utilised by the international team behind the cross-nation Journalistic Role Performance project (JRP), supervised by Claudia Mellado from Pontificia Universidad Catolica de Valparaiso in Chile, and Lea Hellmueller from the University of Houston in the US (Mellado et al., 2018, pp. 944–967; Mellado, 2020, p. 300; Secler et.al., 2016, pp. 167–185). The research scheme applied herein refers to news content analyses conducted by means of a model constructed upon normative theories and previous studies on journalism (Stępińska et.al., 2011a, pp. 33–46; Stępińska et.al., 2011b, pp. 17–30; Stępińska et.al., 2011c, pp. 43–62; Stępińska et al., 2017a, pp. 127–142; Stępińska et al., 2016, pp. 37–52).

Since the research objectives herein are similar but not identical to the goals of the aforementioned studies, the authors adapted the scheme of international research on roles of the media and journalists and, on the assessment of their actual performance (JRP), but modified the research tools for the purpose of determining the degree of journalistic interference in news content. Focusing entirely on the printed press, the authors applied the following criteria of newspaper selection: publication schedule (daily, weekly, biweekly, monthly), ownership structure (commercial and local government-funded), and type (general interest). Additional criteria included paid-for titles, a permanent editorial board, and the selection of local government-funded periodicals from the same area as commercial papers. The research area was the region of Greater Poland, owing to the long-standing press tradition there (Jurga-Wosik, 2012), and the selected titles included: *Gazeta ABC* (est. July 1990, commercial publisher, daily); *Nasze Jutro* (est. April 1990, local government-funded publisher, monthly; *Gazeta Kościańska* (est. March 1999, commercial publisher, weekly), *Panorama Leszczyńska* (weekly, est. December 1979, since 1990s – commercial publisher); *Witryna Śmigielska* (est. May 1991, local government-funded publisher, since 2001 – weekly).

The time period included election years (local government elections: 2010, 2014, 2018), and non-election years (2012, 2016). In practice, empirical analyses were conducted every second year, and for each of the selected years one quarter was chosen randomly. Next, within each selected quarter, one issue of each periodical in question was selected, also on a random basis. In the case of *Gazeta ABC*, random-purposive sampling technique was applied for the last two quarters of the year. As a result, a period of 9 years and 25 issues of local papers were analysed, amounting to 897 news items. The authors took into consideration the following quarters: October – December 2010, April – June 2012, April – June 2014, October – December 2016, and July – September 2018. The findings were juxtaposed with the data from the literature, namely the results recorded for four national periodicals: *Gazeta Wyborcza, Rzeczpospolita, Nasz Dziennik*, and *Fakt* between 2012 and 2013, consisting of a constructed two-week sample of 1,130 press items. These were all news articles from the main section of a given periodical (Jurga-Wosik et al., 2017, pp. 137–142).

11.4   Presentation of Findings

11.4.1   *Journalistic Reliability*
As shown in case law and the literature (Sobczak, 2008, Note 1–6 to Article 1; Maciejewski, 2014; Stratilatis, Costas, 2011, pp. 725–749), a key criterion to assess the reliability of news journalism is the identification of sources in a given news item. Therefore, the first objective of the quantitative analysis herein was to determine if press material by Polish journalists contained information on news sources. The applied criterion was that at least one source had to be provided, where the source was defined as: 1) a natural person, or a natural person representing a legal person, who speaks, is quoted, or provides information in a given news item, 2) documents created by public institutions, social organisations, or business entities, 3) news content obtained from other mass media.

Importantly, the analysis showed that local journalists were relatively well aware of the obligation to provide at least one source – the majority of journalists in commercial (88.7%) and local government-funded (71.8%) periodicals identified news sources (cf. Figure 11.1) even if there was a notable difference between the two groups (16.9%). Interestingly, the average for the national press amounted to 80% (Jurga-Wosik et.al., 2017, p. 137).

Another significant aspect of journalistic professionalism that conditions the right of citizens to information is the verifiability of data and facts in the

■ PP: local, funded by local government   ■ PP: local, commercial   ■ PP: national, commercial

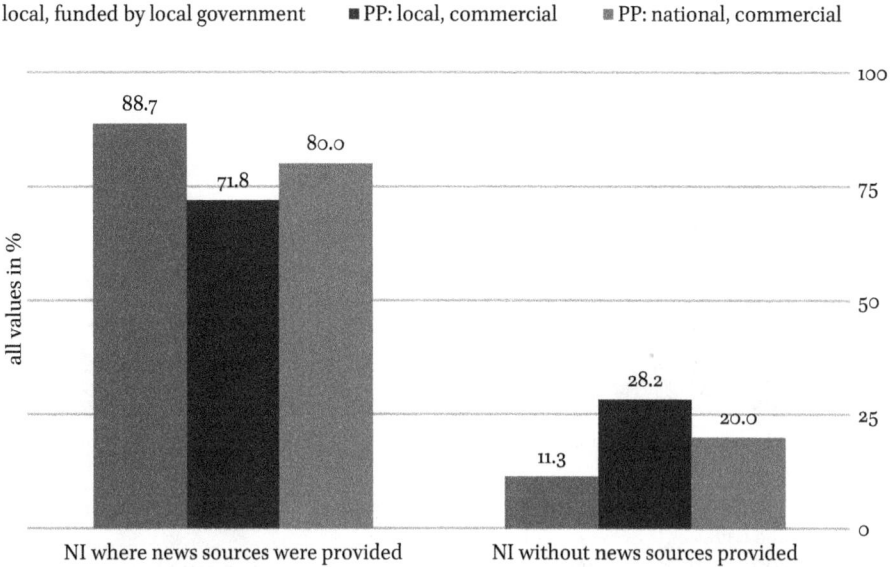

FIGURE 11.1   Data on news items where sources were provided. The Polish press between
2010 and 2018
SOURCE: OWN ELABORATION BASED ON: LOCAL PRESS (FUNDED BY
LOCAL GOVERNMENT, COMMERCIAL): OWN STUDY; NATIONAL PRESS:
JURGA-WOSIK ET AL., 2017, P. 137

press. Therefore, the collected research material was analysed in terms of data validation in other sources. The authors applied the definition of sources as in Point 1 above, excluding all press items that contained only the journalist's subjective views or predictions. It was established that local journalists mostly created verifiable press items, i.e., containing more verifiable than unverifiable data. In this respect, the statistics speaks more favourably of the commercial press, since 84% of items therein contained verifiable data, as opposed to 76% for the local government-funded press (cf. Figure 11.2). Notably, the difference in verifiability between the two types of the press is less distinct than when it comes to providing news sources. Importantly, the analysed percentage was 81.4 % for the national press (Jurga-Wosik et al., 2017, p. 138).

11.4.2   Journalistic Objectivity

As stated earlier in the paper, professional journalism is based on a description of reality only if the news content it presents meets the requirements of objectivity. In this respect, two essential questions arise. First of all, do journalists present reality regardless of their opinions? In this matter, it is even more

■ PP: local, funded by local government   ■ PP: local, commercial   ■ PP: national, commercial

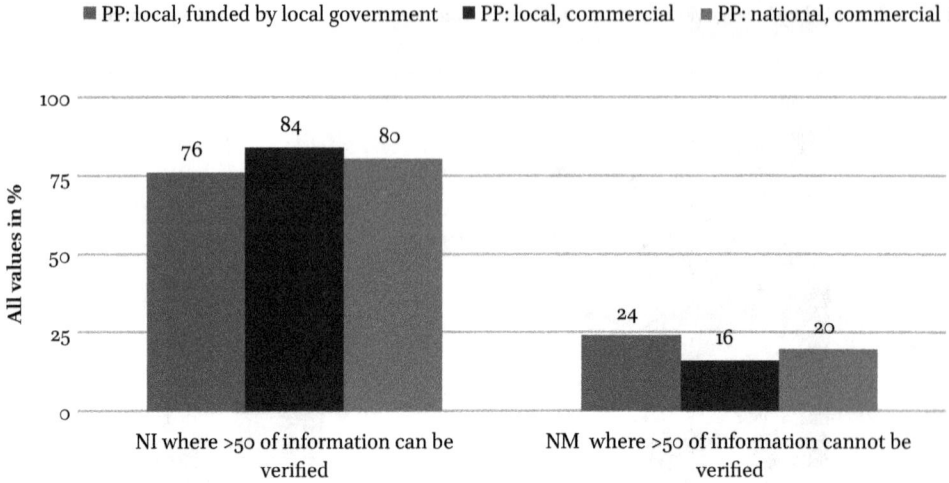

FIGURE 11.2   Data on news items that contained verifiable content. The Polish press between 2010
                and 2018
                SOURCE: OWN ELABORATION BASED ON: LOCAL PRESS (FUNDED BY LOCAL
                GOVERNMENT, COMMERCIAL): OWN STUDY; NATIONAL PRESS: JURGA-WOSIK ET AL.,
                2017, P. 137

important to establish whether the opinions expressed are differentiated from information. Due to its quantitative nature, this study focuses on determining the number of press items that contain the author's opinions. Secondly, does the news content include evaluative statements? In the light of CJEU case law, a journalist's interference in the informative layer of the text is evidenced by evaluative elements, a significant manifestation of which are adjectives (CJEU ruling of 22/2/2007, Krasulya against Russia, 12365/03, Zaremba 2021, pp. 871–879). Thus, when analysing the collected material, the authors tried to determine whether journalists assessed or classified people and phenomena by using adjectives. Importantly, the selection did not take into account adjectives already used in original news sources.

The analyses revealed that in the selected local periodicals the degree of interference in the informative layer of the text was comparable to that reported for the national press (Jurga-Wosik et al., 2017, pp. 137–142)[4]. The

---

4   Jurga-Wosik et.al., 2017, pp. 137–142. The highest percentage was recorded for *Gazeta Wyborcza*, where nearly half the items (48.4%) contained the author's personal opinion, followed by 1/3 of items in *Nasz Dziennik* (28.3%), ¼ in *Rzeczpospolita* (22.4%), and slightly less in *Fakt* (19.8%). In general, journalists used adjectives in 28.1% of press items. These were reported in over 30% of all texts in *Gazeta Wyborcza* (37.6%) and *Nasz Dziennik* (33.9%), and in approx. 20 % of items published in *Rzeczpospolita* (22%) and *Fakt* (18.2%).

■ PP: local, funded by local government   ■ PP: local, commercial   ■ PP: national, commercial

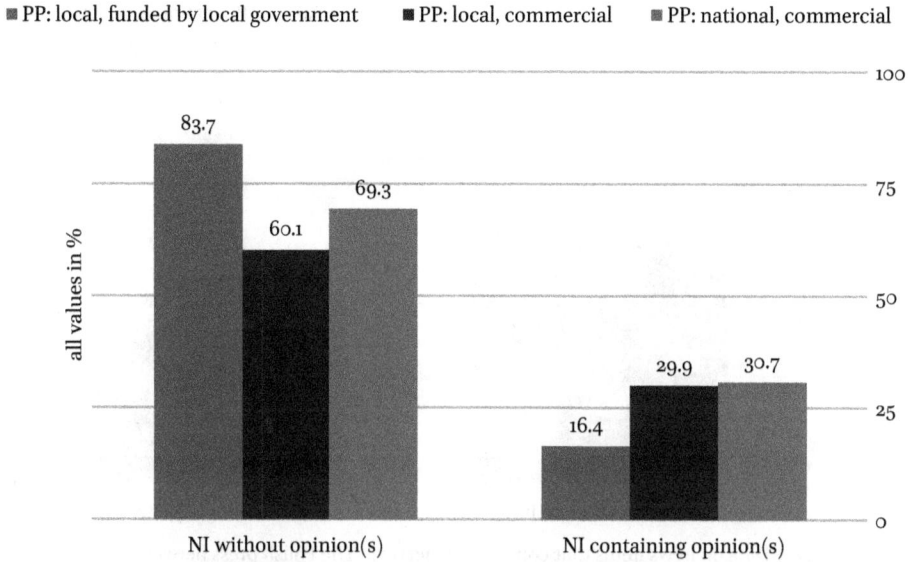

FIGURE 11.3   Data on news items that contained the journalist's opinion(s). The Polish press
between 2010 and 2018
SOURCE: OWN ELABORATION BASED ON: LOCAL PRESS (FUNDED BY LOCAL
GOVERNMENT, COMMERCIAL): OWN STUDY; NATIONAL PRESS: JURGA-WOSIK
ET AL., 2017, P. 139

percentage of opinions in news items amounted to 30.7% and 26% for the
national and local press respectively, while journalists working for commercial
papers were relatively more eager to include opinions (29.9%) than their colleagues from local government-funded periodicals (16.4%) (cf. Figure 11.3). As
for evaluative adjectives, journalists of the national press used them in 28.1%
of press items, while their local counterparts in 44.5% of texts, including 48%
of articles in papers controlled by local governments and 41% in commercial
titles (cf. Figure 11.4). These results may prove that evaluative language is often
used in news coverage.

11.5   Conclusion

Guaranteed by the Polish constitution, freedom of the press is not an autotelic
value, as it is meant to ensure the right to reliable information for all citizens.
Since access to reliable and unbiased information has gained greater importance under democracy, the primary objective of the study was to assess journalistic professionalism with this issue in mind.

Taking into account the normative assumptions that arise from the Polish
Constitution (Article 54) and the Press Law (Article 1), the authors conducted

■ PP: local, funded by local government   ■ PP: local, commercial   ■ PP: national, commercial

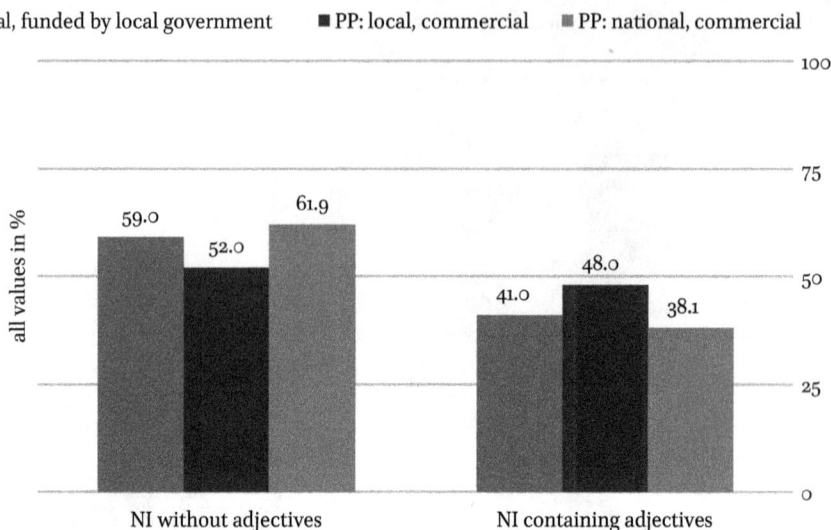

FIGURE 11.4   Data on news items that contained adjectives. The Polish press between 2010
and 2018
SOURCE: OWN ELABORATION BASED ON: LOCAL PRESS (FUNDED BY LOCAL
GOVERNMENT, COMMERCIAL): OWN STUDY; NATIONAL PRESS: JURGA-WOSIK
ET AL., 2017, P. 139

a quantitative analysis of content published in the news media. They applied
random and random-purposive techniques to select a representative sample of
897 news items from the local press between 2010 and 2018, and used a modified version of the codebook, originally developed for the JRP project, in order
to assess the selected news content in terms of reliability and objectivity. The
findings were then juxtaposed with the results of studies on news material
from national daily newspapers.

    The innovative research approach allowed the authors to formulate the
following methodical conclusions: (1) the JRP codebook was deemed a functional tool, improving the quality of scientific debate in the sphere of social
and political communication; (2) the JRP research scheme had to be adjusted
to normative assumptions, which narrowed the scope of research to the actual
actions taken by journalists (role performance); (3) criteria for analysing news
content had to be redefined with regard to obligations imposed on journalists
by the Press Law (Article 1). In this context, the authors specified the indicators of media professionalism, taking into account criteria that determine the
essence of the news content – namely reliability and objectivity. In a substantial dimension of the study, the analysis of the results shows that the level of
professionalism of the local press in terms of citizens' rights to information is

comparable to that of the commercial national press. Reliability of news journalists as a premise of the right to information was assessed on the basis of an analysis of the effects of their work, and deemed satisfactory. Overall assessment was based on the analysis of news items with sources provided (80.2%) and the analysis of items with verifiable data (80.5%). With regard to citizens' rights to information, the lowest indicator related to the local government-funded press and referred to the verifiability of data in news items.

In the literature, the unfavourable impact on professionalism is considered to stem not only from journalists' limited work experience, but also from the diverse objectives of the commercial and local government-funded press (Jurga-Wosik, 2012; Szostok, Rajczyk, 2013). Another ponderable issue is the possibility to ensure economic security to local media workers by implementing legal instruments that formally regulate working conditions (e.g., obligation to hire staff pursuant to a valid employment agreement, and not a pay-by-line contract, as the latter is, in fact, another form of junk contract).

As for objectivity, the authors performed a quantitative analysis of comments and evaluative statements, listing 77.8% news items where journalists did not include their own opinion (13.5% more for the local government-funded than commercial press), and 50.5% news items containing no evaluative statements (adjectives). As a result, the authors concluded that opinions are definitely visible in news coverage. In the light of the aforementioned literature and case law, this confirms that standards of professional news journalism are insufficiently rigorous, which has a negative impact on the citizens' access to information. Focusing exclusively on the Polish printed press in the second decade of the 21st century, the study proves that there is need for further, more profound research of various genres of news material with the citizens' right to information in mind.

References

Legislative Acts and Documentation
The Constitution of the Republic of Poland of April 2, 1997, Journal of Laws, 1997, No. 78, item 483, as amended.
The Act of January 26, 1984 on the Press Law, (consolidated text, Journal of Laws, 2018, item 1914).
The Code of Ethics in Media, http://www.dziennikarzerp.pl/wp-content/uploads /2010/06/karta_dziennikarzy.pdf (accessed: 20/03/2021).
The Code of Ethical Practice by Polish Journalists Association, https://sdp.pl/kodeks -etyki-sdp/ (accessed: 20/03/2021).

the Code of Journalistic Ethics by Catholic Association of Journalists, http://www
.katolickie.media.pl/informacje-ksd/do-kumenty-ksd/53-kodeks-etyki-dziennikar
skiej-ksd, (accessed: 5/04/2021).

Literature

Barańska M. (2011). Dylematy współczesnego dziennikarza/dziennikarstwa: wybrane
zagadnienia, *Przegląd Politologiczny*, Issue no. 4.

Bauer Z. (2000). Gatunki dziennikarskie. In: Dziennikarstwo i świat mediów, Z. Bauer,
E. Chudziński (eds.), Krakow: Universitas.

Chorązki W. (1994). Obraz niezależnej prasy lokalnej w Polsce, w I połowie 1994 roku,
Krakow: Instytut na rzecz Demokracji w Europie Wschodniej.

Donsbach W, Klett B. (1990). Subjective Objectivity. How Journalists in Four Countries
Define a Key Term of their Profession, Gazette (Leiden, Netherlands), Vol. 51, Issue
no. 1, pp. 53–83, https://doi.org/10.1177/001654929305100104

Dobek-Ostrowska B., Barczyszyn P., Michel S. (2013). Zmiana w dziennikarstwie. Kultura zawodowa polskich dziennikarzy (badania ilościowe), *Studia Medioznawcze*,
Issue no. 1.

Dobek-Ostrowska B., Barszczyn P. (eds.) (2016). Zmiana w dziennikarstwie w Polsce, Rosji i Szwecji. Analiza porównawcza, Wroclaw: Wydawnictwo Uniwersytetu
Wrocławskiego.

Foucault M. (2006). Słowa i rzeczy. Archeologia nauk humanistycznych, Gdansk:
Wydawnictwo słowo/obraz terytoria.

Garlicki L. (2010). Wolność wypowiedzi dziennikarza – przywileje i odpowiedzialność,
Europejski Przegląd Sądowy, Issue No. 1.

Gierula M. (2005), Prasa lokalna 1989–2000. Typologia i funkcjonowanie, Katowice:
Wydawnictwo Uniwersytetu Śląskiego.

Głowacki M. (2013). Dziennikarze polscy w świetle studiów porównawczych systemów
odpowiedzialności mediów w Europie, *Studia Medioznawcze*, 2013, Issue No. 1.

Habielski, R. (2009). Polityczna historia mediów w Polsce w xx wieku. Warsaw: Wydawnictwa Akcydensowe i Profesjonalne.

Hallin D., Mancini P. (2007). Systemy medialne. Trzy modele mediów i polityki w
ujęciu porównawczym, Krakow: Wydawnictwo Uniwersytetu Jagiellońskiego.

Halmai G. (2006). Freedom of Expression and Information. Commentary of the Char-
ter of Fundamental Rights of the European Union, http://ec.europa.eu/justice
/fundamental-rights/files/ networkcommentaryfinal_en.pdf.

Hess K, Waller L. (2017). Local Journalism in a Digital World, London – New York:
Palgrave and Macmillan Education.

Jachimowski M. (2006). Regiony periodycznej komunikacji medialnej. Studium pra-
soznawczo – politologiczne o demokratyzacji komunikacji medialnej, Katowice:
Wydawnictwo Uniwersytetu Śląskiego.

Jaska E. Werenowska A. (2018) The availability and use of media information sources in rural areas Rural Development and Entrepreneurship Production and Co-Operation in Agriculture, Jelgava (Latvia): Latvia University of Life Sciences and Technologies,.. pp. 115–122.

Jurga-Wosik E. (2012). Dwie dekady przeobrażeń mediów lokalnych południowo-zachodniej Wielkopolski, *Środkowoeuropejskie Studia Polityczne*, Issue No. 1, Poznan.

Jurga-Wosik E., Stępińska A. et al. (2017). Między informacją, a komentarzem: polski model dziennikarstwa w świetle badan empirycznych. In: Współczesne media. Gatunki w mediach. T. 1 Gatunki w mediach drukowanych, I. Hofman, D. Kępa-Figura (eds.), Lublin.

Kaliszewski A., Wolny–Zmorzyński K., Furman W. (2009). Gatunki dziennikarskie. Teoria, praktyka, język, Warsaw.

Kamiński, I. C. (2010). Twierdzenia i opinie w orzecznictwie Europejskiego Trybunału Praw Człowieka w Strasburgu. In: Fakt vs. Opinia. A. Bodnar i D. Bychawska-Siniarska (scientific eds.), Materiały z konferencji zorganizowanej przez Obserwatorium Wolności Mediów w Polsce 2009 roku, Warsaw.

Kononiuk T. (2013). Profesjonalizacja w dziennikarstwie. Między modernizmem a nowoczesnością, Warsaw: Wydawnictwo Uniwersytetu Warszawskiego.

Karatysz M. (2014). W poszukiwaniu rzetelności, Między subiektywizmem a obiektywizmem w dziennikarstwie, *Refleksje*, Issue No. 9.

Kosmus B., Kuczyński G. (2013). Prawo prasowe. Komentarz, Warsaw.

Keller P., (2011). European and International Media Law: Liberal Democracy, Trade, and the New media, Oxford.

Kowalczyk R. (2008). Media lokalne, t.1, t. 2, t. 3., Poznan.

Kristanova E., (2009). Prasa tradycyjna a elektroniczna – próba porównania typologii 'Uniwersum piśmiennictwa wobec komunikacji elektronicznej', K. Migoń, M. Skalska-Zlat (eds.), Wroclaw: Wydawnictwo Uniwersytetu Wrocławskiego, pp. 113–129.

Kristanova E., (2020). Po grudniu ubiegłego roku. Problematyka polityczna w szczecińskim miesięczniku społeczno-kulturalnym 'Spojrzenia' (1971–1973), *Zeszyty Prasoznawcze*, Issue No. 4.

Maciejewski M. (ed.) (2014). Prawo do informacji publicznej. Efektywność regulacji i perspektywy jej rozwoju, Instytut Nauk Prawnych PAN. https://www.rpo.gov.pl/sites/default/files/Prawo_do_informacji_publicznej.pdf

Mellado C. (ed.) (2020). Beyond Journalistic Norms: Role Performance and News in Comparative Perspective, Routledge.

Mellado C., Hellmueller L. et al., (2018). The Hybridization of Journalistic Cultures: A Comparative Study of Journalistic Role Performance, *Journal of Communication*, Vol. 67, Issue no. 6.

Michalczyk S. (2008). Media lokalne a władza i opinia publiczna. In: Polityka lokalna. Właściwości, determinanty, podmioty, E. Ganowicz, L. Rubisz (eds.), Torun.

Mocek S. (2006). Dziennikarze po komunizmie. Elita mediów w świetle badań społecznych, Warsaw: Collegium Civitas.

Młynarska-Sobaczewska A. (2003). Wolność informacji w prasie, Torun.

Nowakowski K., (2008). Media and Corruption, *Studia Medioznawcze*, Issue no. 2.

Nowińska E., du Vall M., Dobosz I. (2008). Prawa i obowiązki dziennikarzy. In: Prawo mediów, A. Matlak (ed.), Warsaw.

Pepliński W. (2001). Zmiany w modelu funkcjonowania zawodu dziennikarskiego po 1989 r. (na przykładzie gdańskiego środowiska prasowego), *Studia Medioznawcze*, Issue no. 3.

Oleksiuk I. (ed.) (2007). Obraz postępu i zagrożeń cywilizacyjnych w mediach., *XXX-VIII Zeszyt Instytutu Problemów Współczesnej Cywilizacji*. Warsaw.

Oleksiuk I. (2009). Wolność słowa na rynku nowych mediów. In: Media i Polityka, J. Sobczak, B. Hordecki (scientific eds.). Poznan: INPiD, UAM.

Olędzki J. (1998). Polish Journalists: Professionals or not? In: D.H. Weaver (ed.), The Global Journalist. News People around the World (pp. 257–276), New Jersey: Hampton Press, Inc.

Ossowski S., Stępińska A. (2011). Dziennikarze w Polsce: wartości, priorytety i standardy zawodowe, *Studia Medioznawcze*, Issue no. 1.

Palczewski, M (2018). Teorie newsa: historia – definicje – konteksty – dyskursy newsa w kręgu kultury zachodniej, Warsaw: Dom Wydawniczy ELIPSA.

Pisarek W. (1993). Gatunek dziennikarski: Informacja prasowa, *Zeszyty Prasoznawcze*, Issue no. 3–4.

Pokrzycka L. (2008). Problemy lokalnego dziennikarstwa na przykładzie rynku prasowego Lubelszczyzny. In: Oblicza polskich mediów po 1989 roku, L. Pokrzycka, B. Romiszewska (eds.), Lublin: Wydawnictwo UMCS.

Sarnecki P. (2001). Komentarz do art. 54. In: Konstytucja Rzeczypospolitej Polskiej. Komentarz, L. Garlicki (ed.), Vol. II, Warsaw.

Secler B., Stępińska A., Jurga-Wosik E., Narożna D., Adamczewska K. (2016). Model zorientowany na obywateli w perspektywie paradygmatu społecznej odpowiedzialności mediów. Przykład prasy w Polsce, *Acta Universitatis Lodziensis. Folia Litteraria Polonica*, Issue no. 2 (32): Stylistyka mediów, R. Siekiera, M. Worsowicz (eds.).

Sobczak J. (2008), Uwaga 1–6. do art. 1. In: Prawo prasowe. Komentarz, LEX.

Stępińska A., Jurga-Wosik E., Adamczewska K., Secler B., Narożna D. (2016). Journalistic Role Performance in Poland, *Środkowoeuropejskie Studia Polityczne*, Issue no. 2.

Stępińska A., Ossowski S. (2010a). Polski dziennikarz – niezależny altruista? In: Etyka w mediach, t.5: Nowe media – stare idee, W. Machura (ed.), Poznan–Opole: Wydawnictwo Scriptorium.

Stępińska A., Ossowski S. (2010b). Dziennikarze polscy – między mitem 'czwartej władzy' a świadomością misji. In: Media – czwarta władza?, R. Kowalczyk, W. Machura (eds.), Poznan–Opole: Wydawnictwo Scriptorium.

Stępińska A. , Ossowski Sz. (2011a). Społeczne oczekiwania a autostereotyp dziennikarzy polskich w XXI wieku. In: Stereotypy w obszarze społecznym i politycznym, B. Pająk-Patkowska (ed.), Poznan: Wydawnictwo Naukowe WNPID.

Stępińska A., Ossowski Sz. (2011b). Kariera, kontrola, służba społeczna – postawy różnych pokoleń polskich dziennikarzy. In: Studia nad dziennikarstwem, I. Hofman (ed.), Lublin.

Stępińska A., Ossowski S., Pokrzycka L., Nowak J. (2012), The Journalists and Journalism of Poland. In: The Global Journalist in the 21st Century, D. H. Weaver, L. Willnat (eds.), New York–London: Routledge.

Stępińska A., Głowacki M. (2014). Professional Roles, Context Factors and Responsibility Across Generations of Polish Journalists. In: Journalism that Matters. View from Central and Eastern.

Europe, M. Głowacki, E. Lauk, A. Balcytiene (eds.), Frankfurt am Main: Peter Lang.

Stratilatis, Costas. (2011). On the Distinction between Statements of Fact and Value Judgments: A Comment on Petrenco v. Moldova, *Annuaire International des Droits de l'Homme*, Vol. VIII, pp. 725–749.

Strömback, J. (2008). Four Phases of Mediatization: An Analysis of the Mediatization of Politics. The International Journal of Press/Politics, Issue no. 13 (3), pp. 228–246.

Szostak P., Rajczyk R. (2013). Komunikowanie lokalne w Polsce. O instrumentach polityki komunikacyjnej samorządów, Katowice: Wydawnictwo Gnome.

Szot L. (2013). Dziennikarze mediów lokalnych. Pomiędzy profesjonalizmem a koniecznością przetrwania, Wroclaw: Wydawnictwo Uniwersytetu Wrocławskiego.

Sypniewska B. (2020). Counterproductive Work Behavior and Organizational Citizenship Behavior. *Advances in Cognitive Psychology*, Issue no.16(4), pp. 321–328. https://doi.org/10.5709/acp-0306-9

Tsfati, Y., Meyers, O., Peri, Y. (2006). What is Good Journalism? Comparing Israeli Public and Journalists' Perspectives. Journalism, Issue no. 7(2), pp. 152–173.

Van der Wurff, R., Schönbach, K. (2014). Civic and Citizen Demands of News Media and Journalists. What does the Audience Expect from Good Journalism?, *Journalism & Mass Communication Quarterly*, Issue no. 91(3), pp. 433–451. https://doi.org/10.1177/1077699014538974

Wacławczyk W. (2019). Dążenie do prawdy a język informacji prasowej, *Studia Medioznawcze*, Issue no. 1, pp. 429–439. doi: 10.33077/uw.24511617.ms.2020.1.149.

Jaska E., Werenowska A. (2018). Instrumentarium public relations stosowane w kreowaniu wizerunku jednostek samorządu terytorialnego In: Społeczno-ekonomiczne wymiary współczesnej samorządności / Jaska Ewa, Skoczek Tadeusz (eds.), 2018, Warszawa, Muzeum Niepodległości w Warszawie, pp. 141–156.

Wojtak M. (2004). Gatunki prasowe, Lublin: Wydawnictwo UMCS.

Wolny-Zmorzyński K., Kaliszewski A., Snopek J., Furman W. (2014). Prasowe gatunki dziennikarskie, Warsaw: Wydawnictwo Poltext.

Zaremba M. (2021). Problem klasyfikacji wypowiedzi jako twierdzeń faktycznych lub sądów wartościujących w orzecznictwie Europejskiego Trybunału Praw Człowieka w Strasburgu, *Studia Medioznawcze*, Issue no. 1, pp. 871–879.

CHAPTER 12

Political Communication in Selected Polish Religious Web Portals (2019–2020)

Rafał Leśniczak

12.1 Introduction

The aim of the issue undertaken in this paper is to analyse political communication processes in selected Polish religious web portals in relation to political events in Poland in 2019–2020. Quantitative and qualitative content analysis was conducted of publications available on the most popular Polish religious websites which deal with the most important events occurring on the Polish political scene in the period from 06.08.2019, i.e. the date of the decision of the President of the Republic of Poland on the ordering of parliamentary elections to the Sejm and the Senate (Decision of the President of the Republic of Poland, 2019), until 30.04.2020, i.e. the period immediately preceding the presidential election. The research can be classified as belonging to the area of analysing interrelationships between politics and religion and media and politics.

The first of the above-mentioned relations, i.e. politics-religion, refers to the discussion concerning, among other things, models of state-church relations and, consequently, is an attempt to determine the place and role of churches and religious organisations in the public space: from the secular state model, through adhering to the principle of autonomy and mutual respect, to the confessional state model (Joppke, 2015, pp. 5–41). The mutual references between politics and religion are therefore expressed in the attempts to define more precisely the essential features of a secular state, which, as Paweł Borecki (2016, p. 173) notes, include: organisational separation from religious organisations, functional separateness of the above-mentioned entities, incompetence of the state in matters of religion, including internal affairs of confessional communities, and at the same time the incompetence of religious organisations in exercising public authority. Piotr Burgoński and Michał Gierycz (2014, p. 20) indicate three reasons why, after a period of atheistic political science in the 20th century, we are now observing the resurgence of the politology of religion. Firstly, theories of political order in a society are tied in the Christian times to both religious and theological ideas. Secondly, human beings are individuals actively involved in political relations and activities, and at the same time have a natural inclination to be religious. Thirdly, we have observed an increased incidence of politically significant events related to religion in the public space. The web portals analysed in the present research constitute a more or less formalised voice of the institutional Church in the processes of political communication. In this sense, the content of publications on these websites is an expression of the political stance of a religious body, even though it is achieved indirectly, through the media.

In the second of the above-mentioned relations, i.e. media-politics, the issue of influence of media institutions and the agenda of the media on the actions of political leaders should be highlighted, as well as the way in which political processes are perceived and communicated by the public, of which the media are an important exponent (Negrine, 2008). The influence of political activities on the editorial line and agenda of a given medium is also noticed, as well as on the manner in which the legal order determining the functioning of the media is shaped (Robinson, 2001; Dragomir, 2018). These relations are nowadays described by such terms as "mediatisation of politics" and "politicisation of the media" (Strömbäck, & Esser, 2014). They are also the object of research into the relationship between the media agenda and the political agenda (Walgrave, & Van Aelst, 2016). An important issue in the analysis of the relation between the media and politics is the agenda-setting theory, exposing the media's ability to change the significance of the public agenda. As Ewa Nowak (2013, p. 189) aptly notes, "most public (political, social) issues are not encountered by citizens in their everyday life, as citizens form their opinions about the important and the unimportant (create their world) on the basis of signals given to them by the media, especially the news media". The media view political processes essentially through the prism of their leaders. The personalisation of politics, and therefore personalisation of electoral rivalry, is a result of the mediatisation of politics. The role of the individual is more important than that of institutions, which reflects a broader process of the individualisation of social life (McAllister, 2007).

12.2   Research Methodology

The research material consisted of publications addressing the issues of Polish politics after the parliamentary elections held in Poland on 13.10.2019, and posted on the most visited Polish religious websites. It was assumed that only those websites which have been assigned an ecclesiastical assistant can be called Catholic, i.e. they exist and fulfil their mission with the consent or support of a competent ecclesiastical authority (Guzek, 2016, p. 24). This results from the fact that there are web portals that deal extensively with religious and ecclesiastical topics, but are not formally overseen by ecclesiastical authorities, and there are also websites that are administered by other denominations or other religions. In relation to the two website types mentioned above (Catholic ones and those that are not formally supervised by a religious/ecclesiastical institution), a single term, i.e. "religious web portals" or "religious websites", was used. The analysis undertaken uses the August 2019 GEMIUS/PBI survey results identifying the most important Polish religious websites. For the purpose of this analysis, five websites with the highest number of real users were selected: deon.pl, gosc.pl, aleteia.pl, stacja7.pl, wiara.pl (tw, 2019, 10 October). Texts containing at least one of the following key words were included in the analysis: "election", "party", "Sejm", "Senate" or names of Polish political leaders ("Morawiecki", "Duda") as well as publications referring to the political situation in Poland in the period of 06.08.2019–30.04.2020. For the selection of research material, search engines located on the sites belonging to the selected and above-mentioned websites were used[1]. In the research, both quantitative and qualitative content analysis was applied (Krippendorff, 2018; Wimmer, & Dominick, 2013, pp. 158–190).

The timeframe of the analysis covered the period from 06.08.2019 to 30.04.2020, during which significant political events were recorded, including the United Right winning the absolute majority in the Sejm during the election held on 13.10.2019, including the success of Jarosław Gowin's and Zbigniew Ziobro's parties, the victory of the opposition parties in the Senate election, the designation of Mateusz Morawiecki as the Prime Minister on 14.11.2019, the government formation, and the 2020 presidential campaign taking place during the coronavirus epidemic (A. Stankiewicz: Ten rok zmienił; Głowacki, 2020; Jakubowski).

The author adopted the following research presumptions. Religion-oriented media are involved in political communication. This is evidenced by the analysis of the content of the Polish Catholic press and Polish periodicals during the last two decades in relation to parliamentary and presidential elections, which is dominated by topics connected with the relationship between religion and politics (Adamski, Jupowicz-Ginalska, & Leonowicz-Bukała, 2020, p. 190; Guzek, 2019; Leśniczak, 2016). However, unlike the printed press, the area of *political communication* on Polish religious websites has not yet become a

---

1   deon.pl https://deon.pl/wyszukiwarka?q=, gosc.pl https://www.gosc.pl/wyszukaj/wyrazy?q=, aleteia.pl https://pl.aleteia.org/search/?q=, stacja7.pl https://stacja7.pl/#search= and wiara. pl https://www.wiara.pl/wyszukaj/wyrazy?o=1&q= (access: 13.05.2020).

subject of systematic media studies. Author's research presumptions concerning the legitimisation, by selected religious web portals, of actions taken by certain political parties are based on their editorial boards' self-declarations published on their websites, as well as on a small number of works that are already being conducted in this area of political and media studies.

The Jesuit website deon.pl declares to be a social and news web portal, whose mission is: "to inform about significant social events and interpret these events from the Church's point of view, as well as to comment on Church events (...)" (Deon.pl. O portalu). The editorial team of deon.pl notes that "being a link between religion and social life is not possible without providing a friendly place for open and inspiring discussions on religious, social, political and cultural issues" (Ibid). Therefore, it was assumed that topics related to Polish politics are a part of the website's agenda. Deon.pl does not define itself as right-wing or liberal, so it can be assumed that it will not explicitly support any political party.

If we presume that the gosc.pl website represents an editorial approach that is convergent with the printed version of the *Gość Niedzielny* weekly magazine, its political support for the United Right should be assumed, along with the legitimisation of the actions undertaken by the Law and Justice party and support for Andrzej Duda as a presidential candidate.

"Aleteia is a modern evangelisation website established in 2013 by the Foundation for Evangelisation through the Media (Fondation pour l'Évangélisation par les Médias), chaired by Prince Michael of Liechtenstein. On behalf of the Foundation, Aleteia is managed by Média-Participations, a European multimedia group specialising in publishing. (...) Although Aleteia was founded by a group of lay Catholics, it cooperates closely with such important institutions of the Holy See as the Pontifical Council for Promoting New Evangelisation and the Dicastery for Communication. Its partner in Poland is KAI" (as, mp/sch, 2016). Considering the international nature of the website, it is unreasonable to expect that Polish political issues would be high on its agenda.

Based on the analysis of the titles and contents of publications posted in the main tabs of the Polish edition of aleteia.pl, it can be concluded that the portal does not address issues of political communication. Some website tabs deal with the issues related to the life of the ecclesiastical institution (among others, current information about the Catholic Church is placed under the "Aktualności" (*News*) tab; selected stories from the life of Catholics – under the "Dobre Historie" (*Good Stories*) tab; spiritual life – under the "Duchowość" (*Spirituality*) tab), other tabs are devoted to culture, art and travel (Aleteia, n.a.).

On the other hand, Stacja7.pl declares to be a multimedia religious web portal being "a response to the hustle and bustle of the modern world. We want to be a place of respite for those who have had enough of the mad rush and unbearable pressure. To proclaim the Gospel where there is no hope left. To show that living the Christian faith not only gives salvation, but is also a wonderful adventure and the best recipe for a successful, interesting life" (Stacja7. pl. O portalu, n.a.). The main portal tabs confirm the lack of thematic connection and direct references to the area of political communication (Stacja7.pl, n.a.). The portal is a place for pastoral activity as well as reliable information and serves as an opinion-forming centre (jp, am/mz, 2015). Therefore, it is difficult to assume that such a clearly self-defined website would take up political issues.

The wiara.pl portal was established in 2001. Since its inception, the guiding idea has been defined as: "to be there for believers, doubters, seekers, but also for non-believers; to create a web portal while faithfully following the teachings of Jesus and the Church, but, simultaneously, to be open to otherness. As we call it: to stand at the gate and welcome" (Wiara.pl. O nas, n.a.). The website received the Bishop Jan Chrapek "Ślad" and TOTUS awards, and the jury verdicts emphasised appreciation for: "the creation of a religious website with a high-quality and rich content, for promoting the teachings of the Holy Father John Paul ii". (Ibid). This can be interpreted as the manifestation of the website's respect for Catholic social teachings, and therefore lack of website's support for any political party[2].

The wiara.pl portal is owned by the GOŚĆ Media Institute, the same one which owns *Gość Niedzielny*. This prompts us to ask the question whether the texts published on the website are involved, as is the case with the printed weekly, in the processes of political communication, and whether they give support to the Polish right-wing political leaders or not.

In the case of the deon.pl, aleteia.pl, stacja7.pl, wiara.pl websites, no scientific publications have been found whose authors, on the basis of their own empirical studies, would prove that any of the political options was supported by these websites[3].

---

2 Catholic social teachings postulate that the clerical representatives of the institutional Catholic Church should be very restrained when it comes to political matters. The Church has not parted with politics radically and continues to be an important voice in the political discourse, addressing social, political and economic issues. "The Church, with its social teachings, permeates the public sphere, but distances itself, at least in declarations, from active participation in politics, separating the sphere of the sacred – religious activities – from the sphere of the profane, which also includes political activity". [Cf. Modrzejewski, 2010, pp. 50–51].

3 The research was performed using the Google Scholar search engine https://scholar.google.pl/ and the ScienceDirect https://www.sciencedirect.com/ search engine, being one of the

The aim of the analysis was to answer the following research questions: Did religious websites include the most relevant issues of Polish politics after the 2019 parliamentary elections in their agendas?; Did the analysed websites legitimise the actions of the United Right and did they pledge political support to its leaders, including Prime Minister Mateusz Morawiecki?; Did they express their political stance regarding Andrzej Duda's candidacy for the office of the President of Poland?; Did they legitimise his actions?

The research hypothesis has been formulated in the form of the following five H1–H5 statements.

H1. The deon.pl, gosc.pl and wiara.pl websites can be treated as active participants of political communication. These websites debated the most important topics on the Polish political agenda[4].

H2. The aleteia.pl and stacja7.pl websites distanced themselves from addressing the issues of Polish politics in the period of 2019–2020[5].

H3. The gosc.pl and wiara.pl websites legitimised the activity of the United Right and pledged political support to right-wing leaders, including Prime Minister Mateusz Morawiecki.

H4. The deon.pl website did not pledge political support to any political party.

H5. The gosc.pl and wiara.pl websites voiced their support for Andrzej Duda in the 2020 presidential campaign.

In order to verify the above-mentioned hypotheses, a categorisation key was constructed, in which the following characteristics were distinguished: "LEGITIMISATION OF THE ACTIVITY OF THE UNITED RIGHT"; "RIGHT-WING LEADERS AND MORAWIECKI'S GOVERNMENT"; "ANDRZEJ DUDA" (Table 12.1). The categories within an examined characteristic are disjunctive.

---

world's largest online databases of reviewed papers and research books published by Elsevier.

4   The following were taken as the most important topics on the political agenda: the United Right winning the absolute majority in the Parliament (Sejm), including the success of Jarosław Gowin's and Zbigniew Ziobro's parties, the victory of the opposition parties in the Senate elections, the designation of Mateusz Morawiecki as the Prime Minister on 14.11.2019 and the government formation, government's activity, and the 2020 presidential campaign.

5   The portal's distancing itself from addressing political issues means that the website has omitted political matters from its agenda.

TABLE 12.1   A categorization key with characteristics and categories

Characteristic under study and definition of characteristic	Categories and definitions within the characteristic under study
LEGITIMISATION OF THE ACTIVITY OF THE UNITED RIGHT – Text authors' assessment of the political activity undertaken by the United Right as activity based on and within the limits of the law	1. legitimisation – a publication evaluates the activity of the "good change bloc" as based on and within the limits of the law; 2. non-legitimisation – a publication evaluates the activity of the "good change bloc" as not legitimate in terms of law; 3. no reference – text does not address the issue of the legitimacy of the United Right's activity – it only serves an informative function.
RIGHT-WING LEADERS AND MORAWIECKI'S GOVERNMENT – A press publication expresses political support for actions taken by right-wing leaders and Mateusz Morawiecki's government	1. political support – clearly visible, opinions expressed in an approving tone; 2. criticism – actions taken by right-wing leaders and Prime Minister Morawiecki are criticised; 3. ambivalence – a text expresses both support and dissent in relation to actions taken by right-wing leaders and Morawiecki's government; 4. none of the above – a text does not address political actions taken by right-wing leaders and the Prime Minister or is only informative in nature.
ANDRZEJ DUDA – a press publication expresses political support for actions taken by President Andrzej Duda	1. political support – a press publications voices support to Andrzej Duda and legitimised his political actions; 2. criticism – a press publication criticises the political actions taken by Andrzej Duda; 3. ambivalence – a text expresses both support and dissent in relation to actions taken by Andrzej Duda; 4. none of the above – a text does not include evaluation of Andrzej Duda's political actions.

SOURCE: OWN STUDY

12.3 Results of Content Analysis and Verification of the Research Hypothesis

In total, the criteria for analysis were met by 697 texts published on the analysed Internet portals, including 62 texts on deon.pl, 289 texts on gosc.pl, 7 texts on aleteia.pl, 19 texts on stacja7.pl and 320 texts on wiara.pl.

Tables 12.1–12.4 present the number of texts published on the analysed web portals, assigned to each category within the framework of analysed characteristics. The percentage of publications assigned to each category is indicated in brackets (percentage points).

The results of quantitative content analysis prove the legitimisation of the political activity of the United Right as actions based on and within the limits

TABLE 12.2   Legitimisation of the activity of the United Right – number of publications assigned to individual categories

Web portal / category	Legitimisation	Non-legitimisation	No reference
deon.pl	51 (82.26)	2 (3.23)	9 (14.51)
gosc.pl	220 (76.12)	15 (5.19)	54 (18.69)
aleteia.pl	4 (57.14)	0 (0.0)	3 (42.86)
stacja7.pl	18 (94.74)	0 (0.0)	1 (5.26)
wiara.pl	258 (80.63)	20 (6.25)	42 (13.12)
Total	551 (79.05)	37 (5.31)	109 (15.64)

SOURCE: OWN COMPILATION

TABLE 12.3   Right-wing leaders And Morawiecki's government – number of publications assigned to individual categories

Web portal / category	Political support	Criticism	Ambivalence	None of the above
deon.pl	36 (58.06)	2 (3.23)	9 (14.52)	15 (24.19)
gosc.pl	111 (38.41)	10 (3.46)	6 (2.08)	162 (56.05)
aleteia.pl	4 (57.14)	0 (0.0)	0 (0.0)	3 (42.86)
stacja7.pl	11 (57.89)	0 (0.0)	0 (0.0)	8 (42.11)
wiara.pl	120 (37.5)	16 (5.0)	6 (1.88)	178 (55.62)
Total	282 (40.46)	28 (4.02)	21 (3.01)	366 (52.51)

SOURCE: OWN COMPILATION

TABLE 12.4   Andrzej Duda – number of publications assigned to individual categories

Web portal / category	Political support	Criticism	Ambivalence	None of the above
deon.pl	26 (41.94)	0 (0.0)	1 (1.61)	35 (56.45)
gosc.pl	48 (16.61)	6 (2.08)	3 (1.04)	232 (80.27)
aleteia.pl	1 (14.28)	0 (0.0)	0 (0.0)	6 (85.72)
stacja7.pl	7 (36.84)	0 (0.0)	0 (0.0)	12 (63.16)
wiara.pl	54 (16.88)	10 (3.13)	2 (0.62)	254 (79.37)
Total	136 (19.51)	16 (2.3)	6 (0.86)	539 (77.33)

SOURCE: OWN COMPILATION

of the law. The percentage of publications assigned to the "legitimisation" category, within the examined "LEGITIMISATION OF THE ACTIVTY OF THE UNITED RIGHT" characteristic, amounted to 79.05 per cent of all texts, while the "non-legitimisation" category was assigned to 5.31 per cent of the total number of texts. Most texts referring to the subject discussed here were published on wiara.pl (320) and gosc.pl (289) websites, and a smaller number on deon.pl (62). Issues concerning the most important events of the Polish political scene in the period from 06.08.2019 to 30.04.2020 were treated marginally by the stacja7.pl (19) and aleteia.pl (7) web portals. These results confirm the veracity of thesis H1.

Quantitative analysis allows us to conclude that gosc.pl and wiara.pl legitimised actions taken by the United Right and voiced political support to the right-wing party leaders, including Prime Minister Mateusz Morawiecki, as well as legitimised Andrzej Duda's political activity during the 2020 presidential campaign. The number of publications classified in the "political support" category was far larger than the number of publications assigned to the "criticism" and "ambivalence" categories. As far as the "RIGHT-WING LEADERS AND MORAWIECKI'S GOVERNMENT" characteristic is concerned, on the gosc.pl web portal, the percentage of texts classified in the "political support" category amounted to 38.41 per cent against 3.46 per cent in the "criticism" category and 2.08 per cent in the "ambivalence" category. On the same website, the percentage values for the "ANDRZEJ DUDA" characteristic were, respectively: 16.61 per cent ("political support"), 2.08 per cent ("criticism"), 1.04 per cent ("ambivalence").

As far as the "RIGHT-WING LEADERS AND MORAWIECKI'S GOVERNMENT" characteristic is concerned, on the wiara.pl web portal, the percentage of texts classified in the "political support" category amounted to 37.5 per cent against

5 per cent in the "criticism" category and 1.88 per cent in the "ambivalence" category. On the same website, the percentage values for the "ANDRZEJ DUDA" characteristic were, respectively: 16.88 per cent ("political support"), 3.13 per cent ("criticism"), 0.62 per cent ("ambivalence").

What is worth noting is the high percentage of texts classified in the "none of the above" category, under the "RIGHT-WING LEADERS AND MORAWIECKI'S GOVERNMENT" characteristic, i.e. gosc.pl portal – 56.05 per cent and wiara.pl – 55.62 per cent. On the other hand, for the researched "ANDRZEJ DUDA" characteristic, the indicators were at the level of 80.27 per cent for gosc.pl and 79.37 per cent for wiara.pl. The cited quantitative empirical results seem to confirm the validity of theses H3 and H5.

The quantitative results of analysis do not confirm the validity of thesis H4. Over 58% of publications on deon.pl were classified in the "political support" category as regards the "RIGHT-WING LEADERS AND MORAWIECKI'S GOVERNMENT" characteristic, and nearly 42% in the case of the "ANDRZEJ DUDA" characteristic. These categories were most extensively represented in the above-mentioned characteristics.

The deon.pl, aleteia.pl, wiara.pl and gosc.pl web portals took up the topic of the limits to the involvement of the clergy and institutional Church in politics and elections, and they recalled the basic principles of the Catholic Social Teachings (KNS). In this context, Dariusz Piórkowski (2019) mentioned, among other things, the teachings of the Council, the concept of the common good, and differences in the manifestation of political views by the laity and the clergy. Artur Stopka (2019) made a distinction between apoliticism and political neutrality of the Church and explained the statement of the Iustitia et Pax Pontifical Council contained in the "Compendium of the Church Social Doctrine" of 2004, why any political party or grouping fully meets the requirements of faith and Christian life, which causes dangerous misunderstandings. On aleteia.pl, the Word of the President of the Polish Episcopal Conference communicated before the parliamentary elections (2019) was published, in which Archbishop Stanislaw Gądecki reminded the basic principles of the Catholic Social Teachings concerning Catholics' responsibility for political life (KAI, 2019, 1 October). As an example of disrespect for these principles and meddling in party and partisan politics, he mentioned a clergyman from the Lublin Archdiocese, i.e. Fr. Eugeniusz Szymański, who encouraged the faithful to vote for specific candidates and parties ("Proboszcz zachęcał do głosowania", 2019). The wiara.pl and gosc.pl web portals cited the words of the Permanent Council of the Polish Episcopal Conference before the 2020 presidential election, in which bishops appealed to "the conscience of those responsible for the common good of our homeland, both the people in power and the opposition, to work out a common position concerning the presidential election in this extraordinary situation" (Wiara.pl. Rada Stała KEP, 2020; Gosc.pl Rada Stała KEP, 2020). In their communiqué, the bishops reminded that the Church has no mandate to participate in purely political disputes concerning the form or the date of the election, let alone to advocate this or that solution:

> However, it is always the mission of the Church in such a situation to remind people, with kindness, of the special moral and political responsibility that rests with the participants of political life. (Ibid; cf. PAP, 2020, 9 March)

The deon.pl website generally legitimised the United Right's actions as lawful. This was the case in 51 publications. In 9 cases, deon.pl did not refer to the issue of legitimacy, while 2 press texts were included in the "non-legitimisation" category under the "LEGITIMISATION OF THE ACTIVITY OF THE UNITED RIGHT" characteristic.

Deon.pl questioned the legitimacy of the decision of the "good change bloc" to hold the presidential elections on 10 May 2020, as well as boldly questioned the constitutionality of the election and pointed out the difficulty of holding it at that time (PAP/kk, 2020, 28 April).

The same web portal also cited the Senate's calling on the government to immediately announce a final decision on the final primary- and high-school exams for the 2019/2020 school year. The resolution that was adopted highlighted the position of opposition senators, accusing the Minister of National Education of announcing the postponement of the exams "to some undefined future":

> "This piece of information is entirely insufficient. Pupils, students, their parents, teachers and local authorities do not know if the exams will be held, when and in what form they will be held, and how the didactic process preparing students to take them will proceed. There are no guidelines for the process of recruitment to secondary schools and universities", the resolution states. (PAP/df, 2020, April 15)

Many publications on deon.pl did not evaluate the political activity of the United Right leaders, and they remained only informative in nature, e.g. publications on votes in the parliament (PAP/ml, 2020, 27 March).

Ambivalent evaluation of right-wing party leaders, Mateusz Morawiecki and Andrzej Duda was noted, for example, in those texts which assessed amendments to judicial laws, quoting arguments given by the opposition, some member of the judicial community, the Ombudsman, the Supreme Court and the Venice Commission, or which commented on the work on the 2020 budget (PAP/df, 2020, 15 April; PAP/ms, 2020, 8 January).

Simultaneous support and dissent for right-wing parties' actions was also noted in publications on the "Stop Paedophilia" civic initiative project (PAP/ml, 2019, 15 October), government's anti-COVID-19 law (PAP/kk, 2020, 5 March), and the possibility that Marian Banaś, the president of the Supreme Chamber of Control, committed a crime (PAP/kk, 2019, 29 November; PAP/sz, 2019, 28 November).

Political support for right-wing leaders was attributed to those parts of deon. pl publications which included the description of initiatives of a patriotic nature or concerning the common good of the nation, e.g. while paying tribute to the victims of the Martial Law, decisions on enforcing restrictions during the state of coronavirus epidemics, enactment of the "anti-crisis shield", Prime Minister's decision to help farmers whose losses caused by the 2019 drought exceeded 70 per cent (PAP/ml, 2019, 11 December; PAP/ml, 2020, 6 April; PAP/pp, 2019, 24 August).

Deon.pl also quoted M. Morawiecki promoting the success of the Law and Justice and United Right governments in the 2015–2019 period:

> Morawiecki stated that if he were to sum up the four years of Law and Justice and United Right running the country together, he would say that "there is no freedom without dignity and there is no freedom without credibility". He argued that it was the fact that promises were kept that translated into more dignified life for Polish families. "Our work is more dignified, our pay, one can also say that the state of public finances is more dignified, our historical policy is more dignified, our international policy is more dignified", he said. (PAP/jb, 2019, November 12)

The President's political actions were commented on quite often on deon.pl, i.e. in a total of 27 publications. In one case, the website expressed only its partial approval, as it highlighted Andrzej Duda's commitment to the implementation of the "anti-crisis shield" (PAP/kk, 2020, 28 February; PAP/ml, 2020, 27 March). In the remaining 26 texts, publications about the president were classified under the "political support" category.

The Polish President was presented in the perspective of the aid Poland gives to other countries during the pandemic, Polish medical and military missions and aid which consists in sending equipment to those in need. These topics became the subject of a conversation between President Andrzej Duda and Pope Francis reported by deon.pl, and they were interpreted by the Bishop of Rome as a sign of international solidarity (PAP/jb, 2020, April 30). The same website also cited the words of Jarosław Kaczyński, presenting the qualities of Andrzej Duda as an incumbent president in the 2020 campaign:

> "The President proved that his connection to our idea – the idea of a strong, law-abiding and just Poland is a very deep connection, which translates into the readiness to act, to take risks, readiness to overcome hurdles, including the most difficult ones. (...) after winning the 2015 presidential election, there was "no honeymoon period". "Right from the very start, there was a fight, a very difficult fight against those who brazenly violated the constitution and perfidiously told others that we are the ones violating it", said the Law and Justice leader. (PAP/kk, 2020, 15 February)

Deon.pl also presented the President from the perspective of his international policy and as being the guardian of the constitution (PAP/ms, 2019, 21 November; PAP/kk, 2020, 15 February; PAP/pk, 2019, 25 September; PAP/kk, 2020, 21 January).

Neither qualitative nor quantitative analysis of deon.pl publications confirms the veracity of thesis H4.

In the aleteia.pl portal, no texts were found that criticised political actions taken by right-wing leaders, Mateusz Morawiecki's government and the President. These actions were presented as actions taken on the basis and within the limits of the law. The aleteia.pl portal addressed two issues related to the activity of right-wing politicians classified under the "political support" category:

– implementation of safety rules during the coronavirus pandemic:

> At an evening press conference, the Prime Minister declared a state of epidemic emergency. Gatherings of more than 50 people were banned, including those of a religious nature. As Mateusz Morawiecki explained, the primary task of the state of epidemic emergency is to stop the high growth rate of the number of Covid cases recorded by neighbouring countries. (W Polsce wprowadzono stan zagrożenia, 13 March 2020)

– President Duda's dialogue with Pope Francis in the context of international aid provided by Poland during the pandemic and the 100th anniversary of the birth of St. John Paul II:

> "It was a very cordial half-hour conversation. First of all, Mr. President informed the Holy Father about the aid Poland provides to other countries

during the pandemic, about Polish medical-military missions, about equipment sent to those in need. The Holy Father recognised these actions as a wonderful manifestation of international solidarity and an example of the Polish spirit driving us to assist our neighbours in difficult times", says Minister Krzysztof Szczerski in a short video posted on the social media profile of the Office of the President of Poland. (KAI, 2020, April 30)

Similarly to aleteia.pl, the stacja7.pl website legitimised the actions of Polish right-wing parties as lawful. No publications criticising the policies of the United Right leaders, M. Morawiecki's government or President Duda were found on this web portal. In the coverage of his father, Kornel Morawiecki's funeral, the Prime Minister was portrayed as a politician coming from a family with patriotic roots:

> The Archbishop of Kraków noted that Kornel Morawiecki's character was forged by patriotic family traditions, which also resulted in Senior Speaker's engagement in opposing the Communist rule. He recalled that, at the Victory Square, Kornel Morawiecki listened to John Paul II while holding a red-and-white banner with the "Faith and Independence" motto on it, which accompanied him and his friends during the Pope's first pilgrimage to Poland. "With a sense of youthful pride, they carried Poland like a firebrand, like a torch of flames," the Archbishop said. He also pointed to the repressions Kornel Morawiecki had suffered during the times of the Polish People's Republic [PRL], which also affected his family. He stressed that Kornel Morawiecki had been indomitable until the very end. (ad/KAI, 2019, October 5)
>
> In June 1982, he founded "Solidarność Walcząca" in Wrocław, which was one of the largest and most uncompromising underground opposition organisations of the Polish People's Republic. Its main demand was the complete removal of the communists from power and restoration of independence to Poland and other communist states. (KAI/ad, 2019, October 2)

Political support for M. Morawiecki in the analysed texts published on the stacja7.pl portal was highlighted in the view of actions preventing the spread of the coronavirus epidemic (ad/Stacja7, 2020, 9 April; ad/Stacja7, 2020, 31 March; ad/Stacja7, 2020, 24 March; ad/Stacja7, 2020, 11 March) and the government's actions in the area of the pro-family policy (ad/KAI/Stacja7, 2019, 5 December).

President A. Duda's profile appeared, e.g. in the context of Poland's assistance to other countries struggling with the coronavirus pandemic (ad/Stacja7,

2020, 30 April), in connection with funeral ceremonies officiated for the January Uprising leaders executed by shooting in Vilnius in 1863 (ad/Stacja7, 2019, 22 November), the 80th anniversary of the World War II outbreak in Wieluń with the participation of German President Frank-Walter Steinmeier (KAI/ad, 2019, September 1) or the New Year's meeting with representatives of churches and religious organisations (KAI/ad, 2020, 14 January). In all these circumstances and events, approval for A. Duda's political actions was expressed.

The analysis of aleteia.pl and stacja7.pl websites, taking into account a very small, quantitatively unrepresentative research sample (7 texts on aleteia.pl and 19 texts on stacja7.pl), is not sufficient to confirm or reject validity of thesis H2, but qualitative analysis inclines the author to assume this validity.

The wiara.pl and gosc.pl web portals presented a wide spectrum of stances represented by the largest party groupings that entered the parliament as a result of the 2019 parliamentary elections by referring to the records of the following electoral committees' programmes: Coalition Electoral Committee for Civic Platform (PO, N, IPL, ZIELONI), Electoral Committee for Confederation Liberty and Independence, Electoral Committee for Law and Justice, Electoral Committee for the Polish People's Party and Electoral Committee for the Democratic Left Alliance (KAI, 2019, 3 October; PAP, 2019, 7 August).

On the wiara.pl and gosc.pl web portals, A. Duda was presented, among others, as:

- a statesman, caring for the historical memory of Poland;[6],
- a president who is attached to Christian values (PAP, 2020, 15 February; KAI, 2020, 27 March);
- one actively combating the coronavirus pandemic (PAP, 2020, 17 April; PAP, 2020, 30 April);
- one concerned about international politics (PAP, 2019, 29 December);
- one that is supportive of social welfare programmes (PAP, 2020, 15 February; PAP, 2020, 27 April);
- one that is concerned about the rule of law and respect for the constitution[7].

---

6   The main theme of the President's meeting with the inhabitants of Bytom on 29.02.2020 was the National Day of Remembrance of the Cursed Soldiers: "I ask you to pay tribute to them tomorrow, I ask you to remember the heroism of the Indomitable Soldiers, how they suffered, how their families, wives and children suffered. They suffered persecution for decades. These are heroic families deserving great respect, these are heroic people to whom the Republic of Poland owes this respect", said the President. "I am glad that modern, free and sovereign Poland is finally paying the Indomitable Soldiers the respect they deserve", Andrzej Duda stated (PAP, 2020, 29 February; Cf. PAP, 2020, 10 April).

7   In the course of the debate concerning the date and conduct of the presidential election, he was presented as a politician who is concerned about preserving the continuity of the state authority: "The presidential term expires on 5 August, the newly elected president should

Texts undermining political actions taken by the Polish President and his political bloc or ambivalently referring to A. Duda's politics and him as a person were publications presenting the profiles and views of his opponents in the 2020 presidential election. These included texts featuring Małgorzata Kidawa-Błońska, Szymon Hołownia and Władysław Kosiniak-Kamysz.

"If we manage to stop Law and Justice's madness on 7 May, there will be no election in May. I will not take part in the mail-in ballot election as organised by the Law and Justice, as it resembles postal services more than a regular election, particularly in May, when the number of people infected [with coronavirus – PAP] is growing," said the presidential candidate. "The election must be fair, secret, secure and conducted by the State Election Commission. (...) Elections are supposed to be elections, not a postal service. A serious person should take part in elections, which are elections, and not in the farce and legalisation of Jarosław Kaczynski's scheme", said Małgorzata Kidawa-Błońska (PAP, 2020, 28 April).

"However, if those in power persist in their stubbornness, they must know that they bear full responsibility for the terrible consequences for the lives and health of citizens," wrote the Civic Coalition's candidate. "In this situation, I appeal to everyone, all voters, to refuse to participate in the election on 10 May 2020. If it is impossible to act otherwise, let a general boycott be the response to the authorities' irresponsibility," Małgorzata Kidawa-Błońska stressed (PAP, 2020, 29 March).

Szymon Hołownia, while referring to changes in the Electoral Code introduced in the amendment, said that the ruling party "simply does what it wants". "Law and Justice privatise the Republic of Poland. Law and Justice transform it into a private state for their electorate. How much longer are we, as citizens of the Republic of Poland, going to watch it? Doesn't it seem both illegal and morally repugnant to you?," he declared. He asked President Duda if he wanted to be "a quarantined president, elected in a quarantined election". "Does he want to go down in history as a coward who was afraid to stand for a normal fair election process in which all candidates could compete fairly on a level playing field? Does he want to be remembered as the one who came to power over compatriots' dead bodies?," Hołownia asked (PAP, 2020, 28 March).

---

be sworn in on 6 August . It is absolutely necessary for the office of the president not to be vacated, in a way that there is no new president and the presidential term ends – this will be absolute violation of the constitution", the President argued. "It is fundamental that before the expiration of the five-year term of the incumbent president, a new president should be elected and that this president should be able to take over the office in an unhindered manner", he said. (PAP, 2020, 24 April)

In his [Hołownia's] view, the changes introduced are aimed at Andrzej Duda's re-election. "What is Law and Justice really up to? Well, in the dead of the night, under the cover of the anti-crisis package, they intend to enforce unconstitutional, illegal amendments concerning changes in the electoral law that have only one objective: to extend Andrzej Duda's term of office. That is the sole objective," Szymon Hołownia pointed out (PAP, 2020, 28 March).

Kosiniak-Kamysz, if elected, wants to build a strong, safe and prosperous country. He sees his role to be taking care of the national community, ensuring compatriots' safety and integrating people (PAP, 2019, 14 December).

It should be noted, however, that there were very few texts criticising the "good change bloc". The wiara.pl portal published 16 texts classified in the "criticism" category under the "RIGHT-WING LEADERS AND MORAWIECKI'S GOVERNMENT" characteristic (which constitutes 5% of all publications on this portal), and 10 texts also in the "criticism" category under the "ANDRZEJ DUDA" characteristic (which constitutes 3.13 per cent of all publications on this website). By analogy, the gosc.pl web portal data was as follows: under the "RIGHT-WING LEADERS AND MORAWIECKI'S GOVERNMENT" characteristic, there were 10 texts classified in the "criticism" category (which constitutes 3.46 per cent of the total number of publications on this portal), while under the "ANDRZEJ DUDA" characteristic, there were 6 texts classified in this category (which constitutes 2.08 per cent of the total number of publications on this portal).

Criticism of actions taken by the "good change bloc" and lack of legitimisation for its activities were found in a discussion of several issues undertaken in texts published on the gosc.pl and wiara.pl web portals, including: Law and Justice's attempt to bribe some opposition Senate members in order to gain the majority in the upper house of the parliament (PAP, 2019, 17 October; PAP, 2019, 16 October); the Marian Banaś scandal (PAP, 2020, 15 January; PAP, 2019, 29 November; PAP, 2019, 17 October; PAP, 2019, 4 December); the Marek Kuchciński airplane travel scandal (PAP, 2019, 9 August); United Right's legislative initiatives to hold a mail-in ballot election during the coronavirus outbreak (PAP, 2020, 23 April).

Both qualitative and quantitative research results confirm the validity of theses H3 and H5.

12.4   Conclusions

The analysis results confirmed the validity of theses H1, H2, H3 and H5, and did not confirm the validity of thesis H4. Thus, it can be concluded that the research hypothesis is false because one of its theses (H4) proved to be invalid.

It is worth asking why right-wing politicians enjoy so much support from the religious web portals analysed in this paper.

According to the author, the reason for legitimising right-wing parties' actions and for the high level of political support granted by authors of the analysed religious-themed websites to the United Right leaders, Prime Minister M. Morawiecki and President A. Duda, is the fact that they relied significantly on two sources: The Catholic News Agency [KAI] and the Polish Press Agency [PAP].

In the case of the aleteia.pl and stacja7.pl websites, a significant input of the Catholic News Agency as a source of information was noted (4 publications on aleteia.pl, accounting for 57.14% of the total number of publications on this web portal, and 8 publications on stacja7.pl, accounting for 42.1% of the total number of publications on this web portal).

As far as deon.pl, gosc.pl and wiara.pl websites are concerned, it was found that the Polish Press Agency was the main source of information for over 80 per cent of texts published there (respectively: 55 out of 62 texts on deon.pl, i.e. 88.71 per cent; 258 out of 289 texts on gosc.pl, i.e. 89.27 per cent; 308 out of 320 texts on wiara.pl, i.e. 96.25 per cent).

It seems reasonable to accept the thesis that the Catholic News Agency granted political support to the United Right, given that the Agency is owned by the Polish Episcopal Conference and knowing the results of the empirical studies of the nationwide Catholic press after 2000 regarding the political involvement of Polish Catholic media (Leśniczak, 2018; Leśniczak, 2020; Leśniczak, 2021).

The Management Board, Supervisory Board and National Council of the Polish Press Agency are appointed by the National Media Council [Rada Mediów Narodowych] (Polska Agencja Prasowa. Władze). Magdalena Wnuk notes that the dominant model of the interaction between the media system and the political system after 1989 in Poland is the model of instrumentalisation, in which "successive political blocs attempt to subordinate public media channels to themselves, both personally, (...) and in terms of content" (Wnuk, 2016, p. 78). Karol Jakubowicz (1990, p. 10) and Bogusława Dobek-Ostrowska (2010, p. 17) highlight the fact that the role of the media in new democracies (and Polish democracy should be perceived as such) is to put special emphasis on pluralism and take into account the multicultural character of societies. Since the establishment of the National Media Council in 1992 under the Broadcasting Act, there have been attempts to politicise the media and consequently undermine the fundamental principles of their functioning, which include: responsibility for expression of opinions, reliability, pluralism, respect for Christian values, consideration of the Polish intellectual heritage (Wnuk,

2016, p. 80). Under the MP enacted bridging bill on the National Media Council (RMN) of 22.06.2016, the Council is entrusted with the appointment of management and supervisory boards of TVP, Polish Radio and Polish Press Agency. Representatives to the five-member National Media Council are elected by the Sejm and President (Ibid). It can be presumed that the rules of selection of Council members provide an opportunity for exerting political influence over the media appointed to carry out public missions. Thus, the question about impartiality, objectivity or seeking the truth by TVP, Polish Radio and Polish Press Agency becomes relevant. Will the representatives of the "good change bloc" in the National Media Council care only about the good image of the United Right or will they allow polemical voices? This question is relevant if an attempt is made to assess whether the Polish Press Agency, in reporting political events in the period of 2019–2020, adopted such a perspective of interpreting political actions that is favourable to the Law and Justice party (Guzek, & Grzesiok-Horosz, 2021).

The empirical research results lead to the conclusion that the most important Polish religious web portals (which, in the analysis undertaken in this paper, are all, without exception, Catholic) grant political support to the right-wing party leaders, to President A. Duda, and legitimise their political activity. It can be assumed that the way the National Media Council functions has influenced this research result.

References

Adamski, A., Jupowicz-Ginalska, A. & Leonowicz-Bukała, I. (2020). Polish Nationwide Catholic Opinion-Forming Weeklies on Social Media – From Theoretical Introduction to Empirical Approach. *Religions, 11*(4). DOI: 10.3390/rel11040190

Borecki, P. (2016). Państwo laickie w świetle dorobku współczesnego konstytucjonalizmu europejskiego. *Przegląd Prawniczy Uniwersytetu im. Adama Mickiewicza, 6*(1), pp. 173–191.

Dobek-Ostrowska, B. (2010). System partyjny a media w Polsce – zależności i relacje. *Studia Medioznawcze, 2*, pp. 13–26.

Dragomir, M. (2018). Control the money, control the media: How government uses funding to keep media in line. *Journalism, 19*(8), pp. 1131–1148.

Gierycz, M. & Burgoński, P. (2014). Politologia i religia. Wprowadzenie, In: P. Burgoński, M. Gierycz (Eds.), *Religia i polityka. Zarys problematyki* (pp. 19–24). Warszawa: Elipsa.

Guzek, D. (2016). *Media katolickie w polskim systemie medialnym*. Toruń: Adam Marszałek.

Guzek, D. (2019). *Mediatizing Secular State Media, Religion and Politics in Contemporary Poland.* Berlin: Peter Lang.

Guzek, D., & Grzesiok-Horosz, A. (2021). Political Will and Media Law: A Poland Case Analysis. *East European Politics and Societies,* 08883254211049514. DOI: 10.1177/08883254211049514

(Eds.) Jakubowicz, K. & Puszczewicz B. (1990). *Człowiek a telewizja.* Warszawa: NURT.

Joppke, C. (2015). *The secular state under siege: Religion and politics in Europe and America.* Cambridge: John Wiley & Sons.

Krippendorff, K. (2018). *Content analysis: An introduction to its methodology.* London: Sage publications.

Leśniczak, R. (2016). The communicative role of the Catholic Church in Poland in the 2015 presidential election and its perception by the public. *Church, Communication and Culture, 1*(1), 268–285. DOI: 10.1080/23753234.2016.1234123

Leśniczak, R. (2018). Polish Catholic press and political communication of the Church on the basis of the 2000–2015 presidential election. *Political Preferences, 18,* pp. 37–56.

Leśniczak, R. (2017). Wizerunek prezydenta elekta Andrzeja Dudy w polskich tygodnikach katolickich „Gość Niedzielny" i „Niedziela". *Politeja-Pismo Wydziału Studiów Międzynarodowych i Politycznych Uniwersytetu Jagiellońskiego, 14*(48), pp. 299–318.

Leśniczak, R. (2020). Czy tygodnik katolicki „Niedziela" poparł Prawo i Sprawiedliwość w kampanii parlamentarnej w 2019 r? Studium medioznawcze. *Środkowoeuropejskie Studia Polityczne, 2,* 171–190. DOI: 10.14746/ssp.2020.2.9

Leśniczak, R. (2021). Did Polish Nationwide Catholic Weekly Newspapers Support Andrzej Duda in the Presidential Campaign in 2020? A Case Study. *Social Communication, 7*(1), 42–57. DOI: 10.2478/sc-2021-0004

McAllister, I. (2007). The personalization of politics. In: R.J. Dalton, Hans-Dieter Klingemann (eds.), *The Oxford handbook of political behavior. Oxford University Press.*

Modrzejewski, A. (2010). Kościół a polityka. Rozważania wokół aktywności politycznej duchowieństwa rzymskokatolickiego podczas wyborów prezydenckich 2010 roku. *Środkowoeuropejskie Studia Polityczne, 4,* pp. 45–60.

Negrine, R. (2008). *The transformation of political communication: Continuities and changes in media and politics.* New York: Macmillan International Higher Education.

Nowak, E. (2013). Metodologiczne problemy badania zależności pomiędzy agendą medialną, publiczną i polityczną. *Annales Universitatis Mariae Curie-Skłodowska. Sectio K–Politologia, 20*(2), pp. 187–206.

Przybysz, K. (2016). In vitro, aborcja, eutanazja–zagadnienia bioetyczne w dyskursie „Gościa Niedzielnego". *Media-Kultura-Komunikacja Społeczna, 1*(12), pp. 45–60.

Robinson, P. (2001). Theorizing the influence of media on world politics: Models of media influence on foreign policy. *European Journal of Communication, 16*(4), pp. 523–544.

Strömbäck, J., & Esser, F. (2014). Mediatization of politics: Towards a theoretical framework. In: J. Strömbäck, F. Esser (Eds.), *Mediatization of politics* (pp. 3–28). London: Palgrave Macmillan. DOI: 10.1057/9781137275844_1

Walgrave, S., & Van Aelst, P. (2016). Political agenda setting and the mass media. In *Oxford research encyclopedia of politics*. DOI: 10.1093/acrefore/9780190228637.013.46

Wimmer, R. D., & Dominick, J. R. (2013). *Mass media research*. Boston: Cengage learning.

Wnuk, M. (2016). Media publiczne – obywatelskie czy narodowe? Najnowszy dyskurs parlamentarny o mediach w kontekście zmian w ustawie o radiofonii i telewizji. *Studia Medioznawcze, 3*(66), pp. 77–91.

Internet Sources

ad/KAI. (2019, 5 October). Dziś pogrzeb śp. Kornela Morawieckiego. Retrieved from https://stacja7.pl/z-kraju/dzis-pogrzeb-sp-kornela-morawieckiego/

ad/KAI/Stacja7. (2019, 5 December). Premier powołał Radę Rodziny. Retrieved from https://stacja7.pl/z-kraju/premier-powolal-rade-rodziny/

ad/Stacja7. (2020, 11 March). Premier ogłosił odwołanie zajęć w szkołach całej Polski Retrieved from https://stacja7.pl/z-kraju/premier-oglosil-odwolanie-zajec-w -szkolach-calej-polski/

ad/Stacja7. (2020, 30 April). Prezydent Duda rozmawiał z papieżem telefonicznie. Retrieved from https://stacja7.pl/zwatykanu/prezydent-duda-rozmawial-z-papiezem -telefonicznie/

ad/Stacja7. (2020, 9 April). Rząd przedłuża obowiązujące obostrzenia epidemiczne. Retrieved from https://stacja7.pl/z-kraju/rzad-przedluza-obowiazujace-obostrzenia -epidemiczne/

ad/Stacja7. (2020, 24 March). Rząd wprowadza dalsze ograniczenia zgromadzeń i przemieszczania się. Retrieved from https://stacja7.pl/z-kraju/rzad-wprowadza -dalsze-ograniczenia-zgromadzen-i-przemieszczania-sie/

ad/Stacja7. (2020, 31 March). Rząd wprowadza kolejne ograniczenia w walce z pandemią. Retrieved from https://stacja7.pl/z-kraju/rzad-wprowadza-kolejne -ograniczenia-w-walce-z-pandemia/

ad/Stacja7. (2019, 22 November). Żegnamy Bohaterów. Dziś w Wilnie pogrzeb przywódców Powstania Styczniowego. Retrieved from https://stacja7.pl/ze-swiata/zegnamy -bohaterow-dzis-w-wilnie-pogrzeb-przywodcow-powstania-styczniowego/

Aleteia. (n.d.). Retrieved from https://pl.aleteia.org/

as, mp/sch. (2016, 20 July). Ruszył nowoczesny portal ewangelizacyjny Aleteia.pl. Retrieved from https://ekai.pl/ruszyl-nowoczesny-portal-ewangelizacyjny-aleteia-pl/

n.a. (2019, 30 December). A. Stankiewicz: Ten rok zmienił polską politykę. Podsumowanie najważniejszych wydarzeń politycznych 2019. Retrieved from https://wiado mosci.onet.pl/kraj/najwazniejsze-wydarzenia-polityczne-w-2019-r/bmkfp2n

Deon.pl. O portalu. (n.d.). Retrieved from https://deon.pl/o-portalu

Głowacki, W. (2020, 6 January). Rok 2020. Najważniejsze wydarzenia. Co nas czeka w polityce, kulturze, technologii? Wchodzimy w lata dwudzieste XXI wieku. Retrieved from https://polskatimes.pl/rok-2020-najwazniejsze-wydarzenia-co-nas-czeka-w-poli tyce-kulturze-technologii-wchodzimy-w-lata-dwudzieste-xxi-wieku/ar /c1-14691385

n.a. (2020, 28 April). Gosc.pl. Rada Stała KEP: Apelujemy o wspólne stanowisko rządu i opozycji ws. wyborów prezydenckich. Retrieved from https://www.gosc .pl/doc/6278345.Rada-Stala-KEP-Apelujemy-o-wspolne-stanowisko-rzadu-i -opozycji

Jakubowski, G. (n.d.). Rok 2020. Polityka. Co nas czeka? Retrieved from https://polskatimes .pl/rok-2020-najwazniejsze-wydarzenia-co-nas-czeka-w-polityce-kulturze -technologii-wchodzimy-w-lata-dwudzieste-xxi-wieku/ga/c1-14691385/zd/41023795

jp, am/mz. (2015, 28 September). Nowa ewangelizacja w sieci czyli nowa odsłona portalu Stacja7.pl. Retrieved from https://ekai.pl/nowa-ewangelizacja-w-sieci-czyli-nowa -odslona-portalu-stacja-pl/

KAI. (2019, 1 October). Abp Gądecki o tym, czym się kierować w wyborach parlamentarnych. Retrieved from https://pl.aleteia.org/2019/10/01/abp-gadecki-o-tym-czym -sie-kierowac-w-wyborach-parlamentarnych/

KAI. (2019, 3 October). Postulaty światopoglądowe w najbliższych wyborach. Retrieved from https://kosciol.wiara.pl/doc/5894925.Postulaty-swiatopogladowe-w -najblizszych-wyborach

KAI. (2020, 30 April). Prezydent Duda rozmawiał z papieżem Franciszkiem przez telefon. Retrieved from https://pl.aleteia.org/2020/04/30/prezydent-duda-rozmawial -z-papiezem-franciszkiem-przez-telefon/

KAI. (2020, 27 March). Prezydent RP Andrzej Duda z modlitwą błagalną na Jasnej Górze. Retrieved from https://www.gosc.pl/doc/6232951.Prezydent-RP-Andrzej-Duda-z -modlitwa-blagalna-na-Jasnej-Gorze

KAI/ad. (2019, 1 September). "Chylę czoła przed polskimi ofiarami niemieckiej tyranii i proszę o przebaczenie". Retrieved from https://stacja7.pl/z-kraju/chyle-czola -przed-polskimi-ofiarami-niemieckiej-tyranii-i-prosze-o-przebaczenie/

KAI/ad. (2020, 14 January). Prymas Polski na spotkaniu Kościołów u prezydenta. Retrieved from https://stacja7.pl/z-kraju/prymas-polski-na-spotkaniu-kosciolow -u-prezydenta/

KAI/ad. (2019, 2 October). W sobotę pogrzeb Kornela Morawieckiego. Retrieved from https://stacja7.pl/z-kraju/w-sobote-pogrzeb-kornela-morawieckiego/

PAP. (2019, 4 December). Banaś: Byłem gotów złożyć rezygnację z urzędu szefa NIK, jednak... Retrieved from https://www.gosc.pl/doc/6021265.Banas-Bylem-gotow -zlozyc-rezygnacje-z-urzedu-szefa-NIK-jednak

PAP. (2019, 17 October). Banaś nie rezygnuje. Retrieved from https://www.gosc.pl
/doc/5928634.Banas-nie-rezygnuje

PAP. (2020, 24 April). Duda: Gdyby nie doszło do wyborów, byłby kryzys konsty-
tucyjny. Retrieved from https://info.wiara.pl/doc/6273984.Duda-Gdyby-nie-doszlo
-do-wyborow-bylby-kryzys-konstytucyjny

PAP. (2020, 28 March). Hołownia: PiS w środku nocy wprowadza nielegalne poprawki
do prawa wyborczego. Retrieved from https://www.gosc.pl/doc/6234009.Holownia
-PiS-w-srodku-nocy-wprowadza-nielegalne-poprawki-do

PAP. (2020, 15 February). Kaczyński uzasadnia kandydaturę Andrzeja Dudy na
prezydenta. Retrieved from https://info.wiara.pl/doc/6162145.Kaczynski-uzasadnia
-kandydature-Andrzeja-Dudy-na-prezydenta

PAP. (2020, 28 April). Kidawa-Błońska: W wyborach korespondencyjnych 10 maja nie
wezmę udziału. Retrieved from https://info.wiara.pl/doc/6278646.Kidawa-Blonska
-W-wyborach-korespondencyjnych-10-maja-nie-wezme

PAP. (2020, 29 March). Kidawa-Błońska wzywa do bojkotu wyborów. Retrieved from
https://www.gosc.pl/doc/6234890.Kidawa-Blonska-wzywa-do-bojkotu-wyborow

PAP. (2019, 14 December). Kosiniak-Kamysz: Chcę ubiegać się o urząd prezydenta Rzeczpospolitej. Retrieved from https://info.wiara.pl/doc/6040379.Kosiniak-Kamysz
-Chce-ubiegac-sie-o-urzad-prezydenta

PAP. (2019, 9 August). Marek Kuchciński złożył rezygnację z funkcji marszałka
Sejmu. Retrieved from https://www.gosc.pl/doc/5764555.Marek-Kuchcinski-zlozyl
-rezygnacje-z-funkcji-marszalka-Sejmu

PAP. (2020, 15 Februar). Morawiecki: Prezydent Duda jest gwarantem tego, że naprawa
Polski będzie trwać. Retrieved from https://info.wiara.pl/doc/6162882.Morawiecki
-Prezydent-Duda-jest-gwarantem-tego-ze-naprawa-Polski

PAP. (2019, 29 November). "Myślę, że Marian Banaś poda się dziś do dymisji; jeśli się tak
nie stanie, mamy plan B". Retrieved from https://info.wiara.pl/doc/6011766.Mysle
-ze-Marian-Banas-poda-sie-dzis-do-dymisji-jesli-sie-tak

PAP. (2020, 30 April). O czym rozmawiał prezydent Andrzej Duda z papieżem Franciszkiem? Retrieved from https://www.gosc.pl/doc/6281578.O-czym-rozmawial
-prezydent-Andrzej-Duda-z-papiezem-Franciszkiem

PAP. (2019, 7 August). Partie przygotowują się na wybory. Retrieved from https://www
.gosc.pl/doc/5757938.Partie-przygotowuja-sie-na-wybory

PAP. (2020, 15 January). PO nie poprze wniosku o postawienie Banasia przed
Trybunałem Stanu. Retrieved from https://info.wiara.pl/doc/6108299.PO-nie-pop
rze-wniosku-o-postawienie-Banasia-przed-Trybunalem

PAP. (2020, 10 April). Prezydent: Po katastrofie smoleńskiej pokazaliśmy, że w
chwilach trudnych potrafimy być wspólnotą. Retrieved from https://www.gosc.pl
/doc/6254543.Prezydent-Po-katastrofie-smolenskiej-pokazalismy-ze-w-chwilach

PAP. (2020, 17 April). Prezydent: Mam nadzieję, że nowe przepisy z tarczy antykryzysowej szybko zaczną pomagać pracodawcom i pracownikom. Retrieved from
https://info.wiara.pl/doc/6265015.Prezydent-Mam-nadzieje-ze-nowe-przepisy-z
-tarczy-antykryzysowej

PAP. (2020, 27 April). Prezydent: Póki jestem prezydentem, nie będzie prywatyzacji publicznych szpitali. Retrieved from https://www.gosc.pl/doc/6277105.Prezydent-Poki
-jestem-prezydentem-nie-bedzie-prywatyzacji

PAP. (2020, 29 February). Prezydent: Rzeczpospolita jest winna szacunek żołnierzom
wyklętym. Retrieved from https://info.wiara.pl/doc/6185950.Prezydent-Rzeczpo
spolita-jest-winna-szacunek-zolnierzom-wykletym

PAP. (2020, 9 March). Rzecznik KEP: W kościołach nie ma miejsca na kampanię
wyborczą. Retrieved from https://info.wiara.pl/doc/6205708.Rzecznik-KEP-W
-kosciolach-nie-ma-miejsca-na-kampanie-wyborcza

PAP. (2019, 16 October). Senator PO: W 30 sekund dostałbym tekę ministra, gdybym
taką wolę wyraził. Retrieved from https://www.gosc.pl/doc/5925100.Senator-PO-W
-30-sekund-dostalbym-teke-ministra-gdybym-taka-wole

PAP. (2019, 29 Decemeber). Szczerski: W najbliższym czasie uzgodnione z prezydentem
oświadczenie premiera ws. słów Putina. Retrieved from https://info.wiara.pl
/doc/6065128.Szczerski-W-najblizszym-czasie-uzgodnione-z-prezydentem

PAP. (2019, 17 October). Ujazdowski o Senacie: Uważam, że nikt nie zostanie przekupiony.
Retrieved from https://www.gosc.pl/doc/5928262.Ujazdowski-o-Senacie-Uwazam
-ze-nikt-nie-zostanie-przekupiony

PAP. (2020, 23 April). Włodarze polskich miast protestują przeciwko wydaniu spisu
wyborców Poczcie Polskiej. Retrieved https://www.gosc.pl/doc/6272444.Wlodarze
-polskich-miast-protestuja-przeciwko-wydaniu-spisu

PAP/df. (2020, 15 April). Senat podjął uchwałę wzywającą rząd do decyzji ws. egzaminu
ósmoklasisty i matur. Retrieved from https://deon.pl/swiat/wiadomosci-z-polski
/senat-podjal-uchwale-wzywajaca-rzad-do-decyzji-ws-egzaminu-osmoklasisty-i
-matur,844235

PAP/jb. (2019, 12 November). Premier Mateusz Morawiecki złożył dymisję rządu.
Retrieved from https://deon.pl/swiat/premier-mateusz-morawiecki-zlozyl-dymisje
-rzadu-,645900

PAP/jb. (2020, 30 April). Prezydent Andrzej Duda rozmawiał z papieżem Franciszkiem.
Retrieved from https://deon.pl/swiat/wiadomosci-ze-swiata/prezydent-andrzej
-duda-rozmawial-z-papiezem-franciszkiem,856442

PAP/kk. (2019, 29 November). CBA skierowało do prokuratury zawiadomienie o
możliwości popełnienia przestępstwa przez szefa NIK Mariana Banasia. Retrieved
from https://deon.pl/swiat/wiadomosci-z-polski/cba-skierowalo-do-prokuratury
-zawiadomienie-o-mozliwosci-popelnienia-przestepstwa-przez-szefa-nik-mariana
-banasia,668922

PAP/kk. (2020, 21 January). Duda: ochrona klimatu bardzo ważna, ale trzeba działać chroniąc stabilność gospodarki. Retrieved from https://deon.pl/swiat/duda-ochrona -klimatu-bardzo-wazna-ale-trzeba-dzialac-chroniac-stabilnosc-gospodarki,728472

PAP/kk. (2020, 15 February). Kaczyński: Andrzej Duda to kandydat marzeń dla tych, którzy chcą Polski sprawiedliwej i silnej. Retrieved from https://deon.pl/swiat /wiadomosci-z-polski/kaczynski-andrzej-duda-to-kandydat-marzen-dla-tych -ktorzy-chca-polski-sprawiedliwej-i-silnej,758295

PAP/kk. (2020, 28 April). Komisje senackie przełożyły zajęcie stanowiska w sprawie głosowania korespondencyjnego na 4 maja. Retrieved from https://deon.pl/swiat /komisje-senackie-przelozyly-zajecie-stanowiska-w-sprawie-glosowania -korespondencyjnego-na-4-maja-,854177

PAP/kk. (2020, 28 February). Kosiniak-Kamysz: w Senacie powinna powstać nowa ustawa ws. tarczy antykryzysowej. Retrieved from https://deon.pl/swiat/kosiniak -kamysz-w-senacie-powinna-powstac-nowa-ustawa-ws-tarczy-antykryzysowej, 820458

PAP/kk. (2020, 15 February). Prezydent Duda: moim najważniejszym celem jest podniesienie poziomu życia Polaków. Retrieved from https://deon.pl/swiat /wiadomosci-z-polski/prezydent-duda-moim-najwazniejszym-celem-jest -podniesienie-poziomu-zycia-polakow-,758355

PAP/kk. (2020, 5 March). Senat bez poprawek do rządowej ustawy przeciwdziałającej COVID-19. Retrieved from https://deon.pl/swiat/senat-bez-poprawek-do-rzadowej -ustawy-przeciwdzialajacej-covid-19,783855

PAP/ml. (2020, 27 March). Prezydent: zaapelowałem do marszałka Senatu o jak najszybsze procedowanie tzw. tarczy antykryzysowej. Retrieved from https://deon .pl/swiat/wiadomosci-z-polski/prezydent-zaapelowalem-do-marszalka-senatu-o -jak-najszybsze-procedowanie-tzw-tarczy-antykryzysowej,819939

PAP/ml. (2019, 15 October). Sejm będzie kontynuował prace nad obywatelskim projek-tem inicjatywy "Stop pedofilii". Retrieved from https://deon.pl/swiat/sejm-bedzie -kontynuowal-prace-nad-obywatelskim-projektem-inicjatywy-stop-pedo filii,610948

PAP/ml. (2019, 11 December). Sejm oddał symboliczny hołd ofiarom stanu wojennego. Retrieved from https://deon.pl/swiat/wiadomosci-z-polski/sejm-oddal-symboliczny -hold-ofiarom-stanu-wojennego,688296

PAP/ml. (2020, 27 March). Sejm udzielił wotum zaufania rządowi Mateusza Morawieck-iego. Retrieved from https://deon.pl/swiat/wiadomosci-z-polski/sejm-udzielil -wotum-zaufania-rzadowi-mateusza-morawieckiego,653661

PAP/ml. (2020, 6 April). Senat za poprawkami do specustawy dot. wsparcia dla firm w związku z epidemią koronawirusa. Retrieved from https://deon.pl/swiat/wiado mosci-z-polski/senat-za-poprawkami-do-specustawy-dot-wsparcia-dla-firm-w -zwiazku-z-epidemia-koronawirusa,822618

PAP/ms. (2019, 21 November). Prezydent Andrzej Duda rozpoczął dwudniową wizytę na Litwie. Retrieved from https://deon.pl/swiat/prezydent-andrzej-duda-rozpoczal-dwudniowa-wizyte-na-litwie,657414

PAP/ms. (2020, 8 January). Sejm nie zgodził się na odrzucenie w pierwszym czytaniu projektu budżetu na 2020 r. Retrieved from https://deon.pl/swiat/wiadomosci-z-polski/sejm-nie-zgodzil-sie-na-odrzucenie-w-pierwszym-czytaniu-projektu-budzetu-na-2020-r,714303

PAP/pk. (2020, 24 March). Premier Morawiecki: wdrażamy ograniczenia w przemieszczaniu się [AKTUALIZUJEMY]. Retrieved from https://deon.pl/swiat/premier-morawiecki-wdrazamy-ograniczenia-w-przemieszczaniu-sie-aktualizujemy,811668

PAP/pk. (2019, 25 September). Prezydent Duda wystąpi na 74. sesji Zgromadzenia Ogólnego ONZ. Retrieved from https://deon.pl/swiat/prezydent-duda-wystapi-na-74-sesji-zgromadzenia-ogolnego-onz,576322

PAP/pp. (2019, 24 August). 1000 zł dopłaty do hektara w związku z suszą, jeśli straty są wyższe od 70 proc. Retrieved from https://deon.pl/swiat/wiadomosci-z-polski/1000-zl-doplaty-do-hektara-w-zwiazku-z-susza-jesli-straty-sa-wyzsze-od-70-proc,540558

PAP/sz. (2019, 28 November). Prezes i wiceprezes PiS oczekują od szefa NIK podania się do dymisji. Retrieved from https://deon.pl/swiat/czerwinska-prezes-i-wiceprezes-pis-oczekuja-od-szefa-nik-podania-sie-do-dymisji-opis,667572

Piórkowski, D. (2019, 11 October). Partia polityczna nie może stać się bożkiem. Retrieved from https://deon.pl/kosciol/komentarze/kosciol-ma-inne-cele-niz-partia,601913

Polska Agencja Prasowa. Władze. (n.d.). Retrieved from https://www.pap.pl/o-agencji/wladze

n.a. (2019, 6 August). Postanowienie Prezydenta Rzeczypospolitej Polskiej z dnia 6 sierpnia 2019 r. w sprawie zarządzenia wyborów do Sejmu Rzeczypospolitej Polskiej i do Senatu Rzeczypospolitej Polskiej (Decision of the President of the Republic of Poland of August 6, 2019 on ordering elections to the Sejm of the Republic of Poland and to the Senate of the Republic of Poland). Retrieved from http://prawo.sejm.gov.pl/isap.nsf/download.xsp/WDU20190001506/O/D20191506.pdf

n.a. (2019, 28 September). Proboszcz zachęcał do głosowania na konkretną partię. Został upomniany. Retrieved from https://pl.aleteia.org/2019/09/28/proboszcz-zachecal-do-glosowania-na-konkretna-partie-zostal-upomniany/

Stacja7.pl. (n.d.) Retrieved from https://stacja7.pl/

Stacja 7.pl. O nas. (n.d.). Retrieved from https://stacja7.pl/redakcja/o-nas/

Stopka, A. (2019, 5 October). Partie i wypaczona misja Kościoła. Retrieved from https://deon.pl/kosciol/komentarze/partie-i-wypaczona-misja-kosciola,592249

tw. (2019, 10 October). Deon.pl liderem serwisów religijnych, mocno w górę Gloria. tv. Retrieved from https://www.wirtualnemedia.pl/artykul/religia-wiara-serwisy-najpopularniejsze-deon-pl-przed-gosc-pl-liderem-mocno-w-gore-gloria-tv n.a. (2020, 13 March). W Polsce wprowadzono stan zagrożenia epidemicznego. Sprawdź, co to oznacza w praktyce. Retrieved from https://pl.aleteia.org/2020/03/13/w -polsce-wprowadzono-stan-zagrozenia-epidemicznego-sprawdz-co-to-oznacza-w -praktyce/

Wiara.pl. O nas. (n.d.). Retrieved from https://www.wiara.pl/info/o_nas

n.a. (2020, 28 April). Wiara.pl. Rada Stała KEP: Apelujemy o wspólne stanowisko rządu i opozycji ws. wyborów prezydenckich. Retrieved from https://kosciol.wiara.pl /doc/6278345.Rada-Stala-KEP-Apelujemy-o-wspolne-stanowisko-rzadu-i-opozycji

CHAPTER 13

Fake News and Image Crises in Politics in the Social Media Space

Monika Kaczmarek-Śliwińska

13.1 Introduction

When analysing scientific literature on fake news, one can certainly notice the diversity of issues addressed and their interdisciplinarity. This is directly related to the essence of fake news, a phenomenon which can be described as a combination of various factors: cultural, social, political, economic, generational and other. The nature of fake news, apart from studies of attempts to define the phenomenon (Bąkowicz, 2019; Rosińska, 2021), is most often studied by setting a situation, person, or organisation in a given context.

Researchers also observe the nature of fake news, the reasons why it occurs, and the effects it produces; they analyse the possibility of identifying its sources and distribution channels. Thus, there are studies on the market of goods and services and the specific relations between the consumer and the brand, with fake news being examined in the context of consumer trust in the brand (Farte, Obadă, 2021).

The phenomenon of fake news is also analysed by embedding it in the media space, where analyses go in multiple directions. On the one hand, media space is presented as a distribution place for fake news, on the other hand, the media are seen as a place where fake news is created (Al-Rawi, Groshek, Zhang, 2018). Attempts at counteracting it at the audience level (for example, through media education) or finding legal solutions (both at the level of international and national structures) are also made (KRRiT, 2020). Fake news also undergoes scientific analyses from the perspective of the potential image risk (Kaczmarek-Śliwińska, 2021) of an organisation or institution.

Fake news is also analysed as a new category of threat to the economic security of the state, where a difficult situation caused by an external threat (such as the pandemic) is overlapped by threats related to the spread of fake news (Mroczka, 2022); as a result, the primary crisis is reinforced by a secondary crisis - an infodemic, which intensifies the difficulties in normalising the situation at the management level (Di Domenico, Tuan, Visentin, 2021; Jupowicz-Ginalska, Kaczmarek-Śliwińska, 2021). The interdisciplinary nature of the areas in which the fake news phenomenon is analysed is also demonstrated by scientific studies touching on topics that, on an individual level, are interesting research spheres in their own right (for example, combining the analysis of fake news with infodemic during the COVID-19 pandemic among the elderly; Rocha, de Moura, Desidério, de Oliveira, Lourenço, de Figueiredo Nicolete, 2021; Jupowicz-Ginalska, Kaczmarek-Śliwińska, 2021).

In the area of political analyses, fake news is most often studied from the perspective of media processes. In this case, the question arises whether and to what extent public opinion can be shaped by fake news and how it influences political actions (Palczewski, 2019). There are also studies which try to establish the relationship between political polarisation and content identified by users as fake news. Within this scope, the relationship between polarisation and the political narratives created is also explored (Ribeiro, Calais, Almeida, Meira, 2017). There are attempts to establish the relationship between fake news content and the impact on society of these political narratives, which in turn may be reflected in the results of political elections at various levels (from local government level to national parliamentary elections or European structures); such attempts are also made by institutions human rights monitoring (The Helsinki Foundation for Human Rights, 2020).

At the same time, the analysis of the scientific literature has shown a research gap regarding the impact of fake news on potential image crises of politicians or organisations in the context of the typology proposed by William Timothy Coombs. This typology suggests three types of crisis situations and corresponding degrees of responsibility attribution by observers – message recipients. The consequences may be different management strategies adopted by crisis-affected entities, as well as image risks that may affect the functioning of a politician.

13.2   Fake News in Political Communication

Media are indispensable for contemporary political communication in order to effectively implement information policy and manage image strategies. Currently, the media space is defined in two ways, i.e. by media areas that interact and interpenetrate each other: institutional media and social media. Although these spaces may have some common features (e.g. the recipient or the sender), it should be assumed that in considering the space of institutional media we shall understand them as entities that operate on the basis of legal regulations. Moreover, they implement their mission and social goals by applying codes of professional ethics, as well as principles of professionalism. Descriptions of social media spaces, on the other hand, tend to indicate the dominant role of the user as an entity who does not remain under any institutional constraint and who has the power to create or distribute content.

As written by Katarzyna Drogowska and Jacek Wasilewski:

> In the public sphere, it is often not about facts, which may be true or false, but about the perspective of the narrative, the direction of interpretation, or, to put it briefly, spin. (Drogowska, Wasilewski, 2009)

In an attempt to determine which category of lie fake news belongs to, the typology proposed by Paul Ekman can be referred to. He indicated that lying can be performed: [1] passively, [2] actively, [3] by admitting an experienced emotion, [4] by using false truthfulness, and [5] by deceit (Ekman, 2007). With such defined categories of lies, fake news represents a lie which may be implemented for a variety of intentions and purposes.

It makes us wonder why lying in politics hardly ever excludes a person from further functioning in the social space. Sometimes, on the other hand, the use of false information is evaluated in a short period of time or the consequences of this action are drawn. K. Drogowska and J. Wasilewski suggest that it is linked to the separation of the public and private spheres, in the recognition that what is public is attributed to ideology; it is a show, a performance, where lying is permitted, because by its very nature the performance is fiction (Drogowska, Wasilewski, 2009).

The reflection on the separation of private and public spheres may be surprising. It is all the more puzzling because nowadays politicians function mainly in social media and we often see them expose their privacy in public space, intentionally and consciously. However, it might be the case that the so-called 'privacy' is to a large extent fabricated, and therefore it does not reflect the actual situation, but is only an expected presentation created for the purposes of image strategies of politicians.

Fake news is false information produced for a specific purpose by deliberately misleading its recipients. The authors of "Mały leksykon postprawdy" distinguished several types of fake news to describe its specific nature (Drzewiecki & Głębicka-Giza, 2018): [1] false, invented stories, [2] news created for the propaganda, political or commercial purposes (deliberate deception), [3] fake news based on partially true information that has been manipulated, [4] fake news of a satirical nature, [5] real news considered as fake news by people or institutions because of its negative content for these people or institutions. The impact of fake news is significant because, on the one hand, creators and broadcasters (not always the same entities) use institutional and social media channels and, on the other hand, they construct fake news in such a way as to maximise its attractiveness from the perspective of the media user. The fact of distribution through mass media also influences the credibility of fake news, since the recipient (especially with a lower level of media competence) may assume the authenticity of media content and assume that the journalistic profession excludes the intentional creation of false information. Less trust is given to information distributed through social media, where anyone can be a sender. This means, in fact, that in the absence of enforced ethical regulations, the tendency to create and distribute fake news can be considerable.

13.3   Fake News as Perceived by Respondents

"Fake news" was declared the world of the year for 2017 by Collins Dictionary (defined as "false, often sensational, information disseminated under the guise of news reporting") ("What is 2017's word of the year?", para. 1).

According to the Payback Opinion Poll, more than 60% of Poles are familiar with the term "fake news", and 80% of respondents have had personal contact with such messages ("Badanie: Fake news najczęstsze w show-biznesie i polityce", para.1). Among other things, the respondents indicated that politics comes second among topics where they notice fake news.

In the same study, the respondents also identified the sources of false information: media messages (54%), politicians and public figures (41%) and celebrities (40%). The respondents also noticed fake news mostly in online media: websites (76%) and social media (70%). The space defined as traditional media (the press, the radio, television), on the other hand, was indicated much less frequently: television - 30%, and daily press - 16% ("Badanie: Fake news najczęstsze w show-biznesie i polityce", para. 2).

The main reason for the existence of fake news, according to the respondents, is manipulation (65%). Other reasons were: the desire of politicians or celebrities to attract attention (50%), profits earned by those who publish false information (47%), using the "recency effect" of news and the related impossibility to properly verify information in several sources at the same time in order to guarantee reliable information (35%) ("Badanie: Fake news najczęstsze w show-biznesie i polityce", para. 3).

In the Payback Opinion Poll, 71% of the respondents admitted that the scale of fake news poses a threat to the perception of the media as a reliable source of information, with the very phenomenon of publishing fake news expected to intensify (83%). Almost 40% of the respondents declared that they had never believed fake news, while about 30% of the surveyed group believed false information, although the vast majority (97%) of the respondents declared that they verified information in other media.

The results concerning verifiability of information coming from the media turned out to be equally interesting. They showed that one in two people checked it if the authenticity of the message was uncertain, and 57% of the respondents paid attention to the source of information only if its content raised doubts. One fifth (22%) of the respondents checked the source of information every time.

The results also showed that the respondents noticed significant disproportions between the presence of fake news in online media and in institutional media. This corresponds with the findings of the European Broadcasting Union (EBU). The results showed that trust in traditional media is increasing, while trust in social media is clearly decreasing. The radio was declared the big winner of the survey, as 59% of the respondents considered it a trustworthy medium. Television (the European average) was trusted by 50% of the respondents, newspapers by 47%, the Internet by 32%, and social media by only 19% (at the same time, 63% of the respondents indicated social media as untrusted) ("Radio budzi w Europejczykach największe zaufanie. Social media najmniej wiarygodne", para. 2–13).

Interesting results concerning fake news, but also showing the scale of distribution of fake news, were brought by the Kantar TNS survey. The respondents were asked about the frequency of receiving news or information which in their opinion distorted reality or was false; they answered that such a situation occurred daily / almost daily (48% of the respondents; the overall percentage for the surveyed group in the EU: 37%) or at least once a week (27% of the respondents; for the EU: 31%). The statement "several times a month" was chosen by 7% of the respondents (the EU: 12%). A minority of the respondents (Poland: 14%; the EU: 17%) referred to their contact with fake news as "rarely or never" (the "don't know/no answer" option accounted for only 4% of the respondents in Poland and 3% in the EU).

In the survey being discussed, Poles demonstrated greater awareness and knowledge of the dangers of fake news in the social space. For 49% of them, news which distorts reality or is untrue is definitely a problem, while 35% answered "rather yes". Only 12% of the respondents said that the existence of fake news content was not a problem. An analysis of the EU averages shows that the results are comparable: 85% of the respondents consider fake news to be a problem, while 12% do not see the problem ("Czy żyjemy w rzeczywistości fake newsów?", pp. 3–5).

The problem of distorted and false news and information was also raised with regard to democracy in general. The results obtained were consistent with those presented earlier: 79% of Polish respondents (EU average: 83%) consider such news and information as a problem in democracy, while 16% do not see such a threat.

When summarising the discussed survey, it is also worth noting the respondents' opinion on the responsibility for the distribution of fake news content. They indicated institutions and entities on the media market which should take action to stop spreading fake news. What is surprising, however, is the low declarative responsibility placed on key media market players. None of the indicated entities exceeded 50%, as journalists received 49%, state authorities 40%, citizens themselves 34%, NGOs 22%, press and broadcasting executives 20%, European Union institutions 18%, and online social media 18%.

13.4   Credibility of the Media as Perceived by Their Audiences

Research conducted by PMR Consulting&Research and Attention Marketing (2017) shows that the dominant sources of information about current events in Poland and the world were television (over 50%) and news portals (54%). For 21% of the respondents, however, social media were the source of information about current events in Poland and the world, while for 8% it was blogs and vlogs. For every third person aged 18–34, Facebook was a source of knowledge about the world ("Raport Attention Marketing Research", para. 1–12). The two remaining ones from the traditional media trio, namely the radio (less than 30%) and the press (daily - 22%, opinion-forming - 14%, lifestyle - 5%) are much less important as sources of information.

Slightly different results were obtained in opinions regarding trust in public (20%) and non-public (39%) television broadcasts. In both cases, the largest group was over 55 years of age. A significant difference in viewers' trust, depending on the type of medium, was visible in the 35–54 age group (trust in the public broadcaster was 15%, in the non-public one 31%). Slight discrepancies in the answers concerning trust depending on the broadcaster were noted in the group of the youngest respondents (18–34 years old), where trust in the public broadcaster was at 18%, and in the non-public broadcaster - 23%.

An opposite tendency was noted among the respondents as regards their distrust towards information from a given medium. Almost twice as high a level of distrust in the 55+ age group was recorded in the case of information provided by public television (55%) than by non-public television (28%). In the case of the 35–54 and 18–34 age groups, there were smaller disproportions: in the 35–54 age group, the distrust ratio for information provided by television was 57% (public television) to 38% (non-public television), while in the 18–34 group it was 52% to 42% respectively.

When addressing the issue of fake news in the context of image crises, one should consider the question of trust towards the media. The results of the study "Zaufanie do mediów. Źródła informacji i ich weryfikowanie", in which one of the analysed aspects was the relation between types of information (political, social, economic, hobbies/interests etc.) and types of media (television, the radio, the press, websites), show that TV is the leader in the group of political information, being a source of information for 72% of respondents. Radio was indicated by 37% of the respondents, press by 35%, and websites by 43%. In the social information category, the order of information sources is identical (TV 67%, websites 48%, radio 40%, and press 37%). However, in the economic information category, the first two indications of information sources are consistent with those discussed earlier: television - 59%, websites - 54%, followed by the press (35%) and the radio (31%).

In the survey, the respondents also determined their level of trust and distrust in information provided by the media. The most trusted information categories are: social (68%), economic (57%) ones, while the least trusted is political information (46%). It should therefore not be a surprise that the greatest lack of trust in information provided by the media concerned political information (indicated by 49% of respondents), economic information (40%), and the least - social information (30%).

According to the respondents, the credibility of information in the media is influenced by three factors: [1] opinions of independent experts and authorities (59%), [2] supporting media material with scientific research results (51%) and [3] different sources of information (46%).

Paradoxically, for fake news creators, these three elements may be a 'recipe' for creating information which intentionally misleads the recipient, while the accurate formatting of fake news with the use of experts, scientific research results and diversified sources of information may affect its distribution and the influence on the recipients.

The issue of trust and credibility of information provided by the media is connected with the verification of information by its recipients. Such actions were declared by 79% of the respondents as regards political information, 70% for economic content and 63% for social information. The results of the study also confirmed that - as could be expected - in view of the greatest lack of trust and credibility towards political information, it was indicated least often as unverified by the recipients. The fact that political information from the media was not verified was indicated by 21% of respondents, economic information by 30%, and social information by 37%.

What proved to be a highly intriguing aspect of the survey were the results concerning the ways in which the recipients verified information on specific topics. Four ways of verifying information were indicated by the respondents:

1. Checking other sources (for categories of information: political: 72.1%, economic: 68.8%, social: 70.2%).
2. Comments on the Internet and on social media (for categories of information: political: 47.0%, economic: 54.1%, social: 48.1%).
3. Consulting friends (for categories of information: political: 40.7%, economic: 41.3%, social: 57.0%).
4. Consulting experts on a given subject (for categories of information: political: 12.7%, economic: 23.4%, social: 15.1%).

As can be seen from the research presented above, media information is most often verified by: checking other sources, comments on the Internet and on social media, and consulting friends. There is a concern that such verification may not be sufficient to identify fake news, because other sources (e.g. chasing the news) may duplicate false information, whereas comments on the Internet and on social media may contain erroneous (due to unintentional action) or false information (due to intentional action (Freeze, Baumgartner, Bruno, Gunderson, Olin, Ross & Szafran, 2020)). This is compounded by the problem of the "filter bubble", i.e. remaining in a group of people distributing content of a similar nature, tone and attitude, without using dialogue as a form of criticism in relation to the information obtained.

13.5   Fake News and the Online Communication Space

A crisis situation is defined as a period of time in which, due to an event or events, the effective implementation of the mission and objectives of an organisation, brand or public figure is jeopardised, with the crisis being the climax of the crisis situation (sudden event; foreseeable or not) (Kaczmarek-Śliwińska, 2015).

Certainly, political activity fosters the emergence of such crisis situations which, depending on the intensity of the events triggering them, their course and development and their management and stabilisation, are sometimes referred to as problems or incidents (Kaczmarek-Śliwińska, 2019). When confronted with reputational risk, political entities are usually left in a state of uncertainty as to whether the event that has occurred will become a crisis situation transformed into a crisis, or whether the first symptoms can be managed effectively enough to avoid escalation and the attention of institutional and social media.

On the one hand, therefore, it is interesting to know the impact of fake news on the development of situations that may threaten the image and reputation of a politician or a political group. On the other hand, it is necessary to consider the perspective of the creator and the sender of fake news (the creator and the sender do not have to be the same person/media) and the reactions undertaken by the party being the subject of fake news in a direct or indirect way (fake news does not have to refer explicitly to a politician or political group in order to damage their image and reputation indirectly).

It is also necessary to take into account the nature of crisis situations and crises on social media, which stems from the characteristics of the new media environment and media space, currently created not only by institutional media entities (media registered and operating according to legal provisions), but also by Internet users, who are both senders and recipients. Among the many features of the new media space, it is worth noting: [1] its anonymity (or rather the illusion of anonymity in the online world), [2] the ease with which content can be modified by appearing in the digital form, [3] interactivity, with one of its aspect being the possibility of a mutual and ongoing relationship between the entity affected by fake news and its environment (Kaczmarek-Śliwińska, 2016). With all this in mind, the mechanisms present in online communication are also important, as they are specific enough for this environment to be indicated as distinctive (Baptista & Gradim, 2020). Three of them that can accompany distribution and benefit from its strength (Kaczmarek-Śliwińska, 2016) are: [1] networked public, [2] disinhibition; Kenneth Joinson, and [3] cockpit effect. These three mechanisms are clearly present in the case of hate speech, when an online hater takes advantage of the anonymous support of his/her group or of the apparent lack of responsibility that comes with indirect communication in order to attack his/her victim. These mechanisms can also be observed with regard to the distribution of fake news, as some of these messages are accompanied by hate speech (Kaczmarek-Śliwińska, Pyżalski, 2011).

When considering the subject of fake news in politics, it is also important to note the consequences of the transforming roles of users in the online media space. As pointed out earlier, in the situation of a dynamically changing media space, it is not only institutional media that perform the role of a content sender; therefore, it is not only traditionally perceived media broadcasters that can be a source of fake news or a channel for its distribution. Another area of considerable power and sometimes even avalanche distribution of content is social media, where the recipient of content may also be its sender and/or creator. Therefore, it becomes important to pay attention to the area related to potential abuse of entities creating and sharing content online, as it should be assumed that some of such content may be consciously constructed in order to manipulate the recipient. It should also be assumed that some manipulative content will be constructed as fake news. In the activities of institutional and social media, manipulation may be carried out using various techniques and forms. The following are often observed in the online space: gatekeeping, framing, agenda setting, the strawman method, or red herring (Kaczmarek-Śliwińska, 2018). Naturally, then, the question arises about the ethics, legal bounds, and responsibilities involved in such message formatting. In both situations (institutional media and non-institutional users of social media) we can use legal grounds to interpret their activities (such as criminal and civil law, or laws on the activity scope of the media and market entities); however, as far as the ethics of online communication is concerned, it is only possible to refer to a part of the media space, namely the institutional media, which are bound by professional codes of ethics. It is the same with accountability: in the case of institutional media, it is related to the principles according to which editorial-based media operate (e.g. the roles of an editor-in-chief, a managing editor or another gatekeeper) (Kaczmarek-Śliwińska, 2013), whereas as regards social media users, appeal could be made to their individual sense of responsibility or to the principles of social coexistence, which are not legal norms but are morally justified rules of conduct of people towards others in social life.

13.6   Fake News in Political Crisis Situations

According to the typology of crisis situations according to the Situational Crisis Communication Theory (SCCT) by W. T. Coombs (Coombs, 2007), a politician or a political group may be affected by three clusters of situations:

1. The organisation (the politician, the political party) is also a victim of the crisis situation.
2. The organisation (the politician, the political party) has caused the crisis situation unintentionally, accidentally.
3. The organisation (the politician, the political party) has caused the crisis situation deliberately, knowingly.

The analysis of political crisis situations shows that fake news related to political topics is observed - although it is not always possible to confirm the facts - in all of the three clusters of situations defined above (Kaczmarek-Śliwińska, 2020).

In the first situation (the politician and/or the political group are victims of the crisis situation) fake news is created and distributed in order to generate a situation raising doubts as to the politician's honesty, work, behaviour (both in his/her public and private life) or the values and activities of the political party. Such a message is supposed to arouse interest of the media and the audience, generate further journalistic content, and provoke the audience's involvement, either through redistributing the content, creating original content on the basis of the already existing fake news, or through triggering discussions and disputes which are not really intended to clarify, exchange arguments, develop a debate, or reach a compromise. Fake news in this cluster of crisis situations is meant to cause a problem for the politician and/or the political group.

The two remaining clusters of crisis situations, in which the politician and/or political group has caused the crisis situation either unintentionally (by accident) or intentionally, can be difficult to distinguish in political-media reality (Kaczmarek-Śliwińska, 2019).

The first cluster (crisis situations caused accidentally) may be due to the mistakes (Tworzydło, 2017) of the media (haste, failure to verify the source, but also deliberate release of fake news stemming from the particular interests of a given medium) or may be caused by inappropriate actions of the politician and/or the political group (inconsistent communication, information leaks, failure to verify information, etc.). Errors on the part of the media and the political scene are linked to the mediatisation of politics and the confusion between political logic and media logic. This was aptly put by Małgorzata Adamik-Szysiak: "In the times of mediatisation of politics, the media, whose content is dictated solely by media logic, are the main source of political information for the citizens; in the activities of political entities, political logic is being replaced by media logic. Thus, politics can hardly be seen as part of a reality functioning beyond the media; moreover, politics increasingly takes the form of events which are planned and organised specially for the needs of the media" (Adamik-Szysiak, 2018). In such a reality, mistakes or crisis situations due to factors that are independent or difficult to predict by a politician or political group become highly probable.

In the case of the deliberately created crisis situations, which have been planned and aimed at achieving certain effects (usually the manipulation of the audience (Alibašić & Rose, 2019), it is most often difficult to prove such a fact, because proving and publicly announcing it (and perhaps also criminal sanctions) could entail social ostracism (at least of a part of the potential electorate) or - at the very least - embarrassment. Therefore, even when there are allegations of such a fact in the public space, it is a common tactic to make the politician or political group a victim or to accept part of the 'blame' by explaining and proving the lack of deliberateness, other intentions, i.e. to shift towards crisis situations caused unintentionally and by accident.

When discussing crisis situations related to fake news in the political space, the description should be supplemented with a time factor. While observing crisis situations, an attempt is made to divide particular events into stages (Grocki, 2012; Mitroff, Pearson, 1998; Jaques, 2010). When analysing the impact of fake news on crisis situations and crises in the political arena, the events between the pre-crisis and post-crisis state are a crucial issue. These events can occur in two forms (Kaczmarek-Śliwińska, 2019): [1] the fading crisis and [2] the growing crisis. The first one - the fading crisis - means that the crisis situation is disappearing thanks to effective process management. On the other hand, the growing crisis involves the escalation of events and the addition of secondary events to the primary crisis, which continue to sustain institutional and social media interest and destabilise the entity's image. Fake news can be an effective trigger in the case of the growing crisis.

13.7   Conclusions

Reflecting on the issue of crisis situations and crises involving politicians and/ or political groups related to fake news on social media requires taking into account the general nature of the media space, the characteristics of the online media space, the issue of recipients and recipient-senders versus their trust in the media, as well as political scene activity and crisis management skills.

Fake news, being a piece of misleading information, can cause an entity's image to be tarnished and can have a long term impact on their reputation; therefore it requires special scrutiny. This is because most crisis situations in their initial stages are related to a lack of information; it is not known who the creator of fake news is, what their intentions are, and what further actions the creator of fake news may take. Managing a crisis situation in such specific conditions is like walking on thin ice, as is taking no action at all.

It is therefore increasingly important to monitor the media space in order to detect the first symptoms of impending problems and incidents, and then to implement preventive policies which provide an opportunity to minimise the risk of a crisis. What is also crucial are the activities of politicians and parties aimed at increasing awareness, competence and responsibility in communicating with the public and the media (e.g. knowledge of the principles of content distribution in the media space - content migration between different types of media).

Managing crisis situations when faced with fake news also means implementing a responsible image management policy, which should, in practice, mean: diagnosing threats, analysing risks, modelling crisis scenarios and crisis-preventive actions, building individual media space (in-house media and the identification of opinion leaders) in order to maximise the effectiveness of reaching the audiences with messages, regardless of the distribution of content by institutional media.

References

Literature

Adamik-Szysiak, M. (2018). *Strategie komunikowania podmiotów politycznych Polsce w mediach społecznościowych*. Lublin: Wydawnictwo Uniwersytetu Marii Curie-Skłodowskiej.

Alibašić, H., Rose J. (2019). Fake News in Context: Truth and Untruths. *Public Integrity*, 21, 463–468, doi.org/10.1080/10999922.2019.1622359.

Bąkowicz, K. (2019). Wprowadzenie do definicji i klasyfikacji zjawiska *fake newsa*. *Studia Medioznawcze*, 3(78), 280–289.

Coombs, W. T. (2007). Protecting Organizational Reputations During a Crisis: The Development and Application of Situational Crisis Communication Theory. *Corporate Reputation Review*, 10, 163–176.

Drogowska, K., Wasilewski, J. (2009). Kiedy kłamstwo uwiarygodnia, a prawda dyskredytuje, In B. Sobczak, H. Zgółkowa (Eds.), Retoryka i etyka (pp. 102–125), Poznań 2009.

Drzewiecki, P., Głębicka-Giza, B. (Eds.) (2018), *Mały leksykon postprawdy*, Warszawa: Fundacja Wolność i Demokracja.

Ekman, P. (2007). *Kłamstwo i jego wykrywanie w biznesie, polityce i małżeństwie*, Warszawa: Wydawnictwo Naukowe PWN.

Fârte, G-I., Obadă D.-R. (2021). The Effects of Fake News on Consumers' Brand Trust: An Exploratory Study in the Food Security Context , *Romanian Journal of Communication and Public Relations*, vol. 23, no. 3 (54), 47–61.

Grocki, R. (2012), *Zarządzanie kryzysowe. Dobre praktyki*, Warszawa: Difin.

Helsińska Fundacja Praw Człowieka, (2020). Fake newsy i dezinformacja w kampaniach wyborczych w Polsce w 2019 roku - raport z obserwacji. Warszawa: HFPC.

Jaques, T. (2010). Reshaping Crisis Management: The Challenge for Organizational Design. *Organizational Development Journal*, no. 28, 9–17.

Jupowicz-Ginalska, A., Kaczmarek-Śliwińska, M. (Eds.) (2021). Medialno-społeczny obraz COVID-19: Solidarność czy polaryzacja – podsumowanie, diagnoza, rekomendacja. Warszawa: SBP.

Kaczmarek-Śliwińska, M. (2020). Hejt jako źródło sytuacji kryzysowych podmiotów w przestrzeni społecznej. *Zarządzanie Mediami*, 2, 75–87, doi:10.4467/2354021 4ZM.20.023.11802.

Kaczmarek-Śliwińska, M. (2021). Kryzysogenny potencjał fake newsa. In K. Rosińska, P. Płatek (Eds.), Oblicza fake newsa. Perspektywa naukowych analiz zjawiska fałszywych wiadomości (pp. 15–32). Warszawa: UKSW.

Kaczmarek-Śliwińska, M. (2018). Medialna przestrzeń online. Dziennikarz versus internauta w procesie tworzenia i dystrybucji komunikatów. In M. Kaczmarek-Śliwińska (Ed.), Relacje. Media. Konteksty. Praktyka komunikowania się (pp. 37–46), Warszawa: Oficyna Wydawnicza ASPRA-JR.

Kaczmarek-Śliwińska, M. (2015). *Public relations organizacji w zarządzaniu sytuacjami kryzysowymi organizacji. Sztuka komunikowania się*. Warszawa: Difin.

Kaczmarek-Śliwińska, M. (2013). *Public relations w przestrzeni mediów społecznościowych. Działania organizacji i jej pracowników*. Koszalin: Wydawnictwo Politechniki Koszalińskiej.

Kaczmarek-Śliwińska, M. (2019). Specyfika zarządzania sytuacją kryzysową w przestrzeni mediów społecznościowych w perspektywie typologii Situational Crisis Communication Theory W.T. Coombsa. *Studia Medioznawcze, 4*(79), 318–332, doi: 10.33077/uw.24511617.ms.2019.4.72.

Kaczmarek-Śliwińska, M. (2016). Zarządzanie komunikacją kryzysową w przestrzeni mediów społecznościowych w kontekście zjawiska hejtingu. *Kultura - Media - Teologia*, no. 25, 46–58.

Kaczmarek-Śliwińska, M., Pyżalski, J. (2011). Media społeczne (social media) jako narzędzie realizacji agresji elektronicznej. In K. Augustyniak, A. Piotrowski (Eds.), Edukacja dla bezpieczeństwa. Cywilizacyjne problemy bezpieczeństwa (pp. 61–68). Poznań: Wydawnictwo Wyższej Szkoły Bezpieczeństwa.

Krajowa Rada Radiofonii i Telewizji, (2020). Fake news -dezinformacja online. Warszawa: KRRiT.

Mitroff, I., Pearson, C, (1998). *Zarządzanie sytuacją kryzysową czyli jak ochronić firmę przed najgorszym*. Warszawa: Business Press.

Mroczka, K. (2022). Fake newsy jako nowa kategoria zagrożenia systemu bezpieczeństwa ekonomicznego państwa w dobie kryzysu epidemicznego. *Przegląd Bezpieczeństwa Wewnętrznego*, 26 (14), 86–128. DOI: 10.4467/20801335PBW.21.036.15696.

Palczewski, M. (2019). Fake news w polityce. Studia przypadków. *Mediatization Studies*, 3, 137–150. DOI: 10.17951/ms.2019.3.137–150.

Tworzydło, D. (2017). *Public relations praktycznie*. Rzeszów: Newsline Sp. z o.o.

Webography

What is 2017's word of the year? (n.d.) Retrieved November 3, 2018 from https://www.bbc.com/news/uk-41838386

Al-Rawi, A., Groshek, J., Zhang,L. (2018). What the fake? Assessing the extent of networked political spamming and bots in the propagation of #fakenews on Twitter,

Online Information Review. Retrieved November 7, 2021 from https://doi.org/10.1108 /OIR-02-2018-0065.

Badanie: Fake news najczęstsze w show-biznesie i polityce (n.d.), Retrieved April 12, 2018 from https://www.signs.pl/badanie%3A-fake-news-najczestsze-w-show -biznesie-i-polityce-,35087,artykul.html

Baptista J. P., Gradim, A. (2020). Understanding Fake News Consumption: A Review. *Social Sciences*. 9 (10). https://doi.org/10.3390/socsci9100185

Di Domenico G., Tuan A., Visentin M. (2021). Linguistic drivers of misinformation dif-fusion on social media during the COVID-19 pandemic. *Italian Journal of Marketing*. Retrieved May 3, 2019 from https://www.researchgate.net/publication/351975801 _Linguistic_drivers_of_misinformation_diffusion_on_social_media_during_the _COVID-19_pandemic. DOI: 10.1007/s43039-021-00026-9

Freeze, M., Baumgartner, M., Bruno, P., Gunderson J. R., Olin, J., Ross, M. Q. & Szafran J. (2020). Fake Claims of Fake News: Political Misinformation, Warnings, and the Tainted Truth Effect. *Political Behavior*. https://doi.org/10.1007/s11109-020-09597-3

Kantar Public. (2019). Czy żyjemy w rzeczywistości fake newsów? Retrieved May 3, 2019 from http://www.tnsglobal.pl/archiwumraportow/files/2018/03/K.013_Fake _news_O03a-18.pdf

Radio budzi w Europejczykach największe zaufanie. Social media najmniej wiary-godne (n.d.). Retrieved June 10, 2019 from https://www.wirtualnemedia.pl/artykul /radio-budzi-w-europejczykach-najwieksze-zaufanie-social-media-najmniej -wiarygodne

Raport Attention Marketing Research (n.d.). Retrieved July 14, 2017 from http:// attentionmarketing.pl/news/skad-polacy-czerpia-informacje-o-wydarzeniach-w -kraju-i-na-swiecie-raport-z-badan

Ribeiro M. H., Calais P. H., Almeida V. A.F., Meira Jr W. (2017). "Everything I Disagree With is #FakeNews": Correlating Political Polarization and Spread of Misinformation. Retrieved July 14, 2017 from https://www.researchgate.net/publication/317673508 _Everything_I_Disagree_With_is_FakeNews_Correlating_Political_Polarization _and_Spread_of_Misinformation

Rocha, Y. M., de Moura, G. A., Desidério, G. A., de Oliveira, C. H., Lourenço, F. D., & de Figueiredo Nicolete, L. D. (2021). The impact of fake news on social media and its influence on health during the COVID-19 pandemic: a systematic review. *Zeitschrift fur Gesundheitswissenschaften*, . Retrieved July 20, 2021 from https://doi.org/10.1007 /s10389-021-01658-z.

Zaufanie do mediów. Źródła informacji i ich weryfikowanie (n.d.). Retrieved December 10, 2017 from http://pressclub.pl/wp-content/uploads/2017/09/Raport-z-badania.pdf

The Presidential Campaign of Małgorzata Kidawa-Błońska in Media Discourse: Analysis Based on Statistical Corpus Analysis and Topic Modelling

Weronika Świerczyńska-Głownia, Jan Wieczorek, and
Tomasz Walkowiak

14.1   Introduction

14.1.1   *The Candidate*

Małgorzata Kidawa-Błońska comes from a family with a political background, being the great-granddaughter of two distinguished statesmen: President of the Republic of Poland Stanisław Wojciechowski (President in 1922–1926) and Prime Minister Władysław Grabski (*www.platforma.org*).

During her more than twenty years of presence on the Polish political scene, Małgorzata Kidawa-Błońska has held many important offices and functions. For the purposes of this analysis, we will only cover what the authors believe to be the key milestones and events. In 2001, Małgorzata Kidawa-Błońska joined the political party called Platforma Obywatelska (Civic Platform, abbreviated name: PO). In 2005, she was elected Member of the Sejm from that party's list, with 4,615 votes (*National Electoral Commission's website*). In 2007, after the Sejm's term of office was curtailed, she again won a parliamentary seat, with 13,057 votes (*National Electoral Commission's website*). In 2011, she was elected MP from the Civic Platform list for the third time, having received 45,027 votes (*National Electoral Commission's website*). On June 25th 2015, Małgorzata Kidawa-Błońska was elected Speaker of the Sejm (*Resolution of the Sejm of June 25th 2015*). In the next parliamentary election, held in 2015, she once again successfully ran for re-election as an MP, with support for her candidacy continuing to grow. In 2015, she could count on as many as 80,866 votes (*National Electoral Commission's website*). At the first sitting of the Sejm on November 12th 2015, she was elected Deputy Speaker of the Sejm (*Resolution of the Sejm of November 12th 2015*). On September 3rd 2019, she was put forward by the Civic Coalition (former Civic Platform) as a candidate for Prime Minister if that party was to win in the parliamentary election held on October 13th 2019 (*Malgorzata Kidawa...*) Although her party failed to win power in that election, Małgorzata Kidawa-Błońska achieved the best individual result in Poland, running as the Civic Coalition's candidate and winning 416,030 votes (*National Electoral Commission's website*). On November 12th 2019, Małgorzata Kidawa-Błońska was elected Deputy Speaker of the Sejm (*Resolution of the Sejm of November 12th 2019*).

An important fact in the context of this analysis is that Małgorzata Kidawa-Błońska was twice appointed government spokesperson. The first time, between January and September 2014, she was the spokesperson for the government headed by Donald Tusk (*Nowy rzecznik...*). She was appointed government spokesperson for the second time by Prime Minister Ewa Kopacz in February 2015 (*Małgorzata Kidawa-Błońska nowym...*) and held this position until June 25th 2015, when she was elected Speaker of the Sejm, as mentioned above. Moreover, she served as press spokesperson of the Civic Platform Electoral Committee in the parliamentary election in 2011.

On December 14th 2019, the Civic Platform National Convention decided in the party's presidential primary election that Małgorzata Kidawa-Błońska would be the Civic Platform's candidate for the office of President of Poland. 475 electors took part in the election, with 125 casting their votes for the challenger, Jacek Jaśkowiak, and 345 voting for Małgorzata Kidawa-Błońska. 5 votes were invalid (*www.platforma.org*).

Based on opinion poll results, Małgorzata Kidawa-Błońska began the campaign for the office of President of Poland with support sufficient to warrant the assumption that she was in a position to compete against the incumbent President. In February 2020, support for her candidacy was at 20% (*Survey report No. 23/2020*). It is worth noting, however, that in the same month only 9% of respondents said that they thought Małgorzata Kidawa-Błońska would win the upcoming presidential election (*Survey report No. 26/2020*). Only a month later, in March, the polls began to show a significant drop in support for Małgorzata Kidawa-Błońska, estimating it at some 15% (*Survey report No. 35/2020*) while in April, based on the polls, it fell to a mere 5% (*Survey report No. 54/2020*). On May 15th 2020, during a press conference at the Sejm, Małgorzata Kidawa-Błońska announced her decision not to run for president.

14.1.2 Electoral Programme

Małgorzata Kidawa-Błońska's electoral programme was not to be found on her website at the beginning of the presidential campaign, with the candidate presenting its main points during conventions, press conferences and meetings with voters. On the basis of Małgorzata Kidawa-Błońska's statements, the foundation of her presidency was to be the security of Poland and Poles. Security here understood very broadly, and including effective health care, prosperity, a friendly state, a friendly environment, a modern army and alliances (restoring relations with the EU and the US, returning to the Weimar Triangle). The candidate pointed out that her priority would be to uphold the Constitution and put forward initiatives to restore constitutional order and defend the law. She also spoke of the law on civil partnerships, the reasonableness of maintaining the abortion compromise, and the need for climate action (Oworuszko: 2020; *Małgorzata Kidawa-Błońska. Program wyborczy...*)

She stated that the first thing she would do as President of Poland was to submit a bill that would guarantee the best available treatment to all children with a serious illness, regardless of where they lived, how rich their parents were, or what the status of their parents' relationship was. Furthermore, she spoke of the need for changes in the healthcare system. She declared an intention to put forward a bill that would guarantee allocation of an additional one percent of GDP from the state budget for healthcare, and pledged that health spending would reach six percent of GDP as early as 2021. She also spoke of free prescriptions for senior citizens (Oworuszko: 2020).

In May, the candidate expanded her electoral programme to include a package for all those affected by the coronavirus. She pointed to the need for financial assistance and support in the form of tax reliefs and waivers of social insurance contributions for businesses and the self-employed. She spoke of the need for increased testing for Covid-19 and a state-funded financial award for healthcare personnel for working under difficult conditions (Żurek: 2020).

14.2   Theoretical Background

The considerations in this paper derive from the position that political discourse analysis (Van Dijk, 1998) is a branch of discourse analysis that aims to explicate from speeches and debates the salient features of political discourses. A presidential election, therefore, provides interesting datasets to study. Indeed, being a major political event in a country, it gives rise to many political meetings where candidates discuss personally selected societal problems and detail their own solutions. In that context, the identification of the preferred topics of candidates as well as how they evolve throughout the campaign is a worthwhile task (Gautrais, Cellier, Quiniou, Termier: (2017).

A tool supporting such analysis is the topic modelling method. Topic modelling has applications in many fields and research areas, including medical sciences, software engineering, geography, and political and social sciences. This has been discussed extensively by Jelodar, H., Wang, Y., Yuan, C. et al. (2019). In political science, topic modelling is used, among other things, to analyse large corpora created from political speeches delivered over time. This method can be used to identify both prominent and long-term topics as well as niche topics related to events at a specific point in time (Jelodar, H., Wang, Y., Yuan, C. et al.: 2019). As Greene and Cross point out, some topic modelling methods have been adopted in the political science literature to analyse political focus. In settings where politicians have limited time-resources to express their views, such as the plenary sessions in parliaments, they must decide what topics to address. Analysing such speeches can thus provide insight into the political priorities of the politician under consideration (Greene, Cross: 2015).

This statement seems to be corroborated by the research conducted by Quinn K. M., Monroe B. L., Colaresi [et al.] on plenary speeches delivered in the U.S. Senate. The authors used topic modelling to examine the agenda in the U.S. Senate from 1997 to 2004, identifying the thematic categories addressed in the speeches and the main themes of the speeches. Since this method assesses, rather than assumes, the substance of topics, the keywords that identify topics, and the hierarchical nesting of topics, it found that a rich and meaningful political agenda emerged from the collected speeches, where topics evolved significantly over time in response to both internal and external stimuli (Quinn, Monroe, Colaresi et.al.:2010).

Another study using topic modelling in political discourse is Jacques Savoy's paper entitled *Lexical Analysis of US Political Speeches*. The author presents an analysis of the evolution of topics in political speeches by comparing the words that are overused or underused by Obama and McCain during the 2008 U.S. presidential campaign. The dynamics of the particular usage of these words is analysed over monthly periods to identify the underlying dynamics of the campaign topics. A limitation of this approach is that the period is fixed (monthly) whereas predictable (votes, debates) or unpredictable (scandals) events usually give the rhythm to a political campaign (Savoy, 2010).

Another example is the study by Clément Gautrais, Peggy Cellier, René Quiniou and Alexandre Termier, in which the authors attempt to identify the most common topics in the political speeches of each candidate as well as how and when they evolve throughout the campaign. The above study concludes that this gives critical clues to identify and to explain each candidate's main ideas and their evolution. They describe an approach to extract the topic signature of a candidate from their political speeches, i.e., the set of topics discussed by a candidate over time. In this particular case, however, the authors used a standard topic modelling technique with signature mining to analyse Hillary Clinton's and Donald Trump's speeches during the 2016 U.S. presidential campaign (Gautrais, Cellier, Quiniou, Termier: 2017).

Given that the 2020 presidential campaign in Poland took a different form from that used before (due to the Covid 19 pandemic), it was media reports and the social media space that became the main campaign platform for the candidates to communicate with the electorate. Hence, our study focuses on an analysis of media reports concerning candidate Małgorzata Kidawa-Błońska.

14.3   Research Methodology

14.3.1   *Application of Topic Modelling*

Topic modelling (Graham, Weingart, Milligan: 2012), also referred to as: *topical analysis, topical modelling,* is a procedure used to detect sets of co-occurring words in a corpus, i.e., in a set of texts. The tendency of the words to co-occur is interpreted as a sign that they are thematically (semantically) related. In each study, this relation is an assumption that the researcher should verify manually. A topic should therefore be understood as a set of words that are potentially related to one another in terms of distribution and semantics. Statistical methods (WordRank in this case) are employed to extract sets of words where the co-occurrence is likely not to have been caused by chance. Distributional correlation of words is usually accompanied by thematic coherence, although this need not be the case. Distributional correlation is a fact, while thematic (semantic) coherence is a hypothesis to be verified.

Topic modelling with the LDA methodology (Blei, Ng, Jordan: 2003), which is used in this study, involves two principal steps. In step one, the measure of word co-occurrence in the corpus texts is calculated. This is done using the WordRank algorithm (Ji, S., Yun, Yanardag, Matsushima, Vishwanathan: 2015), which is a derivative of the PageRank algorithm developed and used by Google to rank search results. This algorithm, after minor modifications, proved to be an excellent tool for detecting co-occurring words in texts. This step allows researchers to divide the vocabulary into groups of co-occurring units between which there is distributional correlation. The number of groups depends on the researcher and should be optimised when reviewing the results. Topics which are semantically too general mean that it is possible that there are more groups, while topics which are semantically incoherent indicate that too many groups have been set.

Step two of the modelling process involves arranging the results obtained in step one. For each word in the groups obtained, the probability of that word occurring in a corpus text is calculated. The value arrived at should be interpreted as the answer to the question: what is the chance that a particular word will be found in a text selected at random from a given corpus? The information obtained in this way is then used to arrange the results: from each group of words (chosen in step one, distributionally related) a representation is selected so that the sum of the occurrence probabilities of the words is 1. This means that at least one word from the group thus selected should occur in every text in the corpus. This step is intended to shorten the list and eliminate random or less relevant vocabulary – without it, the list would be very long and uninformative.

Steps one and two yield ready-made topics, which should be verified by the researcher/annotator, who can then assess the thematic coherence of the topics. At this stage, the researcher/annotator can decide to create a stop list, containing undesirable words that should be ignored during the research (typically, it is a list of asemantic words, i.e., conjunctions, pronouns, prepositions, particles, or a list of words whose high frequency is due to technicality of the texts or editorial elements: page numbers, names of website sections, abbreviations of source names, etc.). The conclusions made by the researcher/ annotator are also the basis for a possible decision to increase or decrease the number of topics.

After such an evaluation, the researcher should decide whether to analyse the texts again or accept the results. In the first case, the whole procedure should be carried out using new parameters (a stop list, the number of desired topics, etc.). If the results are accepted, the research should be repeated at least twice, and the results from all three iterations (series of experiments) should be averaged. This reduces the influence of the chance element on the final test results. This element is present in the second step. If in any group of words the sum of occurrence probabilities for all elements of the group is greater than 1 (and it usually is), some of the words are rejected at random from among the words with lower probability factor (more on the subject in: Blei, Ng, Jordan: 2003). This means that the exact content of the topics may vary slightly between the iterations – the differences are not fundamental but are noticeable.

The LDA methodology is not the only one that can be used to perform topic modelling. An example of an alternative solution is the Additive Regularization of Topic Models (ARTM) method. However, taking into account the number of studies on the two methods and their description in the literature; the number of practical applications of LDA and ARTM to date and the fact that the team from Wrocław University of Technology (whose members co-authored this study) has the greatest experience with this method, the LDA method was selected (see: Walkowiak, Gniewkowski: 2020). It is worth noting that an experiment using the ARTM method was carried out for the purposes of this paper for the sake of comparison. However, the topics obtained with that method turned out to be clearly less thematically coherent (compared with the ones obtained with LDA). Therefore, the idea of using that method was abandoned.

14.4   Data Analysis and Results

14.4.1   *Corpus Characteristics and Sample Selection*

The corpus subject to analysis consists of 995 samples, which were published on the Internet between February 29th 2020 and May 31st 2020. The samples are articles posted on six influential websites publishing news in Polish, including three main news websites: Onet, WP and Interia, and three major online platforms of news television channels: TVN24, PolsatNews, and TVPInfo.

All samples were obtained from http://monco.frazeo.pl/, which is a corpus search engine (Pęzik: 2020) that enables the perusing of texts that were sourced on an ongoing basis from Polish online media for research purposes. Texts can be accessed in various ways: by chronology, source, authors, etc. What proved of most importance for the purposes of this study was the possibility of selecting texts based on metadata: time of publication, source, and presence or absence of certain keywords set as criteria (presented below). MONCO and FrazeoPL (sister websites, using the same text database) are monitor corpora. This means that their resources are updated with new content every day. In the case of those corpora, the content is sourced from Polish news websites via RSS feeds.

The articles making up the corpus had to meet the criteria of time, source, and presence of keywords. A list of the keywords and combinations is presented below:

Kidawa + Błońska + kandydat
Kidawa + Błońska + kandydatka
Kidawa + Błońska + KO
Kidawa + Błońska + Koalicja Obywatelska
Kidawa + Błońska + PO
Kidawa + Błońska + Platforma Obywatelska
Kidawa + Błońska + wybory
Kidawa + Błońska + kampania
Kidawa + Błońska + wycofać
Kidawa + Błońska + rezygnować
Kidawa + Błońska + wycofywać
Kidawa + Błońska + zrezygnować

For example, 'Kidawa + Błońska + kandydat' means that the article had to contain the words: *Kidawa, Błońska* and *kandydat.*

Since the Polish language is very rich in inflections of nouns and proper names, texts may contain inflected forms of the words (*Kidawie-Błońskiej, kandydatce, kandydatką,* etc.). All grammatical forms were taken into account so that the inflected forms also met the condition set for the research.

The criteria referred to above were met by 995 samples, with the following representation of the various sources:

Number of documents	995
Breakdown:	
interia.pl	131
tvp.info	144
polstatnews.pl	40
wp.pl	197
tvn24.pl	288
onet.pl	195

In terms of the time criterion, most of the samples represent the period before Małgorzata Kidawa-Błońska decided to withdraw from the election (May 15th 2020). Distribution of the samples based on this date is as follows:

Time	Number of documents
before May 15th	912
on or after May 15th	74

The extracted samples were then manually reviewed for the quality of the linguistic material. None of the samples was rejected since they met all the necessary technical criteria. The samples were suitable for topical analysis (they were longer than three sentences and contained a coherent verbal message expressed in natural language – which was Polish). In terms of substance, the collection of texts was verified based on a manual analysis of the samples. 15% of the documents that met the criteria were reviewed. In the case of the samples from MONCO, the following were removed: any parts of code, inclusions from other texts, meta text, advertisements, and the technical framework of the websites from which the texts were originally sourced.

The results are presented in the form of word clouds. Each presents the words that make up a specific topic. Although the geometric arrangement of the words in the word clouds and their order are random, the size of the characters in each word does matter. Letter size reflects two (experimentally selected) variables: the probability of the word occurring in the corpus (subjective frequency) and the number of occurrences in the corpus (objective frequency). The size depends in 80% on the first variable, and only in 20% on the other.

Topics: From February 29th 2020 (Małgorzata Kidawa-Błońska's election as candidate for President of Poland at the national convention of PO) to May 15th 2021 (date of the candidate's withdrawal from the election)

FIGURE 14.1   Evolution of topic activity from February 29th 2020 (Małgorzata Kidawa-Błońska's election as candidate for President of Poland at the national convention of PO) to May 15th 2021 (date of the candidate's withdrawal from the election)

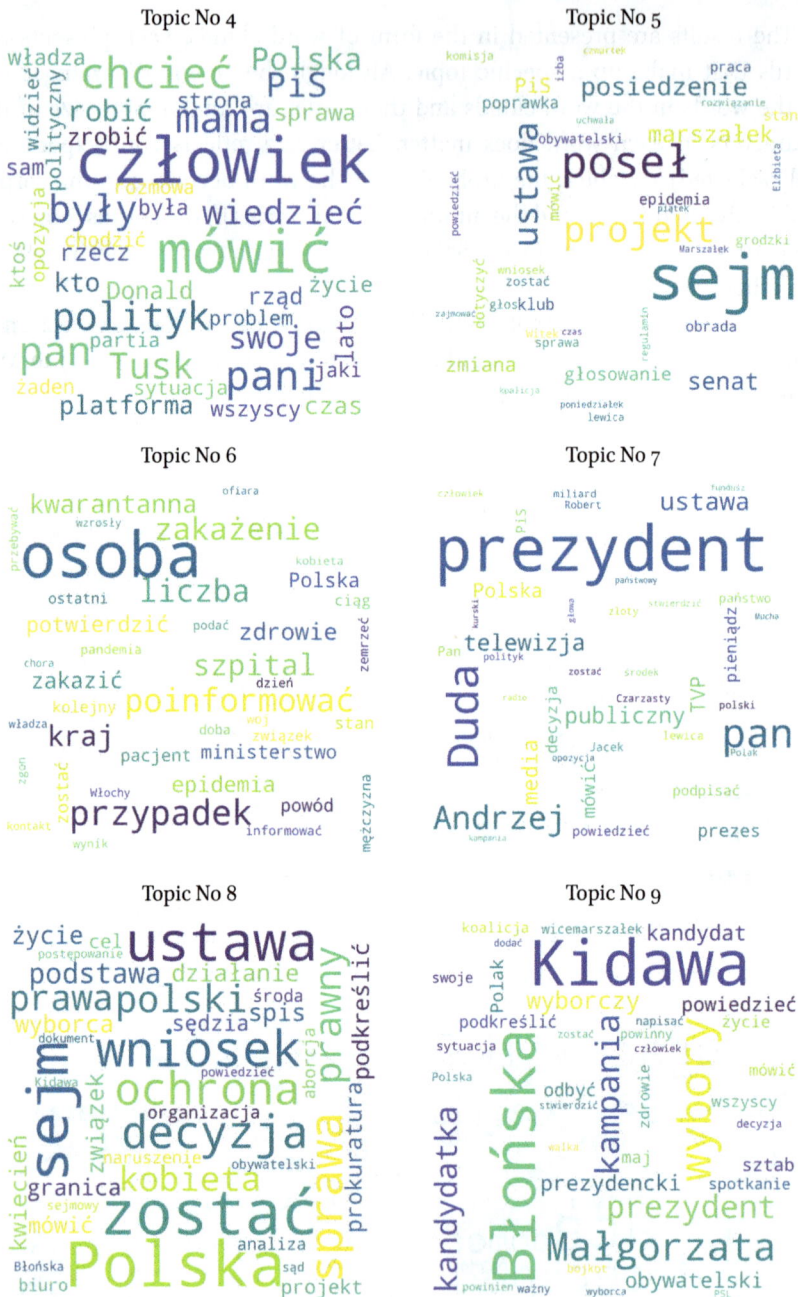

FIGURE 14.1 Evolution of topic activity from February 29th 2020 (*cont.*)

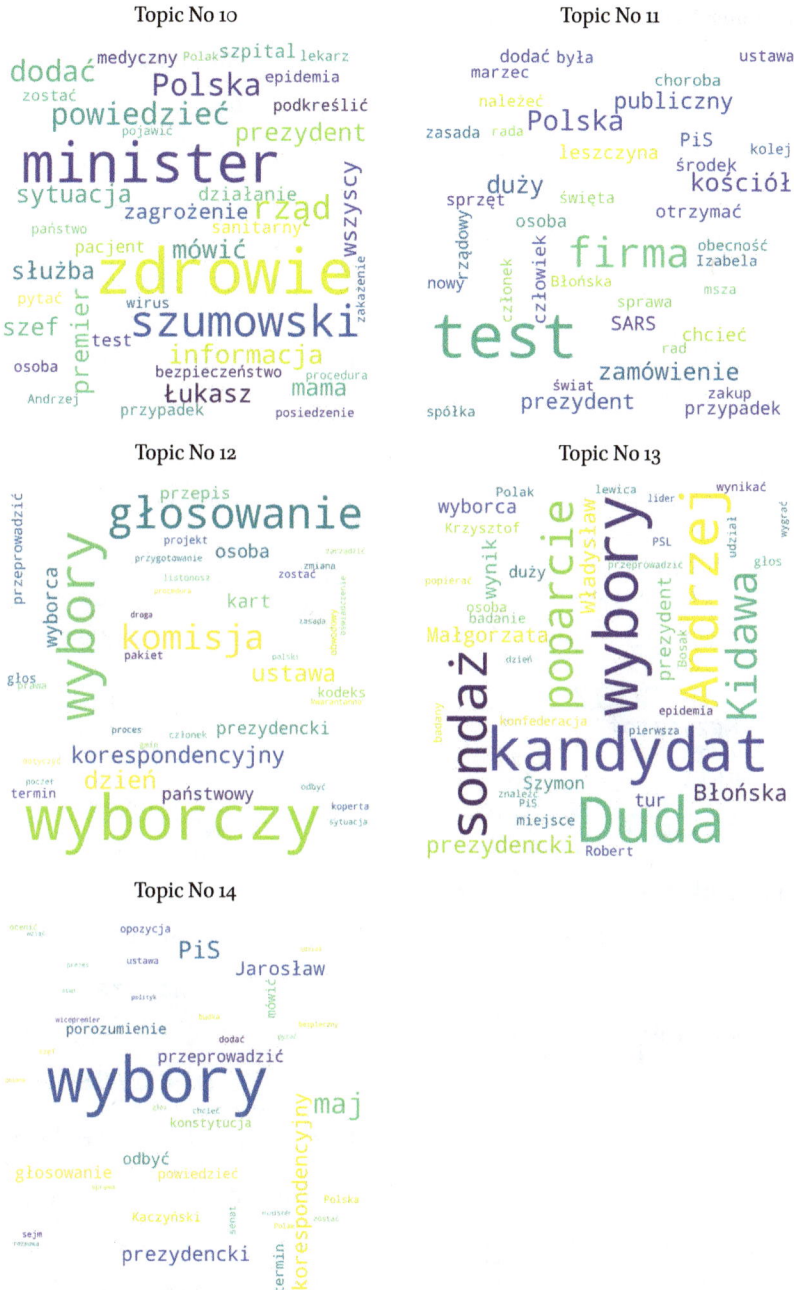

FIGURE 14.1   Evolution of topic activity from February 29th 2020 (*cont.*)

Topics from May 16th 2021 to May 31st 2021

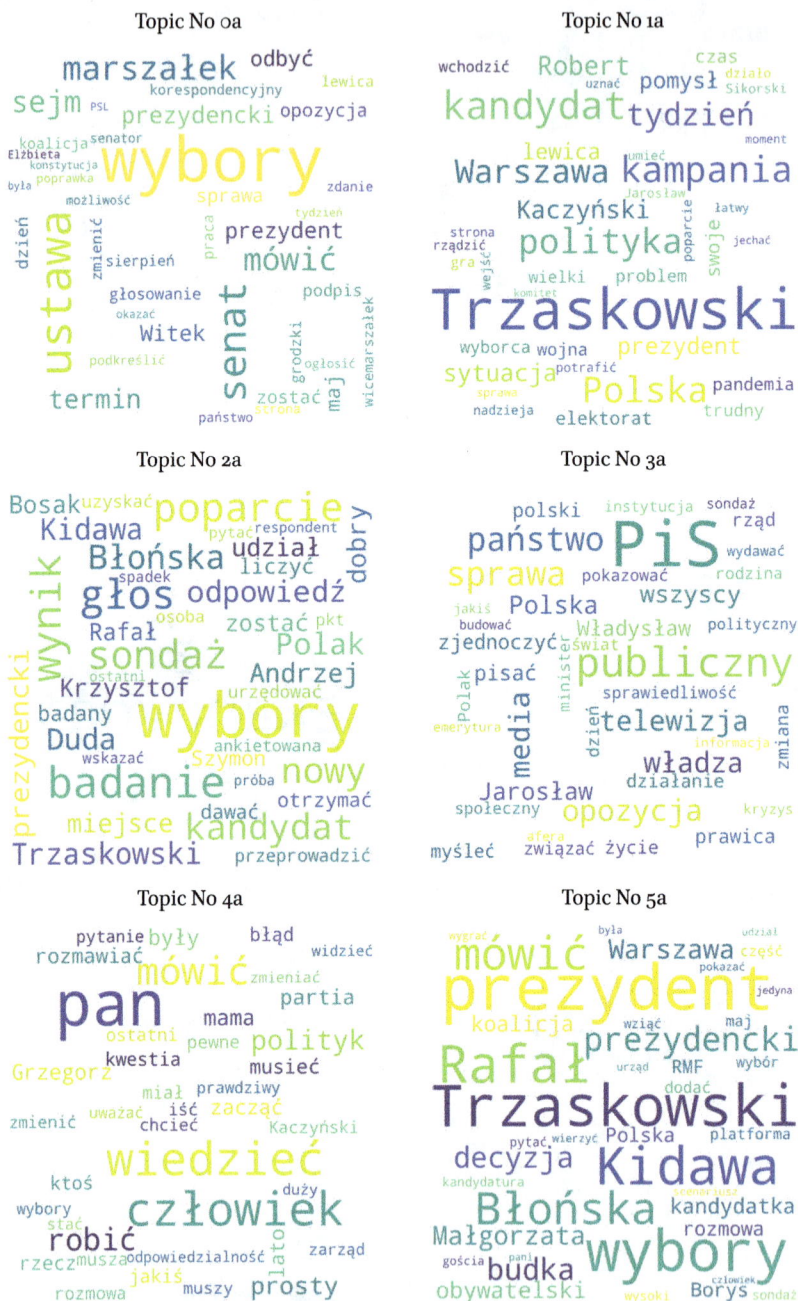

Topic No 0a

Topic No 1a

Topic No 2a

Topic No 3a

Topic No 4a

Topic No 5a

FIGURE 14.1   Evolution of topic activity from February 29th 2020 (*cont.*)

Topic No 6a

Topic No 7a

Topic No 8a

Topic No 9a

Topic No 10a

Topic No 11a

FIGURE 14.1   Evolution of topic activity from February 29th 2020 (*cont.*)

Topic No 12a

Topic No 13a

Topic No 14a

FIGURE 14.1   Evolution of topic activity from February 29th 2020 (*cont.*)

14.4.2   *Evolution of Topic Activity over Time*

The graphs showing changes in topic activity over time should be read as an illustration of the saturation of the material under analysis at a given time. For each topic the probability of its occurrence in a text file (sample) is calculated. The 'saturation' value is the sum of the probabilities of a given topic occurring in the samples. It is calculated as the sum of the probabilities of files from the period divided by the number of files in that period.

14.4.3   *Collocation of Words in the Corpus*

Three words (collocation centres) were selected to analyse the co-occurrence of lexical units: *wybory, kandydatka* and *Małgorzata Kidawa-Błońska*. The task was performed using simple language processing tools provided by the CLARIN-PL research infrastructure.

The research consisted of counting all words occurring next to the collocation centres within a sentence. This means that the software identified all

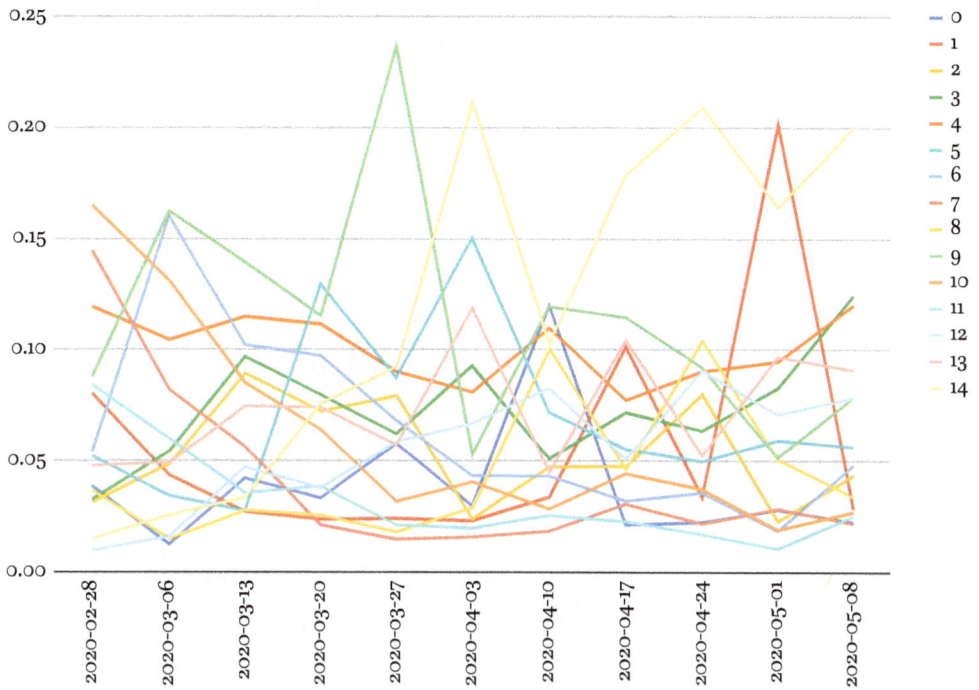

FIGURE 14.2   Evolution of topic activity from February 28th 2020 to May 8th 2020

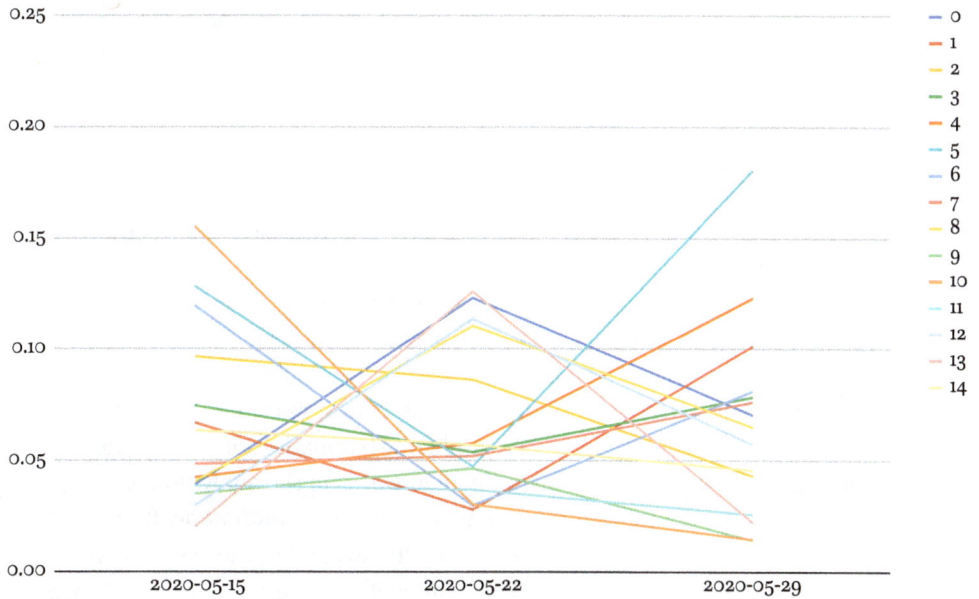

FIGURE 14.3   Evolution of topic activity from May 15th 2020 to May 29th 2020

FIGURE 14.4   Collocation centre: Małgorzata Kidawa Błońska

FIGURE 14.5   Collocation centre: kandydatka

textual occurrences of a particular collocation centre and then counted all words co-occurring with the selected word in the same sentence. After analysing all sentences containing a specific collocation centre, a frequency list was created to illustrate all occurrences of words found next to it.

At this point, it should be noted that Polish is a highly inflected language, which makes it difficult to conduct such statistical research. To address this issue and somewhat mitigate the problem, lemmatisation was performed before the process of identifying individual words in the analysed corpus was started. This means that all grammatical forms were automatically reduced to dictionary forms (infinitives for verbs and participles, the nominative singular for nouns and adjectives). For example, the sentence: *Ala ma kota* after

FIGURE 14.6   Collocation centre: wybory

lemmatisation is: *Ala mieć kot*. This is a standard solution adopted for research in the digital humanities and social sciences community.

14.5   Discussion and Conclusion

This study analysed 955 media reports posted on six influential Polish-language news websites in the period from February 29th 2020 to May 31st 2020. The main purpose of the study was to analyse discourse in the media space and attempt to identify the possible reasons behind the candidate's slump in opinion polls. To this end, the following research questions were posed:

1.   How did the media discourse about Małgorzata Kidawa-Błońska's candidature for the office of President of the Republic of Poland develop and change over time?
2.   How was the candidate's electoral programme presented in the media?

The research was divided into two time periods. The rationale for using the time periods as opposed to processing the entire corpus was twofold. Firstly, given the subject matter of this study, it was important to identify the topics present in the media reports during Małgorzata Kidawa-Błońska's campaign and to determine whether they contain the candidate's programme proposals. Secondly, the thematic content of the media reports following Małgorzata Kidawa-Błońska announcement of her decision to withdraw from the election was cognitively interesting. With an analysis of the entire corpus, extracting short-term topics triggered by specific decisions of the candidate or her proposals would be impracticable.

The application of the topic identification model based on the LDA method made it possible to obtain information (in both periods examined) on the thematic threads that prevailed in the media reports (of the analysed corpus) at a specified time during the election campaign.

For the period from February 29th 2020, when Małgorzata Kidawa-Błońska was elected candidate for President of Poland at the national convention of PO, to May 15th 2020, the date she announced the decision to withdraw from the presidential race, the study identified the principal and most common topics that should be considered with similar intensity throughout the entire period under analysis. This group includes, for example, *wybory* in the context of a state of emergency and a state of natural disaster (topic No. 3) and in the context of voting (topic No. 12), as well as in the context of candidate Andrzej Duda, incumbent President of Poland at that time (topic No. 13). The study also made it possible to extract topics related to specific events and the actions of candidate Małgorzata Kidawa-Błońska. An example is *Kidawa-Błońska* (topic No. 9) and its distribution over time. It is interesting that from the election convention on February 29th 2020, topic No. 9 was constantly present in the media (in the corpus under analysis) and the probability of its occurrence was high. It reached a peak on March 29th 2020, when the candidate published her *Open Letter on the Presidential Election on May 10th 2020'* (*List otwarty w sprawie wyborów prezydenckich 10 maja 2020*), in which she wrote:

> As a nation, as a community, we are facing a danger unprecedented in our recent history. The life and health of Poles are in danger.

She further appealed:

> That is why the election on May 10th 2020 must not take place. If those in power persist in this stubbornness, they must know that they bear full responsibility for the terrible effects on the lives and health of citizens. In this situation, I appeal to all voters not to participate in the elections on May 10th 2020. If nothing else, let the response to the irresponsibility of the authorities be a general boycott. (Raciborski:2020)

After this letter topic No. 9 largely faded away. The trend coincided with a deterioration of the candidate's poll ratings. As a result, with support of about 2 percent on May 15th 2020, Małgorzata Kidawa-Błońska stated that she takes responsibility for the party's falling ratings
and decided to withdraw from the election (Białczyk: May 15th 2020). Perhaps Małgorzata Kidawa-Błońska paid the price for a strategy based on a paradox: boycott the election, although I am not withdrawing my candidacy. The

rational argument that her withdrawal would also mean no longer running for president in the postponed elections, e.g., in the autumn, was not put across to the public, and Małgorzata Kidawa-Błońska remained a "non-candidate", even in "normal elections" (Pacewicz: May 3rd 2020).

Notably, in that period there was *de facto* no prominent topic that described or referred to the electoral programme of Małgorzata Kidawa-Błońska. This is all the more surprising, since – as indicated above – Małgorzata Kidawa-Błońska was a three-time press spokesperson. This warrants the assumption that with her experience she should have had an understanding of how the media works and should have known the strategies for "breaking through" with information to the media agenda.

In the period from May 16th 2020 to May 31st 2020, marking the end of the research timeframe, it was possible – as in the first period examined – to extract the principle and most common topics which should be considered with similar intensity throughout the period under analysis. These are – as in the case of the first period – the topics *wybory* (topics No. 0a, 2a, 8a). In the second period the prevailing topics were *Trzaskowski* in the context of candidate, (1a) (6a), in the context of president (5a), which seems only natural as it was Rafał Trzaskowski who became the new Civic Coalition's candidate for the office of President of Poland. It is worth noting, however, that (in the period under analysis) the new candidate was presented in the media in the context of the former candidate Małgorzata Kidawa Błońska.

Thanks to the research, both Małgorzata Kidawa-Błońska and (at the time of potential next elections) her campaign staff will be able to plan and conduct a more effective election campaign to present the candidate's programme more clearly in the media. In addition, the campaign staff of other candidates may use this study to minimise the risk of insufficient visibility of their candidate's programme in the media.

This study may be a starting point for further research on both media discourse and political discourse on the Polish political scene using the topic identification model based on the LDA method.

References

Białczyk, P., (May 15th 2020), *Małgorzata Kidawa-Błońska: nie będę brała udziału w tych wyborach* [*Małgorzata Kidawa-Błońska: I will not take part in this election*], https://wiadomosci.wp.pl/malgorzata-kidawa-blonska-nie-bede-brala-udzialu-w-tych-wyborach-6510698176702593a

Blei D. M.; Ng A. Y., Jordan M.I., (2003), *Latent Dirichlet Allocation*, Lafferty J., (ed.) Journal of Machine Learning Research, 3 (4–5): pp. 993–1022.

Ceron A., Curini L., Iacus. S.M., (2015), *Using sentiment analysis to monitor electoral campaigns: Method matters—evidence from the United States and Italy*. Social Science Computer Review 33, 1 (2015), 3–20.

Gautrais C., Cellier P., Quiniou R., Termier A., (2017), *Topic Signatures in Political Campaign Speeches*, Proceedings of the 2017 Conference on Empirical Methods in Natural Language Processing, pages 2342–2347 Copenhagen, Denmark, September 7th–11th, 2017.

Głosowanie nr 5 na 1. posiedzeniu Sejmu [*Vote No. 1 at the first sitting of the Sejm*]; https://sejm.gov.pl/Sejm9.nsf/agent.xsp?symbol=glosowania&NrKadencji=9&NrPosiedzenia=1&NrGlosowania=5

Graham S., Weingart S., Milligan I., (2012), *Getting started with topic modelling and MALLET*. The Editorial Board of the Programming Historian.

Greene D., Cross J.P., (2015), *Unveiling the Political Agenda of the European Parliament Plenary: A* http://www.discourses.org/OldArticles/What%20is%20Political%20Discourse%20Analysis.pdf

https://archiwum.premier.gov.pl/wydarzenia/aktualnosci/malgorzata-kidawa
-blonska-nowym-rzecznikiem-rzadu.html

https://archiwum.premier.gov.pl/wydarzenia/aktualnosci/nowy-rzecznik-rzadu
-malgorzata-kidawa-blonska.html

https://isap.sejm.gov.pl/isap.nsf/download.xsp/WMP20150001144/O/M20151144.pdf

https://onlinelibrary.wiley.com/doi/10.1111/j.1540-5907.2009.00427.x

https://platforma.org/aktualnosci/malgorzata-kidawa-blonska-kandydatka-w
-wyborach-prezydenckich-2020

https://polskatimes.pl/wybory-prezydenckie-2020-warszawa-konwencja-malgorzaty
-kidawyblonskiej-program-kidawyblonskiej/ar/c1-14824812

https://www.radiozet.pl/Co-gdzie-kiedy-jak/Malgorzata-Kidawa-Blonska-poglady
-PROGRAM-WYBORCZY-I-POLITYCZNY-wybory-2020-wiek-wzrost-kontakt

Jelodar H., Wang Y., Yuan C. *et al.* (2019), *Latent Dirichlet allocation (LDA) and topic modelling: models, applications, a survey. Multimed Tools Appl* 78, 15169–15211

Ji, S., Yun, H., Yanardag, P., Matsushima, S., Vishwanathan, S. V. N. (2015). WordRank: Learning word embeddings via robust ranking. arXiv preprint arXiv:1506.02761. https://arxiv.org/abs/1506.02761

Małgorzata Kidawa-Błońska kandydatem KO na premiera [*Małgorzata Kidawa-Błońska as Civic Coalition's candidate for Prime Minister*], (September 3rd 2019) http://300polityka.pl/live/2019/09/03/malgorzata-kidawa-blonska-kandydatem
-ko-na-premiera/3 września 2019

Małgorzata Kidawa-Błońska nowym rzecznikiem rządu [*Małgorzata Kidawa-Błońska appointed new government spokesperson*], (February 3rd 2015) www.premier.gov.pl

Małgorzata Kidawa-Błońska. Program wyborczy kandydatki Koalicji Obywatelskiej [*Małgorzata Kidawa-Błońska: electoral programme of the Civic Coalition's candidate*].,

(April 20th 2020), https://wiadomosci.onet.pl/kraj/malgorzata-kidawa-blonska
-program-wyborczy-i-informacje-wybory-2020/njqgxl7

Monitor Polski Dziennik Urzędowy Rzeczypospolitej Polskiej [Official Journal of the
Republic of Poland], Warsaw, July 7th 2015, item 578, https://isap.sejm.gov.pl/isap
.nsf/download.xsp/WMP20150000578/O/M20150578.pdf

*National Electoral Commission's website - Wybory do Sejmu i Senatu Rzeczpospolitej Pol-
skiej 2019 [Elections to the Sejm and Senate of the Republic of Poland 2019]*; https://
sejmsenat2019.pkw.gov.pl/sejmsenat2019/pl/wyniki/komitet/26075/sejm/okr/19

National Electoral Commission's website: https://parlament2015.pkw.gov.pl/349
_Wyniki_Sejm/3/0/20.html

National Electoral Commission's website; https://wybory2005.pkw.gov.pl/SJM/PL
/WYN/M/19.htm

National Electoral Commission's website; https://wybory2007.pkw.gov.pl/SJM/PL
/WYN/W5/19.htm

National Electoral Commission's website; https://wybory2011.pkw.gov.pl/wsw/pl/sjm
-19.html

*Nowy rzecznik rządu: Małgorzata Kidawa-Błońska [New government spokesperson:
Małgorzata Kidawa-Błońska]*, (January 7th 2014) www.premier.gov.pl

Oworuszko, J., (February 29th 2020), Wybory prezydenckie 2020. Warsaw: Konwencja
Małgorzaty Kidawy-Błońskiej. Program Kidawy-Błońskiej [Presidential election 2020.
Warsaw: Małgorzata Kidawa-Błońska's convention. Kidawa-Błońska's programme],

Pacewicz P., (May 3rd 2020), *Hołownia w II turze z Dudą. Katastrofa Kidawy-Błońskiej
i KO. Normalne wybory w sondażu OKO.press [Hołownia in the 2nd round with Duda.
Defeat of Kidawa-Błońska and Civic Coalition. Normal election in the OKO.press opinion poll]*, https://oko.press/w-normalnych-wyborach-duda-z-holownia-w-ii-turze/

Pęzik P., *Budowa i zastosowania korpusu monitorującego MoncoPL [Structure and application of the MoncoPL monitor corpus]*, (2020), Forum Lingwistyczne, No. 7 (7), 133–150.

Quinn K. M., Monroe B. L. , Colaresi M., Crespin M. H., Radev D. R., (2010), *How to
analyze political attention with minimal assumptions and costs.* American Journal of
Political Science, 54(1): 209–228.

Raciborski, J., (2020), *Bojkot majowych wyborów prezydenckich i jego uzasadnienia.
Komentarz [Boycott of the May presidential election and its justifications. Com-
mentary]*, Warsaw, Fundacja Batorego, https://www.batory.org.pl/wp-content
/uploads/2020/09/Bojkot-majowych-wyborow_Komentarz.pdf

Resolution of the Sejm of the Republic of Poland on the election of the Speaker of the
Sejm of June 25th 2015.

Resolution of the Sejm of the Republic of Poland on the election of the Deputy Speaker
of the Sejm of November 12th 2015, Monitor Polski Dziennik Urzędowy Rzeczypospolitej Polskiej [Official Journal of the Republic of Poland], Warsaw, November
26th 2015, item 1142.

Resolution of the Sejm of the Republic of Poland on the election of the Deputy Speaker of the Sejm of November 12th 2019, Monitor Polski Dziennik Urzędowy Rzeczypospolitej Polskiej [Official Journal of the Republic of Poland], Warsaw, November 20th 2019, item 1114 https://isap.sejm.gov.pl/isap.nsf/download.xsp/WMP20190001114/O /M20191114.pdf

Savoy J., (2010), *Lexical analysis of us political speeches*, Journal of Quantitative Linguistics 17(2):123–141.

Survey report No. 23/2020, February 2020, https://cbos.pl/SPISKOM.POL/2020/K_023 _20.PDF

Survey report No. 26/2020, February 2020, https://www.cbos.pl/SPISKOM.POL/2020/K _026_20.PDF

Survey report No. 35/2020, March 2020, https://www.cbos.pl/SPISKOM.POL/2020/K _035_20.PDF

Survey report No. 54/2020, April 2020, https://www.cbos.pl/SPISKOM.POL/2020/K _054_20.PDF

Topical Analysis, https://arxiv.org/pdf/1505.07302.pdf

Van Dijk T., (1998), *What is Political Discourse Analysis?*, Belgian Journal of Linguistics 11:11–52.

Walkowiak T., Gniewkowski M., (2020) *Distance Measures for Clustering of Documents in a Topic Space.* In: Zamojski W., Mazurkiewicz J., Sugier J., Walkowiak T., Kacprzyk J. (eds.) *Engineering in Dependability of Computer Systems and Networks*, DepCoS-RELCOMEX 2019. Advances in Intelligent Systems and Computing, vol 987. Springer, Cham.

Żurek, P., (May 7th 2020), *Małgorzata Kidawa-Błońska: PROGRAM WYBORCZY I POLITYCZNY [POGLĄDY, WYBORY 2020] [Małgorzata Kidawa-Błońska: ELECTORAL AND POLITICAL PROGRAMME [OPINIONS, ELECTION 2020]*

CHAPTER 15

Gender Stereotypes in Polish Presidential Campaigns Based on the Case of Małgorzata Kidawa-Błońska

Monika Wawer

15.1 Introduction

In the last few years, we have noticed many facts that indicate a more extensive participation of women in political life:

- two women have taken the post of prime minister in Poland,
- the representation of women in the parliament has increased (in the Sejm of the 9th term, 132 seats in 29% of seats, in the Senate 24%),
- we have observed significant political activity of women during mass protests in the years 2016 and 2020.

It is also worth noting many female politicians do not see themselves as discriminated against and excluded. Former Polish Prime Minister Ewa Kopacz stated in her speech at the 6th Congress of Women that women's success in political activity depends on their competence, knowledge, and determination. She questioned the limitations of the so-called "glass ceiling," indicating that it is due to the feminine mentality. These words sound as if women are themselves guilty of being excluded from political life. (Krzyżanowska, p.64) Therefore, can we say that the stereotypes about women's Polish political role are gradually ceasing to exist?

Most researchers do not share the optimism resulting from a broader representation of women in power structures. On the contrary, they still indicate strong stereotypes and patterns of thinking present in the discourse on women's activity in politics. (Piontek, 2017) We are still dealing with stereotypes relating to women's features, the expected attitudes, skills, and competencies limiting their activity to specific ministries: health and social policy (Post, 2019).

Therefore, it should be emphasized that the stereotyping of women is one of the determinants that has a significant impact on the discrimination against women in public life.

The Convention on the Elimination of All Forms of Discrimination Against Women emphasizes that taking only legal steps is not enough to combat gender inequality successfully. The social perceptions and stereotypes underlying discriminatory practices should change. (Frańczak, 2016) This article aims to investigate the presence of stereotypes in the media discourse accompanying the presidential campaign of Małgorzata Kidawa-Błońska, one of the opposition's key politicians. The mere disclosure of a set of stereotypes and simplifications that appeared in the media reporting the activity of the presidential candidate will make it possible to notice the ideological structure contained in the media discourse.

At the heart of the analysis is the assumption that the media, using simplification, create a world order consistent with the image of what the recipients (Allan 2010) want. Media discourse serves the dominant social interests "through the production of truth" (Foucault, 1980, p. 93). Of course, this truth is an ideological construct contained in the discourse to uphold and legitimize common sense.

Therefore, determining whether and what gender stereotypes about Kidawa-Błońska appeared in the media discourse will allow the discovery and disclosure of its preferred ideological assumptions. And as a consequence, the exposure of the network of power and hegemony still determines the media discourse about women leaders in Polish politics.

Since 2001, Kidawa-Błońska has associated with Platforma Obywatelska, the main party opposing the present government. Currently, she is the Deputy Marshal of the Sejm, Lower Chamber of the Polish Parliament. She was previously the Marshal of the Sejm and served in many ministerial functions, such as Secretary of State and Press Spokeswoman in cabinets of both Donald Tusk and Ewa Kopacz.

It should therefore be stressed that Kidawa-Błońska has expert knowledge and broad political experience. In December 2019, right after the start of the presidential campaign, the election polls gave her the second place, after the incumbent president, and also a significant advantage over other rivals. However, her position in the polls dropped after she decided to withdraw from running in the elections. Her decision to suspend the campaign was a response to the ruling party's presidential election date during the spreading pandemic. Kidawa, together with her group's leaders, decided to boycott the elections because of threat it posed to citizens' health.

Kidawa-Błońska is, therefore, an example of a female candidate who built her position for a long time, was recognizable to voters, and had extensive political experience. Nevertheless, in the media discourse accompanying her election campaign, we can find an entire repertoire of stereotypes about women in politics.

15.2   Theoretical Framework

The broadest theoretical perspective for the considerations contained in this article is provided by social constructivism (Berger, Luckmann, 1967), understood as a tendency to perceive reality as being created, reproduced, reproduced and susceptible to change. Therefore, the image of reality that the media shows selectively reproduced particular meanings. The framework of this reproduction is determined by the patterns of building journalistic materials, e.g. rules and codes that constitute the value of a journalistic topic. One is predictability, stereotyping, continuity and consistency. (Galtung, Ruge, 1965, Allan, 2010).

The presented reality is thus consistent with the authors 'ideas and with the authors' ideas about potential recipients; it should confirm their understanding of the world and fall within the scope of their interpretive repertoires. At the same time, the article follows the model of mass communication based on the encoding and decoding of media discourse. The essence of this orientation is the assumption that the recipient constructs the meaning of the media message, although the sender equips this message with the so-called preferred reading. This reading is always ideologically coded and legitimizes the world order approved by the dominant and powerful social groups. (Hall, 1974, 1980) The media provide linguistic patterns and facilitate articulating specific points of view. In turn, the articulation theory is related to the post-structuralist discourse theory (Laclau & Mouffe, 1985) and cultural studies (Hall, 1986) and points to the productive forces of discourse. According to Hall, articulation has two meanings: pronouncing and accentuating certain expressions as is' the form of the connection that can make a unity of two different elements, under certain conditions (Hall, 1986, p. 53).

Thus, articulation theory is a way to understand, on the one hand, "how ideological elements come, under certain conditions, to cohere together within a discourse", on the other hand, "how they do or do not become articulated, at specific conjunctures, to certain political subjects. (Hall, 1996, p. 153)

Ideology is therefore ubiquitous in media texts. We can reveal it in the language itself and the discursive strategies used. It is worth recalling several research traditions that have gone down in history by analyzing how the language of the media constructs meaning. Both Glasgow University Media Group and the Birmingham Center for Contemporary Cultural Studies have produced significant interpretations of "media's representations" of social problems since the late 1970s. In semiotics, Hartley, Hodge and Kress analyzed various types of media messages. Van Dijk and Fairclough have proposed a systematic analysis of the journalistic text. From the CDA Critical Discourse Analysis perspective, researchers created a program that explores the role of discourse in the production and transformation of social representations of reality and social relationships. The CDA has set itself to look beyond the media text and find the institutional and socio-structural context.

15.3   Methodology

We used the presidential campaign of Małgorzata Kidawa-Błońska as a case study to notice gender stereotypes distribution in media discourse. We have used Discourse Analysis as a conceptual framework and MAXQDA as an analytical framework.

We understand discourse as a coherent system of perceiving and conceptualizing the world. The cultural definition of the discourse allows revealing the interpretative framework present in the text.

According to the researchers gathered around the KAD, each aspect of social life is discursive, involved in power relations, organized according to ideology. The reality shown by the media is a cognitive construct, an interpretative proposal addressed to the recipient, which strongly influences his understanding of the world. Gatekeepers (media owners, producers, publishers, journalists) are responsible for selecting information and construct it.

The understanding of discourse is usually presented in three dimensions, focused on:
– text or speech structures
– communication and its cognitive determinants
– cultural and social dependencies. (Dijk, 2001, p. 34)
In this article, we will use the third understanding of discourse, which determines how the world is perceived and conceptualized at a given time and place. Such understanding of discourse presupposes a search for the interpretative framework of the world existing in the language, emphasizes the social and cultural context.

Therefore, discourse analysis goes beyond linguistic structure, interpreting what is happening around and through a given statement.

Many researchers have made gender stereotypes in the field of politics the subject of their research. For this reason, in the literature review, we can easily find typical areas of stereotyping of politically active women.

Therefore, we will start with the question of what stereotypes researchers primarily perceived in the media discourse devoted to the participation of women in political life.

Then we are relating these patterns to the research material included 505 press releases, articles, and audiovisual materials published between December

14, 2019, and June 28, 2020 - between the start of the Kidawa-Błońska election campaign and the first presidential election round. It is essential to mention that Kidawa-Błońska indeed withdrew from participating in the elections on May 15, 2020; however, the media kept commenting on her candidacy.

We collected these materials using web browsers, archives of individual media titles. The materials obtained in this way were encoded in the MAXQDA application, which allowed for further analysis.

15.4   Repertoire of Stereotypes about Women in Politics

In this part of the article, we would like to identify and describe these crucial stereotypes based on the literature review. Researchers unanimously mention four areas of stereotyping:
- Traits attributed to women
- Competences attributed to female politicians
- Diminished role of female politicians (puppets in men hands)
- Effects of showing counter-stereotypical traits by female politicians. (Cassese,Holman 2018; Krupnikov, Bauer 2014)

Women are still stereotypically perceived as the embodiment of warmth, as emotional, capable of sacrifice, and striving to alleviate conflicts (Gawor, Mandal, 2007, p. 80). Men are ascribed versatility, erudition, and intelligence (Buć, 2009, p. 61). Men are considered competent, rational, non-pressured, easy to make decisions, endowed with self-confidence. The profession of a politician requires more characteristics stereotypically ascribed to men. Both stereotypes are resistant to change. Researchers underlay - these studies conducted among female and male students, incl. Political directions, i.e., a more aware group in this respect (Pająk-Patkowska, 2016).

Hence, probably, the belief that women are not suitable for politics (Kotlarska–Michalska, 2011, p. 30).

Politicians themselves admit that men and women make politics differently. They pointed qualities and behaviors typical for good employees in everyday life. (Post, 2019) They are related to the so-called ethics of caring, which refers to "caring and kindness" (Szymala 2017, Post 2019).

Politicians are often supposed to warm up the image of the party. They are considered "busy bees" performing necessary but not spectacular tasks (Niewiadomska-Cudak, 2012, p. 53).

Often behind their nominations, there is an immediate party interest in attracting an electorate who is not interested in the "male" confrontational version of politics (Piontek 2015). We noticed this mechanism in the example of two prime ministers: Ewa Kopacz and Beata Szydło. Both candidatures proposed in a particular political situation reminiscent of a political crisis. The candidates' job was to show a different style of politics, a different "face" of a given party (Piontek 2017).

Both Ewa Kopacz and Beata Szydło criticized for their lack of independence and submission to solid leaders. (Musiał, 2017) Ewa Kopacz presented as absolutely loyal to Donald Tusk. In 63% of respondents, Beata Szydło was not independent in making decisions and let herself managed too much.

Let's analyze now what happens when female politics go against these stereotypes. According to Kotlarska-Michalska women tend to justify their oppositional behavior. It usually happens because they are afraid of losing their attractiveness or they don't want to suffer social rejection. (Kotlarska–Michalska, 2011).

Recent research analyses the effect of counter-stereotypic gender strategies on candidate evaluations (Bauer 2017, Krupnikov&Bauer, 2014). Authors indicate that voters do not automatically attribute female characteristics to female candidates (Bauer 2015a, Brooks 2013, Dolan 2014). However, they do not see in them the masculine qualities that are often associated with leadership. Therefore female candidates are often assigned to a category called "neither a leader nor a lady" (Brooks, 2013). What happens when female candidates overcome this frame and show masculine characteristics typical for leaders?

Research shows female politicians may experience a backlash effect for breaking with gender stereotypes. Voters could evaluate them as firm and competent and as cold and distant (Rudman & Glick, 1999). These double standards where especially visible during the presidential campaign of Hillary Clinton.

On the one hand, Donald Trump accused her of not being strong enough to be president:

> Hillary is a person who does not have the strength or the stamina, in my opinion, to be president... (ABC News, 2015)

On the other hand, she was criticized for being over-prepared for presidential debates, for her ambition and determination, for changing the way of speaking from "feminine" to "masculine", and even for wearing trousers all the time.

However, female politicians should choose counter-stereotypic gender strategies in order to achieve success. The backlash effect does not occur in two circumstances. Counter-stereotypic traits will shift the categorization of female candidates as leaders: "Voters will interpret masculine qualities as positive leadership qualities rather than undesirable qualities in women." (Biernat & Manis, 1994).

Voters will not evaluate female candidates based on how warm or likable they are as women but how warm or likable they are as leaders (Bauer, 2017).

Second, voters' response to the counter-stereotypic gender strategies of the candidate depends mainly on whether they are among the supporters or opponents of her party.

Voters will often accept counter- stereotypic female candidates that belong to their political party but will be more critical of such politicians from the opposition party. although they will see them more in terms of leaders, they will punish them for breaking the stereotype. (Bauer 2017) On the one hand, these findings mean their gender does not constrain that female candidate in all circumstances. However, Bauer finds that female candidates gain little from emphasizing stereotypical feminine strengths. It means that:

> female candidates still have to manage their gender to downplay feminine stereotypes and play up masculine stereotypes. (Bauer, 2017)

Cassese and Homan also analyze counter-stereotypic gender strategies in connection with party affiliation. Researchers use the expectancy-violation theory (EVT) in their approach and say that "candidates may be evaluated more harshly when attacks suggest the candidates have violated stereotypic assumptions about their group." (Cassese, Holman) Thus, attacks on a candidate's "home turf," or those traits or issues traditionally associated with their party or gender, may be more effective in reducing support for the attacked candidate (Cassese, Holman).

So Democratic voters have different expectations than Republican voters. Research shows that Americans consider Democrats competent on feminine policy issues and Republicans on masculine policy issues. (Petrocik, 1996; Wouter, 2004; Sapiro, 1981). Consequently, voters associate Republicans with masculine Traits and Democrats with feminine traits (Winter, 2010; Hayes, 2005). (...) voters often stereotype Republican men as especially strong leaders given redundant expectations regarding their sex and party, while stereotypes of Democratic men and Republican women are more muddied, given divergent expectations associated with their sex and party (Holman et al., 2015).

The research described above allows us to look at the problem of stereotyping a bit wider, emphasizing the expectations of voters of the party to which the candidate belongs.

15.5 The Presence of Stereotypes in the Media Discourse Accompanying the Presidential Campaign of Małgorzata Kidawa-Błońska

In this chapter, we will try to identify the stereotypes surrounding the presidential campaign of Małgorzata Kidawa-Błońska.

While analyzing the media discourse accompanying Małgorzata Kidawa-Błońska's campaign, we focused on those cognitive frames that filter women's perception in political life. Based on the literature on the subject discussed above, we have distinguished four primary areas of stereotyping of female politicians:
– Traits attributed to women
– Competences attributed to female politicians
– Diminished women role in politics (puppets in men hands)
– Showing counter-stereotypical traits

We are using these categories to identify recurring stereotypes in media discourse about the Małgorzata Kidawa-Błońska campaign. We noticed 230 media extracts (out of 505 all collected documents) to assign them to distinguished categories.

15.6 Traits Attributed to Women

Party leaders have consistently pointed out that the candidate is caring and responsible. In this way, they presented her at the election convention:

> everyone who knows Małgorzata Kidawa-Błońska knows that she is responsible and caring; this is what Poles need today

Both party colleagues, journalists, and Internet users emphasized these features of the candidate. This image of her dominated in the media favorable to her.

She is a holy woman, patient, but very systematic and very hardworking (this is what former Prime Minister Ewa Kopacz said about the candidate).

TABLE 15.1   M. Kidawa-Błońska's Campaign Stereotypes based on Maxqda Code System

Code system	Excerpts 230
Traits atributed to women	69
Caring, Empathetic, Responsible	25
„Matka Polka", Lady	12
„Aunt Małgosia"	32
Competences atributed to female politicians	41
The diminished role of women in politics (puppets in men hands)	78
Showing counter-stereotypical traits	42

She is a warm, cordial, and kind person who, when she becomes president, will have every reason to be the president of all Poles.

The smiling Deputy Marshal of the Sejm arouses sympathy, has respectable ancestors, and does not give the impression that she wants to do something wrong to the voters.

Media emphasized her ability to mitigate conflicts and elegantly fight disputes.

For supporters, it is a textbook example of a political culture that does not happen very often. She talks so as not to offend hers opponent. The less sympathetic say that nothing comes from her round and elegant sentences, because of that so you lose interest; everything seems empty. PO[1] politician: - There are no fireworks at her place. However, she is a decent, nice lady who does not look for strife, sails calmly on the wave.

In interviews, she likes to mention the story of her great-grandmother's plate, which she broke in anger. Only once in a lifetime, because there is no aggression at all. Her husband describes that during the debates even the biggest cockerels will melt in front of her. They suddenly pay attention to see if they are holding their hands well and if they have a tight tie. - However, this is an achievement because she can somehow indicate with the mere glance that someone has the wrong shirt on for today.

Many media texts were devoted to the Kidawa-Błońska family, particularly her ancestors - strong women, heroic figures who could withstand all hardships and burdens. They lived in a spirit of dedication to their homeland and family. References to the symbol of the "Matka Polka" (Polish Mother) were apparent in this narrative (Titkow 2007). The candidate spoke about these female characters in the tone of a family legend as role models:

> Once, my dad got a very lucrative job offer, and those were times when we lived modestly: dad - a scientist at the Polytechnic, mom ran the house. It was tough, and then this excellent offer came. Then, it was my mother who said, "No. After all, science is important to you. We can do it without the money."
>
> In turn, Grandma was a painter, and when my grandfather was forbidden to publish books during the Stalinist period, she supported the family by painting. It was she who instilled in me the belief that you have to be independent.
>
> Moreover, I still remember that there had to be absolute silence when I was a child at certain times in the house because Grandpa Władek

---

1 PO – abbreviation of the name Platforma Obywatelska, the largest opposition party and M. Kidawa-Błońska party.

wrote. There were three of us then: me, my brother and our cousin. We knew that during these hours, you do not scream, sing, or stomp. When Grandma Zosia was working, there was no silence. She was also an artist. However, it was natural that while Grandma was painting, the children could drop by the studio. As if her job was less important. Such a fate of women?

After Małgorzata Kidawa-Błońska resigned from participating in the elections, her counter-candidate, Szymon Hołownia, welcomed her successor, criticizing her election campaign and calling her "Aunt Małgosia."

The campaign will be more polarized and sharper. Now we had uncle Andrzej and aunt Małgosia. Here comes a player who starts fighting hard in PiS[2], Kidawa-Błońska replied to Hołownia on Twitter:

Aunt is a great institution. Unfortunately, not for everyone. There is responsibility in my family, respect for the Constitution and the law.

Hołownia's statement sparked hundreds of comments, in which voices of indignation and surprise prevailed.

In the call about "Ciocia Małgosia" 'you can see a patronizing pattern - putting a woman in a good role is a good example of the low feminist sensitivity of Mr. Hołownia.

Szymon Hołownio, intellectual, media man, writer, journalist, social activist, and all in all, a nice (though not from my fairy tale) guy! Can you explain to us what is so difficult to assimilate information that texts like: "Ciocia Małgosia" (about Małgorzata Kidawa-Błońska) or "politics are not a female gymnasium" belittle, depress, and offend the female half of the society?

Finally, Hołownia apologized and explained that his words referred to the candidate's image created during the election campaign rather than to herself, whom he likes and respects. It is worth noting, however, that hundreds of Internet users widely commented on his statement. It is difficult to say whether it strengthened or weakened a woman's stereotype in politics as being gentle, caring, and kind-hearted.

---

2   PIS – abbreviation of the name of Prawo i Sprawiedliwość, the ruling party.

15.7   Competences Attributed to Female Politicians

There was a straightforward narrative in media content that undermined the candidate's ability to act as president based on her gender.

According to Poles, even the simplest studies on what the ideal president should be like indicated that he should rather be a middle-aged man with a wife and children. It not to mention the more detailed characteristics of the head of state, i.e. seriousness, experience, knowledge, and, above all, the presidency.

Let us start with the fact that, contrary to politically correct declarations, assurances, and denials - gender does matter. As soon as Kidawa-Błońska's candidacy appeared on the table, passionate discussions started in the journalistic and political backstage. I was surprised at how many men I know, including journalists and politicians, claimed it would be difficult for her to win with Duda because she is a woman.

After her decision to suspend the campaign media intensified undermining her competencies.

An old saying says that you cannot be a little pregnant, and Małgorzata Kidawa-Błońska tries very hard to maintain her candidacy, and simultaneously she is contesting the election. (...) Małgorzata Kidawa-Błońska's communication is internally contradictory, and the candidate herself cannot convey a clear message on this matter. It looks as if she does not know what to do in this situation.

Almost every male politician in her position would end up rearing, seeing – for example in the polls flying head and neck - the effects of a nonsensical manner of conducting campaigns, the end of which could only be a ridiculous scale of failure or the withdrawal of the candidacy under any pretext.

The candidate herself also indicated that her competencies are assessed more severely because she is a woman:

> No other candidate has all the statements so traced. People on Twitter make sure I know what wrong I did. It is not about content errors - because I understand it - but about laughing at the usual slip-ups, which also happen to others. At first, I was concerned about it, but when I thought about how many years I had been in politics and how many times. I was wrong, I can sleep well. It seems that many of these remarks would not have been made if I were a man. I am not saying that I am treated in a completely different way, but for other candidates, and these are the men themselves, certain things pass unnoticed.

On another occasion, Kidawa described these competencies, which she considers typically feminine, giving women an advantage over men, such as performing several activities at the same time and hardworking.

We are better than men because our brain allows us to do many things at once - she said. - We are entrusted with giving birth to children and raising them. We take care of the children, write a research paper and cook for our husbands at the same time.

She also quoted a maxim adequate to the topic of the forum: "If you want something to be loud - tell the man. If you want something done - tell the woman.

Thus, Kidawa-Błońska, in her statement, reinforced the stereotype of "female" competencies in politics mention above.

15.8   The Diminished Role of Women in Politics (Puppets in Men Hands)

In the media favorable to the candidate's political camp, one can read that her husband encouraged her to take up politics, and supported her at the beginning of her career.

In the world of politics, Kidawa-Błoński was the first - who, among other things, he made commercials for the Liberal Democratic Congress. - He involved his wife, who got the task: to organize a party circle in his hometown of Ursus.

Our interlocutors say that she coped brilliantly. Despite this, there is an opinion in the Civic Platform in Warsaw that she entered politics thanks to her husband's protection.

Many statements indicate that the party leaders treated Kidawa-Błońska's candidacy instrumentally and objectively.

However, the truth is that Grzegorz Schetyna exposed the politician to the so-called glass cliff. In the face of a probable defeat, it is a phenomenon when men finally decide to hand over the reins to women - a possible loss will credit their account.

There are repeated opinions that the candidate was dependent, dominated by party leaders.

However, the killer nonsense about the boycott of the elections in which she continued to participate was not invented by herself but by the PO's leadership, to which she obeyed. One could say she was right - she was naive about it. It is true. When, at the gate of the Sejm column hall, Budka whispered to her: "now say this and that" - she followed the instructions uncritically. However, having never been a subjective politician, what else could she do other than obey the party line?

The comments emphasized that she did not receive genuine support from her party but was an unknowing subject of leaders' games.

Her spectacular career ends not due to losing elections or some sudden embarrassment but due to her party's intrigues - Platforma Obywatelska. More precisely, the recognition by the current party authorities that putting Kidawa in the fight for these offices was, in fact, one of the "mistakes and distortions" committed by the previous leadership. This truth has been wrapped up in the bush of due courtesy in the apparent party interest. However, after all, no one who observes politics more closely could overlook the cynical tossing of Kidawa's political fatherhood to one another, like some hot potato, by the current head of the PO and his predecessor.

Another woman is treated as an object in politics. Women in Poland constitute over 50 percent of society. Men still treat us like a whim, as a statistic, like pretending that they need us with their opinion. When we have our opinion, we have to set it aside.

Of course, I am admiring and appreciating such an incredible, typically feminine gesture to step off the stage after you have cleared the ground with dedication for a serious leader.

This theme of stereotyping appeared most often in the media discourse. The image of a woman who cannot independently and consciously manages her career is present both in the media favorable to and opposed to the candidate's political line. According to this vision, behind every woman politician, there is a man, a director, and her career creator.

15.9 Showing Counter-Stereotypical Traits

Media statements show that the candidate has been repeatedly encouraged to behave inconsistently with the gender stereotype.

The research shows that they want her to be more resolute, more frequent, and more severe in attacking Duda and Kaczyński. However, she does not stick to marketers. She will be herself; she will never be aggressive. At most, she will put a pin in elegantly - convinces the staff member.

Kidawa-Błońska herself said even her friends put her in a drawer with the words "Too gentle." She kept hearing that she should be different because she would not achieve anything. She then kept telling them: "You will see again."

The media noted one behavior of the candidate in particular, which can be described as confrontational and inconsistent with the image of a warm, smiling politician, mitigating disputes. After the demonstrators in Puck attacked the incumbent President with invectives, the candidate approached them, talked, and smiled. Politicians and journalists representing the government side condemned her behavior with anger.

Mrs. Małgorzata Kidawa-Błońska, lady, (a model of elegance and style?), Great-granddaughter of the President of the Republic of Poland Stanisław Wojciechowski and Prime Minister Władysław Grabski, beaming with happiness after her supporters interrupted the speech of the President of the Republic of Poland.

Despite numerous appeals, the candidate did not apologize for her behavior, arguing:

> People have the right to express their emotions, and we politicians should respect both those who support us and those who do not accept us.

On the example of this counter-stereotypical behavior of the candidate, we could observe the mechanism described by Bauer. The candidate's supporters supported her, seeing in this ability to confront her leader's attitude, and the opponents attacked, punishing her, among others, for breaking the stereotype (Bauer, 2017).

15.10   Conclusions

In the media discourse accompanying Małgorzata Kidawa-Błońska's presidential election campaign, one can see many examples of stereotypes regarding women's role in politics. Most often, politicians, journalists, Internet users used two interpretive frameworks: The Diminished Role of Women in Politics (Puppets in Men Hands) and Traits Attributed to Women.

Media comments about the candidate's lack of competence were often empty allegations, not supported by any arguments. Their meaning was limited to the simple statement:

> she has no competence to be president because she is a woman.

In the media discourse, we also noted the breaking of the stereotype regarding the warm, disputes-alleviating profile of women in politics. In this case, we observed a clear polarization in media reports, accepting the candidate's behavior by clear opposition titles and criticism by the ruling party's supporters.

We should highlight two regularities in analyzed excerpts that deserve particular emphasis.

First, the candidate herself actively reinforced gender stereotypes. In addition to the quoted statement about the specificity of the female brain that allows women to perform many activities at the same time, there are many other situations in which gender is the proper determinant, e.g., to the author of a critical statement about Ewa Kopacz: "So you accuse her, really, for a man for a journalist, you have crossed the line. "Does this mean that a woman in the same situation would not overstep the boundaries? If not, why not?

Also, referring to the symbol of the "Polish Mother" she could strengthen the stereotypical image of a woman who sacrifices herself, working in the background, in the shadow of a man.

Second, it is worth emphasizing that the female candidates' narrative about their gender should be consistent with the party strategy and the electorate's preferences. The studies confirm this by Cassese and Holman, who analyzed recipients' behavior towards both sexes' candidates, breaking stereotypes. The authors emphasized that the most severely assessed were counter- stereotypical female politicians representing the Democrats. It was due to that Democrats are considered to be stereotypically associated with the female gender. Thus, breaking the gender stereotype by female politicians was also perceived as breaking the party stereotype.

Does this mean that Kidawa-Błońska, reinforcing certain stereotypes about women in politics, was in line with the party's strategy?

Her successor in the presidential campaign, Rafał Trzaskowski avoided and avoids the pitfalls of gender stereotyping. He is consistent and credible in the narrative on gender equality. However, the same cannot be said of the entire political formation. After all, politicians and journalists representing the media supporting the opposition reinforced gender stereotypes. From the very beginning, party colleagues used a whole set of stereotypes when describing Kidawa-Błońska's candidacy. Szymon Hołownia, the author of the most brutal attack directed against the candidate, is a politician who is visually close to her formation. Even Gazeta Wyborcza subtly depreciated her candidacy, consistently drawing a lady's image from the manor who brings "pierogi" to party meetings.

Does this mean there was no readiness in the PO camp for Kidawa-Błońska herself applying for president's role or a problem with accepting a woman running for the state's highest position? Alternatively, perhaps in an even broader sense, the resistance to recognizing that gender stereotypes hurt all men and women.

References

Allan, S. (2010). News culture. New York: Open Univeristy Press.

Banaś, M. (Ed.) (2007). Kobiety w polityce. Kraków: Księgarnia Akademicka.

Bauer, N. M. (2015a). Who stereotypes female candidates? Identifying individual differences in feminine stereotype reliance. Politics, Groups, and Identities, 3(1), 94–110.

Bauer, N. M. (2015b). Emotional, sensitive, and unfit for office: Gender stereotype activation and support for female candidates. Political Psychology, 36(6), 691–708.

Bauer N.M. (2017). The Effects of Counterstereotypic Gender Strategies on Candidate Evaluations. Political Psychology, Vol. 38, No. 2.

Berger P.L., Luckmann T. (1967). The Social Construction of Reality: A Treatise in the Sociology of Knowledge, New York: Anchor

Biernat, M., & Manis, M. (1994). Shifting standards and stereotype based judgments. Journal of Personality and Social Psychology, 66(1), 5–20.

Braden, Maria. 1996. Women Politicians and the Media, Lexington: University of Kentucky Press.

Brooks, D. J. (2013). He runs, she runs. Princeton, NJ: Princeton University Press.

Buć M. (2009) Wpływ zaprogramowania kulturowego na stopień maskulinizacji społecze- ństwa polskiego. [w]: Wincławska M., Brodzińska B. Płeć w życiu publicznym. Toruń: Wydawnictwo Naukowe Uniwersytetu Mikołaja Kopernika 55–66.

Byerly, Carolyn and Ross, Karen. 2006. *Women and Media. A critical introduction*, Malden, MA: Blackwell Publishing.

Cassese, E. C. & Holman, M.R. (2018). Party and Gender Stereotypes in Campaign Attacks. Political Behavior, 40, 785–807.

Dajnowicz M. (2013) Kobiety w politycznej przestrzeni Europy Uwarunkowania i zróżnicowanie regionalne uczestnictwa w polityce. Białystok: Wydawnictwo Uniwersyteckie Trans Humana.

Dolan, K. (2014). When does gender matter? Women candidates and gender stereo-types in American elections. New York, NY: Oxford University Press.

Druciarek M., Niżyńska A. (2014) (Nie)obecność kobiet w polityce. Czy wspólna strate-gia dla Europy Środkowo-Wschodniej jest możliwa? Warszawa: Instytut Spraw Publicznych.

Fairclough, Norman. 2003. Analysing Discourse: textual analysis for social research, London: Routledge.

Foucault, M. (1980). Power/Knowledge: Selected Interviews and Other Writings, 1972–1977. New York: Pantheon.

Frańczak, O. (2016). Zagadnienie stereotypów płci w Konwencji w sprawie likwidacji wszelkich form dyskryminacji kobiet (CEDAW). Folia Iuridica Universitatis Wrati-slaviensis, Vol. 5 (2), 53–74.

Fuszara, M. (2006). Kobiety w polityce. Warszawa: Wydawnictwo TRIO.

Fuszara, M. (2013a). Wstęp. Nierówność kobiet i mężczyzn w wyborach i sposoby jej przezwyciężania. In: M. Fuszara (Ed.) Kobiety, wybory, polityka. (pp. 7–24) Warszawa: ISP PAN.

Fuszara M. (2013b). Udział kobiet w sejmie Rzeczpospolitej Polskiej. In: M. Fuszara (Ed.) Kobiety, wybory, polityka. (pp. 85–96) Warszawa: ISP PAN.

Galtung, J., Ruge, M. (1965). The Structure of Foreign News: The Presentation of the Congo, Cuba and Cyprus Crises in Four Norwegian Newspapers. Journal of International Peace Research 2: pp. 64–90.

Gawor A., Mandal E. (2007). Kobieta, czy polityk? Treść i struktura stereotypu kobiety zajmującej się polityką. *Chowanna*, V.1 (28) pp. 79–93. Katowice: Wydawnictwo Uniwersytetu Śląskiego.

Hall S. (1996). On postmodernism and articulation: an interview with Stuart Hall. Edited by Lawrence Grossberg Critical Dialogues in Cultural Studies Edited by David Morley and Kuan-Hsing Chen, London Routledge pp. 131–151.

Hayes, D. (2005). Candidate qualities through a partisan lens: A theory of trait ownership. American Journal of Political Science, 49(4), 908–923.

Holman, M. R. & Merolla, J., & Zechmeister, E. (2011). Sex, stereotypes, and security: An experimental study of the effect of crises on assessments of gender and leadership. Journal of Women. Politics & Policy, 32(3), pp. 173–192.

Holman, M. R. & Schneider M.C., Pondel K. (2015). Gender Targeting in Political Advertisements. Political Research Quarterly, 68 (4), pp. 816–29.

Kasińska-Metryka, A. (2017). Karuzela z madonnami… czyli wizerunki wybranych kandydatek w wyborach parlamentarnych w Polsce 2015 r. In: M. Kolczyński (Ed.)Polskie wybory 2014–2015. Kontekst krajowy i międzynarodowy – przebieg rywalizacji – konsekwencje polityczne. V. 1 (pp. 341–351) Katowice: Wydawnictwo Uniwersytetu Śląskiego.

Kotlarska– Michalska, A. (2011) Społeczne role kobiet, Edukacja Humanistyczna nr 1 (24), pp. 25–35.

Krupnikov, Y. &. Bauer N.M. (2014) The Relationship Between Campaign Negativity, Gender and Campaign Context. Political Behavior Vol. 36, No.1, (pp. 167–188).

Krzyżanowska, N. (2015) Elityzacja i stygmatyzacja w polskim ruchu kobiet po 1989 r In: Dąbkowska M.I. (Ed.) Odkrywając współczesną młodzież: Studia interdyscyplinarne. (pp. 103–133). Toruń: Wydawnictwu Adam Marszalek.

Kumelska, M. & Modzelewski, W.T. & Schmidt P. (2017) Kobiety w przestrzeni społeczno-politycznej. Wybrane zagadnienia. Olsztyn: Wydawnictwo INP UWM.

Kuperberg, R. (2018) Intersectional Violence against Women in Politics. Politics & Gender, (2018), (pp. 1–5).

Laclau, E., & Mouffe, C. (1985). Hegemony and Socialist Strategy: Towards a Radical Democratic Politics. London: Verso.

Lewin, K. (1947) Frontiers in group dynamics. Human Relations 1(2) (pp. 143–153).

Loke J., Harp D. & Bachmann I. (2011) Mothering and Governing, Journalism Studies, 12:2, 205–220, DOI: 10.1080/1461670X.2010.488418

Malarczyk, M. (2019) Dysproporcje w reprezentacji kobiet i mężczyzn w środkach masowego przekazu na podstawie badań Stowarzyszenia Kongresu Kobiet. Media i społeczeństwo Nr 10 (pp. 19–34).

Musiał-Karg, M. (2014), Polacy o aktywności kobiet w polityce. Czy należy wprowadzać dodatkowe mechanizmy zwiększające udział Polek w życiu politycznym? Political Preferences no 8/2014, pp. 61–74.

Niewiadomska-Cudak, M. (2012) Stereotypowe postrzeganie ról kobiet i mężczyzn w społeczeństwie przyczyną niskiej partycypacji płci żeńskiej w sferze polskiej polityki Pedagogika Rodziny 2/4 (pp.49–61).

Pająk-Patkowska, B. (2016) Kobiety jako uczestniczki sprawowania władzy w Polsce po 1989 r. Środkowoeuropejskie Studia Polityczne, nr 4, s. 205–2016.

Petrocik J.R. (1996) Issue Ownership in Presidential Elections, with a 1980 Case Study. American Journal of Political Science, Vol.40, No 3, pp. 825–850.

Piontek, D. (2017) Seksmisja, czyli płeć w polskiej polityce pp. 303–319, In: M. Kolczyński (Ed.)Polskie wybory 2014–2015. Kontekst krajowy i międzynarodowy – przebieg rywalizacji – konsekwencje polityczne. V. 1 (pp. 341–351) Katowice: Wydawnictwo Uniwersytetu Śląskiego.

Post, B. (2019) Płeć i polityka. Między pozornymi różnicami i różnorodnością. Dyskursy Młodych Andragogów 20/2019.

Post, B. (2010). Płeć kulturowa w polskim parlamencie. In: I. Pańków, B.Post (Eds.), Kobiety u władzy? Spojrzenie z sejmu. (pp.17–42). Warszawa: ISP PAN.

Ross, Karen. 2002. *Women, Politics, Media. Uneasy relations in comparative perspective*, Cresskill, NJ: Hampton Press. Ross, Karen and Sreberny, Anabelle. 2000. "Women in the House: media representation of British politicians". In *Gender, Politics, and Communication*, Edited by: Sreberny, Anabelle and Van Zoonen, Lisbeth. 79–99. Cresskill, NJ: Hampton Press.

Rudman, L. A., & Glick, P. (1999). Feminized management and backlash toward agentic women: The hidden costs to women of a kinder, gentler image of middle managers. Journal of Personality and Social Psychology, 77(5), 1004–1010.

Sapiro, V. (1981) If Senator Baker were a woman: An experimental study of candidate images. Political Psychology 3(1/2), 61–83.

Shoemaker, P. & Eichholz, M. & Kim, E. & Wrigley, B. (2001) Individual and routine forces in gatekeeping. Journalism & Mass Communication Quarterly, 78 (2) (pp.233–246).

Sriwimon, L. & Zilli P. J. (2017) Applying Critical Discourse Analysis as a conceptual framework for investigating gender stereotypes in political media discourse. Kasetsart Journal of Social Sciences, Vol. 38, Issue 2, pp. 136–142.

Szymala K. (2017), Etyka troski. Wkład teorii feministycznej w myślenie o państwie, Civitas. Studia z Filozofii Polityki, nr 21, s. 207–226.

Titkow, A. (2007). Tożsamość polskich kobiet. Ciągłość, zmiana, konteksty. Warszawa: Wydawnictwo IFIS PAN.

Titkow, A. (Ed.) (2003). Szklany sufit. Bariery i ograniczenia karier kobiet. Warszawa: Instytut Spraw Publicznych.

Van der Brug, W. (2004). Issue Ownership and Party Choice. Electoral Studies 23 (2) pp. 209– 233.

Van Dijk, T. (2006). Discourse and Manipulation. Discourse & Society 17(3) pp. 359–383.

Vavrus, Mary D. 2002. *Postfeminist News: political women in media culture*, Albany: State University of New York Press.

Winter, N. J. G. (2010). Masculine Republicans and feminine Democrats: Gender and Americans' explicit and implicit images of the political parties. Political Behavior, 32(4) pp. 587–618.

Witkowska, I. (2016). Kobieta w polskiej kampanii prezydenckiej. Wizerunek kandydatek na urząd Prezydenta RP w latach 1995, 2005 i 2015. In: A. Kalisz, E. Tyc (Eds.), Dyskurs autopromocyjny dawniej i dziś. V. 2 (pp. 63–74). Katowice: Wydawnictwo Uniwersytetu Śląskiego.

Index of Names